Charlie Finley

Charlie Finley

The Outrageous Story
of Baseball's Super Showman

G. MICHAEL GREEN

and

ROGER D. LAUNIUS

WALKER & COMPANY
NEW YORK

Published by Walker Publishing Company, Inc., New York

All papers used by Walker & Company are natural, recyclable products made from wood grown in well-managed forests. The manufacturing processes conform to the environmental regulations of the country of origin.

LIBRARY OF CONGRESS CATALOGING-IN-PUBLICATION DATA HAS BEEN APPLIED FOR.

Green, G. Michael.
Charlie Finley : the outrageous story of baseball's super showman / G. Michael Green and Roger D. Launius. — 1st U.S. ed.
p. cm.
Includes bibliographical references.
ISBN 978-0-8027-1745-0
1. Finley, Charles Oscar, 1918– 2. Baseball team owners—United States—Biography.
3. Oakland Athletics (Baseball team)—History. I. Launius, Roger D. II. Title.
GV865.F43G74 2010
796.357092—dc22
[B]
2010002645

Visit Walker & Company's Web site at www.walkerbooks.com

First U.S. edition 2010

1 3 5 7 9 10 8 6 4 2

Typeset by Westchester Book Group
Printed in the United States of America by Worldcolor Fairfield

Contents

Prologue

With the bases loaded in the 12th inning of game two of the 1973 World Series, the Oakland A's trailed the New York Mets by one run. A's reserve second baseman Mike Andrews misplayed a high bouncing grounder that should have been the final out of the inning; instead the ball skipped under Andrews's glove and between his legs into shallow right field. Two runs came home. Little League coaches across America thought in unison, "Glove to the ground, glove to the ground. Block the ball. Don't let it roll between your legs." The next batter, Mets slow-footed catcher Jerry Grote, hit a slow chopper over the pitcher to Andrews's right. Andrews fielded it cleanly, but his cross-body throw sailed to the right of A's first baseman Gene Tenace, who may have pulled his foot off the bag as he caught the throw. Another run crossed the plate. The A's now trailed 10–6. To many television viewers, it appeared that Tenace's foot remained touching the bag while he stretched for the ball, but umpire Jerry Neudecker called Grote safe. As Mike Andrews recalled, "I saw a video of this later on . . . It showed that his foot was actually on the bag when he caught the ball. I thought it was kind of ironic after everything else that transpired after that."[1] Andrews walked slowly around the diamond between second and first base, manicuring the dirt with his feet, frustrated and embarrassed by his miscues. Two easy ground balls, which would be sure outs 99 percent of the time, in this game resulted in two errors and three runs for the Mets. Andrews, a late-inning replacement, felt a queasy knotty ache in his stomach. He felt it *keenly*.

In the stands behind the Oakland dugout, the A's bombastic 55-year-old owner, Charles O. Finley, known to all as either Charlie or Mr. Finley, began to seethe. The "O" was variously said to stand for *owner, obnoxious*, or *outrageous*, but it was actually for his middle name, Oscar. He had controlled the fortunes of the A's since 1960, and with success now coming after years of frustration, he was not about to let a second baseman's errors sidetrack it. Charlie Finley, the eccentric insurance millionaire turned A's owner, was an intense and complex person who expected everyone around him to give 110 percent. He was a creative innovator, a self-made salesman and businessman, and a megalomaniacal puppet master. Finley believed his team's success was tied to his personal mantra, "Sweat plus Sacrifice equals Success." This is how he lived his life; he expected the same from his team. Finley had stocked the A's with homegrown talent who had matured into players who could perform under intense pressure. Andrews had, in Finley's estimation, failed that test. One error he could maybe forgive, but two errors meant something had to be done.

Finley picked up the phone next to his seat, called A's physician Charles Hudson, and asked him to have the team's orthopedic specialist, Dr. Harry Walker, meet him in the clubhouse after the game. Finley tried to appear outwardly calm, though his heart raced with shock, anger, and disappointment. Only eight weeks earlier, Finley had suffered a serious heart attack. Doctors warned him to take it easy during the playoffs and World Series. Finley's doctor prescribed rest, with minimal agitation or excitement. But this patient was no ordinary person; he thrived on agitation, excitement, and, most of all, attention. Charlie Finley could not help himself—heart ailment or not.

He wanted his second consecutive world championship. After his team had won the 1972 World Series over the favored Cincinnati Reds, Finley had been the toast of the baseball world. The *Sporting News* named him "Man of the Year." He also seemed to be making progress toward his elusive goal of winning the hearts of Bay Area sports fans. Finley had added three important assets to his already dangerous team prior to the 1973 season: speedy outfielder Billy North, catcher Ray Fosse, and former Phillies first baseman Deron Johnson as his designated hitter—the latter a new position in the lineup, thanks to an American League rule change strongly supported and advocated by the A's owner.

The A's had seemed to be cruising in first place in the American League West until the All-Star game, when ace starting pitcher Jim "Catfish" Hunter broke his thumb and was sidelined for six weeks. The A's began to slide. Finley, who was the A's general manager as well as owner, began working the phones and making numerous deals to strengthen the club. He quickly added three quality utility players: Mike Andrews, Jesus Alou, and Vic Davalillo. The A's righted the ship as they won 12 out of 13 games during mid-August. When Hunter returned from injury, he won 21 games and gave the A's three 20-game winners, along with pitchers Vida Blue and Ken Holtzman. Star outfielder Reggie Jackson paced the offense as he led the American League in home runs and runs batted in, and was on his way to winning his first and only Most Valuable Player award. Finley's wheeling and dealing, along with excellent field leadership by manager Dick Williams, pushed the A's into the playoffs and past the tough Orioles in five games for the American League pennant.

But in game two of the World Series, one of Finley's new hires failed him. Finley knew Andrews shouldn't have even been in the game. His team was a player short of the normal 25-man roster because of Finley's mishandling of a late-season transaction. Finley, despite his controlling nature and his wearing many hats in the organization, amazingly made few transactional errors, but his trading of Jose Morales in late September left many wondering if his heart ailment had clouded his judgment.

Before the World Series started, Finley tried to add the slick-fielding Manny Trillo to the A's postseason roster. Major League Baseball rules stated that the A's opponent for each playoff series had to approve such a move. In the American League championship series, the Orioles allowed Trillo's activation to complete the A's 25-man roster. The Mets, as was their right, refused to allow the A's to use Trillo as their 25th player. Finley, ever the blusterer, demanded that MLB commissioner Bowie Kuhn allow Trillo to play. But Kuhn, who despised Finley, refused to overturn the Mets' decision. Before game one of the World Series, the irascible Finley tried to embarrass the commissioner by announcing over the public address system at the Oakland Coliseum that the A's would play the series one player short because of the Mets and Kuhn. The commissioner fumed and admonished the A's owner for his insubordination, but did not change his ruling. Thus, with no Manny Trillo, Mike Andrews was forced to play second base late in game two.

Mike Andrews, whom Finley had acquired in late July on advice of Dick Williams, was there to help shore up second base—the weakest position on the team. He came to the A's from the Chicago White Sox, where he had been used mostly as a designated hitter. Andrews, who was a key infielder for the pennant-winning and Williams-managed 1967 Boston Red Sox, suffered from the same psychological throwing ailment that years later afflicted infielders Steve Sax and Chuck Knoblauch. Physically he was sound; he just inexplicably at times could not make an accurate throw to first base. Andrews would later recall, "I was having throwing problems . . . They called it 'throwing yips.' Nobody knows why it happens, but on balls hit right to me where I had a second or two to think about it, I just couldn't make the throw."[2] Game two of the 1973 World Series was a marathon; combined, the two teams used 38 players in the four-hour-and-thirteen-minute contest. Normally, Andrews wouldn't have taken the field on defense at such a critical moment in a game, but both teams were forced to go deep into their bullpens and benches.

An A's rally in the bottom of the 12th inning fell short; they lost game two by the score of 10–7. The Mets had tied the series 1–1. After the game, the A's players expressed disappointment but also sympathy for Mike Andrews, who felt worse than anyone about his errors. Of course, plenty of other subpar performances contributed to the A's loss. The team had committed five errors in the game, as the bright, hazy sky played havoc with many flyballs and pop-ups. No doubt, the fate of the game did not turn solely on the play of Andrews.

Still, reporters gathered around Andrews in the locker room after the game for his reaction to his performance. He was dejected but philosophical about his two misplays and the game's outcome. He answered all of the reporters' questions. "I plain kicked things around," he explained. "I'm the goat and I am sorry as hell about it."[3] One reporter asked him if his shoulder was bothering him. "Injured?" he responded to this question. "My shoulder bothered me last year, but it's been fine this year."[4]

Then someone asked Andrews to go see Dr. Harry Walker in the training room. Andrews thought the request was bizarre, but he complied. When Andrews entered the room, Walker examined the second baseman's arm. It took less than five minutes. Andrews later said, "He examined my arm, and he was pushing it all over and turning it like they would do. He said, 'Do you feel any pain?' and I said, 'No, no, no.' We go through all this, and he says, 'Okay, fine. I find nothing.'"[5] Andrews left the room believing everything was fine, but a few minutes later he was summoned to manager Dick Williams's office. There stood Charlie Finley in his signature kelly green jacket with an intense look on his face.

A's farm director John Claiborne recalled the scene: "Finley told me he wants to put Mike Andrews on the disabled list, and he asks my opinion. Now, you knew that was a loaded question. I sat down and said, 'I think the commissioner of baseball will ask what kind of bull are you trying to pull now?' And of course he wasn't too enthralled with my attitude, but he listened. He said, 'I don't give a bleep what people think. I'm still gonna try to do it.' Then I told him the only way you're gonna get him on there is if Andrews will sign a letter saying his arm is no good . . . [and] he can't play."[6]

Finley quickly told Andrews that they wanted to place him on the disabled list because of the injury to his shoulder and that Walker had written a report saying his shoulder was injured to a point where he could not play effectively. Andrews shot back to Finley, "You want me to lie?"

"No," said Finley.

Andrews asked, "How else can you explain it?"

Finley blasted back, "Do you want to help the ball club?"

"Yes, but not this way," Andrews answered.[7]

Meanwhile, Williams sat in a chair with his head down, silent. He felt responsible for what was happening. Though rotating his second basemen during game two was not an unusual move (Williams had done it all year, and with the strong support and urging of Finley), the game had been so lengthy he ended up with the wrong second baseman in the game at a critical moment. And now Andrews, whom Williams respected and liked from his days with the Red Sox, was receiving the Finley treatment.[8]

For more than 30 minutes, Finley continued arguing with Andrews. Finley finally said, "I have a statement from the doctor upstairs in my office. At least go up and read it." Charlie the salesman could be relentless. Andrews went upstairs with Finley and read the statement.[9]

The statement, signed by Dr. Walker, read, "Mike Andrews has a history of chronic shoulder disability. He attempted to play but was unable physically to play his position because of a biceps groove tenosynovitis of the right shoulder. It is my opinion he is disabled for the rest of the year."[10]

Andrews still refused to sign it and falsely admit to being injured. Finley hammered him for another 30 minutes, explaining how Manny Trillo could help the team. Finley the salesman was trying to close another deal and, in his mind, help his team. But Andrews resisted. Growing desperate, Finley began threatening his player. He told Andrews that if he did not sign, he would never play baseball again. When this didn't work, Finley abruptly quit the discussion, saying, "Okay, fine, don't sign it. I'll get it through without it."[11] Finley told his staff to send out copies to the press, without Andrews's signature.

Andrews began to panic. He wondered what he could say or do to prevent the statement from being released. He felt demoralized and exhausted. He later told the media, "I was dead anyhow. Maybe Trillo could help the team . . . I said, give me the damn thing. I'll sign it . . . I was embarrassed . . . I was beaten."[12] He signed the statement. Thinking the World Series was over for him, Andrews left Oakland for his home in Peabody, Massachusetts.

On the team's flight to New York, the rest of the A's started to feel a slow boil of outrage and anger toward Finley when they realized what he had done to Andrews. Players talked of boycotting the third game of the World Series. Williams tried to calm them down by reciting the Finley line that Andrews had a nagging shoulder injury, but no one bought the story. "There were a lot of guys who were outright angry on the plane coming out here," said star outfielder and A's union representative Reggie Jackson to reporters after arriving in New York.

By the time the A's took the field for their off-day workout at Shea Stadium, most of the boycott talk had evaporated. In support of Andrews, however, his teammates taped his number, 17, on their shirtsleeves for the workout. Most remained very angry and outspoken in their criticism of Finley's actions. "This is a bad time to dump Mike. We got him as a pinch hitter, not as a fielder, and his arm doesn't bother him to swing the bat," said regular second baseman Dick Green. Others were more pointed. "Who ever heard of firing a guy in the middle of the World Series," questioned reliever Darold Knowles.[13]

Finley became visibly annoyed when he saw his players with Andrews's 17 on their sleeves. Later, after the workout, Jackson unloaded on his owner: "This thing is a real embarrassment and disappointment. A team is a team. Finley doesn't seem to understand that . . . The other players won't stand for it. We won't just take it and shut up."[14] He said the A's would likely file a grievance through the Major League Baseball Players Association on Andrews's behalf if he wasn't reinstated. That evening, Finley called a press conference at the team hotel in New York. In his folksy, carefully worded style, he explained his side of the cascading controversy: He was disappointed in Andrews's play in game two and had him checked by the team doctor—who concluded he was injured and unable to play. He ended the press conference by denying that Andrews had been fired; rather, he was merely put on the disabled list. Finley said that he hoped Commissioner Bowie Kuhn would allow the A's to replace Andrews on the roster with an able-bodied player.

Newspapers and radio talk shows from the country focused on the controversy, casting the once-acclaimed Finley as a mean-spirited, manipulative tyrant. *New York Daily News* columnist Dick Young compared the A's owner to Ebenezer Scrooge.[15] Columnist Art Spander believed the Andrews controversy could be "laid at the feet of Charlie Finley, who, like the queen from Alice in Wonderland, would simply repeat: 'Off with his head.'"[16] Even sportscaster and former Yankees shortstop Tony Kubek, who covered the Series on NBC television, questioned the veracity of Finley's claim about Andrews's injury and the overall fairness of the situation.

The next morning, Commissioner Bowie Kuhn ordered that Mike Andrews be reinstated immediately. After an investigation that included discussions with Andrews and Dr. Walker, Kuhn issued a statement that rebuked Finley's request to replace the "injured" Andrews. Kuhn used the logic that Andrews's injury did not occur during the World Series but was a preexisting condition. He went on to release a public statement condemning Finley for "unfairly embarrassing a player who has given many years of service to professional baseball."[17] Though he didn't take any action against Finley, Kuhn hinted that he would reexamine the issue after the Series.

With Andrews at his home in New England, the A's and Mets took the field for game three of the World Series. The A's were now two players short and facing the best starting pitcher in the National League, Tom Seaver, at Shea Stadium. The Andrews-Finley controversy dominated the coverage of the Series, but the Oakland A's had a unique ability to compartmentalize outside distractions and concentrate on winning baseball games, especially important games. They did so masterfully during game three. A's captain Sal Bando handed out black armbands to his teammates in support of Andrews, which they all wore during the game. On a cold, windy night, A's ace pitcher Catfish Hunter battled the Mets' flame-throwing Seaver. Both pitchers were sharp. The Mets scratched two runs off Hunter in the 1st inning, but Catfish and the bullpen shut the Mets down the rest of the game. Seaver struck out 12 A's hitters through 8 innings, when he surrendered the lead as Bert Campaneris scored on a Joe Rudi single. The game extended into extra innings again, but this time the A's would not be denied. Mets catcher Jerry Grote's passed ball set up the game-winning RBI single by Campaneris in the top of the 11th inning. The A's won the game 3–2 and took the lead in the World Series. Despite the exciting game, the focus again returned to the Andrews issue in the locker room afterward.

Prior to game three, with Andrews expected to rejoin the team the following day, A's manager Dick Williams had held a closed-door meeting with his players to clear the air. The pressure of the Series, the Andrews-Finley affair, and the national spotlight in the Big Apple were affecting Williams. No doubt the pressure of working for Charlie Finley for three years was also getting to him. Finley repeatedly marched Williams before the media to give the "Finley line" throughout the Andrews controversy.

Though Williams was a loyal colonel to Finley, constantly covering for his boss and sometimes lying to support his boss's antics was frustrating. He disagreed with what Finley had done. At the team meeting before the game, Williams had again given the Finley version of the Andrews issue. The players had listened but remained agitated. Then he'd firmly stated that he disagreed with the decision and disliked the circus it had generated. Williams had shocked the defending champs when he'd said, "I'm going to deny this if it leaks out of this room, but I'm resigning after the Series—win, lose, draw," wiping tears from his eyes as he finished.[18] The players, a few reporters, and even Charlie Finley had heard rumors about Williams's leaving the A's for the newly open New York Yankees managerial job, but to hear him say he intended to quit had been stunning. The A's players now had additional motivation, other than their collective desire to repeat as champs and their common dislike of their owner, to win the '73 Series. They'd win it for Dick Williams.

At a national press conference in New York the day after game three, Mike Andrews publicly confirmed for the first time that Finley had coerced him into signing the disability statement. Andrews said, "I should have walked out on the doctor and Finley in the first place. But I was tired and ashamed and I just hung my head." He went on to say, "I'm sorry I signed, but if I was in the same state of mind again, I'd do the same thing." He explained he was not offered any financial incentive to sign the document and was never threatened by Finley. However, Andrews's attorney, Harold Meizler, who also attended the press conference, said his client "had not been in complete control of his emotions. He had reached the lowest level of humiliation. At that point, he might have signed over the deed to his home." Nonetheless, Kuhn reinstated Andrews and rebuked Finley. All parties wanted to return the focus of the Series to the field of play.[19]

With Andrews back in uniform for game four, the A's tried to concentrate on playing baseball and winning the Series. But the media frenzy and distractions of the past several days continued—and took a toll on the defending champs. The Mets, led by the strong pitching of lefty Jon Matlack and the four-for-four hitting performance of popular outfielder Rusty Staub, easily defeated the A's 6–1. The A's played slow afoot and distracted, seemingly never in sync. The A's sole highlight was the pinch-hitting appearance by Mike Andrews in the eighth inning. Dick Williams sent in Andrews to hit for the pitcher to lead off the inning. The capacity crowd in Shea Stadium and everyone in both the A's and Mets' dugouts stood and cheered as Andrews appeared at home plate; everyone wanted to see him get a hit and stick it to old Charlie. Andrews grounded out harmlessly to the third baseman, but as he jogged off the field, the fans stood and cheered once again. Reggie Jackson, also cheering, was the first to meet him in the dugout. The ovation persisted and Andrews's teammates pushed him out of the dugout to wave to the crowd. A's first baseman Gene Tenace was surprised by the response from the Mets crowd, saying, "I couldn't believe they would treat him like that in a visiting city, like he was Mickey Mantle." Catcher Ray Fosse believed Dick Williams was sending a twofold message: "Mike, we stand with you . . . and fuck you, Charlie."[20]

Finley, seated behind his team's dugout, was not amused by the A's performance or the crowd's show of support for Mike Andrews. *New York Times* reporter Joseph Durso eloquently described the scene in the next day's newspaper. "The cheers got bigger and bigger—from everyone except Finley, his lord and master, sitting in a green jacket and hat under a blanket near the Oakland dugout . . . But, at last Andrews's moment was complete. Finley yielded to the judgment of history, applauded tentatively, then more boldly and finally gave it a flourish by twirling a green and gold pennant around for the prodigal son."[21] Almost lost in the emotions of the moment was the fact that the Mets had evened up the Series, which was now at two games apiece.

The next night, the A's bats fell silent once again. Two Mets lefties, starter Jerry Koosman and reliever Tug McGraw, stymied the A's hitters. With the A's trailing 2–0 in the ninth inning, McGraw struck out the last two A's hitters to end the game, slapping his thigh with his glove (a McGraw habit that would become legendary) as he shook catcher Jerry Grote's hand. Meanwhile, the sellout crowd of 55,000 screaming Mets fans began serenading the A's owner, singing, "Goodbye, Charlie . . ."[22] The Mets headed west to Oakland leading three games to two. The A's were down, but still not out. A confident Reggie Jackson reassured A's fans and his teammates. "We've had our backs to the wall before, and we win when we have to win," he said. "We're not gonna let the Mets beat us. We're the best. We've just been toying with them . . . We'll win in seven."[23] It did not help that Jackson was as cold as the New York weather, going 1 for 12 in the three games at Shea Stadium.

On the flight back to Oakland, Charlie Finley stewed. His world champions were on the brink of being eliminated by a team that had won only 82 games during the regular season. The A's were distracted and upset by all the negative attention from the New York media—most of which was the direct result of Finley's own antics. At a press conference in Oakland before game six, the A's maverick owner spun things once again, Charlie Finley style—rewriting history and appearing as the victim. He always wanted the last word, especially when he felt wronged by Bowie Kuhn. Finley defended his treatment of Andrews and railed against Kuhn. "It is my ball club, my money and I don't appreciate anyone telling me how to spend my money to run my business. As long as I own this club, I will operate it my way," Finley said. "I don't think the baseball commissioner treated us fairly in turning down this request . . . He released his letter, a formal letter denying the A's request to put Andrews on the disabled list, before I ever received it."[24]

Later in the press conference, which everyone agreed was bizarre, Finley told a new version of how things had transpired with Andrews after game two. Finley said he thought he was helping his team by replacing an underperforming and injured player. Feeling he had been poorly portrayed during the whole episode and trying to shift the negative focus to others, Finley said, "I am not a doctor. I have never attempted to practice medicine . . . Dick [Williams] thought it would be a good idea to have Andrews examined by a doctor. Dick Williams agreed with me 100 per cent. I asked Mike [Andrews] if he would affix his signature to the letter attesting that the medical report was true . . . Mike stated he would sign the letter if I would guarantee him a contract next year. I said I could not . . . I told him he did not have to sign the letter. He decided to sign it."[25] Andrews denied that he asked Finley for a contract the next season.

The next few questions shifted to Dick Williams's rumored decision to leave the helm of the A's. Finley said, "I've never had a manager who was more co-operative and understanding . . . I told Dick two things: One, 'I'd like to keep you with me. However, should you prefer to go to the Yankees if you're offered the Yankee job, I certainly won't stand in your way.' "[26] These words would soon prove hollow and again cast Finley as untrustworthy. With Finley, there was always a catch.

The A's tried to focus on game six in Oakland, while their fans turned on the team's maverick owner. Filling the balconies in the stands were signs ripping not only Finley but also the outspoken A's superstar Reggie Jackson: WE LOVE OUR A'S, BUT FINLEY GO HOME, KEEP A'S, TRADE FINLEY, and REGGIE JACKSON, L.V.P. A's fans were tired of both the owner and the star outfielder talking the talk but not walking the walk.

A capacity crowd turned out for game six, and the A's played with purpose. Catfish Hunter provided clutch pitching and a resurgent Reggie Jackson drove in two runs with two deep doubles to pace the offense—finally delivering on his boastful newspaper oratory. The Mets' Tom Seaver was effective but did not have his exploding fastball, and the A's evened the series at three games apiece with a 3–1 victory. The newly committed A's were again one victory away from the championship. During the postgame locker room interviews, the press focused on where Dick Williams would be next season. Williams named Ken Holtzman as his starter for game seven, but reporters inquired only about Williams's possible move to the Yankees and the team's young new owner, George Steinbrenner.

Another capacity crowd turned out on a bright, sunny Northern California Sunday afternoon for game seven. However, newspapers and television networks around the world were focused on a new story, not the final game of the 70th World Series. Late the previous evening, President Richard Nixon had committed his infamous "Saturday Night Massacre" in Washington, D.C. Nixon fired special Watergate prosecutor Archibald Cox. Attorney General Elliot Richardson and Deputy Attorney General William Ruckelshaus resigned rather than carry out the president's orders. Cox had refused to accept Nixon's summary transcripts of the secret White House tape recordings. As the nation teetered near a constitutional crisis, Nixon, perhaps the only public figure then more despised by the general public than the A's owner, knocked Finley and an exciting World Series off the nation's front pages.

Game seven was the third time in the series that A's southpaw Ken Holtzman battled Mets lefty Jon Matlack. It was also when A's outfielder Reggie Jackson became known as "Mr. October." A's shortstop Bert Campaneris ignited the defending world champs by launching a two-run homer, the club's first home run in the series in the A's half of the third inning. Even so, most fans remember the inspired play of Reggie Jackson. He also hit a monster two-run shot to deep right field and then dropped his bat at home plate, joyfully danced around the bases, and made a final emphatic jump and thump with both feet on home plate. These actions are etched in the minds of baseball fans who watched the deciding game. A new, outspoken superstar had been born. Jackson also added to his lore by making two spectacular outfield catches that kept the Mets at bay and propelled the defending champs. A's pitchers Holtzman, Rollie Fingers, and Darold Knowles (in his Series-record seventh appearance) silenced the Mets batters. Shortstop Bert Campaneris caught a lazy pop-up for the final out, and a throng of frenzied fans poured onto the field at the Coliseum. The A's prevailed 5–2 and were again World Series champions.

The victory celebration seemed more muted than the one the previous year. Commissioner Bowie Kuhn presented Charlie Finley and Dick Williams with the championship trophy, and their frosty relationship permeated the exchange. Then, before a national television audience, with champagne spraying the makeshift stage, Dick Williams made his announcement. "There's no way I can describe the thrill of winning a second World Series, but in my heart it is a sad thing for me," Williams said, finally disclosing the worst-kept secret of the Series: He was quitting as manager of the A's. He said he did so for "personal reasons, and not out of any dissatisfaction over my relations with Mr. Finley. He has been wonderful to me. I have nothing but the highest regard for him."[27] Few believed Williams's words. He went on to credit Finley's trades that brought the A's Ray Fosse and Billy North as the key to their second championship.

At this point, the attention-hungry Finley grabbed the microphone and thanked everyone associated with the ball club for their success, and predicted that the A's would win a third championship in 1974. He told manager Dick Williams, "Even though you're not going to be with us next year, I want to thank you for the great job you've done for the three years you've been with me."[28] Finley tried to take the high road by wishing Williams the best of luck in the future.

Several players, including Joe Rudi, tried to convince Williams to stay, but his mind was made up. They all blamed Finley for Williams's departure. A's pitcher Catfish Hunter was direct: "He [Finley]created an atmosphere that drove the best manager in baseball away from a championship team." Catcher Gene Tenace, the hero of the '72 series, said, "Williams can quit. The players can't."[29] Jackson was more interested in making amends with Williams. They hugged on national television and told Williams, "I'm sorry, I'm sorry, I'm sorry." Williams, with tears in his eyes, told Reggie he was as well.[30] Williams and Jackson had not always seen eye to eye, but each knew what the other meant.

A reporter commented to Jackson that Finley deserved significant credit for driving the team to excel. The A's outfielder shot back, "Please don't give that man the credit. It takes away from what the guys have done . . . He spoiled what should have been a beautiful thing."[31]

Then it was announced that Reggie Jackson, with his .310 average and five extra-base hits, was chosen as the Series' most valuable player by *Sport* magazine. The locker room showed signs of life as more bottles of champagne were uncorked and consumed. Suddenly, Finley found himself standing next to Jackson and said to him: "Congratulations on a great job. Thanks for an outstanding performance. You are the greatest player in the game." Finley seemed sincere, but the fed-up Jackson matter of factly responded, "Thank you, I appreciate it."[32] An awkward silence followed before Finley slowly walked away. Then Reggie took a large swig from a bottle and sprayed it out of his mouth. "What lousy, cheap stuff," he said. "Well, what can you expect on this club?"[33]

As the celebration began to lose momentum, Mets manager Yogi Berra entered the A's locker room to offer congratulations. Surveying the room, Berra remarked, "This doesn't look like a winning dressing room to me."[34] Charlie Finley might have won another championship but his players were in rebellion. A triumphant moment was tainted by mistrust, anger, sarcasm, and general sadness. As Finley headed upstairs to join friends and family for a continuation of the victory party he ran into Vida Blue. Finley asked if he would go as well, reminding him, "It's open to all the players and their wives."

"I only drink milk," Blue replied. Finley told Blue milk was on hand.

"Homogenized or pasteurized?" Blue inquired. Putting on a smile, Finley told him both were available and asked which he preferred.

"Chocolate," Vida said with a cold stare.[35]

Blue turned to leave and Finley walked toward the victory party down the hall.

Charlie Finley and his A's reigned again as champions of the MLB world. He did not realize it at the time, but this was the zenith of his baseball career. One more championship awaited his team, but for Finley this series began a bumpy and combative decline from the top of the baseball world. Once revered as an iconoclastic, eccentric maverick owner by the national media, after this October Finley increasingly came to be known as an arrogant, mean-spirited megalomaniac. His treatment of Mike Andrews forever cast a shadow upon him as a man of dishonesty and poor sportsmanship. The quarrels with his players only increased, especially as they gained more negotiating power.

Charlie Finley was a man of inconsistencies—miserly and autocratic one minute, charitable and paternal the next. The one characteristic that ran through his entire soul was control; it was how he brought order to his different worlds. Control meant everything had to be done the Finley way. The baseball establishment vilified him for his new maverick ideas intended to improve the game, but the baseball world was changing. The baseball lords were losing control. And it would be the iconoclastic yet old-fashioned Charlie Finley and his rambunctious players who would unwittingly lead the baseball world into a new, uncertain era.

Chapter One

```
S + S = S
```

"Sweat plus Sacrifice equals Success," or more often "S+S=S," was Charles O. Finley's core belief, and it dominated his life. He practiced it himself, and he admonished others to do likewise. Finley was not born into money or privilege but came from what might charitably be called a working-class background. The son and grandson of steelworkers, Finley, after achieving astounding fame and fortune, still wore his humble origins on his sleeve. "My God," said Bill Dauer, who worked for Finley when he owned the Kansas City A's, "I've heard the Philosophy of the Three S's about 1,000 times. I've heard the story of how he made his money 500 times. There isn't a man who ever worked for him who hasn't heard the philosophy and his story so often they could recite them by heart."[1]

Charles Oscar Finley's story encompasses a winding path through myriad interweaving and disjointed circumstances. His grandfather Randolph Finley had settled in northern Alabama to work in the steel mills after arriving from Ireland. He and his wife, Emma Caroline Finley, had 11 children. Randolph and Emma's son Oscar was a young apprentice at the steel mill when he met Emma Fields, a transplanted Georgian. They married and raised three children, Thelma, Charles, and Fred, whom they brought up to accept their place in life and to accept a reward in heaven, as taught in the Southern Baptist church, which they embraced.[2]

Born into this poor working-class home in Ensley, not far from Birmingham, Alabama, on February 22, 1918, Charlie Finley loved to tell people that he shared a birthday with the "father of our country," George Washington. Finley believed he was a great man like Washington, though he thought he was perhaps more like Lincoln. Finley claimed the mantle of the self-made man of humble origin, and he never let others forget it. Both his grandfather and his father were lifelong employees in the steel and iron industry. They spent their lives in the mills, and never got away; perhaps they never really wanted to. When Finley was growing up, Birmingham, with its iron and steel refineries, was leading the state's industrial revolution. Working in the mills was backbreaking, and most workers were unskilled and, as likely as not, functionally illiterate. The companies employing them paid poorly, often less than two dollars a day, and working conditions were desperate.[3] Like John Wayne's character, Sean Thornton, said in *The Quiet Man*, the steel workers of Birmingham poured sweat into "steel and pig iron furnaces so hot a man forgets his fear of hell."[4]

Finley grew up knowing that he wanted to do more than manual labor, and he had the ability to achieve his desire. He had a rare talent for selling virtually anything. As a boy, Finley earned a little spending money by mowing lawns; he recalled working six days a week, taking Sunday off for church, and making a dollar fifty to three dollars a day. But soon he organized some of his buddies to do most of the manual labor, while he went door to door to line up yards for mowing and took a percentage of all the grass-cutting money. Other examples of his entrepreneurial nature abound. He sold newspapers and magazines, and claimed to have received prizes for his industriousness.[5] Like many personal biographies, his got better, more elaborate, and less grounded in reality with each repetition. His persona became that of the self-made man, the hustler who achieved greatness. He thought of himself as an Horatio Alger–like character who succeeded through hard work, perseverance, imagination, and sheer will.

One scheme from his childhood suggests both his enterprising nature and the ethical flexibility that he would repeatedly demonstrate. Finley loved to tell the story of how he saw—and most important, seized—an opportunity to make money buying eggs that had failed a "candling" test for 5 cents a dozen from a poultry producer. Candling is a common process in which producers shine a light through an eggshell to see if a chick is being incubated. If they detect a cracked shell or an interior defect, they discard the egg. Finley bought these discarded eggs and sold them to office workers in downtown Birmingham for 15 cents a dozen. Unfortunately, many of the eggs that had failed the candling test had partially formed chicks inside. Finley, who was well aware of this, told a reporter in 1959, "The only disadvantage was that I could never go back for a resale."[6]

In the great egg escapade, and as he would demonstrate many times thereafter, it did not seem to bother Finley that the product was something less than what he had advertised. It was not that he flagrantly violated the law; he simply skirted it to gain a short-term advantage. He tended to skirt legalities all the time, and in his dealings in Major League Baseball, as well as in other business arrangements, this flexibility in his practices repeatedly landed him in court.

In 1933, Finley's father lost his longtime job in the Birmingham steel plant. He was in good company. In that year, the most desperate of the Great Depression, 24.9 percent of Americans were out of work. The massive federal spending during the New Deal helped to turn around an economy on the verge of total collapse, but its impact wasn't immediate.[7] Out of work and penniless, Oscar Finley was lured to Gary, Indiana, by his brother Bill, who pulled strings to get him a job at the steel plant where he worked. So Oscar Finley relocated his family to Gary, that great-working class town at the southeastern doorstep of Chicago. Later Charlie Finley liked to tell people that all they had to eat on the trip north was home-grown peanuts. He might even have been telling the truth.

What was obvious to all was that the southerner Finley fit into the streetwise Gary culture about as well as raw garlic in ice cream. Sam Joseph, a friend Finley made in Gary, said: "Boy, when he first came to Gary he had that thick, syrupy southern accent. He really had it . . . He couldn't pronounce my name. He'd say Saaalman. He'd get the 'l' in there. Every once in a while, he'd say, 'Saaalman, do you think I've lost my accent?' " Eventually he did, but he had to work at it, speaking slowing and deliberately in a stentorian, heraldic voice to hide his origins. When he got worked up, his voice would get a tad higher, he'd drop his *y*'s and *g*'s, and his drawl would return.[8] This led to his briefly used nickname, "Alabama," which Finley worked to shuck as quickly as possible.

He had a devilish sense of humor that seemed to pop up all the time. Attorney Neil Papiano, whom Finley employed during one of his many legal battles as A's owner, told the story of how he and Finley were panhandled on the street in Chicago one day, and Finley told a beggar, "Look, I've been working this side of the street for years, and I make a lot of money over here. So here's twenty bucks—you just go work the other side." The panhandler gleefully ran across the street, no doubt thinking that he might be able to turn that sidewalk into the same type of cash cow as Finley's side.[9]

Charlie Finley underwent the first of many transformations between his junior and senior years in high school. It was the summer of 1935, and Finley transferred to Horace Mann High School, a public school serving the upper-class neighborhood of Morningside. It was on Gary's west side, one of the most exclusive residential areas in northwestern Indiana. It was home to a large percentage of Gary's business and professional leaders, as well as those who commuted to work in Chicago. The schools serving this area were excellent, and Charlie Finley wanted to be a part of them, so he engineered his transfer. After graduating in 1936, Finley went to work at a steel mill, just like his father and grandfather had before him. At first he unloaded boxcars. Finley recalled, and this was no doubt heartfelt, that for all the hard work, it was "a blessing in disguise." "I'm thankful for having the opportunity to learn the facts of life," he said. But Finley saw a way out, and he had the courage to pursue it.[10]

He enrolled at Gary Junior College to study engineering but soon transferred to the Indiana University branch campus at Gary, taking classes toward a degree—though he would never graduate—while he continued working at the steel mill.[11]

He worked, he studied, and he occasionally indulged in his passion for baseball. He had played first base from the time he could first pick up a glove in Alabama and watched games as time permitted. He later liked to say that he regretted not transferring to the main Indiana University campus at Bloomington because he was sure he could compete well in Big Ten baseball. The path he took, however, proved critical to his future success. He parlayed his early experiences in the steel mill into a management post in the industry just as the United States rearmed and upgraded its warmaking capabilities in response to a rising fascist threat in Europe and Asia.

In the midst of this youthful climb toward success, Charlie Finley met, fell madly in love with, and married a young woman from the Horace Mann school district of Gary. Shirley N. McCartney had graduated from Horace Mann High School a year ahead of Finley, though there is no indication that the two knew each other while high schoolers. She was from a middle-class family whose connections would prove helpful to Finley during his rise to business success. They began dating while both were enrolled at Indiana University's Gary campus. And while at first she was one of several young women that he dated, soon their relationship became serious. They married on May 5, 1941. Shirley became a compass, guiding him both in business and in his personal life. It is hard to overestimate her influence on him. Charlie's friends expressed nothing but high regard for the quiet, reflective, attractive, elegant Shirley Finley.[12]

The young couple, like so many other newlyweds, struggled to make ends meet. Charlie took a second job, in a butcher shop, and Shirley apparently worked there for a while as well. Although Shirley's father had broad business interests, including an insurance business, the young couple tried to make it on their own, without family help. They moved into a basement apartment not far from Shirley's parents.[13]

When the United States declared war on the Axis powers in December 1941, following the Japanese attack on Pearl Harbor, Charlie Finley tried to enlist in the Marines but was refused because of an ulcer. Instead, he went to work in the defense industry, taking a job in the Kingsbury Ordnance Plant (KOP), near La Porte, Indiana, about 60 miles east of Gary. Built between 1940 and 1941, the plant produced 20 mm to 105 mm artillery shells. Finley worked there around the time of its peak workforce, which in May 1942 was 20,785 employees. A month or so after he started at the KOP, Finley and 27 others were sent to New Jersey for management training. Upon his return, he became a foreman and soon rose to division head of one of the five major units at the plant. He worked harder than most, usually coming into the plant every day of the week, and often putting in 10 to 12 hours per day. These promotions suggest that Finley's superior work ethic and capabilities were apparent to his bosses, who recognized his innate talent as an organizer and a leader.[14] Meantime Finley's family grew with the birth of his first child, Sharon, in 1942, followed in succession by Charles Jr., Kathryn, and Paul. Then, in the middle and late 1950s came Martin (1955), Luke (1958), and David (1959).

During World War II, Charlie Finley began to sell life insurance on the side. Days he would work at the ordnance plant, and nights he would make appointments and talk to families about ensuring their future livelihood should the principle breadwinner die or become incapacitated. His father-in-law, who sold insurance, encouraged him to enter this profession.[15] Louis Duke, whom Finley met at the plant, also sold insurance and helped him get into sales. One of Finley's great strengths, demonstrated throughout his life, was the ability to convince others to do what he wanted: in this case, purchase insurance policies.

When the war ended with victory over Japan in August 1945, the ordnance plant began winding down its operations. Finley left this job in 1946, after working to transition the facility to reserve status, in case it should be needed again; it would be used during the Korean War, but by then most of the World War II workforce had moved on. It was an easy move for Finley, who was doing well in the insurance business and appeared to have found his niche. Thanks to his superior salesmanship qualities, he won awards from the Traveler's Life Insurance Company almost immediately, writing $15,450 in accident insurance premiums along with an additional $2,412 in health and life insurance premiums in 1946.[16]

Those were some of the happiest days of his life. He was a young man with a growing family, a sweet and supportive wife, and enough success to make him feel satisfied. He enjoyed both work and play. He had enough money to make ends meet, more than enough leisure time to play baseball or softball in the evenings, and enough standing in the community to be seen as a person of substance and value. It looked like things were working out.

But tragedy struck Finley and his young family in December 1946. At age 28, he contracted tuberculosis and had to stay in a sanatorium for more than a year, though it took him much longer than that to make a full recovery. Finley could not breath, could not get up without assistance, and essentially had to lie in bed while others did everything for him. He was fortunate that during the World War II years, considerable advances in medicine, such as penicillin and other antibiotics, had revolutionized the treatment of tuberculosis. Previously, it was often a fatal disease. But with these new drugs, patients could be successfully treated, even if it was a long and difficult process.[17]

Charlie Finley lay in a bed over the winter of 1946–1947 at the J. O. Parramore Hospital, in Crown Point, Indiana. Martin Finley, born in 1955, discussed how his father told him about his experiences with tuberculosis: "He was so weak and nauseous all the time that he could not keep up a meal. He finished one meal, and then all of sudden, he puked the whole thing up and thought he was going to die." While there, Martin Finley added, all his father "could do was read and lay there in bed, and all he thought about was insurance, insurance, insurance, and he was talking to doctors about their insurance needs, and that's when he came across that doctors did not have group insurance for disability."[18]

Eventually Charlie Finley lost more than 100 pounds, recalling: "I had the sweats about three times a day. I made a game out of it. I'd whisk the sweat from my forehead with a forefinger and snap it at the wall, trying to make a big circle. Some days I did."[19]

He had neglected the cardinal rule in selling insurance, one Finley had given to countless others. He did not purchase insurance for himself. This led to regrets: The illness ruined him financially. His young wife had to go back to work to make money for their family—taking a job as an editor at the Gary newspaper. He lost his apartment, and Shirley and their two small children moved back in with her parents.[20]

The situation, however, also led to the insurance innovation that made Finley a multi-millionaire and launched him on his career as baseball magnate, innovator, and gadfly.

For the first six months Finley was at Parramore, he was not able to leave the sanitorium for even one day. During these many months of recovery, he began to assess the tragedy that had befallen him and his family. "I figured it was a bad enough situation for the average guy, but what a calamity it'd be for a fellow with a big income who suddenly found himself without money to meet his high standard of living."[21] He began to question the doctors treating him at Parramore about their insurance plans. He asked how they would survive if they were seriously injured or disabled. To his surprise, most had no clue, let alone a plan about how to support their families. Finley said that he asked himself "what group of people had such standards [of living] and could be interested in a special sort of insurance program to cover the sort of problems I'd run into. I thought of doctors. You know, suppose a surgeon loses a finger or gets crippled? His expenses go on, but his income dwindles."[22]

As he recovered, Finley began to develop his new insurance idea. He studied actuarial tables and insurance statistics. He learned how much money the average doctor made, his average expenses, and what funds were needed to maintain a certain standard of living. He devised how much coverage a doctor would require and how much of a premium a doctor might be willing to pay that would still provide an insurance broker with a reasonable profit. Finley knew his idea could revolutionize the insurance business and potentially make him rich. As he would often say, "All you got to do is lose your health and you do a hell of a lot of serious down-to-earth thinking."

In March 1949, Finley left Parramore for good. Over the previous 27 months of recovery, he had regained his stamina and his weight, which by then was up to 217 pounds. He also left with the idea of selling affordable group disability insurance to doctors, but he needed financial backing. "I left [the hospital] with this idea that seemed a natural," he said. "At first the insurance companies weren't buying any such suggestions, but I'm stubborn about such things. I'd practically exhausted the list of companies that might underwrite such a new program, so I went back to the first company that had turned me down."[23] Finley remained a first-class salesman. Provident Life and Accident Insurance decided to back Finley's new idea. Soon thereafter, he formed Charles O. Finley and Company to administer the insurance and rented offices on the 10th floor of the Gary National Bank building.

In 1950, Finley sold his first group disability policy to the Lake

County Medical Society; it provided $100 a week in disability income plus other benefits for an annual premium of just $176. He used his persuasive sales pitch and his understanding of the professional man's financial situation to close the sale. Soon, medical societies from adjacent counties were purchasing his policies as well. Within a couple of years of his release from Parramore, Finley had sold disability policies to 92 percent of the doctors in the Chicago area.[24]

Finley knew he was sitting on a gold mine. He wanted to take his program national, but he needed a larger underwriter. Most large insurance carriers were reluctant to increase the length of such long-term disability insurance while reducing the price. Ever the shrewd salesman, Finley negotiated with several companies for nearly two years before striking a deal with Continental Casualty Company to underwrite his program. He then persuaded the leaders of the American College of Surgeons (ACS) to make the organization's membership list available to him at a meeting in San Francisco in 1951. He was so desperate to pursue this opportunity that he took out a loan, using an old DeSoto as collateral, to scrape together the money for an airline ticket and new suits so he would be presentable.[25] Salesman Charlie Finley became a super salesman that day as he closed the deal. It was a bonanza for the once-destitute Finley, and it became the foundation of his future insurance empire. The ACS group policy sale totaled $6 million of potential premiums and yielded Finley nearly $450,000 in commissions, according to the U.S. Tax Court.

With the ACS deal in hand, Charles O. Finley and Company reaped ever-larger sales. He became a millionaire in less than two years after starting his company. His business continued to expand. He sold a group policy in 1953 to the Southern Medical Association, a group of doctors in 17 states, for eventual annual premiums of more than $3 million. In 1961, Finley added the mammoth American Medical Association to his insurance empire, along with its $8 million in annual premiums. More and more state and local medical associations signed up for his disability insurance. Finley's disability policies were simple and practical. They protected a professional's earning power over a period of years in the event the person was sick or injured and unable to work. If the injury or illness was permanent, the policyholder received payments for life. "The idea wasn't new, but the policy offered a great deal more coverage than my rivals' for a modest increase in premiums," said Finley.[26] In 1952, Finley severed ties with his early backers and moved Charles O. Finley and Company from Gary to 310 South Michigan Avenue in downtown Chicago. He believed he needed a big-city address to have true national success.

During this time, Finley's soon-to-be-legendary caustic and overbearing personality began to emerge. While he was charming when attempting to land potential insurance clients, he exhibited two negative personality traits to his employees and family: a quick, intense temper and the constant need to control everything. An early employee remembered Finley hollered a lot in the office. "He screamed because, I think, he was shy. If you looked him straight in the eye, he'd shut up. He'd shut up quick if you yelled back . . . I noticed that he hollered the loudest when he wasn't sure about something. Once he told me to shut up when I wasn't even talking. What a horrible temper."[27] In spite of these personality traits, the Finley insurance empire would soon cover more than 50 medical associations, with memberships of more than 70,000 doctors, and generate $20 million worth of business annually.[28]

In 1952, Finley purchased a 20-room house for his family in Morningside, one of Gary's most prestigious neighborhoods. He drove around town in a new Cadillac and hired two employees to help Shirley and him at home. His former neighbor John Mihelic did odd jobs at the new house, and Mildred Day worked as a maid and nanny, helping Shirley with their growing family. Mihelic and Day would play important roles in the personal lives of the entire Finley family for more than 20 years. Mihelic remembered, "He was always good to me. He seemed to like me a lot. He took me to ball games . . . He was a nice man then."[29]

Finley shrewdly invested his insurance profits in the stock market and accumulated a personal fortune of more than $5 million by 1954. Though he was now fully recovered from his tuberculosis, doctors cautioned him not to overextend himself. He tried to slow down, but there was just too much money to be made. "I get my six hours sleep a night, or the equivalent," he said. "I'm like a horse. I can sleep anywhere. And I keep my belly full. I smoke too many cigars, but hardly drink at all. My main vice is fried chicken."[30]

By happenstance, Finley's insurance offices in Chicago were in the same building as the American League offices under the leadership of league president and chairman Will Harridge. Finley, with his avid interest in baseball, soon sought out Harridge and the two found they had much in common despite their strikingly different backgrounds. Finley, the self-made man, lobbied the patrician Harridge to make baseball more friendly to the "workingman," a generic term that he often used to stand in for his personal background and experience. Harridge recalled, "Charlie never was short on ideas. He had a lot of ideas, and some of them were good. And he was persistent about them."[31] Harridge appreciated Finley's enthusiasm for baseball and encouraged the insurance magnate to pursue buying a MLB team. Finley wasted little time acting on Harridge's advice.

The lowly Philadelphia Athletics became Finley's first target. By 1954, the once mighty Athletics were in shambles. Longtime owner Connie Mack had retired as manager four years earlier, after selling off much of the franchise's talent. Mack and his two sons, Roy and Earle, put the team up for sale after several years of failure on the field and in the stands at ancient Shibe Park—named Connie Mack Stadium in 1953. Finley eagerly jumped into negotiations with the Macks. He appeared at a league meeting in Chicago in October 1954 waving a certified check for $450,000 and bragging about his considerable credit line. During the next several weeks, a circuslike atmosphere reigned over the negotiations, with several proposed ownership groups, some with partners in multiple groups, making bids for the Athletics. The Mack family fell into strife and indecision.

Ultimately, Finley faced two serious competitors: One group, headed by successful Chicago businessman Arnold Johnson, was offering $3.3 million and had the support of civic leaders in Kansas City, where Johnson wanted to relocate the team. The other group, headed by oilman and businessman Clint Murchison, also offered $3.3 million, but with less cash up front. Murchison promised to move the club to Southern California. Finley offered $3 million for the Athletics, but he ruffled some feathers in the baseball establishment by brazenly offering minority shares in his ownership group. In mid-October, the American League owners agreed on the proposed sale of the Athletics to Arnold Johnson's group and on the team's relocation to Kansas City. The league gave the Mack family a deadline to sell their shares to Johnson. But Roy and Earle Mack reneged and tried to sell their shares to an underfinanced local group headed by advertising executive Jack Rensel. As chaos reigned, Finley saw an opening to reenter the fray and formed a new syndicate with Philadelphia drugstore magnate Harry Sylk. While still a long shot, the 36-year-old Finley again became a serious bidder for the Athletics.[32]

A November 4 breakfast meeting was scheduled with the ailing 91-year-old Connie Mack for each group to make their final bid. Finley recalled, "I was so hungry for a ball club I could taste it. I thought I'd be cute and show up 10 minutes before the scheduled time. But Johnson was even cuter. He showed up an hour before the scheduled time. The meeting was supposed to be at nine. He got there at eight. Mack's daughter verified his credit with a phone call, and Johnson had his ball club. I had a check, just as big as Johnson's, but I never got a chance to wave it."[33] Arnold Johnson, a close business associate of Yankees co-owner Dan Topping, had better league connections and ultimately access to more money than the young upstart Finley. The Macks sold to Johnson, and soon the Athletics headed west to Kansas City.

A disappointed Finley claimed to have learned a few lessons from his first foray into Major League Baseball and redoubled his efforts to buy a ball club. He began frequenting MLB meetings, and he quickly realized that he went to more of these meetings than the majority of the actual owners. Many of these owners found Finley to be pushy and overly persistent and were annoyed by his desperation to join their exclusive club. Many disliked his unorthodox ideas about the game and business and feared he might ultimately try to take over their league if he was allowed to buy a team.

Joe Inglehart, chairman of the Baltimore Orioles, was given responsibility of "checking Finley out" and warned his fellow owners that "under no condition should this person be allowed into our league."[34] However, over time Finley's enthusiasm was overwhelming, and he began to win a few converts. Finley had money, smarts, and bravado. The baseball lords needed new blood with deep pockets. But they wanted someone less nouveau riche—someone less Rodney Dangerfield and more Cary Grant.

Still, the lords of baseball knew that their ownership ranks had to be expanded for the business to survive, and they had few other options. They only hoped they could contain Finley.[35]

In 1956, Finley bought a 21-room farmhouse for his growing family on 260 acres near La Porte, Indiana, for $125,000—not an insignificant sum at the time. He immediately set about renovating the house and some of the outbuildings. He bought expensive Georgia marble for the construction of a cabana, a fence, and other additions to the main farmhouse. He added a large, comfortable family room with a flagstone fireplace that had a large *F* on the chimney outside. And he added additional acreage to the farm. John Mihelic's son Ron, who worked on Finley's farm, recalled that the large amount of open land was ideal for hunting. Past the front gate, which was almost never closed, was a large, manicured lawn.[36]

John Mihelic, the farm's caretaker and handyman, worked as hard as anyone to turn the farm into a showplace. Finley uncharacteristically trusted John with many business decisions at the farm. Ron Mihelic said, "I think he might have trusted my dad more than anyone I can think of. He could relax around my dad." In 1962, after the Finley family relocated permanently to the La Porte farm, John Mihelic would chauffeur Finley from the farm to his Chicago office. This lasted for about two years, until the 90-minute one-way commute began to wear on Finley. He began spending the business week in Chicago, staying in a luxury suite at a Michigan Avenue hotel near his office.[37] "Charlie really cared about the farm, I think," recalled Ron Mihelic. "He spent a lot of money fixing it up, but he didn't spend that much time there. It's confusing. And when he was home on the farm, he'd spend lots of time on the telephone."[38]

David Finley recalled that his parents essentially lived apart from the time he was a young boy, pursuing different lives but remaining married. His father visited only periodically from the 1960s on. "My parents basically weren't married since I was three years old," he said. "It wasn't like, '*Dad's coming home!*' It was like, 'Dad's coming home.' We had our life on the farm and liked it that way."[39] Rick Knoll, a friend of the Finley boys, noted, "When he would come home, I don't want to say that everybody was nervous, because everybody was happy to see him, but everything was cleaned. Mildred ran a tight ship. And he came in, and he'd take over."[40]

The centerpiece of the farmhouse was the spacious and inviting family room, which was dominated by windows on three sides and a massive fireplace. Shirley Finley would organize art gatherings and hold teas and other events in that very pleasant and airy room. As *Parade* feature writer Robin Orr reported:

> The room, which has its own separate kitchen, was designed by Shirley, whose talents extend to oil-paintings and who has had exhibitions in La Porte and Chicago. "That gal can do anything," says Charlie proudly. He especially likes the huge fireplace in the room. "It's five-foot long and logs are cut to fit," he explains. "If I want a bright red fire I burn cherry. For a fast fire I burn pine. If I want aroma I burn hickory. If I want a slow fire, oak, a crackly fire, apple. We have all five types of wood right here on the farm."

Finley commented, "I don't spend as much time there as I'd like . . . My wife will tell you I'm like a bad penny—I'm liable to show up anytime."[41]

He continued to expand the La Porte farm's acreage over the years by purchasing additional farmsteads; by the early 1970s, it would reach 1,280 acres. He stocked it with animals of all varieties, farm critters and those a bit more unusual. He had cattle and hogs for a time, as well as monkeys. He had John Mihelic and others farm some of the land, so in a literal sense it was a working farm. It was not, however, anything approaching a classic farm on which those living on it made their livelihoods. This was more of a hobby than a business, but Finley enjoyed playing the gentleman farmer.

Tom Corwin recalled that the farm animals might have provided some food for the family and their friends, but the animals were there more as an opportunity to have fun. He said one year Finley bought a stock of albino turkeys, apparently just for the novelty of them. "He invited my family," Corwin said. "I was at college during that time, but he invited the family down to pick up a turkey. And the caveat was, you had to go and catch the turkey. So here was my dad running around in, evidently, a muddy field, trying to tackle the turkey. And they brought it home, and we had it in our backyard for a while, which was a thing interesting for kids to walk by on the way to school, seeing an albino turkey in our back-yard."[42]

Finley's first three children remembered moving to the farm and liv-ing there for a time before going to college. The four younger children, all sons—Paul, Martin, Luke, and David—knew the farm as their only home. They all enjoyed it and saw it as wonderful place to grow up, this showplace farm made homier by the efforts of their mother. David Finley said, "It was a really fun place . . . [It] was like a summer camp . . . I raised chickens and sold eggs to get an allowance to go bowling or play golf, whatever I needed to do. I baled hay." He added, "The neat thing was we had a lot of fun things at the farm, and I always had friends coming to my house and had home-court advantage at all times."[43]

The farm had a swimming pool that became the scene of many teenage parties over the years. The children built a basketball court in the hayloft of the big barn, where many a pickup game took place. They even recalled occasionally playing members of the A's team when they visited the farm.[44]

Finley acquired an old railroad caboose and had it pulled onto the property for the kids to play in. They used it as a clubhouse fort, among other things. Rick Knoll said that they all played in it. "Every caboose comes with these little dynamite charges that they're supposed to put on the tracks. So us kids got all those dynamite charges, and, of course, trying to figure out how to set them off, we were dropping concrete blocks on them and everything else," he remembered. They played tag there, Knoll said, "and you'd run around that caboose, and it had almost like a widow's walk on top, around the cab, and you'd get up there, and the whole thing . . . It'd just be a blast."[45]

Finley continued to pursue other baseball teams during the late 1950s, first the Detroit Tigers and then the Chicago White Sox. He made serious bids and lost, and was feeling a little snakebit. Finley participated in the American League meetings in 1960, seeking to acquire the rights to one of the expansion teams the league was proposing. If that bid failed, he hoped to lay claim to an existing team. He knew that former All-Star Hank Greenberg, who owned part of the White Sox along with Bill Veeck, wanted an expansion team in Southern California. So Finley schemed to obtain the White Sox. "Finley is sitting in Chicago reading about all this in the papers," remembered sportswriter Jerome Holtzman. "He'd been anticipating that Greenberg would get L.A., and that Veeck would go with him. And that would leave the White Sox for sale."[46] In anticipation, Finley purchased an option on Veeck's shares with a final offer of $4.2 million for the White Sox. However, the American League's plans to put an expansion team in Los Angeles suffered a severe complication when baseball commissioner Ford Frick ruled that the Los Angeles Dodgers would be entitled to significant financial indemnification for the invasion of their market territory. Dodgers owner Walter O'Malley also wanted other conditions, including that the new American League franchise sign a lease to play in Dodger Stadium upon its completion in 1962. Suddenly, Greenberg and Veeck believed that acquiring the new Los Angeles franchise wouldn't be financially profitable.[47] So Finley, still holding an option for Veeck's shares of the White Sox, assumed Veeck wouldn't sell that team. Sensing an opportunity, Finley began focusing his considerable fortune and efforts on a Southern California franchise. He believed he had the resources and resolve to successfully purchase and operate a new American League expansion team in Los Angeles.

While Finley was pursuing the White Sox, the Kansas City Athletics were in need of a new owner. Arnold Johnson, who had moved the team from Philadelphia, had died suddenly of a heart attack on March 10, 1960. The ball club was in turmoil, with the Johnson estate in probate and potential new local ownership desperate for funding. As many as 12 groups—5 of which wanted to move the team to another city—expressed interest in buying the Athletics when the team was officially put up for sale on July 31, 1960, by the executors of the Johnson estate and the team's minority owners. Veeck told Finley, "Charles, you can go to Kansas City right now and buy the majority interest in the ball club from Arnold Johnson's widow."[48] But Finley did not get involved with any group; he was too distracted with pursuing an expansion franchise in Southern California.

To bid for the Athletics, Kansas City Chamber of Commerce president J. W. Putsch and *Kansas City Star* sports editor Ernest Mehl put together the strongest local ownership group, led by attorney Byron Spencer and prominent local businessmen and investors from Kansas

City and the nearby cities of Topeka and Wichita. The city, of course, wanted local ownership for the team, but Spencer's group appeared under-capitalized and struggled to find additional investors.[49]

By October 1960, only two groups had emerged as viable candidates to purchase the Athletics. The group led by Byron Spencer had eight firm investors and had placed in escrow $250,000 in earnest money. Elliot Stein, a minority owner of the White Sox and former treasurer of the St. Louis Browns, led a second group, from St. Louis. Both groups submitted proposals to keep the team in Kansas City with bids of $3.5 million, $1.8 million of which would go to the Johnson estate.

St. Louis hosted the 1960 baseball winter meetings in early December, and there the issue of A's ownership came to a head. For the first time in months, the Kansas City ownership group appeared to be the favorite for purchasing the Athletics. On December 5, the American League gave conditional approval for the Kansas City group to buy the team. This occurred after much wrangling and behind-the-scene negotiations with other owners and league officials. Most owners felt the Kansas City group was underfinanced and lacked a strong, deep-pocketed leader. Indeed, the group had raised only $2.6 million in cash and pledges, well below its $3.5 million offer. Further, no individual person had contributed more than $50,000, and no corporation provided more than $200,000. The group hoped to raise the additional funds with a public stock offering once the deal was finalized. After receiving the American League's approval, many of the group's backers celebrated by sending a radio broadcast back to Kansas City announcing the league's favorable decision and their pending purchase. But was it a done deal?

At this moment, Charlie Finley finally realized the Kansas City Athletics provided his best chance to purchase a Major League Baseball team. As the Kansas City group celebrated and tried to finalize the paperwork and financial agreements for the purchase, Finley seized the opportunity. He knew the American League owners were not satisfied with the financing of the Kansas City group. He also knew that the probate court was not required to sell Johnson's majority interest in the team to the local group if a better offer appeared; the probate court's mission was to seek the highest possible dollar amount for all assets of the Johnson estate. So, after losing his bid for the Southern California expansion team to Gene Autry, Finley quietly talked up support for his possible purchase of the Athletics at the winter meetings.

On December 6, Finley struck, submitting a $1.85 million bid to the Johnson estate and the probate court for Johnson's majority stake in the Athletics. Finley's bid was $50,000 above the Kansas City group's offer to the estate and undercut its efforts to finalize its purchase deal. For months, the attorneys representing the Johnson estate had pressed Finley to submit a bid for the majority stake in the club, but Finley was preoccupied with trying to acquire the California expansion team. He also hoped that if he lost out and the Veeck and Greenberg syndicate eventually obtained the California expansion team, he could emerge as the new owner of the White Sox—the team closest to his home and the team he truly desired. "I was interested (in the Athletics)," explained Finley, "but I couldn't move then because I had this option to buy the (White Sox) stock owned by Veeck and Greenberg."[50]

After announcing his bid, Finley went before the Cook County Probate Court on December 19, 1960, for a final hearing on the sale of the Johnson's shares in the Athletics. Only two bidders remained: Byron Spencer's group and Finley. Spencer and his Kansas City backers scrambled to find additional funding, eventually receiving the authority to increase their bid to $1.9 million. Their efforts did not deter Charlie Finley. Flush with cash and prepared to increase his bid, Finley told Spencer, "I don't care how high you go. I'm prepared to go higher."[51] Finley had decided he would go as high as $2.5 million; he did not intend to come up short this time.

Finley increased his bid to $1.975 million on December 19, forcing the Kansas City group to withdraw its offer and Judge Robert Dunne to approve the sale of the Johnson stock to Finley.[52] The next day, the American League president announced the formal approval of the sale of the Kansas City Athletics to Charles O. Finley. After six years of frustration, Charlie Finley finally owned a Major League Baseball club.

At a press conference from his Chicago offices, Finley held court with reporters on his initial plans for the Athletics. He intended to signal a new era for the team and tried to soothe the uneasy feelings of Kansas City civic leaders and fans. With the limelight firmly planted on the new owner, Finley initially charmed the local Kansas City media with his folksy demeanor, his enthusiasm for the team's future, and his candor. "Kansas City will no longer be regarded as a Yankee farm team," explained the new owner. "We'll trade with every club in the league if we think we're getting a fair deal."[53] Finley closed his comments to reporters by assuring everyone that his intentions were "to keep the A's permanently in Kansas City and build a winning ball club."[54]

Chapter Two

The Savior of Kansas City?

In January 1961, after purchasing a controlling interest in the A's, Charles O. Finley arrived in Kansas City. He believed he was the "savior" of the lowly Athletics Major League Baseball franchise and wasted little time in turning on his famous "Finley charm" as he met with Kansas City civic leaders and citizens; despite his quick temper and megalomaniacal tendencies, Finley could be equally charming, gregarious, and warmhearted. But he had a tough crowd in Kansas City. After years of the A's losing and finishing in the American League cellar, the city had naturally grown disenchanted with the team. They especially disparaged former owner Arnold Johnson's propensity to ship rising young A's players, such as Clete Boyer, Hector Lopez, Ralph Terry, and particularly Roger Maris, to the New York Yankees in exchange for aging Yankees heroes, including Billy Martin, Don Larsen, and Hank Bauer. Finley earned points by immediately proclaiming that Kansas City would no longer be "regarded as a Yankee farm team."[1]

In 1961, Finley was 43 years old; of average height and weight, though with the residue of too much fried chicken around his belly; reasonably healthy for a chain-smoker and serious drinker; moderately handsome; and a good conversationalist when he wanted to impress others. He could make a good first impression when motivated. He whirled into Kansas City, greeting all he encountered as a hail-fellow-well-met and inspiring a feeling of trust in the fans and business leaders with what he said and how he said it. In his first interview there, Finley proclaimed, "This ball club is going to stay in Kansas City . . . When I was chasing the Detroit Tigers I wasn't going to move the Tigers out of Detroit. When I was chasing the White Sox I wasn't going to move the White Sox out of Chicago. And when I got a place to roost in Kansas City—brother, I mean to tell you, I'm here to stay!"[2] Finley, the ultimate salesman, soon charmed the jaded Kansas Citians with his optimistic announcements about the A's and their future on Missouri's western border.

Finley promised that he wouldn't be an absentee owner, which was a priority for the city fathers, and pledged to move his family to Kansas City after his eldest son graduated from high school two years hence. He rented a fancy suite at the famous Muehlebach Hotel in downtown Kansas City, using it as a prop in his courtship of the Kansas City media and business elite. Finley promised to increase the A's lackluster attendance by implementing a large and aggressive direct mail campaign— which he had used to good effect in his insurance business—to increase the number of season ticket holders. He also said he would provide innovative ticket offerings, such as nine-game ticket plans, a first for MLB. It was a masterful performance. Finley sold himself as a man of honor, someone the fans of Kansas City could trust. He swore he would never move the team out of Kansas City. He promised to turn the lowly A's into winners—no matter the cost. Perhaps these were not outright lies, but his promises quickly proved elusive, especially his pledge to turn the A's into winners no matter how much money it took.

On a local radio program, interviewer Monte Moore, who would later be hired by Finley and have a long and controversial career as the A's radio broadcaster, said to Finley, "You've mentioned you wanted to do one thing . . . instill in the people of Kansas City the confidence that you hoped you could. Do you feel you've achieved that goal?"

"I felt it would take about six months to get the faith and confidence of the fans in this area," Finley answered. "They have been so exceedingly nice to me that I have their faith and confidence already."[3] Indeed, Kansas City fans seemed to have a growing confidence in the new A's owner. Worries that the Chicago-based insurance magnate was a big-city carpetbagger set to move the ball club elsewhere seemed overly exaggerated. Even the Kansas City mayor, H. Roe Bartle, jumped on the Finley bandwagon, saying, "Charlie Finley has put more spirit into the city than anyone [in the past decade]. He holds the heart of the city in the palm of his hands."[4]

In addition to his selling himself to the city, Finley worked on finalizing the management of his new team. He pledged to hire the "best baseball brains" and devoted considerable energy running the team—few at the time really appreciated how much control Finley would insist on holding when it came to the running the A's. In December he had announced that he would retain A's manager Joe Gordon for the 1961 season, but he refused to keep general manager Parke Carroll, saying he needed a more experienced GM.

Even as he sacked him, Finley went out of his way to praise the popular Carroll, insisting that he remain with the organization. The real motivation for this maneuver, it turned out, was financial. Carroll still had two years left on his $25,000-per-year contract, and Finley was obligated to pay him unless Carroll found a comparable job with another club. Frank Lane, who succeeded Carroll as GM, later recalled, "Finley told me that since he would have to pay Carroll he would stick him in an office and force him to clip items out of papers for his pay."[5] Carroll's time as a Finley employee turned out to be short-lived. The 56-year-old Carroll died of a massive heart attack on February 4, 1961, less than six weeks after Finley purchased the team. Carroll's widow tried to press Finley to pay the $50,000 owed on his two-year contract with the A's, but Finley refused. Carroll's family then sued, but Finley prevailed in court.[6]

To replace Carroll, Finley tried to hire New York Yankees general manager George Weiss, but Weiss declined. On January 3, 1961, Finley announced the hiring of Frank Lane as the A's new general manager. Known to everyone as "Trader Lane" because of this penchant for making deals, the new GM also wanted to wheel and deal in Kansas City. He loved the adrenaline rush that came from aggressive negotiating and making big, creative business decisions. In 1948, Lane joined the Chicago White Sox with instructions to turn a losing team (the Sox lost 101 games the previous season) into a winner. He made 241 trades involving 353 players during his seven seasons as GM and pried such franchise players as Billy Pierce, Nellie Fox, and Minnie Minoso from other clubs in exchange for lesser talent. Lane repeatedly feuded with Sox owner Chuck Comiskey throughout this process and left the team in late 1955, long before the White Sox won the American League pennant in 1959. Some gave Lane considerable credit for that success, but others, such as new White Sox owner Bill Veeck, believe the team won in spite of Lane.

Lane escaped to the St. Louis Cardinals just before being booted out by Comiskey, and quickly angered Cardinals fans in 1956 by trading fan favorite and future Hall of Fame second baseman Red Schoendienst, a cherished link to the glorious teams of the 1940s, to the New York Giants for Alvin Dark. He then tried to deal St. Louis icon Stan Musial to the Philadelphia Phillies for pitcher Robin Roberts. But when word of this proposed deal leaked and the public expressed anger, Cardinals owner August Busch intervened to stop the trade. Busch, after a few too many drinks, publicly criticized Lane at a St. Louis sports dinner, and the two entered extended warfare until Lane departed. Amid this fight, Lane had the balls to demand a three-year extension as Cardinals GM; Busch responded in a telegram: "KISS MY ASS."[7]

After leaving St. Louis in the winter of 1957, Lane went to Cleveland, where he quickly ran afoul of Indians fans as well. He publicly feuded with field manager Joe Gordon, the same Joe Gordon who was managing the Kansas City A's in 1961. Lane fired and then rehired Gordon, but before the end of the 1960 season, he carried out his most unusual trade: dealing manager Joe Gordon to the Detroit Tigers in exchange for their manager, Jimmie Dykes. It was purely to get rid of an enemy, and most thought the Gordon fiasco was a result of Lane's pettiness and vindictiveness. In addition, whatever small amount of goodwill Lane might still have left in Cleveland disappeared when he traded away popular slugger Rocky Colavito. Lane left a wake of anger and strife in both St. Louis and Cleveland. One conclusion is clear; Lane's trades were more about grabbing newspaper headlines than improving his ball teams. Lane never guided a team to a World Series, and in many cases, his teams' record declined during his tenure.

Lane had two years left on his contract, and if he were to be fired, he would have to be paid in full. Indians owner Nate Dolin did not want to do that, but he did want to get rid of Lane. So Dolin did what so many other employers had done: He convinced someone else to hire Lane. His sucker was neophyte baseball owner Charlie Finley, who knew he needed help with the A's but had no clue where to get it. Eager to unload Lane, Dolin told Finley, "You need a general manager. Frank will help you learn the business." Finley offered the GM position to Lane, despite his baggage. Amazingly, Lane hesitated to accept the job, not sure that he wanted to work for the lowly A's. Dolin had to convince Lane to take it, telling him in every way short of firing him that he needed to move on.[8] Lane reportedly signed a four-year contract with Finley and the A's for a salary of $100,000 per year, four times what his predecessor, Parke Carroll, had earned.

At the press conference announcing the hiring of Lane, Finley stated, "I had several men in mind, but Lane was my first choice. We had several conferences on the phone and finally came to terms. I wanted, for one thing, something to arouse the baseball fans in Kansas City . . . I can't think of anyone who could do a better job of pumping life into a ball club than Frank Lane."[9]

Lane quickly sought the adrenaline rush of the trade and, just weeks after his hiring, engineered a major swap with the Baltimore Orioles. On January 24, 1961, he sent Russ Snyder, Whitey Herzog, and a player to be named later to the Chesapeake Bay team for Clint Courtney, Al Pilarcik, Wayne Causey, Bob Boyd, and Jim Archer. Needless to say, the trade was inconsequential to both clubs. All were spare parts, and only Causey had much of a career with the A's. But it did cause the first blowup between Lane and Finley. Lane did the deal but did not bother to get Finley's approval. Finley fumed, "I want to know about the deals before they were made, not after." This rule may have pleased the owner, but it did not slow down Lane. He dealt more than 10 players that year, and from then on kept Finley informed.[10]

Finley cautioned A's fans that it was going to take time to build a winner, but he confidently predicted Lane's salary was money well spent. "I know it isn't going to be easy building a club into a contender. But we'll be wheeling and dealing. That's one of the primary reasons I sought Lane: I wanted an experienced baseball man and especially one who has an outstanding record as a trader. To me Lane is the best trader in baseball . . . Even at $100,000 a year Lane is an exceptional bargain. We won't be cheap. I believe in hiring the best men—regardless of their price."[11] But despite Finley's early infatuation with Trader Lane, he would soon come to agree with his fellow owners in Chicago, St. Louis, and Cleveland about the GM's shortcomings

Throughout the spring, Finley and Lane consolidated power and reorganized the A's baseball operations. Finley named one of his insurance subordinates, Pat Friday, as the club's executive vice president. Both Friday and Finley drew no salary from the A's organization, as they were well paid by the Charles O. Finley and Company's insurance division. Finley touted this nonsalary status in the local media, pledging to make the club's future success the first priority. "We're going to plow every cent of profit back into the club," he said. "Our main objective is to build the team into a contender."[12] Lane brought in veteran St. Louis baseball executive Bill Bergesch as assistant general manager. Finley hired former Notre Dame football star Jim Schaaf to be the new traveling secretary for the team. Schaaf, fresh out of college, later ran team promotions for Finley. Finley also retained George Selkirk as director of player personnel and a young baseball executive named Hank Peters as the team's minor-league director.

Peters knew how to judge baseball talent. He began his career in the scouting department of the St. Louis Browns (which became the Baltimore Orioles in 1954) and slowly worked his way up over the next decade. In 1956, he moved to the Athletics and ran their minor-league operations at the time Finley arrived on the scene. But Finley and Peters got off to a very inauspicious start.

During the spring of 1961, Peters received a call from a scout looking at a young pitcher on the West Coast named Bill Landis. The scout wanted to sign Landis for approximately $35,000. In the pre-Finley days, Kansas City A's scouts had to have permission from the general manager for a signing, but not from the owner himself. Peters agreed with his scout that this kid sounded like a good prospect, but he needed approval from new GM Frank Lane. Peters called Lane in West Palm Beach, where the

A's were training for the season, but could not track him down. He finally got hold of George Selkirk, the player personnel director, and told him about this prospect and that they needed to act promptly to get him under contract. Selkirk gave the go-ahead. Later, Peters told Lane in a phone conversation of the signing and the amount. Lane agreed it was a good deal. None of them bargained on the firestorm this would cause when Finley found out about it.

As Hank Peters recalled, "Well, now I get back to Kansas City after spring training, and they say, 'Finley wants to talk with you.' So I go over there, and he's on the phone and he said, 'Who gave you the authority to go out and spend my money for signing this player?' I tried to explain to him, but he wasn't interested in that. He said, 'You're fired . . . You're finished.'"[13]

Peters told Finley that he needed to honor his personal contract, which the blustery Finley eventually did, but only after playing the virtuous victim. Immediately, Peters called Reds GM Bill DeWitt and caught on as that team's farm director for the balance of the 1961 season. A few months later, Finley called Peters once again with a shocking proposition. As Peters said:

> I guess it was September or October, out of the clear blue sky, Charlie calls me one day, and he said, "I owe you an apology." He said, "I finally found out that Lane lied to me. I'd like for you to come back and work for us." And I said, "I'm not too sure about that." So he called again and said he'd give me my old job back plus make me the assistant general manager and a pretty sizable increase in salary.

Finley kept upping the ante until Peters could not refuse any longer. As was typical of Finley throughout his life, he trusted few subordinates, tried to control all aspects of the A's operation, and kept his own counsel. Over time, Peters was able to convince Finley that the only way for the A's to win was to invest heavily in finding, signing, and developing young baseball talent. There were no shortcuts to success, Peters taught Finley, who eventually came to accept Peters's approach to MLB operations as his own.

In addition to working to put his mark on the A's front office, Finley began pressuring in the spring of 1961 to gain complete control of all shares of the franchise. Upon acquiring the majority ownership of the team from Arnold Johnson's estate, he still controlled only 52 percent of the club. A Kansas City group that had lost its bid to purchase majority ownership to Finley retained an option with the club's minority owners to purchase the remaining 48 percent of the team's stock.[14] This irked Finley, who wanted sole control so he could do as he pleased with the team. The Kansas City group, fearing that Finley might try to move the franchise, offered to release its option to Finley if he agreed to keep the club in Kansas City for at least four seasons. Finley quickly seized on that offer. As a show of goodwill, he promised to waive the attendance clause in the stadium lease, which gave the A's owner the right to void that lease and potentially move the franchise if paid attendance fell below 850,000 per season. When he promised this, the Kansas City group waived its option to purchase the minority shares.

Finley then bought out all the other minority stockholders. For this 48 percent minority interest, he doled out an estimated $1.9 million, bringing the value of his total stake in the team to nearly $4 million and making him sole owner of the A's. Finley and Red Sox owner Tom Yawkey were the only two individual owners in the American League.[15]

Finley created a board of directors to quell any remaining uneasiness that he might want to move the A's to another city. But this board, for the brief time it existed, had no real power; it was merely a division of Charles O. Finley and Company. What's more, Finley quietly dissolved the board after the 1961 season, just seven months after he'd created it. He eventually distributed the A's stock holdings between the members of his immediate family. His wife, Shirley, and their eldest four children received 69 percent of the stock holdings, with Finley retaining the balance. In later years Finley would state, "Only 30 percent of the stock is in my name, so the family can fire me at any time. But where would they find someone else to do all this work for no salary?"[16]

Never one to miss a public relations opportunity, Finley demonstrated his promise of keeping the A's in Kansas City with a show of burning the stadium lease—or so it appeared. He called a press conference in the office of Mayor H. Roe Bartle before the start of the 1961 season to "burn the lease" on the stadium, thereby making the point that the attendance clause was obsolete. He invited dozens of civic and business leaders, including an official from the fire department, to witness the burning. "I gave my word that once I had obtained the full 100 per cent, this clause in the contract would be stricken," he asserted. "We're going to accomplish this with a little drama. Maybe at heart I am an arsonist. At any rate, I'm going to strike a match and set fire to the contract. Then I will sign a new contract. This will prove I am not in the slightest concerned about the 850,000 minimum. I am not concerned, as a matter of fact, with the attendance at all."[17]

In the coming months, his promises rang increasingly hollow, but on that cold mid-February 1961 day, the audience loved it. The former steelworker from Gary, Indiana, became the toast of Kansas City. Little did anyone at the press conference know that Finley had burned blank stationery paper, not the stadium lease. The attendance clause of the lease remained in effect. Finley hoodwinked the press and had no intention of signing a new lease.

Later that month, Finley staged another publicity stunt by commandeering an old school bus, dousing it with gasoline, and publicly burning it in the left-field parking lot of Municipal Stadium. Talking to reporters as flames engulfed the old yellow bus, Finley explained that the burning symbolized the end of the A's shuttling good young players to the hated New York Yankees in exchange for their aging castoffs. "Fans have not wanted to be known as a farm club of the Yankees," he said. "They have resented the many deals that have been made between these two organizations . . . I don't mean we won't make deals when we believe they will help us . . . But a new era will start in Kansas City and that I can promise . . . No more deals with the Yankees."[18]

Finley seemed to have a penchant for arson. At his farm in La Porte, Indiana, he burned the caboose he bought as a playhouse for his children in a large bonfire because he believed his teenagers and their friends were using it for inappropriate activities. What those inappropriate activities might have been was the source of endless speculation—drinking, marijuana smoking, and making out are the most common beliefs—but what

went through Finley's mind is unknown to all except the actual participants, and they are not talking. Rick Knoll said that one of the Finley's
sons told him, "My dad got pissed off, and away it went."[19] Suffice it to say
that Finley demonstrated his raging temper and took it upon himself to
clear the farm of this playhouse. La Porte local Fern Schultz said that a lot
of people thought the caboose was inappropriate for a showplace like the
Finley farm and probably were not unhappy when he burned it. She heard
comments like, "Why did he put that in front of that beautiful home?"
Schultz said that the neighbors believed that it "doesn't belong here, and
it's out of place."[20]

Finley and his management team's popularity surged during the first
three months of 1961. Everyone wanted to talk with him and hear the
new, young, and flamboyant owner's plans for the struggling A's. Finley
and his front office executives made approximately 150 appearances
throughout the community; Finley himself made more than 120 of them.
He gave speeches, sometimes five a day, at dozens of civic and public func-
tions, church meetings, social clubs, fraternities and sororities, garden clubs,
and political and public events.[21] His message at all the events was the
same: This is Kansas City's team; it will stay in the city; it will become a
winner; the city's patience and support will be needed. Finley thrived on
the breakneck pace and the warm support he received from his new city. "I
don't think I can outdo Veeck," he said, referring to Bill Veeck's reputation for stumping on behalf of his team, "but I am going to try. There is no
substitute for going out and meeting the people. The more speeches the
better."[22]

Finley, taking another page from Veeck's playbook, began to change
Municipal Stadium. While a few upgrades were already under way when
Finley arrived, the new owner embarked on a major renovation of the stadium. First, he moved the bullpen to the right-field line, and he then
moved the left-field fence and added box and bleacher seats down the left-
field line. He added much-needed lighting to the outside of the stadium,
helping to eliminate concerns that muggings might take place on the way
home from ballgames. New concession stands and restrooms were added,
and radio broadcasts of the game were piped into each restroom. He re-
painted the seats throughout the entire stadium bright yellow, turquoise,

and orange. He added new scoreboards, including something he called the "Fan-A-Gram" next to the main scoreboard to post messages. A picnic area was constructed behind the new bleacher seats in left field with maple trees for shade and carriage lights for night games. Feeling that fans wanted to see the game behind the game, he added lights to the dugout. "I look at it from the fans' point of view," explained Finley. "I like to see what's going on in the dugout—the strategy being planned and so on. So I figured everybody would like to see it too."[23] Those who disliked Finley later claimed that he added the dugout lighting so he could manage the game strategy from the owner's box.

While Finley pushed these improvements, not everyone agreed he was interested in making the MLB experience in Kansas City better. A's announcer Merle Harmon said that Finley's aggressiveness was disconcerting to many fans. "He sort of walked into the stadium and says, 'Get rid of all this stuff!' "[24] While most people probably thought what he was doing was fine, a growing number questioned his steamroller approach to running the A's.

Two of Finley's improvements to the stadium stood out. "Finley's two most interesting innovations are a device for supplying the plate umpire with baseballs when he needs them and a mechanism that saves [the umpire] the bother of bending over and dusting off the home plate," Rex Lardner wrote in a *Sports Illustrated* feature article on Finley. He continued:

> The first is a rabbit with blinking eyes, wearing an A's uniform, that rises from an invisible spot in the grass to the right of the plate umpire. Between the ears of the rabbit, who is called Harvey, is a cage of baseballs. The cover magically flings itself open and the umpire helps himself. The ascent of the rabbit is accompanied by an ascending whistle, while his disappearance into the ground is accompanied by a descending whistle. Simultaneously the organist plays "Here Comes Peter Cottontail." The other innovation is a compressed air device whose spout is in the center of the plate. When needed, air jets out to blow dirt off. A few enemy batters have been startled by Little Blowhard or Harvey the

first time they encountered them, one of them leaping nearly one foot in the air.

Regardless of the cuteness of these ideas, some within the A's organization were not amused by them. "He's trying to out-Veeck Bill Veeck," Frank Lane complained. "If the team doesn't do well, I don't think the fans are going to give a damn for Bugs Bunny."[25]

Indeed, Finley patterned many of his upgrades and innovations at Kansas City's Municipal Stadium on the efforts of White Sox owner Veeck, who upgraded Comiskey Park in 1959 and 1960. Veeck's improvements also included a Sox-O-Gram, new restrooms, fresh paint for seats, a picnic area, new radio and PA systems, and a mechanical ball-lift system. "Bill Veeck provided Charlie with a behavioral model of significant proportions—and a lot of new ideas," wrote author Tom Clark.[26] Even Veeck recognized Finley's copycat nature. He once quipped, "If I ever run out of ideas, Charlie Finley will be out of business."[27] But two things Finley never could duplicate were Veeck's ability to attract huge crowds to games and his ability to win friends in MLB, and these two critical shortcomings haunted Finley throughout his baseball career. His teams, even when successful, never generated huge revenue, and Finley never had the support of the other owners to take the actions he believed necessary for his club.

One stadium innovation that Finley did originate was placing sheep on a tall rocky hill beyond the right-field fence. Finley, who loved the peaceful view of the sheep, also dressed an employee in a shepherd's outfit for each home game, and the shepherd would ring a bell after every A's home run. The sheep grazed behind right field for Finley's first four seasons in Kansas City. Then one day, a batter hit a soaring home run that struck one straight on the head, instantly killing it. Moreover, the sheep were targeted continuously by A's players for practical jokes and mistreatment. Moe Drabowsky tried to hit the sheep with fungoes during pregame warm-ups. "I was always taking aim at the sheep up there," he said. "You could scare the sheep . . . One relief pitcher chased one of the sheep up the hill before a game . . . [It] died of a heart attack."[28] For a while Finley also had goats in the outfield.

Maybe the reason for all the practical joking was that some players found the animals demeaning. The players took themselves seriously and thought they were being turned into a carnival sideshow. And Harvey, the sheep, and the goats were just the beginning. Many of Finley's ideas never came to pass, including placing an elevator under the pitching mound that would lift up a relief pitcher entering the game. Sanity prevailed, and Finley dropped the idea, but sportscaster Bill Grigsby recalled that Finley always wanted "another Finley First!"—something brand-new and original. In Grigsby's words, the organization soon realized, "Brother, this is going to be a long season."[29]

Though turning the A's into winners took years, Finley acted quickly to improve the cosmetic and entertainment aspects of his product. However, the improvements he made to Municipal Stadium, which he leased from the city, started his initial problems with, and later his disdain for, the local city council. "I poured a half a million dollars of my own money into improvements on a municipally owned stadium," Finley said. "And now I've got the sexiest looking ball park in the country. The ballpark looked like a pigpen. I asked the council to fix it up. They pleaded poverty but told me they would give me credit if I did something . . . They gave me nothing."[30] Finley actually invested $411,000 in stadium improvements.[31] As Finley complained and bickered with city officials throughout 1961 for reimbursement, the owner's shine faded. By the late summer of 1961, the bloom was most assuredly off the rose. Finley's proclaimed satisfaction with his newly adopted city waned as well, and he surreptitiously began to plan for moving the team.

While Charlie Finley believed he knew the front office and promotional aspects of his new business, the actual baseball side proved challenging. At first he publicly stated his respect for and reliance on newly hired general manager Frank Lane and field manager Joe Gordon in all baseball matters. But he did not hold to it.

Privately, Finley intended to be his own man in baseball, just as he was in the insurance business. His actions proved in keeping with his character; he carefully controlled everything in his life and refused to allow others to run his baseball club. It became evident to both Lane and Gordon that their new boss would dictate most every decision of the A's, be it business, promotion, or game related. As far as the relationship between the field manager and the general manager, Finley either misread the situation or chose to ignore the adversity between his two subordinates. Going into spring training, Lane-Gordon relations were tenuous at best, and there was a long history of animosity. Nonetheless, both men were professionals and did have a measure of respect for each other. In fact, both soon realized that they had a new nemesis to focus their attention on—their new boss, Charles O. Finley.

Lane's problems with Finley began almost immediately. Lane thought he needed to shore up several positions on the field. Finley believed that, as team owner, he had the ultimate authority, and he wanted to place his own mark on the club. "Lane has not been shorn of any authority," stated Finley. "I leave the discussions to making a trade to him and then he makes a recommendation to me. Then we discuss the possibilities."[32] That was a far cry from allowing his baseball professional to oversee the team. Farm director Hank Peters described Finley and his insurance subordinate Pat Friday as very naive in all aspects of professional baseball. "Charlie Finley didn't know beans about baseball," Peters said.[33]

Communication was a problem between Finley and Lane from the beginning. Finley wanted to move the A's spring training facilities from West Palm Beach, Florida, to Chandler, Arizona, for 1962. Acting on instructions from Finley, Lane negotiated a deal with city officials in Chandler. As he prepared to sign the new deal with Chandler officials, he heard a radio report that Finley had just inked a five-year lease extension back in West Palm Beach. Perplexed and annoyed, Lane called Finley and asked, "Are we both working for the same club?"[34] Finley tried to play each city off against the other by asking Lane to see if Chandler would top the West Palm Beach offer. Lane refused. Pitting one city against another soon became one of Charlie Finley's favorite negotiation tactics to extract the best business terms possible. This negotiating tactic and the rancor it invoked led to Finley's negative public image and his eventual reputation as a slick-talking, untrustworthy carpetbagger.

The situation between Finley and manager Joe Gordon was no better. An early confrontation portended a rocky relationship. One evening during spring training in 1961, Finley arrived at the A's hotel around one A.M. and saw A's broadcaster Bill Grigsby, reporters Ernie Mehl and Joe McGuff, and coach Jo-Jo White drinking in the bar. Finley joined them and asked White to call Gordon down from his room to discuss a few issues about the team. White refused and suggested it might be better if Finley called Gordon. Finley rang Gordon's room and told him to join them at the bar to talk about a few of the players. Gordon reportedly told the owner that he was not going to talk about the players in public, least of all at a bar, and that they could discuss things in the morning at the ballpark. Finley did not take kindly to a subordinate refusing his demands and responded, "Look, get your ass down here or you're fired."

Gordon showed up about ten minutes later in a white T-shirt and his stocking feet. Finley yelled that if Gordon was too busy to meet with him, he was fired. Gordon, his face red with rage, grabbed Finley by the neck. "Look you phony son of a bitch, I just work for you," he shouted. "You bought my contract, Mr. Finley, but you don't own me. And if you wanna pay me my $25,000 for the year, let's just get this thing over right now." Finley, choking and trying to catch his breath, defused the situation by changing from a bully to a friend: "I just love a fighter, Joe! I want you as my manager. Okay, let's talk about it tomorrow at the ball park." Gordon released Finley's neck and went back to bed.[35]

As the 1961 season began, the lowly A's stumbled out of the gate. It would take more than Frank Lane's trades to overcome their futility. The tense Gordon-Finley relationship was exacerbated by the team's poor performance on the field. As the A's lost game after game, Finley began "advising" his manager more and more. For example, he ordered Gordon to move pitcher Jim Archer from the bullpen into the starting rotation. Gordon complained to reporters about Finley's interference and his difficulty managing the team under such conditions. Finley reaffirmed his faith in his manager and stated he was only offering advice and suggestions to Gordon. "Mr. Finley's statement clarifies the situation to me," Gordon responded. "I'm pleased. If he and Frank Lane are only offering suggestions to me, then I'm free to accept or reject them as I see fit."[36] Unfortunately for Gordon, they were not suggestions; they were orders traveling under an assumed name. To make matters worse, Finley had a telephone installed between the owner's box and the dugout. Gordon hated Finley's frequent telephonic "suggestions" during games.

The one moment that trumped all other Gordon-Finley controversies involved forged Finley initials on a lineup card. One evening Gordon gave the umpires a lineup card with the notation "Approved by C.O.F." written at the bottom. One of the players had jokingly written it on the card, and Gordon thought it was funny and submitted it. The joke appeared in the local papers the next day, and Finley called Gordon, berating him for the stunt and asking if he had written the initials on the card. Gordon said that he hadn't but did not offer up who might have done it. Finley eventually dropped the matter, but he did not forget the slight and quietly began looking for a new manager.

Finley soon faced a new embarrassment by reneging on his promise not to trade with the Yankees. On June 14, 1961, Frank Lane traded the A's best starting pitcher, Bud Daley, to the hated Yankees for pitcher Art Ditmar, a solid veteran who was off to a slow start, and young power-hitting prospect Deron Johnson. Despite the trade's considerable merit, the uproar in Kansas City came immediately. Lane intentionally did this deal to embarrass Finley. "When he [Finley] pulled that bush league trick of burning the charter bus to Yankee Stadium and announcing he wouldn't even trade the A's batboy for Mickey Mantle, I was determined to make a deal if I could," Lane explained. "I told Finley at the start not to make stupid promises that he would never deal with the Yankees. I deal with any club and always have."[37] Finley's approach was more philosophical, even as he fumed about Lane's dealing behind his back. "My father reminded me one day that a wise man changes his mind, but a fool never does," Finley told the media. "He was right . . . This is a screwy business . . . And right now I'm chuckling at myself."[38] The A's fans were not chuckling.

In an attempt to distract the public from the Yankees deal, Finley tried to showcase his true commitment to turning the A's into winners. Finley and his executives were watching a big young redheaded high school pitcher from Pennsylvania named Lew Krausse Jr. His father, Lew Sr., had been a pitcher for the old Connie Mack Athletics and was now a scout for the A's. The young Krausse appeared to be a pitching prodigy; he hurled 19 no-hitters in high school and struck out 24 batters in one game. Finley had an inside track because of his father's job as an A's scout, but signing the young phenom was not assured. Lew Sr. said his son would sign with the highest bidder. The A's and Finley brought the young Krausse to Washington when the A's were in town to throw batting practice. The flame-throwing youngster turned heads.[39] Friday hustled the young Krausse and his father to the Shoreham Hotel for a private meeting with Finley. Lew Krausse recalled that

> Finley himself had dinner with my father and I, and Finley said to me these exact words: He said, "[Well] I don't know much about baseball, but it sure looked like you threw the ball hard, and other people said you look like you have great potential." But really and truthfully, he didn't have a whole lot of knowledge of who had ability and who didn't. But that was my first meeting with Mr. Finley. As a matter of fact, he had a pair of solid gold cuff links on that he just took right off and gave to my father. My father complimented him on them, and he just took them off and gave them to my dad. I actually signed a contract before that next day, before I graduated from high school, which wasn't legal. He demanded it, and I was looking out more for my dad . . . It just seemed like, well, $125,000 was all the money in the world.

It was one of the highest signing bonuses paid at that point in baseball history. Krausse became Finley's first big-money bonus baby.[40]

Finley, facing a public uproar over the Yankees trade, decided to start his new young hurler at Municipal Stadium just 2 days later and just 10 days after the young Krausse graduated from high school. Joe Gordon protested. He thought starting the young, untested pitcher in his first game at the major-league level could damage not only his arm but also his confidence. Finley dismissed his manager's concerns. He needed a positive story, and the young pitcher would generate much interest and a large crowd.

On June 16, 1961, on a warm humid night before 26,000 fans, Lew Krausse started his first professional game against the Los Angeles Angels. The big right-hander hurled a superb three-hit shutout for a 4–0 victory, and he even collected two hits himself. His performance electrified Kansas City. Finley beamed with pride over his new find. The press forgot about the Yankees trade and focused on this new pitching star, even comparing him to future Hall of Famers Bob Feller and Robin Roberts. Even the skeptical Gordon complimented the kid, saying, "This is the greatest pitching performance by a youngster I've ever seen in the major leagues."[41] Unfortunately for Gordon, this did not assuage Finley, who had decided to replace him with a new, more "cooperative" manager.

Only days after Lew Krausse's big debut, Finley canned Gordon, announcing the firing at a hastily called press conference. "I was the man behind the move," Finley stated. "Lane told me a thousand times during spring training that Gordon was no good . . . It was a cinch to happen because he (Gordon) and Lane proved they couldn't get along together." Lane remained silent at the press conference, but afterward he called Joe Gordon, who was fishing, to give him the news. By the time Lane reached Gordon by phone, Gordon had already heard about the firing on the radio. "Charlie told me he was going to fire Gordon," Lane later recalled. "And he did it right after we had our best road trip . . . But Joe had done a few things to upset Charlie, like the lineup card thing, and you just don't do that. So, I made no real strong fight to keep Joe."[42]

Finley and Lane needed to find a new manager fast, so shortly before the press conference, they approached their 38-year-old veteran outfielder Hank Bauer. The ex-Marine and native Kansas Citian had played 12 seasons for the New York Yankees, helping them win seven world championships. Bauer had a record 17-game hitting streak in the World Series between 1956 and 1958 and made three All-Star teams during his Yankees career. He had joined the A's in the Roger Maris trade two years earlier. Now on the downside of his career, Bauer played as a part-time outfielder for the A's and was rumored to be on the verge of being released. At first, Finley tried to get Bauer to manage in the minor leagues, but he refused. Then Lane suggested he take over for Gordon as manager of the A's. Bauer reluctantly agreed and signed on to manage the A's through the 1962 season. Finley introduced his new manager to the press and boasted, "He will make a great manager . . . He is tough and a winner."[43] Bauer planned on keeping the current coaches and told the press, "I'm going to take it easy for a while until I get my feet wet."[44]

Finley orchestrated Bauer's managerial debut a few hours later by having the public address announcer at Municipal Stadium say, "Hank Bauer, your playing days are over. You have been named manager of the Kansas City Athletics." And with that, Bauer walked to home plate and submitted the A's lineup card. Most of the fans in attendance that day had no idea of the change before the announcement, which was greeted with a few boos. But Bauer and the A's turned the jeers into cheers by winning that first game with him as manager.

Nevertheless, no manager could change the luck of the A's in 1961. The players were young, inexperienced, and not very talented. There were a few bright spots on Finley's team, including a solid season by veteran first baseman Norm Siebern and talented youngsters such as infielders Jerry Lumpe, Dick Howser, and Wayne Causey. Their pitchers were terrible, and the team spent most of the summer in the cellar of the American League. Lew Krausse Jr. soon discovered that being a big-league pitcher was not as easy as his debut game had made it seem. American League hitters began sitting on his fastball, and he got shelled most every outing after his debut. Krausse tried to learn a breaking ball, but, he recalled, "my arm wasn't mature enough to handle those things . . . I felt my arm burning late that season, but I didn't want to tell anybody . . . I was going out there when I had no business being out there pitching . . . By the end of the season my confidence was shattered."[45]

Bauer appeared to have no answers to the troubles of the struggling A's. Finley again became impatient. He wanted to see improvement, not realizing, or not being willing to admit, that improvement with bad baseball teams is mostly incremental. Finley even contemplated firing Bauer in early August 1961, but Frank Lane intervened. "I said 'Charlie, you can't do that. You just got through the firing of Gordon a couple of months ago . . . It would be a horrible thing to do."[46] Finley decided to keep Bauer.

During his ownership of the A's in Kansas City, Finley constantly sought to move the team elsewhere. Finley was, in the words of associate Jim Schaaf, always in search of new possibilities. "He didn't feel, for whatever reason, that he was going to be able to really make it big in Kansas City. He just didn't feel that way. That was his opinion, and so I think when it all boils down, it was a business decision. He wanted to go. He thought there were greener pastures."[47] That business decision dominated

Finley's thinking about the A's from the time he took over until he left the city for Oakland at the end of the 1967 season. The manner in which Finley schemed to move the team proved contentious from 1961 on.

Bill Grigsby thought Finley bought the A's with the intention of moving the team. Grigsby remembered picking up Finley at the airport and chauffeuring him, along with Pat Friday and another associate, around on his first trip to Kansas City in January 1961. Grigsby worked for the Majestic Advertising Agency and the Schlitz Brewing Company, which held the broadcast rights to the A's games. Both companies were eager to meet the new A's owner. Grigsby recalls overhearing the discussion in his car between Finley and Friday. "We went to the brewery, where the meeting went fairly well. But on the way back to the hotel, all he could do was talk about moving the club out of Kansas City. That was the first hint I had of future trouble. I knew I had become privy to something, and I knew I had to keep quiet about it. The only city that was mentioned that day was Dallas, but mostly it was moving anywhere."[48]

Finley's relocation efforts took many different turns over the next seven years and would lead to bitterness and consternation on all sides, including fans, city officials, and the owner himself. During the summer of 1961, Dallas became the first of many cities that Finley eyed as a possible new home for the A's. It was about twice the size of Kansas City and had a steadily growing population. Dallas–Fort Worth officials were planning to build a new 50,000-seat stadium in nearby Arlington, Texas. The city also offered a much larger media market. This appealed to Finley, as radio and television revenue played an increasingly larger role in teams' financial success.

Ernie Mehl, the beloved longtime sports columnist and editor at the *Kansas City Star*, broke the story of Finley's convoluted maneuvers. Mehl had been the driving force in bringing the Athletics to Kansas City, and he had a special affection for the team. He began tracking rumors in the summer of 1961 of Finley's negotiations with other cities about moving the team. Team manager Hank Bauer first leaked him the story, and Mehl immediately began to report on what he considered Finley's duplicity. In August he trumpeted that Finley's famous burning of the stadium lease in the mayor's office in February had been a ruse, that instead he had

burned blank stationery, and that the attendance clause that had precipi-
tated the stunt was still in effect. The city tried all season to get Finley to
sign a new lease, but the wily owner continuously put it off by feigning
scheduling conflicts or saying that he was traveling.

Mehl found out about a secret trip by Finley to Dallas with American
League umpire supervisor Cal Hubbard to view the Cotton Bowl and
Burnett Field. They had investigated the city's ability to accommodate a
Major League Baseball team on a temporary basis until a new ballpark
could be built. Hank Bauer had ratted out this trip to Mehl, out of spite for
Finley's constant meddling with the A's. Bauer told Mehl that Finley had
come into his clubhouse office after returning to Kansas City, threw down
a 10-gallon cowboy hat, and said, "Well, what would you boys think about
playing down in Dallas?"[49] Mehl quickly confirmed the story from sources
in Dallas.

On August 17, 1961, Mehl wrote a spectacular front-page story expos-
ing Finley's relocation efforts. "Finley is considering a move of the franchise to Dallas," Mehl reported.

> Most suspicious of all has been his failure to sign a new lease with
> Kansas City for the use of Municipal Stadium, although he made
> a great to-do about signing a new one at the start of the season . . .
> The old lease, however, wasn't burned . . . Since then the council
> has made repeated attempts to get Finley to sign and on numer-
> ous occasions he has promised he would . . . But as of now the club
> is operating under the old lease that stipulates that in the event
> the ticket sales fall below 850,000 the owner of the franchise
> can exercise the option to move by so notifying the city before
> October 15.

Mehl concluded that at the current pace, home attendance would fall
far short of 850,000, and Finley would probably attempt to recoup his
losses by moving the club to Texas.

Mehl also criticized the manner in which Finley was running the
A's and his treatment of Bauer. "His decisions on the field have been
criticized . . . second guessed by the very men who should have been

sympathetic with him. He has had to alter his pitching rotation to satisfy the whim of the owner, make line-up changes against his better judgment," Mehl wrote. "The players have reacted to the front office discord and they play now as if they no longer cared."[50] Later Mehl commented, "There never has been a baseball operation such as this, nothing so bizarre, so impossibly incongruous."[51]

Finley read Mehl's story while he was in Dallas, attending a meeting of the Texas Medical Association, which was a client of his insurance firm. He responded with a broadside that had just enough truth in it to be good propaganda. "I know nothing about the rumors," he declared. "They're rather disgusting. It's just a coincidence that I'm in Dallas. I've certainly indicated a desire to operate in Kansas City."[52]

Charlie Finley's ego and outspokenness confounded the issue even further only a few hours later as the *Dallas News* reported the details of Finley's touring sports facilities in the area while declaring his love of Dallas as a potential home for a major-league franchise. "A team here (in Dallas) would be a tremendous asset to major league baseball," Finley boasted.[53] "Mehl's stories were based on rumor and not fact," Finley later said to the Kansas City papers. "Never once did he call me to check out what he was writing about. The truth is what I have said and I will stand behind it . . . It makes me so sick it almost makes me want to take the club out of here."

After Finley's love of media attention and forked-tongue quotes to the Kansas City and Dallas newspapers exposed his secret relocation scheme, he backtracked and tried publicly to discredit Mehl and the Kansas City papers. The practice of quick denials, shifting blame, and publicly disparaging his critics became common Finley tactics in dealing with controversies for the rest of his baseball career—most of them caused by the owner himself.

Finley insisted that Mehl's negative writing about his club and management amounted to no more than payback for Finley's refusal to pay travel expenses of *Kansas City Star* and *Times* reporters. Finley went on to imply that Mehl, as the *Star*'s sports editor, acted inappropriately by accepting $1,000 to edit the team's yearbook for the team's previous owner. The newspaper quickly denied Finley's assertions, claiming that

Mehl never asked for nor received any travel expense money from Finley, and Mehl explained that he had edited the team's yearbook on his vacation.[54]

The Finley-Mehl feud came to a head on August 20, 1961, when Finley held an "Ernie Mehl Appreciation Day" between games of a doubleheader with the White Sox. Finley ordered billboards that said ERNIE MEHL APPRECIATION DAY—POISON PEN AWARD FOR 1961, with a cartoon of Mehl sitting at a typewriter with a quill pen next to a bottle labeled "poison ink." He had the billboards mounted on both sides of a flatbed truck, which was driven around the playing field. As the truck circled the field the organist played "Who's Afraid of the Big Bad Wolf?"[55]

Few of the 10,000 fans in attendance that day really understood or paid attention to the truck and the inflammatory billboards. Before the game, Finley badgered broadcasters Bill Grigsby and Merle Harmon to promise to announce a description of his big "promotion" between games. Grigsby and Harmon, neither of whom worked for Finley or wanted anything to do with this stunt, said the best they could do was mention the promotional event before the game.

The circling of the billboard truck was followed by an actual "Poison Pen Award" presentation ceremony on the field. Ernie Mehl did not attend the game, so Finley presented it to him in absentia. After the ceremony, Finley ran into Harmon and asked, "Hey, did you give my big promotion a good plug?"

Harmon responded, "No, I did not."

An angry Finley said, "What did you mean you didn't? You promised me you would do it!"

"I promised you we would do anything to be cooperative as long as it was in good taste," Harmon asserted. "Those are my orders."

Finley shouted back, "Well, it was in good taste."

"I think it was the most despicable thing I've ever seen in my life," Harmon told him.

Finley fumed and launched into a tirade, cussing at Harmon and threatening to fire him. Harmon held his ground, insisting that he did not work for Finley and thus could not be fired by him, and Finley eventually stormed away.[56]

Major League Baseball commissioner Ford Frick disapproved of the whole escapade. Frick told the Associated Press, "Such things do not belong in baseball and I called Mr. Mehl this morning to apologize to him both personally and in the name of baseball."[57] For his part, Finley was unapologetic. He said it came in response to "Mehl's vicious campaign against the team."[58] He then strong-armed the Kansas City government, especially mayor pro tem Tom Gavin, to send Frick a cable avowing the city's strong support of Finley's ownership of the A's. "We have always had and still have complete confidence in Mr. Finley's integrity and sincerity, and we feel that this attitude more correctly reflects the sentiments of the vast majority of the people of this city than does the unfortunate adverse publicity of recent date," it read.[59]

Finley added fuel to the fire by instructing his team's traveling secretary to cease making travel arrangements for *Star* and *Times* reporters for road games. He further attempted to isolate and punish the newspapers by instructing that no team information or press releases be given their reporters. Publicly feuding with journalists in Kansas City, especially a sportswriter as powerful as Ernie Mehl, may have been Finley's cardinal sin. Most owners do everything possible to maintain good press relations, even if they privately loathe the media. Finley had abrogated this time-honored agreement.

Finley further stoked the fire just two days after the "Poison Pen" affair by calling a press conference at his Chicago office. He specifically invited all the Chicago sports media but excluded any *Kansas City Star* or *Times* reporters. Mehl got the message; Finley had no intention of backing down.

Reporters at the hastily called press conference buzzed over what Finley might do next. The owner did not disappoint: He fired Frank Lane. "I've waited for him to quit and save face," Finley explained. "But now I'm firing him . . . He did nothing but create dissension on my club. Any fool can sit on the telephone and make deals. I wanted someone to oversee and run the entire organization. But all he did was make deals. Pat Friday and myself—we did the G.M.'s work." The owner also assured reporters that Lane would be paid in full. He disputed his earlier pronouncements of Lane's salary being $100,000, insisting now that he was not the highest-paid general manager in baseball. "He got only $50,000 a year from us and there was no bonus clause attached for attendance," Finley said. He claimed he tried to reach Lane to inform him of his firing but could not get ahold of him before the press conference. Finley went on, "If I had known then what I know now, Gordon would be my manager. It was Lane who poisoned my mind on Joe Gordon . . . and Lane also has been knifing Hank Bauer. The biggest mistake I ever made was firing Gordon. I fired the wrong man. Lane was the man who should have been fired."

Though Mehl was not present, other sportswriters grilled Finley about his rumored move of the A's to Dallas. He denied it and insisted his relations with Kansas City officials were excellent.[60]

Finley ended the conference by announcing that Pat Friday would be the A's general manager. Finley decided that Friday, his former insurance business subordinate, would handle the business operations of the club and that Finley himself would make all future trades. Friday remembered the surprise of his appointment, saying, "Mr. Finley called and said, 'I've held a press conference up here in Chicago and have decided the time has come for Frank Lane and me to have a parting of the ways. By the way, you're the new general manager.' "[61]

Meanwhile, Frank Lane, who was at a Kansas City hotel giving a speech promoting the virtues of owner Charles O. Finley and the future fortunes of the A's, finally got word of his firing. "When I came out to get a cab to go to the ball park the cab driver said, 'Gee, that's tough luck, Mr. Lane.' I asked him what had happened—was a ballplayer hurt? He said, 'No, you got fired. Didn't you know that?' "[62]

The next day Lane held a press conference to "set the record straight" and unburden his conscience regarding his former boss. He discussed many topics, including the potential move to Dallas, the team's operations, and Finley's feud with the *Star*.

> Beyond a shadow of a doubt Charles Finley has been considering a move of the Kansas City Athletics to Dallas . . . This move has been in Finley's mind for some time. Now that he knows it cannot be done he is saying he never contemplated it. But he is not telling the truth and he knows it . . . I am glad to be out. I was warned not to take the job, but I took it anyway. Now I wish I had listened to the advice.[63]

Not surprisingly, Finley and Lane traded barbs and lawsuits for years after they severed their relationship. Finley refused to pay the remaining salary on his contract, and Lane filed a lawsuit against him in federal court in Chicago on October 8, 1963. Lane contended that his contract called for him to be paid as general manager for four years, followed by payment as a consultant for an additional four years. Finley dragged out the case for four years. Lane sued for $144,000, but the two eventually settled for $113,000.

Meanwhile, with his relocation scheme exposed and his management of the ball club under intense criticism by the media and fans, Finley needed to do something to repair his public image. Many Kansas City fans and city officials doubted his motives and increasingly viewed him as a manipulative carpetbagger. On August 26, 1961, Finley finally signed an amendment deleting the attendance clause from the stadium lease, but he remained bitter and sanctimonious about his treatment by the local media. "It was my idea to take the clause out and . . . it took some time to draw up the agreement," he said. "Now, it has been done and is signed. I think this should be a sufficient answer to those who doubted my veracity . . . It is a shame that when someone spends $500,000 of his own money on a city owned stadium, works night and day and sacrifices, and then is criticized as I have been criticized. It makes me sick enough to want to take the club out of Kansas City."[64] Finley transformed complaints about his surreptitious efforts to move the A's from Kansas City into the reason for moving the A's from Kansas City.

The play of the 1961 A's on the ball field also likely sickened the Kansas City fans. The A's finished tied with the expansion Washington Senators for last place, with a 61–100 record, 47.5 games out of first place. The A's poor performance on the field and Finley's constant off-field antics negatively affected attendance at Municipal Stadium. Finley's plans to heavily promote the A's before the season and his innovative direct mail ticket campaign had also failed. By the end of the 1961 season, the A's had sold only 775,000 total tickets, and only 684,000 fans actually showed up at the stadium. Finley stopped most customary promotional activities and player appearances, focusing solely on direct mail promotions, and only within the metro Kansas City area—he didn't reach out to fans in the outer suburbs or neighboring towns and counties.

This resulted in disappointing season ticket sales. To make matters worse, Finley disbanded several popular youth programs during the season as well, including a popular booster-club system with a network that stretched to four states that offered discounted tickets to high school fans.

Finley's first season as owner of the Athletics served as a microcosm of his future behavior and personality as a major-league owner. On the one hand, Finley demonstrated his persuasive charm, perseverance, strong work ethic, generosity, innovation, spirit, showmanship, and commitment to winning. However, he also possessed a significant and powerful negative side: his need to control everyone and everything in his world, his untrustworthiness and proclivity to deceitfulness, his hot temper and bullying of subordinates and colleagues, his capricious decision making, his attempt to move the ball club to Dallas, and his penchant for rewriting history whenever it suited his needs. For better or for worse, all these traits would be on display for A's fans for many years to come.

Chapter Three

In the Doldrums

Kansas City's winter of discontent after the 1961 baseball season brought rumors of a move for the A's and a behind-the-scenes effort to mend fences between Charlie Finley and Ernie Mehl. It succeeded to some extent, as the head of the Kansas City Chamber of Commerce engineered a public kiss-and-make-up between Mehl and Finley at the 1962 home opener. As a symbol of their "burying the hatchet, Mehl threw out the first pitch to Finley behind the plate."[1] The good humor, however, did not last long.

All through the 1962 season, Finley continued to work a deal to pull the A's out of Kansas City. The city councilmen learned that Finley refused to sign a two-year deal with the Schlitz Brewing Company to broadcast the A's games because he wanted the flexibility to move the A's to Dallas at the end of the season. He also refused to discuss any stadium lease extensions with the city.[2] On May 18, 1962, he applied to the American League for permission to move the team. His request was ruled out of order for a simple reason: He had raised it at a meeting that was entirely about minor-league issues. Finley's reaction to the rebuff was typically belligerent: "Those goddamn club owners think they can keep me from moving the team. I'll show them a thing or two. I've got some tricks I haven't used yet."[3] He believed he could sue MLB if necessary, overturning the antitrust exemption put into place by Congress in 1922 and moving the team on the grounds that his competition was engaging in restraint of trade.

Soon, city leaders began their own campaign to counter Finley's moves. Ernie Mehl proved a willing accomplice. He published a lengthy report of the maneuvering in the *Sporting News*, calling the fans of the A's "the most abused in the major leagues" and denouncing Finley as a tyrant seeking to rob the loyal fans of their team. He repeated the demand of the city leaders that the other owners end this debate with "a simple, forthright, clear-cut statement from the nine other owners that the Athletics' franchise is not going to be moved."[4] The principal concern, Mehl argued, was that the stadium lease expired at the end of 1963 season and at that point there would be nothing to hold the A's in Kansas City without strong pressure from the other American League owners. For his part, Finley repeatedly said he had no plans to move the team unless necessary. Finley refused to define what "necessary" really meant.

Later that summer, sports columnist Red Smith announced, "There are at least five men in Kansas City prepared to buy out Finley at a fair price."[5] As with the definition of "necessary," a "fair price" had the possibility of a wide divergence of meanings. Regardless, having spent the better part of a decade trying to purchase a major-league franchise, Finley would not have sold the A's despite the fairness of any offer.

Finley asked for a meeting of American League owners on September 18 to discuss a possible relocation of the A's. Arriving in New York City, he pressured his fellow owners on the Dallas–Fort Worth area's merits to host a major-league franchise. Representatives from the Texas urban powerhouse showed up to make a sales pitch, and Finley supported their positive assessment with a report of his own travels there. He also introduced a set of grievances against his current situation in Kansas City. He recited long-standing concerns: complaints about the stadium (opened in 1923), the lease, the cut on concessions, the failure to draw large audiences, and the difficulties in obtaining repayment for improvements to the venue. He also added a few new ones: poor availability of parking near the stadium, inadequate roads to access the stadium, and fan safety. But he did not officially ask his fellow owners for permission to move, in no small measure because he had counted noses beforehand and knew he did not have the votes to gain approval. No action resulted.[6]

Seeing his efforts come to nothing, Finley tried a new approach. He went back to Kansas City leaders and demanded a new stadium, claiming that, without one, the city's "days as a major league city are numbered." He complained about the seats, the amenities, the vendor accommodations, the locker rooms, the training facilities, the access, the parking, and the location. Nothing, as far as Finley was concerned, could make Municipal Stadium acceptable. He concluded that Kansas City could be an outstanding baseball town, "but it's like fishing—you can have all types of hooks in your tackle box, but without bait they're no good. A new stadium is the bait."[7] Finley said he wanted a new edifice completed as early as 1964.

The city council took Finley's call for a new stadium under advisement and appointed a group to study it. This standard practice of putting off decision making satisfied most of those in the American League; the city promised to improve parking accessibility to Municipal Stadium and to undertake the development of a master plan for the construction of a large sports complex that could handle both baseball and football. When briefed on the city's efforts in the Chicago office of American League president Joe Cronin on September 27, Finley reeled with displeasure. He resented what he considered the subterfuge of city officials, who claimed that there were more than 5,000 parking spots within walking distance of the stadium. Finley and the league had agreed that only about 1,800 were both in a safe neighborhood and acceptable for A's fans. The Kansas City Council members offered a carrot: "We would at least double the capacity for parking if we were assured of keeping the club." They wanted Finley to sign an extension on the current stadium lease, which wouldn't expire for another year, but Finley refused.[8] At an owners' meeting on October 5, the league also accepted the Kansas City strategy on the study, stating, "It was agreed a study would be made of how to correct these two faults, which are obvious, and compare that cost with the building of a 50,000-seat stadium with parking spaces for 15,000 cars."[9]

One issue arising from these discussions infuriated Finley. Kansas

City Chamber of Commerce head Earl Smith intimated that new facilities would be provided when the A's attendance increased. Finley rightly charged that attendance could not increase as long as going to the games was such an unappealing experience. "If the A's moved into the first division," Ernie Mehl reported in the *Sporting News*, "it was felt new facilities would be provided the club."[10] But probably not sooner. Smith countered that a better team would draw more fans and that Finley should address the problem of the A's finishing at or near the bottom of the league since arriving in Kansas City for the 1955 season. Finley responded that fielding a better team would be his most important objective but that he did not have the money to sign good players because of the small revenue generated at the gate.

The team on the field did not generate much in the way of fan support during this time. Both 1961 and 1962 were horrific seasons, in which the A's earned records of 61–100 and 72–90, respectively, finishing ahead of only the hapless Washington Senators. With first baseman Norm Siebern and second baseman Jerry Lumpe leading the offense, and nothing spectacular behind them, the A's did not inspire much confidence. There was no superstar to watch every night as he chased some record, nor was there the zany wretchedness of a team like the New York Mets, which attracted a loyal following who came to see the next boneheaded method of defeat. The A's lengthy losing streaks made going to the ballpark an exercise in frustration for the fans. Not surpisingly, the team finished eighth in attendance, out of ten teams, in 1961 and dead last in the league in 1962.

As his team slogged through the 1963 season, Finley thought strategically about the problems of Major League Baseball and offered comments on how to deal with them. Not long after the World Series, Finley sent a letter to MLB commissioner Ford Frick arguing for playing the series at night. He made the case that evening games, and weekend afternoon games, would draw a greater attendance and would allow the "working man" to participate in the experience. This was important, he noted, because "it is the working man who supports baseball throughout the entire season." He recommended that MLB take action to ensure that the workingman could take part in all aspects of the game. "In essence," he wrote, "we have been saying for years to the working man, 'thanks friend, we appreciate your support during the season and now that it's time to stage America's Greatest Sport's Spectacle, we are going to stage it at the most inconvenient and unreasonable time for you to see it. We are going to start it on a Wednesday afternoon when you are working at the steel mills, coal mines, factories, or offices. You can get the details when you get home from work.'" He made the same case for children, who could not see these games because they took place during school hours, and argued that the league must make fans of children so they will also be fans when they grow up. He brought to bear his sales background, adding, "We are selling baseball and if we are wise, we will do everything possible for the greatest exposure of America's Greatest Sport's Spectacle—The World Series."[11] Nothing came of his proposals at the time.

Finley was correct about the Kansas City stadium, and the dreadful team coupled with a decrepit place to play made matters all the worse. Municipal Stadium had been a makeshift arrangement all along. Opened in 1923 as a minor-league park, it had to be enlarged in 1955 to accommodate the A's with the addition of a double-decked grandstand that extended from home plate to the right-field foul pole and down the third-base line. With this, as well as bleachers in right field, it still handled only 30,611 fans. Not that this was much of a problem, since the A's rarely sold out. But the amenities and intangibles were depressing. As a major-league facility, it was marginal at best. Finley knew the stadium in Kansas City needed to be replaced.[12] Ernie Mehl did not agree and insisted repeatedly about the stadium that "there is the feeling that it is exactly what many have said: one of the most attractive in the major leagues."[13] In this case, Finley was on the better side of the argument, even if persuading community leaders of it would take time.[14]

In the fall of 1962, Finley gained few concessions from the league or the city. Indeed, Cronin forced Finley to back off and make nice with Kansas City officials. Finley told Mehl that he was happy to stay in Kansas City, even saying in a moment of uncharacteristic candor, "I have done some thinking [about moving the team], but the fact is that if the fans will support me here and we can come up with a good club, our problems are over." Then came his mea culpa to the Kansas City fans, who had turned on him when they'd heard about his discussions with Dallas: "I can understand their feelings. They had a major league club and they didn't want to lose it." Finley said that he thought the A's were better than when he bought them and that they would improve in the future. He tried to subvert the idea of moving the team. "We're in Kansas City to stay," he stated, "and we're going to make the best of it. I think the fans will come out and support us." Finley also played up the supposed losses that the A's had experienced since he took ownership, which he claimed amounted to $1.55 million in 1962. (There is anecdotal evidence that he made at least a small profit every year that he owned the team.) To combat these alleged losses, Finley vowed austerity in player signings and bonuses and forced the city to make concessions on the stadium lease.[15]

Finley did make efforts to improve the situation in Kansas City during the 1963 season. At the same time, though, he happily courted other cities as a possible home for the A's. Janus-like, Finley repeatedly swore fealty to Kansas City while threatening to move the team if he did not get what he wanted: Finley's A's would stay in Kansas City only if the city built him a new publicly financed stadium with generous lease terms that would line his pockets with money.[16] In so doing, he pioneered what became the standard ploy in all professional sports: to shake down the local government for funding for these initiatives by threatening to leave the city for greener fields.

Finley's flap with Kansas City politicos over Municipal Stadium took a new turn with the great stadium-lease escapade of 1963. It caused him to complain about the lease throughout the year and led Ernie Mehl to charge him with abusing the Kansas City fans because, as the city council claimed in a letter to the American League, "there has seemed to be little interest by the owner in developing a dynamic baseball operation in Kansas City."[17] Finley certainly did not see it that way, and it seems that his organization was largely successful in signing and developing the young talent that would make the A's into a contender.

The controversy began with the twin events of the A's lease coming up for renewal and the move of the American Football League's Dallas Texans to Kansas City, where they became the Chiefs. On February 8, 1963, the cagey owner of the soon-to-be Chiefs, Lamar Hunt, negotiated a stunning agreement to play football in Municipal Stadium for one dollar per year for the first two years in Kansas City, with very favorable conditions to follow. Finley wanted to know why his deal wasn't at least as good as Hunt's. "If we had the same kind of lease given the Texans (now Chiefs)," he told Joe McGuff, reporting for the *Sporting News*, "we would have to draw 2,000,000 fans a year before we had to pay a cent of rent."[18] He also demanded the $411,670.64 he spent on stadium improvements and thought that the city owed him. The city council disavowed responsibility for these improvements but offered to negotiate with Finley on what compensation might be appropriate. They eventually agreed to a $300,000 reimbursement.

Even Hank Bauer, who had resigned as the A's manager at the end of the 1962 season because he could no longer deal with Finley's antics, agreed that Finley had gotten a raw deal from the city. "The city built a practice football field for the Kansas City Chiefs, and they only charged the Chiefs one dollar," Bauer said. "And Charlie got mad because he was paying a good hunk of his money to the city, and they wouldn't do nothing for him. But he [Finley] was a prick too."[19] Lew Krausse agreed. The city mistreated Finley by failing to give the A's the same kind of deal that the Chiefs had. The scandal eventually became more of an irritation than a salacious bit of news, though. Krausse recalled that "it just seemed like the headlines in the paper had nothing to do with who won or lost the game, but it was about Finley [fighting with someone]."[20]

Finley found a confederate who also wanted to fast-track the stadium-lease renewal in Mayor H. Roe Bartle, who was concerned that the nine-member city council would turn over in April and wanted to get the lease completed before the current leadership departed. Mostly, the city leaders wanted to ensure the A's retention through a lengthy contract; they considered other terms more flexible. On April 10, just before the turnover of the council, Finley and Bartle signed a lease extension, and the city council ratified it by a 6–1 vote. Finley thought he was home free, and that it would help to resolve all the difficulties between the A's and the city. "It was so wonderful," he said, "that no one in his right mind would have ever wanted to leave Kansas City."[21] However, as soon as the new city council members took office, they voided the contract, ruling that it had been improperly ratified. City manager Ben Powers said that the contract was the business of the new council, and since it had been expanded to 13 members, ratifying it would now require seven affirmative votes. The new council summarily killed the deal.

Finley threw a tantrum. He called *Atlanta Journal* sportswriter Furman Bisher, who had been courting several teams to move to his city, to vent. "These goddamn city councilmen voted in the kind of contract I wanted for the stadium here this morning, then left office," he told Bisher. "A new council took office then and these bastards just killed the contract the other council voted to accept this morning."[22] His public statements were only modestly less inflammatory. He told reporters, "I signed this contract in good faith. Then the new City Council came in and told me I had no contract. They said it was not a valid contract. Then they invited me to come down and negotiate a new contract with them. I've come here. I've negotiated and I've gotten no place. I want to say now that this new City Council is not going to push Charlie Finley around and give him a rotten deal."[23] He even sent Pat Friday over to try to pay two years' rent, with two one-dollar checks, on the voided contract.

Finley might have been duplicitous in his dealings with city officials— he might have too often acted the jerk—but with this turn of events, he was now the abused rather than the abuser in the relationship. Rebuffed, he vowed not to discuss the contract again until the end of the 1963 season.

Instead Finley began a magical mystery tour of prospective major-league cities. He visited Atlanta and allowed Bisher to show him potential sites for a new stadium for the proposed Atlanta A's. He even caught up with Kansas City Chiefs coach Hank Stram and asked him to take a proposal to owner Lamar Hunt that the two teams move from Kansas City to Atlanta together. "This is a horse-shit town," he said of Kansas City. "No one will ever do any good here."[24] The Chiefs leadership chose to ignore Finley's offer. Finley also went back to Dallas and to Oakland to talk to city leaders.

Hank Peters recalled how Finley added a new prospective city where he might move the A's:

He called me one day on the phone, and he said, "Where is there a good-size minor league stadium that's not in baseball right now?" So I thought about it for a while . . . I said, "Well, the biggest stadium that I know that does not have a minor league team is in Louisville, Kentucky." And he said, "Will you get me all the particulars on it?" He wanted to know how many people it held and the outfield distance. So I assembled all that data and sent it on up to him. About a week later, I hear that the Athletics are going to move to Louisville.[25]

Finley constantly joked about taking the A's to Louisville—or perhaps he wasn't joking. "We have these caps that have K.C. on the front," he trumpeted, "and we don't want to throw them away, so I think we'll call ourselves the Kentucky Colonels. And before every game, after 'The Star-Spangled Banner,' everyone will sing, 'Oh, the sun shines bright.' "[26]

The race was on to get out of Kansas City, and Finley would not rest until he had done so. Everyone else looked forward to Finley getting out of Kansas City as well, but they wanted him to leave the Athletics there when he left. Finley would have none of it. League president Joe Cronin warned that Finley would not be allowed to move. "Under the league constitution he is bound to operate in Kansas City unless he receives a three-fourths vote of approval to move," he said. And there was no way the league, which constantly had to clean up after Finley's messes, would allow that to happen.[27] Finley repeatedly tried to cut deals to move the team to other cities.[28]

As this played out, the situation with Municipal Stadium remained unsettled through the end of 1963. The haggling over the stadium in the winter of 1963–1964 proved to be most vexing for those interested in MLB in Kansas City. Both Finley and Kansas City officials argued back and forth over the expiring lease and the team's future in the city. Neither side seemed willing to compromise.

Finley was willing to talk with city officials about the stadium deal, but much of what he did was admittedly for show. He began one early-February meeting by asking if anyone had poems to recite or songs to sing, "or any autographed baseballs to give out?" He then said that everyone should be ready to get down to "brass tacks" and proceeded to hand out brass tacks to each of the participants, presumably for their lapels. All this made for great theater, and the sportswriters loved it, but it yielded nothing.[29]

The stalemate led to threats from Cronin and members of the Missouri congressional delegation, and it was inevitable that Finley would eventually be forced to surrender. That surrender came only after Finley vacated the stadium. When the lease expired at the end of 1963—and after the mayor's efforts prevented team employees from moving into office space offered by Civic Plaza National Bank president Alexander J. Barket—Finley set up the A's business offices in the garage of team scout Joe Bowman. Over the winter, the few full-time A's employees moved the team's files and office furniture into the garage, where they spent seven weeks in exile. Finley promised to play in a cow pasture rather than in Municipal Stadium unless he got what he wanted.

Hank Peters recalled that Finley moved "offices into the garage." He continued, "We moved a couple desks out there and our files, and we set up spring training and took care of contracts and everything else out of that garage."[30] Bowman recalled that Finley didn't even bother to put in a telephone, and A's employees had to go into the kitchen to make calls. Finley got angry that Bowman's wife did not keep the line clear for the use of the team, and Bowman had to tell him to back off. "You want a telephone in there that nobody's on," he said, "you put one in." Team employees tramped around the yard so much going to and from the garage that they killed the grass. Bowman said that he complained to Finley about that too, and the next thing he knew, a 15-pound bag of bluegrass seed showed up on his doorstep, courtesy of Charlie Finley.[31]

The public got into the act as well. The talk of the city revolved around Finley's nastiness and lack of grace on this issue. On January 11, 1964, the *Sporting News* published a photograph of a lawn jockey that was painted in the A's team colors by Roy T. L. Cox and holding a sign that read FINLEY GO HOME. A fan summed up the general view: "Finley is using the impasse over the stadium lease as a new wedge in his long campaign to move the franchise."[32] The atmosphere remained toxic a couple of years later. Young outfielder Joe Rudi remembered driving to Municipal Stadium for the first time and seeing "dummies dressed like Finley hanging from the houses."[33]

All the while, Finley participated in seven negotiating sessions with Kansas City officials and had to answer for the impasse in two American League meetings, in which he was grilled by league president Cronin and fellow club owners. At a meeting on February 21, it was reported, "the league members, after carefully weighing the facts put before them, determined by a vote of 9 to 1 that the offers made by Kansas City for a lease were fair and reasonable." They also concluded that Finley had failed to comply with earlier directives to settle this dispute. By the same vote, the league put Finley on notice that unless he came to terms with Kansas City officials, they would meet "for the purpose of considering and acting upon the termination of membership of Charles O. Finley & Company in the American League." On February 23, Finley sent a telegram to the Kansas City mayor agreeing to a four-year lease to play in Municipal Stadium. The terms required the A's to remain in the stadium four years, but the team had to pay no rent. Instead the city would get 5 percent of all admissions and 7.5 percent of all concessions. Should attendance fall under 575,000, the A's would owe nothing to the city.[34]

Ernie Mehl called the stadium negotiations "a situation without precedent in the history of baseball" and laid the blame for its prolongation firmly at the feet of Finley. Mehl did not even give Finley credit for finally bowing to the wishes of his fellow owners. The league's total lack of support— perhaps it might more accurately be characterized as opposition—for Finley's legitimate concerns about the poor condition of the stadium played a pivotal role in the length and testiness of the dispute. Chicago White Sox owner Arthur C. Allyn said, "Finley is a fool and his action is inexcusable."[35] Baseball scion Red Smith characterized Finley's fellow owners as collectively telling him, "Down boy! Back in your box."[36] In this debacle, the city and the league got together to squelch valid concerns voiced by Finley, but this was overshadowed by Finley's obnoxious behavior throughout the episode. He had a point about Kansas City's need for a new stadium—a point that the city council would eventually understand—but he lost the public relations battle. He was his own worst enemy, something he demonstrated repeatedly throughout his career.[37] As one observer noted, and many others would testify over the years, Finley "is a very strange man—a real Jekyll and Hyde. He says one thing one day and entirely the opposite the next day."[38]

At some level, Finley knew he had gone too far and worked to make amends. He constantly tried to bring fans back to the A's. Continued efforts to sell season tickets and the usual round of special activities at games helped to increase attendance. In 1963 he scrapped the standard home whites and road grays in favor of colorful uniforms for his players. Clothed in Finley's favorite colors, kelly green and Fort Knox gold, the Athletics were the subject of ridicule for years. Ron Mihelic remembered being called into the family room at the La Porte farmhouse during the winter of 1963, where Finley "had all these uniforms spread out. I think my mom was there too. He said, 'What do you guys like best?' Not that our opinion would have changed his mind at all, but that's when he decided on kelly green and gold."[39]

Jerry Lumpe, the A's second baseman between 1959 and 1963, told of his shock at first seeing these new uniforms. Finley called Lumpe and asked to meet with him in his suite at the Muehlebach Hotel in Kansas City. "I guess we were talking contracts," he said.

> But anyway, this was when he told me we were gonna have new uniforms. And he said, "This is really something. This is just a fabulous new thing." And he went in his bedroom, and he brought 'em out, and I guess my jaw probably dropped a foot when I saw 'em . . . When I saw the first gold and green, [they] were not very pretty. In fact, they were ugly . . . I didn't know what to say, except I had to say that I liked them because I still hadn't signed the contract.[40]

Despite the new uniforms, the A's seemed to be in a holding pattern on the field. In 1963 Lumpe and Norm Siebern were the most stalwart of the everyday players, with batting averages of .271 and .272, respectively, and 21 home runs between them. Among the starting pitchers, only Diego Segui, who would make the transition to the championship teams in Oakland in a few years, posted a winning record, at 9–6. And Orlando Pena earned a 12–20 record while recording a respectable 3.69 earned run average. The team posted a 71–91 win-loss record, finishing eighth out of the 10 teams in the American League and eighth in attendance in the league. While not a great record, it appeared the team was making headway. In November 1963, Finley traded for sluggers Jim Gentile and Rocky Colavito, also netting cash payments of $75,000 in these two deals, which he used to sign a selection of young players who eventually rose to the majors.

For the 1964 season, Finley dreamed up yet another bizarre stunt for the enjoyment of Kansas City fans. After hearing manager Ed Lopat wax eloquent about the New York Yankees' success resulting from their stadium's 296-foot right-field wall, a gift to left-handed power hitters, Finley decided to build one for the A's and dubbed it the "K.C. Pennant Porch." He did not mind that he had violated a 1958 rule that no fence could be shorter than 325 feet. He got away with it for two exhibition games before being forced to move it back, grousing all the while about the Yankees receiving preferential treatment by being grandfathered in at the time of the rule's adoption. "Finley pitched his typical fit," baseball historian Steve Treder commented, "but reluctantly dismantled the Pennant Porch. But he moved the fence back only to the 325-foot limit, and ensured that the overall right field configuration at Municipal Stadium would still be extremely home run–friendly. Finley dubbed the revised setup the 'One Half Pennant Porch.'"[41] Finley then decided to have a white line painted on the field at the original K.C. Pennant Porch distance. He directed the public address announcer to say, "That would have been a home run in Yankee Stadium" whenever a ball flew past the line. This practice was quietly dropped when other teams hit more balls past the white line than the A's did. Other team owners thought Finley was a buffoon for taking these actions; the sportswriters loved the colorful copy he provided. Many Kansas City fans enjoyed that he thumbed his nose at the baseball establishment, especially at the hated Yankees.[42]

Finley's strategy of trying to develop more power on the A's team was not wrong, but in 1964 it backfired. Both Colavito and Gentile added pop to the lineup, hitting 34 and 28 home runs, respectively, when the most homers by an A's player in 1963 was 16, by Siebern. But bringing in the fences also helped the opposition. The A's hit a total of 107 home runs at home, a franchise record, but an injury-riddled pitching staff gave up 132 home runs, which set a new major-league record. The team sank to 57–105, the worst record in the American League. The A's in 1964 were a one-dimensional team that had power but lacked pitching, defense, and offensive efficiency and had a low on-base percentage. Until the team improved, Finley tried to lure fans to the games with extravaganzas.

His most infamous event involved the greatest rock band to invade America—the Beatles. Finley tried to gain fan approval by bringing the band to Kansas City for a concert in the fall of 1964. Seeing that the Beatles did not have a Kansas City stop on their first U.S. tour, he tracked down band manager Brian Epstein at the Cow Palace in San Francisco on August 19 to try to bring them to Municipal Stadium. For the modest price of $150,000, Epstein agreed to divert the band's tour to Kansas City for an additional concert at the Kansas City Municipal Stadium on September 17, 1964, just before the Beatles ended that tour on September 20.

Even before the Beatles arrived in Kansas City, Finley had some fun with them. When the Fab Four visited Chicago's International Amphitheatre on September 5, he took Charlie Jr., Paul, and Kathryn to the concert and arranged for them to meet the band; they even had their photographs taken with the lads. The Finleys drove back to La Porte in a limousine wearing Beatles wigs and sent a stir through the community that the band was staying with the Finleys. Rick Knoll said, "You can imagine all along Johnson Road, the entire length of the marble fence, it was probably two people deep . . . all trying to get a glimpse of the Beatles." The myths expanded as some in La Porte claimed to have seen Ringo, or George, or Paul, or John. "That was one of the biggest scams, and to this day, there are people that still believe they were here," he said.[43]

The Beatles played in Kansas City on September 17 for only 31 minutes. They began their set with the song "Kansas City/Hey, Hey, Hey, Hey," and the crowd of about 20,200 went wild. But there were plenty of empty seats.

Drew Dimmel recalled that "when confirmation was announced on my local 'rock' station, WHB, that tickets were going on sale to see The Beatles, live, at Municipal Stadium in Kansas City I persuaded my dad to drive me down to the ticket booth. I bought two field-level tickets, paying $6.50 apiece; one for my little brother and one for me. I was 15 and he was 12."[44] A seat on the playing field cost $8.50, while a seat in the upper or lower deck cost $2. Never shy about publicity, Charlie Finley had a photo of himself wearing a Beatles wig printed on the back of the tickets.[45]

Kansas City was the only concert venue on the tour that didn't sell out. Many potential concertgoers stayed away after the *Kansas City Star* and others urged a boycott of the concert as a way of showing displeasure with Finley. Finley promised to give all of his after-expense profits to a local charity, Children's Mercy Hospital, but because the concert did not sell out, Finley actually lost money—possibly becoming the only Beatles concert promoter ever to do so. Finley nonetheless made a sizable donation—$25,000—to the hospital. Of course some local entrepreneurs did make money on the concert, especially the two people who acquired the bedsheets from the Beatles hotel rooms, which they then cut into small squares to sell as souvenirs. They netted $159,000 for their efforts.[46] For Finley, thanks to years of self-generated acrimony, no good deed went unpunished. There would be many more instances of similar behavior in Kansas City thereafter.

Ever since being forced to compromise with city officials in 1964, Finley had longed for a larger market with more fans, friendlier lease terms, and higher broadcast revenue. Kansas City was, in his estimation, a small-market city that did not appreciate what he offered. Finley tried to field a competitive team and spent hundreds of thousands of dollars on renovations to Municipal Stadium, while believing he was receiving unfair lease terms from the city.

On the other hand, city officials, the news media, and fans in Kansas City grew tired of Finley's constant complaints, his empty promises and double-talk, and his constant wandering eye for a new home for the Athletics. Kansas Citians simply wanted stability and harmony in their Major League Baseball team. Finley's uneven temperament, his feuding with managers and players, and his outrageous nature turned the city's baseball fans against the A's owner, whom they viewed as publicity-hungry and not to be trusted. Even so, many fans loved the A's and saw a talented young team emerging, one that might soon compete for the American League pennant, and were optimistic about the future.

After a tumultuous 1964 season, Charlie Finley and his A's were tired of the bickering and acrimony. For his part, Finley turned the reins of the franchise over to a "legitimate" baseball person to manage. Faced with mounting competition in the insurance business, Finley recalled Pat Friday from his position as A's general manager back to the insurance company's Chicago offices on April 6. This cleared the way for Finley to promote Hank Peters as the new GM of the Athletics. Friday had proven to be a competent business administrator for the A's organization, but he knew very little about baseball and nothing about judging baseball talent.[47]

Peters had run the A's player development and farm system and knew how to build a winning franchise by developing minor-league talent. He had learned his trade from great baseball executive and owner Bill DeWitt and from managing the minor-league system for the St. Louis Browns. Before being fired by Finley in 1961 and catching on with the Reds for one season, Peters had built one of the game's best scouting staffs with the A's. "We had some good players in the organization when Mr. Finley bought the club," Peters said. "We had signed Howser, Wickersham, Wyatt, Segui, and Cletis Boyer. We just didn't have enough good prospects."[48] However, after the chaotic season of 1961, six of Peters's scouts resigned, and two years later Finley and Friday trimmed the scouting department from 22 to 11 positions as a cost-cutting measure, but the scouts who remained were shrewd judges of talent.

Most important, Peters convinced Finley that the only way to turn the A's into winners was to spend money to sign players and develop them in a strong minor-league farm organization. Finley embraced the sound advice of this 40-year-old executive and pursued that approach with enthusiasm thereafter. It took about six years of persistence before the team began showing signs of life on the field, but the A's approach of building through player development proved remarkably successful. Peters commented:

> He [Finley] did come up with the dough. He decided . . . or he discovered that the only way he was ever going to build a ball club and be successful was to have a protected player development program with talent . . . Charlie did provide the capital. We went out and signed a lot of the talent that played on those great Oakland clubs.[49]

Finley signed a few players during his first season as owner, notably high school pitching prospect Lew Krausse and slick-fielding shortstop Ted Kubiak. In 1962 he signed young infielder Tony La Russa; though he had a mediocre playing career, LaRussa would make his mark in baseball as one of its most successful field managers 30 years later. Also that year, A's scout Felix Delgado discovered a skinny 20-year-old from Cuba named Bert Campaneris and signed him for a mere $500 bonus. At the time, he was a pitcher who could throw with both arms. In a minor-league game that season for Daytona Beach, "Campy," as he became known to his teammates, pitched two innings of relief both left-handed and right-handed. He gave up only one run and struck out four batters. Later that year, the A's decided to develop him as a shortstop. The A's called him up to play shortstop in 1964, and in his first major-league game he hit two homers off tough lefty Jim Kaat. Campy anchored the A's infield during their championship reign nearly a decade later. In 1965, A's scouts signed three more impressive prospects, pitchers Jim Nash and Paul Lindblad and catcher Dave Duncan, all of whom went on to make important contributions to the team.

Finley and Peters enjoyed some success in signing prospects in 1962 and 1963 and thereafter redoubled their efforts to steal the march on a Major League Baseball amateur player draft system, instituted in 1965, that would apportion prospects to teams based on their standing during the previous season. Finley announced to Peters that he had made a big profit from his insurance business and needed to spend it quickly or face a huge tax liability. "Let's sign some ballplayers," Finley ordered.[50]

In 1964, Finley, Peters, and the A's scouts signed 80 players for approximately $650,000, which was at the time the most spent by one team in a single season. Of the 80 players, three became important parts in the A's future championship run: pitchers Jim "Catfish" Hunter and John "Blue Moon" Odom and outfielder Joe Rudi.

Eighteen-year-old Jim Hunter, from rural Hertford, North Carolina, pitched with grace, control, and moxie. The Hunter family lived in a tin-roofed sharecropper's house, and everyone worked the farm. Hunter, one of eight children, grew up milking cows and doing chores before going to school. After school, he compiled an impressive 26–2 record on his high school team and hurled five no-hitters. A's scout Clyde Kluttz said, "He knew instinctively how to pitch. There was no way you could give that to him. Those kind of guys are just born, and not very often."[51] He appeared destined for pitching greatness, except for one issue. The young Hunter, who loved to fish and hunt, sustained a serious foot injury in a hunting accident only a few months before his senior season. On Thanksgiving Day 1963, his brother's shotgun accidentally fired—blowing off his little right toe and filling his right foot with 60 buckshot pellets. A doctor mended his foot, but left in the majority of the buckshot. Most scouts feared the injury would prevent Hunter from ever pitching professionally.[52]

Finley, though, was undeterred. He went with Kluttz to the Hunter farm in a black limo led by a police escort to ink the deal. "Mr. Finley started passing out green warm-up jackets and green bats and orange baseballs and it sort of scared off the other scouts," said Hunter. Finley met the Hunter family and left convinced that Jim was not only a good prospect but a nice young man as well.

Finley telephoned Hunter a couple of weeks later to talk about a contract. Hunter remembers, "They [other team's scouts] figured Mr. Finley had me all sewed up . . . Finley said, 'I'm calling today to sign ya . . . I'm gonna sign ya today kid, or never talk to you again.' The money he offered me was fine, but I kind of felt I could get a new car, too . . . I said I'd call up the other scouts to see if they'd top his offer. He got mad and said I [had to] take the money then or not at all. I took it."[53] Finley signed Hunter to a $75,000 bonus contract.

Then Finley decided to give his new young pitcher a nickname. "To play baseball you've got to have a nickname," Finley said. "What do you like to do?" "Hunt and fish," said Hunter. Finley then cooked up a story of how the pitcher got the nickname "Catfish." Finley told him, "When you were six years old you ran away from home and went fishing. Your mom and dad had been looking for you all day. When they finally found you, about, ah, four o'clock in the afternoon, you'd caught two big fish . . . ahh . . . catfish . . . and were reeling in the third. And that's how you got your nickname . . . Now repeat it back to me."[54] Years later Hunter recalled, "I did fish a lot as a boy, but I didn't think much of my name. But I also didn't want to cross this man who was spending so much money on me so I said all right . . . I didn't think the name would stick."[55]

Catfish Hunter did not pitch in the 1964 season; instead Finley sent him to the Mayo Clinic, where surgeons removed 45 pellets from his right foot. Hunter then recuperated for several weeks at the Finley farm in La Porte. Martin Finley said, "In 1964 my dad signed Catfish Hunter. My dad took a chance on Catfish, who blew part of his foot off. He went to Mayo to get his foot recovered, and he left just few weeks later for La Porte . . . He was only eighteen, and I was nine at the time, and it was like having another big brother for a couple of weeks, and he was always very kind to us kids."[56] David Finley also thought of Hunter as essentially another older brother to play with and said that Hunter "remained that throughout the whole time he was with the A's."[57] Hunter recovered from the surgery and made the Kansas City A's roster in 1965 without spending a day in the minors.

Pitcher John Odom's experience was similar, with the personal treatment from Finley assuring the deal with the A's. Odom compiled an impressive 42–2 record in high school with eight no-hitters. "I was almost 19 when the baseball scouts came around. The San Francisco Giants offered me about $40,000. The A's offer was real low. So their scout, Jack Sanford, got on the phone with Finley and Finley came down to see me personally."[58] To sign Odom, Finley did something that worked repeatedly for him: He cooked dinner and used the opportunity to sell the young pitcher on the A's. As he had done for numerous other players, he bought a huge amount of food for the Odom family, so much that it had to be delivered by a pickup truck. Then he cooked them a feast of "fried chicken, corn on the cob, black-eyed peas, collard greens," and assorted Southern delicacies.[59] It put him over the top with the family. Finley and Odom's mother especially bonded in their initial meeting. He signed for $75,000, received the nickname "Blue Moon," and went on to star with the A's during their glory years.[60]

It was during this time that Finley gained his reputation as a connoisseur of Southern cooking and all things fried. Supreme Court Justice John Paul Stevens, who worked with Finley as an attorney in Chicago in the 1960s before ascending to the bench, recalled many instances of his quest for fine fried food:

When we go out to dinner, and he'd do this in the restaurant, I remember him doing it in Montreal, in the Congress ... he'd go into the kitchen! He'd walk into the kitchen and say, "Who's the chef here?" And he'd find the chef and say, "What's good here? Where's your fish?" He'd get the fish out, and he'd inspect it, and then he'd go and sit down and order for the table! I really kind of timidly would follow along behind him. He'd go in, introduce himself to the chef and the assistant chef, and talk about what they had around. He'd look at it and see for himself and size it up, and we'd go in and order![61]

As often as not Finley brought his own fish or steak with him to a restaurant. He loved a restaurant in Chicago called Ireland's, and he sometimes brought the main course with him when he came. He would buy fish at a market, wrap it up like in a scene from *The Godfather*, and cart it around town with him. When he arrived at the restaurant that evening, he would go straight back to the chef and supervise its preparation.[62]

Finley signed another important player in 1965. A's scout Don Pries followed the progress of a big, fair-haired, talented infielder named Joe Rudi from Modesto, California. Rudi's hard play and clutch hitting impressed several major-league scouts, but their interest waned after Rudi was hit by a pitch that fractured his left hand during his senior year of high school. On Finley's instructions, the A's and Pries remain interested in Rudi. To further court him, Pries arranged medical treatments for Rudi's hand. Eventually, Rudi rewarded the A's interest and loyalty by signing a contract. Years later, Rudi shifted position to left field, where he would become an All-Star for the A's.

In 1965, Major League Baseball instituted its amateur draft system, granting the last-place Kansas City A's the first choice in the draft. Hank Peters was impressed by Arizona State University outfielder Rick Monday, who had batted .356 with 11 homers and was selected as college player of the year, and the A's used their choice to get him. Finley signed Monday after the College World Series for an estimated $100,000 bonus contract and a new car. This opened a connection to Arizona State that later brought to the A's both third baseman Sal Bando, who signed for an estimated $30,000 bonus, and the incomparable Reggie Jackson. ASU head coach Bobby Winkles, who would manage the A's for Finley in the late 1970s, said, "They were great players. Bando came to ASU as a short-stop, and he had big legs and strong arms. And I thought . . . I had a shortstop. So I moved him to third base, and that's where he played his career. Rick Monday . . . was the best-looking player as a sophomore that I ever had. All of them good guys and never a problem. Bando's the greatest leader I ever saw in baseball."[63] Years later Finley traded Monday to the Cubs for a tough left-handed pitcher named Ken Holtzman—the move that turned the A's starting rotation into baseball's best.

Two additional players taken by the A's in the 1965 draft played key roles in the team's later success: California native Rollie Fingers and Gene Tenace. Fingers attended Chaffey Junior College but left after being drafted by the A's. Fingers, a tall and lean pitcher with a great fastball and a surprisingly good bat, led his American Legion team to the national championship in 1964. He signed for a $20,000 bonus contract. Tenace impressed the A's with his swing and determination. Scout Dan Carnevale signed Tenace, who played several positions before becoming a catcher in the minors.[64] Finley promoted his new talent quickly. Bando and Monday joined the A's in 1966; Fingers and Tenace made the team in 1968 and 1969, respectively.

During the 1966 and 1967 amateur drafts, the A's also possessed early picks, but Finley began to tighten his wallet on bonuses. Cutbacks in the scouting area also hurt the A's ability to find great talent, but they did draft two players who both became All-Stars and won an American League Most Valuable Player award; and one of them was elected to the Baseball Hall of Fame.

The first of these was ASU outfielder Reggie Jackson, who dominated the 1966 College World Series, prompting Finley to take him as the second pick after the New York Mets wasted their pick on high school catcher Steve Chilcott, one of only two number one draft picks never to reach the major leagues. Jackson was a known talent, and he spurned several teams—including the Dodgers and Giants—that wanted to sign him out of high school. Jackson wanted a larger signing bonus than those teams offered and felt that playing in college would increase his marketability.

"And Reggie, of course, was a football and baseball player, and he had an agreement with Frank Kush, the football coach, that if he could make the baseball team as a sophomore, he didn't have to go to spring football," recalled ASU coach Bobby Winkles. "Well, not only did he make the team, but he made All-American in baseball. And those are three guys [Jackson, Monday and Bando] . . . that was probably our three most outstanding players."[65]

Jackson sparkled in his one varsity baseball season at ASU, hitting 15 homers and displaying Mickey Mantle–esque power. He was the first college player to hit a shot out of Phoenix Municipal Stadium. Reggie possessed speed, power, and a cannon for an arm—he was one of the most complete ballplayers of his generation. The A's owner knew Jackson was the key component to developing a winning ball club. Finley negotiated with Jackson after the College World Series and signed him for an estimated $95,000 and a new car. Jackson recalled Finley's sales pitch: "He came driving up in a big Cadillac. He kept talking about what a big star I was going to be and how we were going to be champions. He really overwhelmed me."[66] Indeed, Jackson's star shined brightly in the coming years with the A's, as his fame and big-game performances transformed him into "Mr. October."

Before the 1967 amateur draft, Finley and his scout Connie Ryan watched an 18-year-old pitcher from Mansfield, Louisiana, named Vida Blue. A tremendous athlete, Blue played football, baseball, and basketball in high school. As a star football quarterback, he passed for more than 3,400 yards and 35 touchdowns and ran for more than 1,600 yards in his senior year. Blue dreamed of playing college and professional football and becoming the NFL's first black quarterback. His strong left arm dazzled baseball hitters as well. He once pitched a no-hitter and struck out 21 hitters in a seven-inning game, but lost because of walks, missed third strikes, and passed balls. Nonetheless, Blue lost only two games in three baseball seasons and led his team to two district titles. Colleges and MLB teams heavily scouted him during his senior year of high school. However, the death of Blue's father during that year and the financial struggles that resulted pushed the young athlete toward baseball, where he would immediately be able to earn an income, rather than into football, where four years of college would prevent him from helping his family.[67]

The A's selected Blue in the second round of the 1967 amateur draft. Ryan offered Blue only a small-bonus contract, and Blue's high school coach advised him to reject it. Blue and Ryan quarreled over the offer; enter Charlie Finley. He immediately fired Ryan and phoned Blue to hammer out an agreement, offering a $25,000 signing bonus. Finley turned on his salesman's charm and closed the deal. Blue recalled later his decision to pursue baseball. "I was forced to do what I did because I was the breadwinner for my mother and my four sisters and brother," he said. "It was just one of those things. I'm a big college football fan. I love college sports, football specifically, but there might have been a part of my youth that I missed out on. But I had to grow up fast anyway. It might have been a tough balancing act to still be the breadwinner and a college student/athlete, so I just used what God gave me—the ability to throw a baseball—and I tried to make it work."[68]

A 1968 *Life* magazine article on Finley and the A's reported that Finley spent $2.5 million on bonus contracts for players. It declared the A's minor-league system tops in baseball. In actuality, Finley spent perhaps between $1.5 and $1.7 million on bonus contracts for approximately 250 ball players between 1962 and 1967. He routinely overstated the money he spent and supposedly lost as owner of the A's. During the mid-1960s, Finley's insurance company achieved its high-water mark—generating tens of millions of dollars in commissions. Finley made money hand over fist and needed to find a way to spend it for tax purposes, but by the late 1960s the insurance market had softened and profits fell considerably. This led to a dramatic reduction in Finley's available money for signing talented young players. Nonetheless, Finley invested wisely when he was flush with cash. The players he signed in the period from 1964 to 1967 included three future members of the Baseball Hall of Fame (Hunter, Fingers, and Jackson) and half a dozen future All-Stars (Monday, Rudi, Tenace, Odom, Bando, and Blue). These nine players, along with Campy Campaneris, formed the nucleus for the A's future success. As a group, they were named All-Stars a remarkable 35 times during their A's years, and 53 total times in their careers.

"It takes a man like Charlie Finley to get a club to the threshold that quickly. It takes somebody with guts, foresight and a willingness to put money into areas where there isn't much glory returned on investments," wrote former manager Alvin Dark. "Finley was willing to pay large bonuses to sign the top prospects and Peters and his scouts found a number of players that eventually become major-league All-Stars. Almost any scout could name the top players in the country, but it took good scouts to find the players nobody else knew about and then see the players wind up in the major leagues."[69]

Though there was little to be proud of on the field, other than the up-coming talent for future seasons, Finley remained committed to bringing fans into the Kansas City ballpark. He figured that more people would come to see a badly played ballgame that had stunts and promotions than would come to see only a badly played ballgame. He outdid himself in 1965 with a series of "Finley firsts," as he liked to call them. Taking a cue from Bill Veeck, Finley also installed a "pitchometer" on the scoreboard to time the pitchers. Rules stated that the pitcher must throw the pitch within 20 seconds after receiving the ball from the catcher when the bases were empty. Finley felt games dragged because umpires did not enforce the rule. The Finley pitchometer ran for several weeks, but since the um-pires refused to enforce the 20-second rule during the time the pitcho-meter operated, it was eventually removed.[70]

Finley also installed a small zoo in the picnic area to entice children to come to the game. This new attraction proved popular with young fans and included six capuchin monkeys named after Finley's father and uncles, six China gold pheasants, six German shorthaired rabbits, two peafowl, and a German shorthaired pointer. While the young fans enjoyed the animals, the players did not. "Catfish Hunter and I would go out to the ballpark early and feed the monkeys grasshoppers. Sometimes we'd give them cough medicine or sleeping pills," said pitcher Lew Krausse. Hunter re-called "combing the outfield grass for grasshoppers . . . [We'd] stuff a pill or two down the hopper's throat and toss it in the monkey cage. See the mon-key catch the grasshopper . . . Wait five minutes. See the monkey go ape-shit, running and screaming all over his cage."[71] Finley also sent some of these animals to his La Porte farm for his children to enjoy.

Several of Finley's promotional events before games drew unusually large crowds. In fact, the crowds at these promotional-night games accounted for a rather large percentage of the season's total attendance. He held Automobile Industry Night, in which cars were given to lucky fans and players arrived on the field in limos. Jim Schaaf, who ran the A's promotion department, recalled these memorable Finley events. "We had several big promotions throughout the year that people weren't doing in baseball in those days," Schaaf said. "We'd have Automotive Industry Night. Charlie had a lot of these ideas. He came up to me one time and said, 'We want cars we can have painted and do things to dress them up, and we're going to give 'em away as prizes during the game.' We would call tickets in certain locations, and fans would win a car. What he promised was you could drive the car off the lot . . . Those types of promotions that he was really involved in . . . he got a big kick out of them. The fans got a big kick out of them too." Schaff added, "Sometimes the person would get in the car and start driving off . . . and the car would just break down halfway out of the gate."

Finley also held regular Farmers Nights, at one of which A's outfielder Ken Harrelson even showed his prowess in a cow-milking contest. "That was a spectacle in itself," Schaaf said. "We'd have greased-pig contests. Fans would come out and try to catch the pigs. He'd give away some sheep and have people dress up in their farm costumes or farm outfits and come to the game."[72] Finley and Schaaf also held Bat Day and gave away green and gold bats.

Always looking for some new promotional angle, Finley decided the A's needed a new mascot. He was tired of the elephant mascot and logo the Athletics had used since they were in Philadelphia and wanted something original and Missouri-focused. One winter day before the 1965 season, Finley called Schaaf at four A.M. and talked nonstop about an article he was reading in the *Chicago Tribune*. Schaaf recalled their conversation:

"Jim, I'm reading the *Chicago Tribune*," Finley said.

"That's great. It's four A.M.," Schaaf responded groggily.

"Well, this is great. I'm reading this paper," Finley went on.

"Well, what is so great about it?" Schaaf shot back, now awake and annoyed.

"Do you know why the Allies won World War I?" Finley asked.

Schaaf responded, "I'm really not a history student. I'm an economics major, but I recall something about General Pershing—"

Finley cut him off. "This story in the *Chicago Tribune* said that one of the factors in winning the war was the Missouri mules!"[73]

Schaaf could not understand the excitable Finley. What was the connection with mules, Missouri, and the war? Finley explained that Missouri mules were used during the war to move ammunition and materiel through the mud and snow of France. The mules could transport things when man and machine could not. The mules' mobility and strength allowed the Allies to move war assets more quickly than the Germans could. Schaaf said Finley told him, "Jim, I don't like the mascot of the A's. I've never liked it. We gotta get something that has to do with Missouri—and who cares about the elephant. We need something that represents Missouri, and this is the perfect deal, a mule. We need to get a mule, and we need to get the finest mule in the state of Missouri . . . That's the job and I want you to do it."[74]

This order dumbfounded Schaaf, but he called Howard Benjamin, who owned a horse farm just outside of Kansas City. Benjamin Stables had connections all over the state and housed the Kansas City Chiefs horse War Paint, which galloped around the stadium after Chief touchdowns. Benjamin soon found a mule and called Schaaf. When Finley and Schaaf went out to see it, Finley fell in love with it right away.[75]

Finley and Schaaf organized a media bonanza around the team's new official mascot—Charlie O., the mule—named by the owner himself. Finley and Schaaf arranged for Missouri governor Warren Hearnes to donate Charlie O. to the team. Hearnes presented the mule to the team on opening night in 1965, and Charlie Finley rode Charlie O. around the stadium to the cheers and laughs of fans. Finley said Charlie O. was a product of the greatest mule search in history. "Everybody's got to see this mule," exclaimed Finley.[76] Many fans, amused by Finley's escapades with his new mascot but tired of his threats to move the team, wondered who was the bigger "ass" of the two. Many players privately complained, as the mule seemingly received better treatment and more perks from the owner than they did. To transport the mascot to home games, Finley bought an air-conditioned trailer equipped with a hi-fi system that played "mule music," such as "Mule Train." Finley built Charlie O. a pen in the picnic area's zoo so fans could pet and visit the mascot. He even created Charlie O.'s own uniform, which consisted of a green and gold blanket, a green and gold bridle, and a green and gold A's cap. On Mule Day, later in the season, the A's starting lineup rode to the field in a mule train, despite some complaints from players.[77]

Finley decided to take Charlie O. on a promotional tour during the 1965 and 1966 seasons. Schaaf remembered Finley telling him, "This is something different. This is unique. Nobody has a mascot like this . . . I want to take him all over the American League!"[78] So off they went to every American League city. Schaaf arranged for Charlie O. the mule to travel in his trailer pulled by a colorful station wagon, and many times the mule stayed in the hotels with the team. Finley paraded the mule down the streets of several cities as players and ball girls passed out pens, bats, balls, and caps—all in the A's colors of green and gold.

Schaaf could never forget Charlie O's 1965 trip to New York, where Finley "register[ed] the mule at the Americana Hotel. He wanted to have a big deal where we would bring the mule down with a police escort on Seventh Avenue. We brought him from Central Park, and we had a police escort all lined up, stopped all the traffic in bringing the mule right to the hotel, and we had a band playing outside. We had the players outside with bats, passing 'em out to the fans, signing autographs . . . We brought the mule into the hotel, registered him in the hotel. We had a place out right by the garage area of the hotel, where we actually had this room set up for the mule in part of the parking lot area, and we had furniture in the room and all these things . . . Charlie had his picture up there and also a picture of the mule in the bedroom there."[79]

Later that day, Finley held a press event. "Everybody in New York was at that press conference, from Howard Cosell to Frank Gifford to everybody," Schaaf said. "Every news outlet in New York was at this press conference . . . We packed this room at the hotel, one of their big exhibition rooms, and we had the mule in there, and it was just an unbelievable experience . . . The mule was in every single paper in New York . . . on the whole back page of the *Daily News*."[80]

Finley also brought Charlie O. to Yankee Stadium for the game and wanted an A's player to ride the mule around the stadium. Young outfielder Ken "Hawk" Harrelson said he grew up with a mule at his grandfather's farm. However, Harrelson exaggerated his riding experience; Harrelson rode his grandfather's mule with a saddle, but Charlie O. did not have one. Nonetheless, they placed a blanket over the mule and hoisted Harrelson onto his back and sent him onto the field. The mule began to trot and Harrelson started to lose his grip and began to fall off. The crowd and other players roared in laughter. Charlie O. began to buck, possibly from the fear of the experience in front of the boisterous crowd, and threw Harrelson to the ground. Charlie O. meandered into the outfield to the roar of the crowd while Harrelson picked himself up and dusted off.[81]

Finley loved it; he was laughing hysterically—nearly in tears. Pictures of Harrelson hanging on for dear life made all the newspapers the next day. Shortly afterward, Harrelson, who fancied himself a hat collector, received a $25 Stetson cowboy hat from Finley.[82]

Thereafter, Finley sent Charlie O. to Chicago for an A's game against the White Sox. White Sox owner Arthur Allyn announced publicly that Charlie O. the mule was banned from entering Comiskey Park. Sox GM Ed Short quipped, "If I let Finley ride that mule around the park, I won't be able to tell which one is the jackass."[83] Undeterred, Finley held a lavish luncheon for Charlie O. and his team at the Sheraton Chicago Hotel, where the local media fawned over the mule and its owner. Finley hatched a plan to one-up Allyn. On Finley's instructions, Schaaf hired attractive young ladies to picket outside the stadium before the game with signs that read WHITE SOX UNFAIR TO MISSOURI MULE. Schaaf rented a vacant lot across from the ballpark, hired a band to play Finley's mule songs, erected a powerful sound system, and hired a sound truck. With Charlie O. the mule in the lot across from the stadium, Finley and Schaaf arranged to have a smaller mule placed in a large crate and delivered to the A's clubhouse.

Schaaf cleared the delivery with Sox officials, who were told the crate contained bats and other training equipment for the A's.

Ken Harrelson, who was not playing that day, said, "I heard a commotion outside the [clubhouse] door, then a knock. When I opened it, there was Charlie giving orders in a stage whisper to a crew of guys pulling and pushing a huge box, five or six feet high and so wide it wouldn't fit through the door."

"Come on, Kenny, help us get this box open," said Finley, panting and excited.

"What's in it?" asked Harrelson.

"Never mind, never mind, just let's get it open quick," Finley responded.

The box opened and to Harrelson's amazement a mule emerged, not Charlie O., but a smaller baby mule that looked just like Charlie O.

"Come on, come on," Finley whispered. "Let's get him out—hurry up."

Finley, Harrelson, and others coaxed the shy mule out of the box and into the clubhouse. Finley said, "Kenny, help me get this thing on the field."

"You can't take him on the field, Charlie," Harrelson protested. "It's right in the middle of the ballgame."

"I don't give a damn when it is," Finley barked. "I got this mule this far and we're going to get him the rest of the way. Now, come on. Are you going to help me or not?"[84]

Finley and Harrelson moved the mule up the tunnel from the clubhouse into the dugout, Finley leading him with a rope and Harrelson pushing its hind end, all the time worrying about getting kicked. The A's players began laughing. At the same time, Schaaf radioed with his walkie-talkie to the sound truck in the lot across from the stadium. "I called a guy, and then we blasted out with 'Mule Train' coming into the ballpark. You could hear the song 'Mule Train' right inside the stadium like you were sitting next to the guy who was singing it. It was that strong coming out of this sound truck."[85]

Meanwhile, the game proceeded with the A's in a tight situation. The Sox had men on base and A's pitcher Jack Aker on the ropes. The mule stopped at the three steps separating the dugout and the field. Few fans had noticed the mule as yet. "Kenny," Finley whispered, "help me push him up the steps to the field so the customers can see him."

"Charlie, we can't do this," Harrelson pleaded.

"The hell we can't," said Finley, and he and Harrelson pushed the mule up the steps and onto the field as "Mule Train" echoed throughout the stadium.[86] The crowd roared at the sight as the umpires called time and began shouting at Finley and Harrelson to get rid of the mule. The mule proceeded to gallop around the infield. Finley hee-hawed until tears streamed down his face, all the while pointing to Allyn's box. Finally, order was restored, and Harrelson and some other players led the mule off the field and back into the clubhouse. The baby mule stepped on Harrelson's foot as they escorted it off the field, putting the young outfielder on the bench for the next three games. Nonetheless, Finley beamed with pride at this stunt. "Getting the mule in the stadium was what Charlie wanted . . . That was his deal because he was in Chicago. Chicago was his town. He wanted to do something spectacular. They said he couldn't do it; he said he's going to do it," said Schaaf.[87] And he did.

Despite such antics, only 528,344 fans came to Municipal Stadium to watch the A's, the lowest attendance in the majors and the lowest ever by the A's in Kansas City. Most fans remained bitter over Finley's efforts to move the team in 1964 and likely did not enjoy the poor quality of the team.

The A's got off to a horrendous start, losing 21 of their first 26 games under manager Mel McGaha. On May 15, Finley and Peters fired McGaha and placed their AAA manager, Haywood Sullivan, in charge. The 34-year-old Sullivan became the youngest manager in the majors. His youth didn't help much. In 1965 the A's again finished dead last in the American League, ending with a 59–103 record, the worst ever for the A's in Kansas City. Rocky Colavito and Jim Gentile were gone, and the offense that remained was anchored by new first baseman Ken Harrelson, who batted only .238 but hit 23 home runs and drove in 66. Harrelson was a product of emphasis on player development that would transform the A's later in Oakland; at only 23, he looked to be a star of the future.

So did three other young players who reached the major leagues for at least part of that year—all of whom would be important to the championship teams in Oakland in the early 1970s. Fleet-footed Bert Campaneris became a solid shortstop and hit a team-leading .270 with 12 triples and 51 stolen bases, while anchoring the defense with improving glove work. Nineteen-year old Jim "Catfish" Hunter stayed with the A's all year, to protect him from the first-year draft, and developed into one of the team's best pitchers. Hunter finished with an 8–8 record, with 82 strikeouts and a 4.26 ERA. Along with Campaneris, steady second baseman Dick Green, who batted only .232 but hit 15 home runs and drove in 55, would anchor the infield throughout the championship years in the 1970s. Collectively, they were part of a youth movement that Finley made his raison d'être throughout this time in Kansas City. He was optimistic about the future, and he had reason to be.

Campaneris was part of another Finley stunt. The owner instructed manager Haywood Sullivan to play Campaneris at all nine positions—a first in modern baseball history—during a September 8, 1965, game versus the California Angels. Finley dubbed it Campy Campaneris Night, and nearly 22,000 fans showed up for the spectacle. Campy played every position, but gave the Angels a 2–1 lead in the sixth inning by misplaying a fly ball in right field. He pitched the eighth inning, giving up just one run on one hit, but also walking two. He moved behind the plate for the ninth inning, only to be knocked senseless by the Angels' Ed Kirkpatrick on a play at the plate. Campy took the relay throw from second baseman Dick Green but positioned himself up the third-base line in front of the plate. Kirkpatrick ran over him, knocking the wiry young Cuban to the ground. Campy left the game, and while X-rays showed nothing to be amiss, Finley's promotional stunt cost the A's their star shortstop for the next five games as he recovered. The A's lost the game 5–3 in 13 innings.

Two days after Campy Campaneris Night, Finley signed 59-year-old pitcher Satchel Paige to help shore up the team's poor attendance and generate excitement. Paige, a future Hall of Famer who had starred in the Negro Leagues, debuted in the majors in 1948 with the Cleveland Indians at the age of 42 and last pitched for the St. Louis Browns in 1953. Finley told the press he hired Paige as a player-coach so the retired star could work the five years he needed to qualify for a MLB pension. Finley, without consulting Sullivan, announced Paige would be the starting A's pitcher on September 25, making him the oldest player ever inserted into a major league game. For the game, Finley placed a rocking chair in the bullpen for Paige's use and hired a nurse to watch over the ancient pitcher. Paige pitched three shutout innings on September 25 versus the Red Sox. He allowed only one hit, a double by Carl Yastrzemski, and threw only 28 pitches. He left the game after the third inning with the A's leading 1–0, although the bullpen could not hold the Sox, and the A's eventually lost 5–2. Finley's stunt did not bring fans to the park: Only 9,289 watched Paige's historic performance. Shamelessly, Finley released Paige after the 1965 season, still short of the years he needed to get a MLB pension, forcing Paige to take a coaching job with the Braves in 1968 to qualify.

With the end of the 1965 baseball season, and with the A's turning in one of the worst performances of any team at any time, Finley decided to spend the off-season reorganizing and restructuring. He had a stock of young talent in the A's farm system who were coming along. It looked like a nucleus of quality ballplayers were just starting to mature, and additional ones would be signed in the next amateur draft, in which the hapless A's would have early picks of the talented players coming out of high schools and colleges. Finley would sign many of them. and the A's would improve as the youngsters made their way on to the big team. The Kansas City version of the A's would not see the full fruits of that development, but in Oakland the A's would rise to the top of the baseball world, taking their owner with them.

Chapter Four

Endgame in Kansas City

Soon after the disastrous 1965 season, turmoil hit the A's front office once again. Charlie Finley knew he needed to make changes and in late October promoted Eddie Lopat from manager to executive vice president of operations and demoted Hank Peters to administrative assistant in charge of the club's minor-league system. Finley viewed the move as nothing more than a simple reshuffling of personnel and a way to add a little more experience to the mix.

Finley's decision profoundly disappointed Peters, who was a rising executive with baseball savvy, had an uncanny ability to judge talent, and was responsible for building one of the strongest scouting departments in baseball. Finley downplayed the front office shake-up in the press. "It may be a step down in your opinion, but in no sense is that a step down," Finley said. "There will be no cut in salary and Peters will work closely with Lopat. Ray Swallows, Peters and myself have tried to run the club, and it is a physical impossibility . . . I don't consider this at all a shake up . . . To build a contender and eventually a championship club it is necessary to have as many capable assistants as you can surround yourself with."[1]

Peters was the one person Finley should have retained at all cost. He didn't. On November 28, 1965, Peters resigned from the A's to become the minor-league director for the Cleveland Indians. Peters would go on to become the general manager for the Baltimore Orioles from 1975 to 1987, turning the Orioles into one of the most successful teams of the period. Before departing, Peters advised Finley not to bother to hire another general manager, as Finley seemed to want to make all the GM decisions himself.[2] Finley took Peters's suggestion, naming himself the general manager. It was a costly mistake.

On the same day Finley made himself general manager, A's manager Haywood Sullivan resigned to become the Red Sox vice president in charge of player personnel. Sullivan, who wanted to move into the business side of baseball, had grown tired of Finley's meddlesome ways and decided to leave on his own terms. Two key scouts, Joe Bowman and Art Lily, resigned with Peters; both were instrumental in signing much of the young talent in the A's farm system.

Finley and Lopat moved quickly to replace Sullivan. Alvin Dark, who joined the A's as a consultant during the 1965 season, became the A's next field manager. A star with the great New York Giants teams of the 1950s, he had earned his managerial bona fides leading the San Francisco Giants to the World Series in 1962, though they lost to the Yankees. Dark's success on the field with the Giants was overshadowed by problems with his players, especially his black and Latino players, who charged him with racism. Certainly, Dark's controversial past did not seem to bother Finley.[3]

"I think it will be a great advantage to the youngsters getting an experienced manager at the helm. A manager like Dark could mean the difference of eight to 10 to 14 ballgames over an inexperienced manager," Lopat said.[4] Dark boasted about the talent in the A's minor-league system and seemed excited by his new young team. Years later Dark recalled, "The one thing I have wanted to do in baseball, my ultimate ambition, is to start from scratch with a young team and take it to a championship . . . In Kansas City, when I took over the job managing Charlie Finley's Athletics in 1966, there was no doubt in my mind we could do it."[5]

The A's lost another member of their front office in early 1966 when public relations director Jim Schaaf left to take on the same job with the American Football League's Kansas City Chiefs. Schaaf held various positions with the A's over the years and became a Finley favorite. Despite his close relationship with the owner, Finley's 18-hour workdays and demands wore on the young Schaaf. "When I started working with Charlie . . . I was just twenty-one. I got married in '63 and started a family," Schaaf said. "It was just . . . all your time from morning to night and all hours of the night . . . phone calls and all those things. You were on-call twenty-four hours a day . . . I said, 'Charlie, I love you like a father, but I can't continue to do this because of my family' . . . And he understood."[6]

Also in 1966, Finley and the civic leaders of Kansas City began working together to resolve the A's poor attendance problems. The shaky détente began as the Greater Kansas City Sports Commission was formed to promote season ticket sales for both the A's and football's Chiefs. Many in the professional sports world questioned whether Kansas City could support major-league sports as both the A's and Chiefs struggled in attracting fans to their games. The Sports Commission partnered with area banks to sell season tickets on a no-interest installment plan. Finley jumped at the opportunity to partner with the Sports Commission and ran an advertising campaign encouraging fans to "Jump on the A's Mule Train." Additionally, the Sports Commission and the A's sold tickets through an innovative new payroll-deduction plan with participating area businesses and industries. The efforts paid off, as the A's sold a team-record 5,735 season tickets for the 1966 season.[7]

Alvin Dark's belief in his young team seemed misplaced early in the 1966 season. The A's lost their opener to the Twins 2–1 on April 12. They rallied and won their April 19 home opener against the Twins 3–2 behind a strong pitching performance from young hurler Chuck Dobson. However, they lost 14 of their next 16 games. Seeing his team sinking when the veteran pitchers were used, Dark decided to put in his talented young pitchers as often as possible and forced Lopat (with Finley's eager approval) to call up several from the A's minor-league system. Soon, the A's rotation featured their very young but talented hurlers: Catfish Hunter, Chuck Dobson, Lew Krausse, Jim Nash, and John "Blue Moon" Odom. The five starters' average age was just 21 years old. Joining the young phenoms in the bullpen were two talented veterans, Paul Lindblad and Jack Aker, who was just 25 years old. The new young pitchers steadied the A's team and began to turn around their hard-luck, losing ways. This staff's impressive 3.56 ERA ranked sixth in the American League for the season. Their immense talent and hard fast-balls overcame their youth and lack of experience, and the A's began to win ball games. From June 19 to the end of the season, the A's played better than .500 baseball, winning 50 games while losing only 49, the first such stretch in history of the A's in Kansas City.[8]

On the strength of their strong pitching, the A's climbed out of the American League cellar for the first time in three years, finishing with a 74–86 record. The team's attendance also surged to 773,929, nearly 250,000 more fans than in 1965. Finley thought the A's had turned a corner. He celebrated his team's newfound success by awarding Dark—the runner-up to Baltimore's Hank Bauer (another Finley managerial cast-off) for the Manager of the Year Award—a new Cadillac. Finley could smell a first division finish in 1967 and possibly his first winning season since purchasing the franchise. He even began thinking of abandoning his dream of moving the club out of Kansas City.

This optimism led Governor Warren Hearnes to form the Jackson County Sports Complex Authority in September 1966 to consider new stadium concepts for the Kansas City Chiefs and the Athletics. An earlier proposal for a downtown domed stadium proved to be too costly, so efforts shifted toward building new twin stadiums away from the more expensive city center. This twin-stadium concept originated with Chiefs owner Lamar Hunt after Finley refused to discuss a shared multiuse stadium. In January 1967, the authority released a report recommending that twin stadiums be constructed on the east side of Kansas City. It estimated the total cost of the stadiums at $54 million. The sports complex would be a part of $102 million bond proposal that would go before Jackson County voters on June 27, 1967. Authority chairman Dutton Brookfield and Kansas City mayor Ilus Davis tried to solicit Finley's support for the proposal, but Finley remained silent.

For months Kansas City Star sports editor Ernie Mehl and other city leaders tried to find a new ownership group for the A's. Mehl and other city leaders feared that Finley would press to move the A's once his stadium lease expired at the end of the 1967 season. They believed the only way to keep the A's in Kansas City was to find someone to buy out Finley. They instigated discussions with a potential new local owner named

Ewing Kauffman, the head of pharmaceutical company Marion Laboratories. Kauffman never really had any interest in baseball, but he did have an interest in purchasing the franchise for the good of the community. Finley responded to the Kauffman rumblings by saying, "Unless he's willing to start the discussion at $25 million, he might as well not even come up to see me."[9] Discussions did take place, but Finley wasn't interested in selling the team. At one point, Kauffman asked to see the A's accounting books, and Finley responded by saying, "Which set of books do you want to see?" The discussions ended with Finley asserting publicly that the A's were not for sale.[10]

The A's 1967 hopes rested on their young and talented pitching staff. Entering spring training, the five A's starters—Jim Nash, Catfish Hunter, Lew Krausse, Chuck Dobson and Blue Moon Odom—represented an investment of more than $300,000 in bonuses by Finley. Expectations began to rise, not just those of Finley and Dark, but of the entire baseball world. Finley and the A's were looking forward to the season; little did they realize that their fast lane toward success was about to be detoured.

The A's started out of the gate fast, as the A's young hurlers continued their winning ways. The team had an 18–18 record on May 25 but began a tailspin in June in which they lost 9 of 10 games before the All-Star break, dropping to last place with a 35–49 record. As the A's pitchers struggled to control their blazing fastballs and to maintain composure night in and night out, the team's hitters began to show promise and solidify the lineup. Speedy shortstop Campy Campaneris led the league in stolen bases for the third year in a row. Outfielder Rick Monday, a number-one draft pick, emerged as a star center fielder, making the All-Rookie team; and second baseman Dick Green provided a steady glove and leadership despite hitting only a paltry .198. Later that summer, zany outfielder and first baseman Ken Harrelson returned to the A's in a trade from the Washington Senators and provided an offensive spark by hitting .305.

Despite their talent, many players struggled in adjusting to the big leagues. "The trouble with . . . committing yourself to a youth movement is growing pains," Dark explained. "Young players require great patience. We had a lot of growing pains in 1967. I have to say this for Charlie Finley.

He never once interfered with my field managing in those two years."[11] Still, several important pieces were missing from the team. A second wave of talent would begin arriving the following year, with the infamous names of Jackson, Bando, Fingers, Blue, and Rudi. Nonetheless, as the summer passed the A's began to sink into last place.

Despite Alvin Dark's pronouncement in his memoir that Finley never interfered with his field managing during 1966 and 1967, other Finley-induced distractions undoubtedly affected the young and inexperienced team. One major distraction that likely played a role in what would become a disappointing 1967 season was the increasing tension between the A's owner and Kansas City municipal officials. Once again, Finley was threatening to move the team.

On May 7, 1967, both the *New York Times* and the *New York Daily News* reported that Finley wanted to relocate the A's to Oakland. The *Times* reported a mutual lack of interest shown by both Finley and the Sports Complex Authority, while the *Daily News* noted the city's apparent indifference to the fate of the A's. In a May 27 *Sporting News* article, columnist Joe McGuff stated, "Neither story could be farther from the truth. Lack of interest in the sports complex has been entirely one-sided. In addition, Kansas City has done everything possible to support the A's." McGuff went on to ballyhoo the efforts of the Greater Kansas City Sports Commission in securing season tickets for the A's over the past two seasons.

Soon, both McGuff and Ernie Mehl began a clandestine counter-information campaign, aimed at the other team owners, touting the strong interest in and support for Major League Baseball in the Kansas City area. They hoped to provide a more accurate view than the one being reported in New York newspapers. They met with several American League owners and tried to expound the virtues of baseball in Kansas City and the need to keep the team in the city.

Despite Finley's lack of cooperation, the voters in Jackson County approved the bond for the twin-stadium complex on June 27. The sports complex proposal won nearly 69 percent of the vote, easily exceeding the two-thirds majority it needed to pass. But Finley still remained coy, saying, "I have no comment whatsoever."[12]

On July 18, Finley began intense discussions with the Sports Complex Authority and Kansas City officials in his Chicago offices. Finley said, "At this moment I do not know what I want to do." All parties described the meeting as cordial, but Finley pressed Sports Complex Authority president Dutton Brookfield for a written proposal. "We came away feeling there was a genuine spirit of cooperation on Mr. Finley's part," said Brookfield. Finley offered only tepid assurances. "I did not present any proposal," Finley told the press after the meeting. "I've requested they make me a proposal in writing." Then he lied: "Through last year my losses in Kansas City were $4,283,000." More to the point, he recited that "the average attendance was 670,000." Finley then gave a hint of his decision timetable. "It will be around the first of October before I know what to do," said Finley. "If I decide I want to move, I will request permission of the American League at that time."[13]

While this played out, various local business interests tried one last time to purchase the A's from Finley and ensure the team stayed in Kansas City. None of them had the cash necessary to get anywhere with Finley. But even if they did, he had no desire to sell the team; he simply wanted out of Kansas City.

Finley might have been right about the need to move elsewhere for the economic good of his team, at least in the short run. As revenues dried up in northern and some eastern cities, new markets, especially those on the West Coast, offered a growing population and attracted an increasing number of baseball teams, as the old way of things changed. With the moves of the Boston Braves to Milwaukee in 1953, the St. Louis Browns to Baltimore in 1954, and the Philadelphia Athletics to Kansas City in 1955, the system truly began to change. The 1958 departure of the Brooklyn Dodgers and the New York Giants for Los Angeles and San Francisco, respectively, destroyed the existing structure of the sport forever.[14] Should the A's take advantage of these opportunities as well, especially with new stadium possibilities elsewhere?

Revered sports columnist Leonard Koppett opined that while the moves of the Braves, Browns, and Athletics upset the fans in their old stomping grounds, few others cared. They seemingly accepted the moves as necessary to meet the economics of the changing times. But when two of the three New York teams fled for the West Coast, bedlam broke loose. "Four centuries earlier," Koppett wrote, "the idea that it was the earth going around the sun instead of the other way around shook the whole culture's sense of mankind's central importance. In baseball's mini-universe, the franchise shifts of the 1950s had an analogous impact."[15]

All of this set up the possibility of franchise relocation for the Kansas City Athletics throughout the 1960s, and Finley played it for all it was worth from the moment that he bought the team.

In July 1967, the *Sporting News* reported Finley wanted to move his team to Milwaukee. Finley met with Milwaukee County officials and received a favorable lease offer for the use of Milwaukee County Stadium and considerable pledges for television and radio rights from the local Schlitz Brewing Company. Finley worked behind the scenes at the 1967 All-Star game in Anaheim to secure the votes required to move the A's to Milwaukee or elsewhere. He needed seven votes from the American League owners to move the A's, but he had only five.[16] The Milwaukee deal collapsed when Finley refused to sell majority interest in the A's to a local ownership group.

Finley then turned to other potential cities. He quickly scratched New Orleans off his list, given that the $65 million Superdome stadium would not be completed until 1972. This led him back to Oakland. City officials there offered Finley a lease of the new Oakland–Alameda County Coliseum. The proposal also guaranteed Finley and the A's radio and television income of more than $1 million per season, a nice upgrade to the paltry $155,000 to $250,000 he was making in Kansas City. Finley upped the pressure on Kansas City, stating, "I'm very much impressed" with the Oakland proposal.[17]

Later that month, Washington state governor Dan Evans and Seattle mayor Dorm Braman telephoned Finley and invited him to come to Seattle to look into the city's major-league potential. However, Seattle did not possess a suitable stadium, and recent bond issues to build one had failed. Nonetheless, Finley visited Seattle on August 1 and announced, "I have known for a long time that the Seattle area would be a great area for major league baseball."[18] Finley met with Seattle officials on August 7 and told them he planned on seeking permission to move the A's in October.

However, Finley refused to sign any formal contract with Seattle and instead played city against city as he tried to get the American League votes necessary to move the A's.

The league owners slowly seemed to be moving in Finley's direction. "Seattle and the northwest territory is the prime territory," said one owner. "The league has said 'no' to Charles so many times that I don't see how we can turn him down again. We'd much rather have him move to Seattle than Oakland."[19]

In addition to the media attention over the adversarial relationship between Finley with the local Kansas City community, another incident brought national attention and embarrassment to the A's during the final seven weeks of the season, and also illustrated the sometimes bizarre behavior of the A's owner and general manager.

The wheels began to come off the A's season after an extra-inning loss in Boston on August 2—though the team had actually enjoyed a successful road trip, splitting 12 games. The team boarded TWA Flight 85 the next day for the return flight to Kansas City, with stops in Baltimore and St. Louis. Because of Finley's legendary penny-pinching, the A's traveled on commercial flights. Players Ken Harrelson, Jim Aker, Lew Krausse, Paul Lindblad, and several other all sat in the back of the airliner, and A's broadcaster Monte Moore sat nearby. Manager Alvin Dark and his coaches sat toward the front of the nearly empty jet. What happened during the five-hour flight remains in dispute to this day.

As the flight progressed, one of the players began to irritate Moore, who was playing cards. Alvin Dark said, "Evidently they did a little kidding-on-the-square during the flight because Moore snapped at one of them for stuffing paper in the air-conditioning vent behind him, creating a racket. Moore was quoted, 'Why don't you guys grow up?'" Moore went up front and reported the problems to traveling secretary Ed Hurley, who passed it on to Dark. Neither Dark nor Hurley thought too much of it at the time. However, Dark did walk to the back of the plane to check things out. "I got up and went back for a look. As soon as I saw their faces, I suspected they were up to something. They were like kids with innocent looks. I asked the stewardess if she was having trouble. She said, 'Oh no, they're a great bunch of guys.' I didn't think any more about it. We landed in Kansas City at around ten thirty that night." Dark recalled that the players were somewhat more cheerful departing the plane than usual, but there were certainly no drunks among them or evidence of bad behavior.[20]

Pitcher Lew Krausse disputes Dark's recollection of events. "Alvin Dark was on the hot seat so bad he never came back [during the flight]. He never said a word," Krausse recalled. He does agree with Dark that nothing serious or out-of-line happened on the flight. "The flight attendants were all sitting down, sitting with us. We were just talking and laughing having a good time, nobody was standing up or dancing," he said.[21]

Nothing was mentioned publicly about the August 3 plane trip for more than two weeks. Then, on August 18, as the A's were preparing to play the Senators in Washington, DC, Finley phoned Dark and asked him to fine and suspend Krausse for his misconduct on the plane. Dark balked and told Finley that nothing serious had occurred on the flight from Boston. But Finley said, "I want you to fine Lew Krausse $500 and suspend him because he was drunk getting off the plane after the last road trip and used bad language around a woman passenger." Dark told Finley that he could not support this decision and checked with several other players, including Harrelson, all of whom said nothing had happened. "Charlie, you can't do it," said Dark. Finley decided to anyway.[22]

"My phone rings at eight in the morning there in Washington . . . Finley," Lew Krausse recalled. "I should have known right away from his tone that something was wrong. He said, 'I'm fining you five hundred dollars for carrying on and drinking on that flight.' And seriously, I had to wait and think what flight it was . . . Finley and I are screaming and hollering at one another and I'm denying everything. I slammed down the phone on him. I went into the bathroom . . . come back into the bedroom, where the phone was ringing again. He says, 'As of today you're suspended indefinitely without pay. You're to go directly to Kansas City.'" Years later Krausse said, "This was no big deal. He [Finley] blamed me for what was going on there [with the flight] because at the time I was the only single person on that flight with those girls. All the other guys . . . were all married."[23]

For a long time, it remained a mystery who had informed Finley about the TWA flight "incident." Some believed it was Moore; others suspected shortstop Bert Campaneris. Years later, according to Monte Moore, Paul Finley said he was the person who told his father of the shenanigans on the flight. Moore said, "After he [Charlie Finley] died, they had a memorial service on a Sunday, and they had me come and speak. As I was walking out of the coliseum with my family, Paul Finley, Charlie's son, who was on that airplane when that thing happened, came running up to me, and he said, 'Monte, I've got to tell you something. This has been bothering me for a lot of years. I did something that caused you a lot of heat, and it's unfair, and I want you to know that I am the one who told my dad about what went on in that airplane. And I know that you were not the one, and I never said anything about it.' "[24] Paul Finley, a teenager at the time, traveled frequently with the A's during his summer breaks and happened to be seated one row in front of Moore on that flight.

After suspending Krausse, Finley had traveling secretary Ed Hurley type up a statement to be read the team. Finley then called Jack Aker, the team's union representative, and asked him to read this statement to the players. The insinuations in the memo outraged Aker, but Finley made sure it was posted in the clubhouse before the game:

> Effective immediately and for the balance of the season, all alcoholic drinks will no longer be served on commercial airlines to members of the Kansas City Athletics.
>
> The Kansas City Athletics will no longer tolerate the shenanigans of a very few individuals who obviously do not appreciate the privilege of playing in the major leagues and being treated like gentlemen.
>
> The attitude, actions and words of some of you have been deplorable.[25]

The statement and Krausse's suspension enraged the players. They asked Aker to try to get it retracted or modified before it made it into the newspapers, but it was too late. Finley had already released it to the wire services.

Evidently, Finley expected trouble from his action and decided to fly to Washington to head it off. He arrived late on August 19, 1967. The players had been busy for the past day coming up with a response to Finley's new air travel doctrine. During the game and after, players met with Aker as he crafted a response. They even informed Alvin Dark of their plans and promised to show him the final copy before releasing it to the press or Finley. Upon arriving at the Shoreham Hotel in Washington, Finley called Dark to his suite and asked for his support in the brewing controversy. He wanted Dark to tell the players he agreed with the suspension of Krausse. Dark refused, fearing that Finley would be open to litigation since there was no real proof that anything happened on the plane. Finley then told Dark, "Alvin, I'm going to have to let you go . . . I want my manager to back me on this and you're not doing it." However, Finley's pronouncement did not end the conversation. "We talked and talked," Dark recalled. "And I found myself telling him what a terrific bunch of boys he had, that with them and the ones he had coming up—Reggie Jackson, Sal Bando, Joe Rudi—he would win a pennant for sure . . . We talked for two and half hours."[26]

Amazingly, Finley proceeded to ask Dark if he would like to continue to manage the A's for two more years. Dark was befuddled because he had just been fired. He asked the owner if he was hiring him back. Finley responded, "How about two more years? With a raise?" Dark agreed. The conversation continued, with several members of the coaching staff, along with Monte Moore and Ed Hurley, joining in. Then, shortly after midnight, *Kansas City Star* reporter Paul O'Boynick barged into the room and asked Finley for a comment on the players' press release. Finley was unaware of any player statement, so O'Boynick read it to him. The statement said:

> In response to the Charles O. Finley's statement of August 18, we, the players of the Kansas City Athletics, feel that an unjust amount of pressure has been brought to bear on several members of the club who had no part whatsoever in the so-called incident on the recent plane trip from Boston to Kansas City. The overwhelming opinion of the players is that the entire matter was blown out of proportion. Mr. Finley's policy of using certain unauthorized

personnel in his organization as go-betweens has led to similar misunderstandings in the past and has tended to undermine the morale of the club. We players feel that if Mr. Finley would give his fine coaching staff and excellent manager the authority they deserve, these problems would not exist.[27]

Finley was flabbergasted by the players' statement. He immediately turned to Dark and asked if he had known anything about it. Dark responded, "About what?" Finley interpreted this to mean Dark had known nothing of its existence. However, Dark had known that the players were working on a statement, but thought they had an agreement for him to review it before it was released to the press. Then Finley demanded that Aker, the A's union representative, come to his suite. Unfortunately, Aker had broken the team's curfew to visit an old friend in Baltimore and was not in his room. He finally returned at two A.M. When they finally met that night, Finley promptly fined Aker $250 for missing the curfew and demanded that the players retract their statement. Aker refused because of the players' unanimous vote to release it.

"Did Alvin see the statement?" Finley asked.

"Yeah," Aker responded. That was not exactly true. Dark had hoped to see their document before it made it to the press, to temper it, but Aker had released it beforehand.

"You knew they were working on this?" Finley roared.

"Yes I did," answered Dark.

Finley accused Dark of disloyalty and demanded to know why he had not told him of the statement. Dark said it had never come up in their conversation. Finley then stormed out of the room and headed for a coffee shop. Dark retreated to his room and awaited his fate. Finley called him an hour later and fired him—again. In the span of eight hours during the evening of August 19 and the early morning of August 20, Alvin Dark was fired, rehired with a raise, and fired once again.

Finley promptly named Luke Appling the A's manager. He also issued a statement about Dark's firing to the press: "I released Alvin Dark as manager because I am convinced he had lost control of his ballplayers." It went on to say that Dark "stated several times that the contents of the statement made by the ballplayers had come as a complete surprise to him. He said that had the player representative consulted him or the players, he would have made every effort to prevent it because it had no basis in fact." It was pure Finley fiction.[28]

The team had a game that day, and Dark went to the stadium to say goodbye to the players. Emotions ran high as he cleaned out his locker. After the game was called because of the rain, the players talked about their next move, but they could not agree on an action. Some wanted to strike; others wanted a different form of protest. Dark then issued his own press release, which had a more complete and accurate accounting of the activities of the night before. "I want to point out that I disagreed with Mr. Finley about the Krausse fine. This was a case of singling out one ballplayer and making him look bad . . . At no time did I make the remark attributed to me by Mr. Finley that the players' statement of August 19 had no basis in fact . . . I knew the players were drafting a statement. They did it with my approval, but I did not instigate it . . . I did know of it, but I had not seen their final draft. I want to say that I think the action of the players is the most courageous thing I have ever seen."[29]

As the team returned to the hotel, several newspaper reporters were waiting in the lobby. Outfielder Ken Harrelson remembers reluctantly talking to the press. "I was in a fog," he said. "I shouldn't have said anything . . . All these guys were crowding around asking for public statements . . . A writer came to me, all I could think of was what Finley had done, not only to Alvin, but to the whole club . . . I said, 'The only thing I know is that Charlie Finley's actions of the last few days have been bad for baseball. I think they have been detrimental to the game.' " Unfortunately for Harrelson, he was quoted later that night on the local evening news as calling Finley "a menace to baseball." Harrelson and several players were watching the newscast. Many of the players thought it funny, but Harrelson did not. The reporter misquoted him, and now he feared Finley's wrath.[30]

Finley called Harrelson at nine the next morning. "Kenny, did you make those statements in the papers?" Finley inquired. "I said everything except you were a menace," Harrelson responded. "What I actually said to the reporter was that I thought your actions of the last few days were bad for baseball."[31]

"I've been good to you," Finley said. "I want you to write a public re-traction and give it to the papers." Harrelson agreed to retract the word "menace" but refused to retract the rest of his quote. Finley fumed and screamed into the phone and threatened to suspend or release him before hanging up. Harrelson stewed about what Finley could do to him. Harrel-son was on a hot streak at the plate and doubted that Finley would trade him. Fifteen minutes later, Finley called back and in a hard, legalistic tone said, "As of this moment, you have your unconditional release from the Kansas City Athletics. As of this moment, you are no longer a mem-ber of the Kansas City Athletics." Then he hung up. Harrelson was dumbfounded. Finley could have sold him to another team via a waiver transaction for at least $50,000. He could have traded him. Instead he was released. Harrelson feared that Finley would blacklist him, but as soon as word of his release reached the newswires, four American League pennant contenders called him and began bidding for his services. Harrelson had in effect become baseball's first free agent because of a temper tantrum by Charlie Finley.[32]

Finley quickly realized his temper had gotten the better of him. He called Luke Appling and asked him to talk with Harrelson. Appling told Harrelson that Finley had lost his temper and that everyone, including Finley, wanted him back. Harrelson, who by now realized the financial windfall before him, responded, "If Charlie wanted me back, he'd have called and asked me . . . There's no way that I'm coming back to play for this man." Shortly thereafter, Harrelson signed with the Boston Red Sox for $150,000 over the next two years, more than 10 times the salary he'd been earning a few days before. Harrelson would help Boston take the pennant in 1967 and have an All-Star season in 1968.[33]

Between the players' feud with Finley and Harrelson's departure, the team limped home with at 10–29 record under Appling and finished in last place again with a disappointing 62–99 record. After the season, Finley fired Appling and accepted Ed Lopat's resignation as executive vice president. Lopat quit before Finley could fire him.

The late-season acrimony sank A's attendance in August and Septem-ber; they drew 726,639 fans in 1967. The Krausse and Harrelson inci-dents left many fans with a bitter taste in their mouth. They were tired of

Finley's acrimony, and Finley was equally tired of Kansas City. Years later, Krausse noted Finley's other motives for inflaming the flight incident. "It was all a game that he was playing to have a legitimate reason to get out of town," he said. "When this shit was going on, people were just staying away from the ballpark. It got nasty." Krausse added, "Finley was just screwing with everybody's minds. He was looking for a way out of Kansas City, so he thought he would just disrupt everything. And sure enough, he did."[34]

In mid-September 1967, Finley began to show his cards. He sent a telegram to Carleton Sharpe, the city manager of Kansas City, stating, "Pursuant to paragraph four of our lease dated February 28, 1964; this is to advise you that it is our present intention not to exercise our option to renew the lease on Municipal Stadium."

Soon city, state, and congressional officials from Kansas City, Oakland, and Seattle were invited by American League president Joe Cronin to the league meeting scheduled for October 18 in Chicago to "discuss an application which is expected to be filed shortly, to transfer the Kansas City Athletics to another location effective for the 1968 championship season."[35] Complicating an already difficult situation was the mounting pressure on the league to increase its number of franchises. Major League Baseball wanted to expand its presence to compete with the increasingly popular National Football League. MLB hoped to expand each league by two teams beginning in the 1970 season. Many owners wanted the new teams to go to four entirely new markets, but with Finley's problems with Kansas City, it became increasingly likely that league officials would need to place one of the four new franchises in Kansas City if they allowed Finley to move the A's. On the eve of the league meeting, White Sox owner Arthur Allyn told the Kansas City Star's Ernie Mehl that he had seven expansion votes in his pocket for Kansas City should the owners let Finley leave. Soon Kansas City officials were split on whether to fight to keep the A's or to let Finley and the team leave and receive a future expansion team.

On September 18, 1967, city officials sent Finley a letter that made a last-ditch attempt to keep the A's and entice Finley into formal discussions to leave the team in Kansas City. In response, Finley sent a September 28 letter to city manager Carleton Sharpe formally ending discussions and stating that he was moving the A's from Kansas City. "During recent years I have given a great deal of consideration to the question of what action should be taken with respect to our franchise upon the expiration of our present lease of Municipal Stadium," Finley's letter stated. "More recently I have sought and obtained expert advice as to what course of action would best serve the interest of the American League as well as the interest of the Athletics . . . Based on that consideration and that advice I have decided to take the steps necessary to transfer the Athletics franchise to another city."[36]

He quickly followed that up by announcing the A's would move to Oakland for the 1968 season. Finley noted, "I based my choice of Oakland on four points: the Oakland–Alameda County Coliseum sports complex provides the finest facilities for all-round sports in the world, the climate in the area is very ideal for baseball and second to none, the population growth in the area is the fastest of any major league area in either league, and the enthusiasm for sports in the area is overwhelming."[37]

As all parties prepared for an October 18 showdown in Chicago, Finley's fellow American League owners tried to figure out an acceptable compromise. They quickly realized that not only would Finley's application be under consideration, but league expansion would likely be on the agenda as well. Kansas City, Oakland, and Seattle were each represented by high-powered attorneys and politicians from Washington, DC. One of the most notable was Senator Stuart Symington from Missouri. Earlier in his career he had served as Air Force first secretary and had battled Joseph McCarthy's communist witch hunt in the Senate during the 1950s; his efforts at standing up to McCarthy earned him the nickname "Sanctimonious Stu." Symington loathed Charlie Finley and explicitly threatened to open hearings in Congress into possibly revoking baseball's antitrust exemption if the league owners allowed the A's to move. Fearing significant legal and legislative repercussions from an A's move out of Kansas City, the American League owners realized that they had only three options:

1. The league could allow the A's to move to Oakland and leave Kansas City without a major-league team—a scenario similar to when the National League allowed the Milwaukee Braves to relocate to Atlanta

in 1965. This decision would likely result in litigation by Kansas City and significant legislative pressure in Congress by Senator Symington.

2. The league owners could turn down Finley's application to move, as they did in 1964 when he wanted to move to Louisville, and force Finley to sign a new lease and remain in Kansas City. In addition, they could attempt to cajole Finley into selling the A's to a local ownership group at a fair market price and be rid of Finley as an owner once and for all. Several MLB owners had never liked nor respected Finley and felt he was a significant liability to baseball. However, most owners knew they could not force Finley to sell.

3. The league could attempt to find a compromise by using its planned expansion as a solution. Kansas City's only real hope for retaining a Major League Baseball team lay in allowing Finley and the A's to move to Oakland and receiving a guarantee of a future team when the league expanded. However, this solution was no panacea, since the timetable for expansion was unsettled; some owners favored an immediate expansion and other preferred waiting for two or three years.

On the morning of October 18, Finley gave the first presentation to his fellow owners on his application to move the Athletics to Oakland. He methodically presented his case for relocation, claiming to have lost more than $4 million in his seven years of running the franchise in Kansas City and postulating that he would likely be forced into bankruptcy if forced to remain in the city.[38]

Then Finley presented the results of his survey of the three cities (Oakland, Seattle, and Kansas City) made by the consulting firm Booz Allen Hamilton. The survey attempted to determine which city was most suitable for a Major League Baseball franchise. Finley presented the survey as an impartial study, but in fact he instructed the consulting firm to favor Oakland. The survey results surprised no one in the room: Oakland–San Francisco was said to be the area best suited to host a second major-league franchise.

Knowing Finley paid for the survey, several owners questioned its conclusions. Most felt the survey shortchanged Kansas City and Seattle while exaggerating Oakland's readiness for baseball. "Very frankly, we felt the A's had not done the proper market studies to look at the various place that were available," said Frank Cashen of the Baltimore Orioles. "And we thought it would certainly hurt the San Francisco Giants to put another team in the Bay Area."[39]

Following Finley's presentation, the owners heard from both Oakland and Kansas City representatives. The Oakland delegation, led by Robert Nahas, the president of the Oakland–Alameda County Coliseum complex, and the powerful William Knowland, a former senator and publisher of the *Oakland Tribune*, focused their presentation on the city's ability to provide baseball and the A's with a modern, first-class stadium facility; the city's great support of major-league sports (the Oakland Raiders); and their ability to hit the ground running for the 1968 season. After their presentation Nahas went on to describe Finley as "a man who plays with his cards up."[40] The Kansas City delegation followed. Led by Mayor Davis, Dutton Brookfield, and Senator Symington, the Kansas City group discussed the city's attendance, sports interest, media market, transportation infrastructure, accommodating lease proposals to Finley, and planned new sports complex. The delegation appealed to the owners for a continuation of their franchise with or without Charlie Finley as owner.

At approximately 5:30 P.M. the owners began their deliberations on the Finley application and the possible expansion of the American League. Several wanted to go ahead and approve the Finley application for the A's moving to Oakland but wait until a future meeting to decide on expansion. Expansion was a delicate balancing act, and several owners felt the American League needed to better coordinate its expansion with the National League. As the discussions dragged on, two ballots were taken on Finley's application to move the team. In the first ballot, Finley received six favorable votes, leaving him one shy of the seven required for approval. Baltimore voted against the move, with Cleveland, New York, and Washington abstaining. Cronin then ordered a second vote. Finley persuaded Yankees' president Mike Burke to support his cause, and the owners voted 7–3 in favor of Finley's moving the A's to Oakland. Soon after, the owners voted to expand the American League by two teams. At around 10:30 P.M. the

American League issued a press release stating that it had "voted to allow Charles O. Finley to move the Kansas City Athletics to Oakland, California, effective for the 1968 baseball season. The league also voted to adopt its expansion plan under which the league would expand to 12 clubs as soon as practical, but not later than the 1971 season, and awarded these two expansion franchises to Kansas City, Missouri, and Seattle, Washington."[41] Charlie Finley prevailed and the A's were headed west to sunny California.

The vote led to additional fireworks when league president Joe Cronin and several owners met with the Kansas City delegation to explain the decision. The outraged KC delegation rejected the terms. They could not accept being without a baseball team for three years. Symington threatened to submit legislation and hold hearings into baseball's antitrust exemption, then stormed out of the meeting. Mayor Davis told Cronin, "Finley deliberately sabotaged the Kansas City franchise to get it out of town . . . He's rewarded by getting permission to move elsewhere and we're penalized . . . We were prepared to sit out one year, but we're not going to be without baseball for three years because of Finley. We'll fight it all the way."[42] Cronin quickly called a second meeting with the remaining owners at the hotel; a few had already left to return home. Cronin then asked that the Kansas City delegation meet in his suite for one last session.

The late-night meeting opened with a rancorous atmosphere. Both sides discussed compromises, and finally an agreement was reached. Cronin then called reporters into the suite and revealed that Kansas City's expansion team would begin play during the 1969 baseball season. Kansas City's threats had forced the league to accelerate its expansion plans.

The next day Senator Symington returned to Washington and, in an uncharacteristic display, took to the Senate floor and publicly chastised Charles O. Finley as "one of the most disreputable characters ever to enter the American sports scene." Symington said that even though Kansas City would be without baseball for one year, "the loss is more than recompensed for by the pleasure resulting from our getting rid of Mr. Finley."[43] He concluded his diatribe with the most popular quote of his political life, sarcastically saying, "Oakland is the luckiest city since Hiroshima."[44]

Meanwhile, back in Kansas City, most citizens and baseball fans were resigned to the A's leaving town. "I'm sorry to see the baseball team leave, but it's good to be rid of Mr. Finley," said Mrs. Clestine Sadler, a weaver for Wardrobe Services Inc. "I hope we get an owner who wants to work with us as a city," said Elaine Grimes, a Kansas City secretary. She added, "With Charles Finley's attitude toward Kansas City, we're better off without him." Kenneth Blakey, a doorman at the Muehlebach Hotel, echoed most fans' thoughts on the A's departure: "I'd like to see the A's stay here under home ownership. But if it took losing them to get rid of Finley—fine, especially since we're getting a new team in a year."[45]

So Finley and Kansas City parted ways with bitter feelings and plenty of blame on both sides. It had been a tumultuous seven-year relationship. On a fundamental level, Finley pioneered the now-standard shakedown approach of MLB owners seeking new publicly financed stadiums, which has been used repeatedly since the 1960s to extract money from cities throughout the nation.

At the same time, though, he failed to capitalize on this campaign because he moved from Kansas City before its stadium was completed. In essence, he was too impatient to wait until the early 1970s for the new stadium to be built in Kansas City, so he moved on to Oakland, which had a new stadium, but perhaps not an ideal one, since it was multipurpose and therefore did not have the best dimensions for either baseball or football. Finley claimed the following as rationale for this move:

- a superb Oakland sports complex
- an ideal regional climate
- the fastest population growth of any major-league area
- overwhelming local enthusiasm for baseball

But the real reasons for Finley's move rested with his long-standing feud with Kansas City politicos and fans and his impatience with the process of stadium development. He lived to regret it.

Maybe the largest mistake Finley made in this matter was fighting with the local media. The battles with the *Kansas City Star* and *Kansas City Times* hurt Finley's reputation and his club's marketability. The viciousness of his attacks toward legendary columnist Ernie Mehl especially hurt

Finley's image. For all Finley's bluster over his marketing and media suaveness, he was really a novice in both areas. He craved to see his name in the newspapers but never understood how to maintain cordial relations with the fourth estate. One of the best ways to earn the respect of the press is to tell the truth—every time. Finley never learned this simple axiom. He became an expert at parsing words and manipulating facts to suit his particular desire at any given moment. "I didn't totally dislike Finley," said Mehl. "There are a lot of things to like about him . . . Unfortunately, many of the things he does are outrageous. He hurts people and then tries to laugh it off . . . He said he was a man of his word and then broke his word . . . Once the community found out it could not trust him, it turned on him. He couldn't seem to understand this."[46]

However, Kansas City deserved some blame for its dealing with the A's owner. Finley never received the financial support he believed was promised him by the city during his initial renovations of the stadium. The city always seemed willing to provide the Kansas City Chiefs with better terms than it gave the A's and Finley. Furthermore, the city exacerbated Finley's insecurities by its bait-and-switch stadium-lease fiasco in 1963 and 1964, which resulted in Finley trying to leave Kansas City for Louisville and the league forcing him to stay put and sign a four-year lease. The bad blood created by this situation assured that Finley would move his team when the lease expired in 1967.

As John Peterson correctly points out in his book, *The Kansas City Athletics*, "had the new council accepted the lease, the ill feelings could have been avoided . . . History somewhat vindicates Finley because Kansas City lost two other major-league franchises [hockey and basketball] within the next 20 years because they refused to make compromises that ultimately resulted in the loss of these teams."[47]

Former baseball executive Cedric Tallis said, "The American League never would have permitted Finley to move if they hadn't conceived of having an orderly expansion and another club in Kansas City. Expansion was a good thing at that time . . . All in all, I think it was best that the marriage between the A's and Kansas City was dissolved."[48]

In reality, the Finley–Kansas City union represented all the unseemly aspects of a shotgun marriage that was forced on each party, both of whom wanted different partners in the first place. It was a union imposed by a federal probate judge in which each party was unwilling to listen to or compromise with the other. Neither side really wanted the other, and like so many shotgun unions, it ultimately failed. Would the experience in Oakland be better?

Chapter Five

Oakland A's Rising

On October 26, 1967, Charlie Finley arrived at the Oakland airport to a hero's welcome. Finley, wife Shirley, sons Charlie Jr. and Paul, and several other A's executives and players were welcomed by more than 400 enthusiastic fans, local reporters, and politicians from the Oakland area. Fans greeted the party with signs that read OAKLAND'S NO. 1 CITIZEN: CHARLES FINLEY and WELCOME CHARLIE O. FINLEY. Never one to miss a media opportunity, Finley took the microphone and declared, "In Kansas City, we played practically all our games before groups this size."[1] He then went on to repeat many of the same promises he'd made seven years earlier to the fans in Kansas City. He pledged that the A's were in Oakland to stay and that his number-one priority was building a winning ball club. He promised not only to move his family to Oakland but to relocate his insurance business from Chicago as well. During the circuslike event, Finley talked about placing his baseball-dispensing mechanical rabbit in the Coliseum, he bragged about spending more than a million dollars on a fancy new fireworks-equipped scoreboard for the Coliseum, he promised even flashier uniforms for his players, and he announced that the team's mascot, Charlie O. the mule, would make his home in Oakland and would visit local schoolchildren. The fans ate up the flamboyant owner's every word and promise.

Finley's oratory excited the fans. He had laid the groundwork for his arrival by making a spectacular announcement only days before. Finley persuaded legendary Yankees icon and Bay Area native Joe DiMaggio to join the A's as the team's new executive vice president and consultant. DiMaggio, who had been out of baseball since his retirement from the Yankees in 1951, needed two more years of baseball service to qualify for the league's maximum pension allowance and also yearned to get back into the game. Upon learning that most in the media believed he would be doing public relations appearances for the A's, DiMaggio said, "That's out. Also, I'm not going around talking to groups or making appearances at banquets. As I understand the job, I'll be busy all of the time with player personnel, working on possible trades, and serving as an advisor."[2] Little did DiMaggio know that Finley never planned on using him that way. Instead, he utilized the "Yankee Clipper" as a part-time hitting coach and roving publicity ambassador—a public relations role. Two years later, DiMaggio would become fed up with his position in the organization and with Finley and leave. But for now, Finley let Joe believe whatever he wanted.

The day after his arrival in Oakland, Finley and some of his players, including bonus baby Rick Monday, held a news conference to introduce the new A's field manager, Bob Kennedy, a former manager of the Cubs. Just as he had in announcing his previous managers, Finley told the press that Kennedy was the perfect man for the job and affirmed his belief that they would have a blissful working relationship. Finley told the press that problems with the players in the 1967 season should be viewed as "water over the dam."[3] He said the A's attendance goal for the upcoming 1968 was a million fans. He downplayed Giants owner Horace Stoneham's pointed comments on the adverse effect the team's relocation to the East Bay would have on Giants attendance. "I wouldn't have fought for five years to come to Oakland if I did not think the area could support two teams," Finley said in response to Stoneham.[4]

Soon, Finley inked a five-year radio and television deal, with ARCO paying the A's approximately $1.1 million a year. Next came the lease for the Oakland Coliseum. In typical fashion, Finley negotiated every aspect of the lease, and it took months to come to an agreement. Coliseum general manager Bill Cunningham said of the lease strategy, "Our approach was to tie him down in the lease to provisions that would protect the Coliseum and our community against the repetition of [another Kansas City] happening."[5] As the negotiations dragged on, Finley continued to state his willingness to sign a long-term lease.

The lease negotiations came down to the wire, with Finley agreeing to terms only two weeks before the season opened. He signed a 20-year lease for an annual rent of $125,000, or 5 percent of the gate up to an attendance of 1.45 million (an attendance number that the Finley A's never reached). The A's also received 27 percent of the parking revenue and 25 percent of the concession revenue. The lease also included an interesting provision— an injunctive relief provision—to protect Oakland and the Coliseum against a Kansas City–type relocation. "Finley agrees to have the A's play exclusively in our stadium and no other place, except as a visiting team, for a period of twenty years," explained Cunningham. "He is further specifically bound by the contract not to enter into discussions with anybody or any city about the transfer of the A's to another location during the life of the contract . . . Under our terms, the first time there's even a public discussion about moving, we could go to court."[6] Despite news reports at the time, the lease did not contain a provision allowing Finley to buy out the remaining years of the lease. It should be noted that there were substantial rumors in 1970 about Finley having clandestine discussions with Toronto concerning again moving the A's. While Finley wanted to show good faith to his new city by signing a 20-year lease, the move severely handicapped his ability to sell the A's 10 years later to several out-of-town bidders.

While Finley finalized the lease, his skeleton front office staff relocated to Oakland and began selling season tickets. He announced a stated goal of selling 5,000 season tickets for 1968. Finley's cousin Carl Finley, who had worked for the team since the early 1960s, was in charge of the front office. Carl was a very likable character, seemingly the polar opposite of the bombastic and quick-tempered A's owner. A former school administrator from Dallas, Carl held numerous front office positions in his nearly 20 years of working for Charlie Finley, including ticket manager, public relations manager, and A's business manager. Mainly, Carl did whatever Charlie wanted him to do at any given time. Players and coaches alike remembered Carl, who died in 2002, with fondness and empathy. Most could never understand how he put up with Charlie's controlling and abusive manner. Carl, like many of Charlie's managers, endured hundreds of late-night phone calls.

Among those working on the front office team in Oakland were two twentysomethings from Charlie's stomping grounds in northwestern Indiana, Tom Corwin and Ron Mihelic. Corwin's parents had gone to school with Finley, while Mihelic's parents, John and Evelyn, lived on and ran Finley's La Porte farm. Corwin began as the A's new traveling secretary, and Ron Mihelic served as assistant ticket manager.

Longtime baseball man Phil Seghi, who would go on to serve as general manager of the Cleveland Indians in the 1970s and 1980s, ran the A's farm system and scouting departments. As the Reds scouting director, Seghi signed future superstar Pete Rose to his first contract.

The final new addition to the front office staff was Bill Cutler, the former administrative assistant to American League president Joe Cronin. Finley convinced Cutler to join the A's staff in the autumn of 1967 and move to Oakland with the team. At the time, Cutler believed he was joining the club as a quasi–general manager, a position similar to the one Joe DiMaggio believed his to be. However, Finley decided that he wanted to utilize Cutler in many different odd jobs with the A's, including stadium advertising sales, public relations, and minor-league player development. Each time, Cutler refused to do the job, saying that his contract stated his position was "vice president with duties of a general manager." After six months of these disagreements over Cutler's duties, Finley fired him with more than three and a half years left on his contract. Cutler took Finley to court, and though he lost the initial trial, an Oakland court eventually awarded him $50,000 on a breach of contract ruling. Cutler's six-year experience in court against Finley, well documented in Herbert Michelson's book *Charlie O.*, painted Finley as an untrustworthy, manipulative bully who took great pleasure in toying with subordinates' careers and lives. Many of the staff and executives who worked for Charlie Finley echoed this sentiment. At the same time, they recognized that Finley could be a charming and generous friend and business colleague. No one was immune to his antics.

Finley and the A's began selling tickets and promoting Oakland's new baseball club in earnest during the winter and spring of 1968. Finley sent promotional season-ticket flyers to every telephone-service subscriber within a 50-mile radius of the Coliseum. "We're also getting the addresses of every automobile owner within the same radius," declared Finley.[7] In total, the A's sent 1.5 million ticket applications to homes within a 50-mile radius of Oakland, a promotion that cost approximately $125,000. He also shelled out an additional $45,000 for newspaper advertisements and player-appearance promotions in the Oakland metropolitan area. Despite all these efforts, the A's never came close to their goal of selling 5,000 season tickets. In the end, barely 1,500 were sold for the 1968 season.

Finley, DiMaggio (in spite of his wishes), and several A's players canvassed the East Bay area during the winter of 1968 seeking support for the A's. The gregarious and optimistic Finley appeared before countless community groups promoting the A's and their chances for the 1968 baseball season. Charlie Finley was an imposing figure, more than six feet tall and solidly built, a far cry from his 96-pound tubercular self. As a public speaker, Finley could be very charming and charismatic. Ladies in particular were attracted to him. However, Finley's darker side always lurked just under the surface. As any moment, his temper could explode, and he would spew forth a mix of profanity, crassness, and sarcasm. No one ever really knew which Charlie Finley they were about to meet.

As the A's entered spring training, many baseball experts were again cautiously optimistic about the young team. Finley predicted the team could contend for a first division finish. "This is the first year I've really believed the team is capable of doing something," said Finley on a trip to spring training. "For the first time, I'm looking forward to opening day . . . If we move up three notches, I'll be very happy." Finley also finally cleared the air over who made the baseball decisions for the A's in a spring training interview. When asked who would be the club's general manager for the upcoming season, Finley replied, "You're looking at him. I think it's going to work out well this year, working with my manager, being that close with no one in between us."[8] After going through four general managers in Kansas City, Finley now publicly announced what everyone had known for seven years—he ran all aspects of the A's. Unfortunately, manager Bob Kennedy had no idea how "close" of a relationship he was going to have with the volatile Finley.

The A's got off to a good start in 1968, playing .500 ball for the first month and a half of the season. The talented new young players, including Reggie Jackson, Sal Bando, and Rick Monday, led their improved offense. Veteran shortstop Campy Campaneris, first bagger Danny Cater, and second baseman Dick Green anchored the infield. However, it was the A's pitching staff who bolstered their emergence as a competitive team in the American League. The A's young starting pitchers began to dominate at the major-league level. In their five-man rotation of Catfish Hunter, Jim Nash, Blue Moon Odom, Chuck Dobson, and Lew Krausse, no one was older than 25 years old. As a staff, they pitched effectively and deep into almost every game during the 1968 season. Hunter, Odom, Nash, and Dobson all threw more than 225 innings that season.

In fact, the 1968 major-league season is remembered as the year of the pitcher. Hitters could not buy hits or score runs, as they were hindered by more aggressive enforcement of a strike zone that had been expanded in 1963 to extend from the top of the shoulders to the knees. For the first time in decades, baseball had a 30-game winner in Detroit's Denny McLain. The American League had its all-time lowest collective batting average (.231) and lowest slugging average (.340) since the dead-ball year of 1915. The A's mirrored the trend.

On May 8, 1968, pitcher Catfish Hunter etched his name in baseball history by hurling the American League's first perfect game in 46 years. Hunter, utilizing masterful control, sat down 27 consecutive Twins on a cool night in Oakland before only 6,298 fans—similar attendance numbers became commonplace on cool, damp evenings in Oakland. The A's won the game 4–0, with Hunter striking out 11 Twins and requiring only 93 pitches. After the game, Hunter's teammates carried him off the field. His performance marked his emergence as the A's ace and his ascension toward becoming one of the game's most dominant hurlers.

Charlie Finley listened to the game late that evening from Chicago. His cousin Carl often fastened a radio to a phone with rubber bands so Finley could hear the radio broadcasts back home. When Hunter returned to the clubhouse after the game, Finley was on the phone from his Indiana home to give Hunter a $5,000 raise for his efforts.

As the season progressed, Finley's supposedly close working relationship with Bob Kennedy deteriorated. By early August, Finley stopped making his customary three or four daily phone calls to his manager. Everyone agreed this was very odd, and players and coaches began to speculate privately about how soon Kennedy would be fired. The A's were still playing .500 baseball, but falling further off the pace of the eventual American League champions, the Detroit Tigers. "I remember Bob Kennedy in 1968," said pitcher Chuck Dobson. "We were fifty-one and fifty-one. He came out, and he said, 'Can you believe we're fifty-one and fifty-one? Who would've thought that as the beginning of the season?' Well, we all looked at Kennedy . . . If he wouldn't go to sleep at nine P.M. at night on the bench, we'd be sixty and forty! He was not our best manager."[9]

The A's finished the season in sixth place with an 82–80 record, just a game out of the first division, but it was an amazing 20-win improvement over their 1967 record. Kennedy felt his young team and he himself, as manager, deserved accolades for the tremendous improvement. But it was clear that others saw things differently. A's beat reporter Ron Bergman recalled that Kennedy was "putting his stuff in a shoebox [after the A's finale, a 4–3 loss to the Twins], and he said he was going up to see Charlie [in the A's offices at the Coliseum]. And a coach says, 'Are you going up to pick up your pink slip?' So he [Kennedy] said, 'No way!' Because, actually, they would have been in the first division except for a bad call that was made in the last game of the season . . . Kennedy thought he'd done a good job. He had done a pretty good job! So he went up, and he got fired. We ran into him in the parking lot. He was getting in his car; he was just dazed. I mean, he couldn't believe it."[10]

Kennedy's firing took less than five minutes. Finley told the press that he had decided to fire Kennedy in early June because he did not agree with many of his on-field decisions, but he had allowed him to finish the season, hoping he would improve. Only an hour after firing Kennedy, Finley, through his publicist, announced the hiring of his former Kansas City manager Hank Bauer to manage the team next season.

Since leaving the A's, Bauer had developed a reputation on the winter banquet circuit by telling funny stories about his time with Finley. One of the most memorable anecdotes involved Finley admonishing Bauer for the condition of his uniform trousers. "One day, I got a call in the dugout. It was Charlie," Bauer would tell his listeners. "Mr. Bauer, I noticed that when you took the lineup card out to the umpire before the game, you had a grass stain on the seat of your pants," Finley had lectured Bauer. "I don't think it befits a big league manager to be seen with a grass stain on the seat of his uniform pants."

"Charlie, that ain't no grass stain," Bauer had replied in a serious tone. "That's mistletoe." Bauer had hung up the phone before a shuddering Finley could respond.[11]

Years later, Bauer, who after leaving the A's in 1962 guided the Baltimore Orioles to the 1966 world championship, remembered Finley calling him with an unexpected offer: "Charlie called me up. He says, 'Hey, buddy. How'd you like to manage Oakland?' I says, 'Charlie, you know I quit on you one time. What's the matter with you?' He says, 'Well, I need a manager out here.' And I said, 'Well, it's kind of funny what we're talking about.' And he gave me a salary, and I said, 'Well, not one year. I'll go for two.' Because I knew he was going to fire me again."[12] The following season, under Bauer, marked the A's ascension into playoff contenders.

While the A's ball club appeared to be knocking on the door of success in the 1968 season, from a business and attendance standpoint, the move to Oakland proved disappointing to Finley. In his haste to get out of Kansas City, Finley overestimated the Bay Area's ability to embrace two MLB teams, the Giants and A's, in the late 1960s and 1970s. The United States was experiencing severe economic difficulties during this period, and the Bay Area was not immune. San Francisco and Oakland, while tied together by the San Francisco Bay, were very different cities with very different inhabitants. Despite being later connected by the light-rail Bay Area Rapid Transit system, there was very little cross-city visiting in the 1970s. San Francisco residents viewed themselves as urban, educated, affluent sophisticates and turned their noses up at their cross-bay blue-collar, largely uneducated, working-class neighbors. Additionally, Oakland had a much more diverse population, with more African Americans, Asians, and Latinos than San Francisco. With its enormous docks, small factories, bars and taverns, and working-class mind-set, Oakland seemed primed for Major League Baseball. But it had only half the city population of San Francisco (365,000 versus 750,000), and in spite of more than 2 million people living in the East Bay region, the A's never drew a solid attendance. Many factors played a role: traffic, poor infrastructure, fan segmentation with Giants, a long traveling distance, poor promotion and marketing by Finley, and the cold, damp evening weather in the spring and summer.

The A's arrival in Oakland did not produce the level of fan interest or rivalry envisioned by Finley and the other American League owners. The A's drew only 837,466 fans in 1968, well short of Finley's public attendance goal of 1 million and only half of his private goal of 1.5 million. The next season, attendance dipped to 778,232, despite a better, more competitive team. Soon, Finley would again look toward other locations, disappointed by Oakland's weak support for his club.

The A's move to Oakland affected the cross-bay Giants as well. The Giants had averaged 1.5 million fans during the early and mid-1960s, but after the A's arrived in 1968, Giants attendance plunged to 837,220. By the mid-1970s, the Giants barely drew 500,000 per season. The A's drew more than a million fans only twice during the Finley years in Oakland, despite winning three world championships during the span. It would be nearly 20 years before either ball club had respectable annual attendance numbers. Finley's vision for baseball and the A's in the Bay Area was well ahead of his time. The 1969 edition of the A's emerged as one of the most talented young teams in the majors, finishing in second place in the newly formed Western Division of the American League. Rule changes that lowered the pitching mound and modified the strike zone, as well as the creation of four new major-league ball clubs—which had the effect of thinning the pitching talent—dramatically increased run production during the season. Baseball became more of an offensive game again. As MLB celebrated its centennial in 1969, Charlie Finley and his Oakland A's were poised to emerge as a new kind of team for Americans to embrace.

At the same time, Americans' perceptions of society were changing concerning race, sexuality, ethnicity, and social class. Divisions were apparent everywhere. The country had careened from one cataclysm to another in the late 1960s. Assassinations of key leaders in civil rights, such as Reverend Martin Luther King Jr., and of politicians, especially presidential candidate Robert Kennedy, shocked the country. Anti–Vietnam War demonstrations took place on campuses and cities throughout the country. Angry protesters rioted and started fires in Los Angeles, Detroit,

Washington, and other major cities in protest of the King assassination and the poor state of race relations in the country. Traditional perspectives were clearly changing, and A's owner Charlie Finley believed he could remake the A's and MLB into something attractive to those embracing new trends in society. He pushed for innovations that he believed would improve the game and make it accessible to a younger generation that was unhappy with the status quo. While Finley pushed orange baseballs, interleague play, and colorful uniforms, one of the most important changes to the A's was rising right under his nose: a young superstar outfielder named Reginald Martinez Jackson. Known to all as Reggie, he differed from many of Finley's past players by being outspoken, money-conscience, self-confident to an extreme, articulate, educated, media-savvy, and sometimes narcissistic, and by having athletic talent to burn. Jackson's on-field performance backed up all his swagger and style. After posting impressive rookie numbers in 1968 (.250, 29 HR, 74 RBI, even while striking out a staggering 171 times), Jackson emerged as bona fide superstar in 1969 as he chased MLB's storied single-season home run record.

Finley and Jackson had a love-hate relationship. They alternated between highly public arguments, in which they fired outrageous comments at each other through the media, and kiss-and-make-up sessions where they professed their profound affection for each other. The reporters knew that, together, Finley and Jackson had the star power, the outlandish personalities, the raw nerves, the love of the spotlight, and the quotable statements to make their work of reporting on the A's both easy and exciting. When Finley and Jackson locked horns, the public loved it, and reporters never had to work too hard to get the story. Both loved to talk, and the more they talked, the more they offered quotable quotes. It was a journalist's dream, and the owner and outfielder played it for all it was worth.

It's a good bet that even if Finley had known of the titanic and very public struggles he would have with his franchise player, he would still have taken Reggie Jackson in the 1966 amateur draft as the A's top pick and second overall. They played off each other like hypergolic fuels, igniting on contact; and like those fuels, when properly controlled, they accomplished seemingly magnificent results.

At first Finley thought he could control Jackson the way he had controlled everything in his life—through sheer force of will. However, Finley soon found that Jackson's will was every bit as strong. When Finley took Jackson to his farm in La Porte to soften him up—as he had done with many other players over the years—Jackson would have none of it. "I felt like I was in Oz," Jackson recalled. The famous Finley charm worked only a little, when he "put on his apron and cooked breakfast for us all on the back patio. Eggs, steak, bacon, ham, sausage, pork chops, and fresh cantaloupe a la mode. It was the first time in my life I had cantaloupe a la mode," Jackson said. "Charlie was in charge of everything, his family, the food, me, my dad, and everything else that was happening. Over breakfast, I said, 'Mr. Finley, if you give me the money you offered yesterday, plus two thousand dollars a semester for my college tuition, and a new Pontiac, I'll sign.'" Finley remained silent and then, at the end of the meal, in his usual big voice, said, "Well, there isn't any more to talk about. We do have a deal. Reggie, you're going to win me a World Series some day." Jackson signed; the deal was reportedly worth close to $95,000, including a new maroon Pontiac Catalina.[13]

At first Jackson seemed to perceive Finley as something of a father figure. In many ways, Jackson and Finley were quite similar in their personality. Both were strong-willed, opinionated, and driven to excel. Both loved the camera and were as much showmen as athlete or businessman. Yet both were enigmatic in their own way—difficult to understand and appreciate. A's pitcher Chuck Dobson roomed with Jackson on the road for three seasons early in their A's careers. Dobson said, "I roomed with him almost three years. Very talented. One thing I really respected about Reggie is that he knew who he was and what he was . . . and he didn't pretend to be a nice guy. He wasn't out to win nice-guy awards. In a lot of ways, he was just pretty arrogant and real self-confident. Knew who he was; knew what he wanted . . . He didn't care [what others thought of him]. He had a lot of anger and thought . . . 'Ah, screw you if you don't like what I'm saying.'"[14]

"I thought he was a real mystery," Dobson said. "But also, I want to say one thing about Reggie. If ESPN was alive and on the air . . . Reggie would've set all kinds of home-run records. When he knew the world was watching . . . he always hit home runs [when the A's played in the nationally televised Saturday] 'Games of the Week.' Yeah, put that red light on, and he turned on. He was great at that."[15]

Reggie Jackson emerged as the complete ballplayer in 1969. He was young, fast, and strong. He possessed a cannon of a throwing arm and explosive speed on the bases. However, the two things he did best in 1969 were crush home runs and talk to the national media. Jackson held out for two weeks in spring training while he bickered with Finley over his salary. He had made the major-league minimum of $10,000 in 1968 and wanted a raise to $25,000. Finley offered a raise to only $15,000. Both refused to budge. Finley told Jackson that he had paid him a large signing bonus and expected him to sign his offer. Eventually, after Jackson missed two weeks of spring training, they compromised at $20,000 for the 1969 season.

Jackson and the A's got off to a tremendous start in 1969. The ball exploded off Jackson's bat nearly every time he swung. He carried the A's on his broad shoulders, hitting homer after homer. As May turned to June, the A's were battling the Twins for first place, and Jackson's homers kept coming. The American public began to take notice of the young left-handed slugger. He hit two homers against the Senators in Washington as President Richard Nixon watched in the crowd. His second homer of the day won the game in the 13th inning. Nixon was so impressed with the young star that he penned him a note after the game. On July 1 (the A's 71st game of the season), Jackson's stats were astonishing, with 30 home runs, 62 runs batted in, a .287 batting average, and an amazing 1.145 on-base plus slugging percentage (OPS). On July 2, in Oakland, Jackson hit three more homers against Seattle. Finley followed his young star into the dressing room, embracing him and showering him with compliments. By this time, Jackson was a national media darling, appearing on the cover of *Sports Illustrated* in a beefcake picture in which, shirtless, he showed off his bulging biceps while holding a bat under one arm. Finley quickly tried to capitalize on his new young star by printing "Reggie Regiment" cards and distributing them to fans at games in hopes of forming a fan club for his slugger. In early July, Jackson was on pace to eclipse Roger Maris's single-season home-run record of 61. "Oh, Lordy, but life is lovely," Jackson told a sportswriter. "I just keep pickin' up them 'taters.'"[16] By the All-Star game in 1969, Jackson and the A's were on top of the baseball world, and owner Charlie Finley could taste the playoffs.

In mid-July, the media crush on the young slugger became frenzied. It is estimated that he gave more than 100 media interviews in the two weeks leading up to the All-Star game. The press hounded Jackson before and after every game, and he loved the attention and fame and the new pulpit the media provided. The press called him on the phone at all hours because he provided them with thoughtful, edgy quotes. In this regard, Jackson had no equal in baseball, but he was not emotionally prepared for the constant adulation. Finley resented it, in part because he had always been the most colorful of anyone with the team. He criticized Jackson for concentrating too much on being a celebrity rather than on playing baseball, and he ordered a halt to all interviews before A's games. Jackson did not agree with this decision and made that clear, but added that "he pays me every first and fifteenth, he can give orders."[17] But Jackson continued giving interviews.

The Twins swept three games against the A's in July as Jackson was outslugged by veteran power-hitter Harmon Killebrew. The A's fell from a first-place tie with the Twins in the AL Western Division and never challenged again that season. They went on to finish second in the AL West. Jackson hit his 40th homer at the end of July, but then his pace declined. He hit only five homers in August and only two in September after being hospitalized with a severe skin rash; some said the rash was brought on by the psychological pressure of the record chase.

As the team sank, Finley took his anger out on manager Hank Bauer. Pitcher Chuck Dobson said, "It was so obvious to us that Finley was not going to let Bauer manage. Finley was our manager. We'd have guys show up on the bench . . . Bauer would look around and say, 'Who are you? What are you doing?' And the guy would say he'd just been called up! Well, Finley called him up. Bauer had nothing to do with it . . . But underneath, we knew who controlled the shots . . . We had a meeting in Chicago one time, and we were playing terribly, and Finley came in . . . He was coming down on us about something. He turned to Hank, who was sitting there, and he says, 'Isn't that right, Mr. Manager?' And Hank said, 'Yeah, yeah, that's right. . . .' He says, 'A little louder, Mr. Manager! They didn't hear you!' Just buried him in front of us. It was terrible."[18]

Finley wanted to make a managerial change, as he had so many times before. Players were beginning to rumble about Bauer's Marine Corps–type managerial style. Once, a hot humid evening in Washington, coach John

McNamara asked Bauer to give an obviously worn-out Sal Bando the night off. Bauer responded, "Fuck him!" and Bando played. With his team running on empty, Finley finally dumped Bauer as the team prepared for a night game in California. Finley, Bauer recalled, "got me on the phone, and he says, 'I want to talk you.' So I stayed in my room, knock on the door, and 'Charlie, how are you?' And he came in, and he sat down; he didn't say nothing. Eventually, I said, 'Haven't you got guts enough to tell me I'm fired?' He said, 'How'd you know?' I said, 'Well, you know your pet peeve is don't lose communications, and you haven't talked to me for thirty days.' "[19]

Finley and Bauer headed to the ballpark to announce the decision before a game with the Angels. Finley told Bauer he was going to appoint coach John McNamara as manager for the balance of the 1969 season. *Oakland Tribune* beat reporter Ron Bergman recalled the two "stumbling" into the stadium. "Finley and Bauer had sat in a hotel room at the Grand Hotel in Anaheim all day talking about the decision to fire Bauer. They'd had a fifth of whiskey. They drank a bottle of it. Then they showed up in the press box in Anaheim and announced it together, and both of them were just plastered out of their minds."[20] Bauer became the first Finley manager to be officially fired for a second time.

The A's rallied behind new manager John McNamara, going 8–5 to end the season but never threatening the Twins for the division lead. Even so, their 88–74 record in 1969 represented a 26-win improvement over their abysmal last-place finish in 1967. Several young players blossomed into stars in 1969; the future looked bright. The 23-year-old Jackson was clearly the standout, finishing with 47 home runs and 118 RBI, batting .275, and leading the league with 123 runs scored. "Although I tailed off, I still had a hell of a year," Jackson remarked after the season.[21] Had the team's pitching improved on par with the club's hitting, the A's might have won the division. But injuries and inconsistency hampered the A's starting rotation. Blue Moon Odom nursed a sore elbow on his way to 15 wins. Chuck Dobson pitched his heart out in 1969, delivering his best season with 15 wins and 11 complete games. Catfish Hunter threw the ball well (with a 3.35 ERA) but served up too many gopher balls and won only 12 games. Jim Nash injured his shoulder, and Lew Krausse performed erratically, moving back and forth from the bullpen to the rotation.

Finley realized his young team was on the brink of playoff contention. Plenty of talent also waited in the minors and on his bench to supplement his improving team, including players that soon would be household names: Rudi, Tenace, Blue, and Fingers. Most important, Finley's A's now possessed a true superstar in Reggie Jackson, whom, along with pitcher Catfish Hunter, Finley viewed as the cornerstone of his push for a championship. Unfortunately for Finley, Jackson's breakout season further inflated the young outfielder's self-confidence and led him to question authority, the status quo, and ultimately his owner's right to dictate a contract offer for the following season. The paternal Finley never expected the rebellion his young superstar demonstrated in the spring of 1970.

Though Finley believed his team was on the cusp of a pennant, the A's were not drawing as many fans as he expected. Attendance for the year had actually declined—a trend Finley found deeply troubling. He decided to tighten belts among the A's. He also chided Oakland's business community for not supporting the team, urging the city's successful businessmen, salesmen, stockbrokers, and store owners to go forth and sell the A's for the overall good of the Oakland economy. The local chamber of commerce agreed to split 100 businessmen into five groups to canvass season-ticket sales from the community. Finley promised a free season ticket for every 75 sold by each group. While sales did increase modestly, the A's fell considerably short of their goal of selling 3,000 season tickets.

In an effort to reach younger baseball fans, Finley sent out a special Valentine's Day greeting to 300,000 teenagers in the East Bay area. Each Valentine contained a pass for one of nine home games in April, May, or June. Finley promised to hire rock bands for those dates as a further incentive to the young fans, who seemed to be turning to faster-paced sports like basketball and football. Indeed, Finley correctly understood that the future success of the A's and Major League Baseball rested with younger fans, whom they needed to bring back into the fold. But Finley's Valentine efforts did not result in a dramatic increase in attendance for the A's. Several players actually yearned for the days in Kansas City. Sal Bando recalled, "We didn't have the support either from the media or from the fans that the Raiders did, and of course the Raiders had been winning. We didn't draw that well. I gave the Coliseum the nickname the 'Mausoleum' . . . the Oakland Mausoleum . . . It was gray. It was big. No fans. It was cold."[22]

Meanwhile, Finley continued to manage every aspect of the A's organization from his Chicago office. He ran a lean organization with less than a third the front office staff of other MLB teams. He approved every expenditure, every promotion, every minute office purchase; he even controlled the complete layout of the A's annual team yearbook. His cousin Carl oversaw the day-to-day operations in Oakland, since Finley visited the A's office only a few times during the off-season.

And, of course, Finley kept on wheeling and dealing as the general manager. Between the 1969 and 1970 seasons, Finley picked up veteran relief pitcher Jim "Mudcat" Grant from the Cardinals to help bolster the A's weak bullpen. He reacquired starter/reliever Diego Segui from the Brewers in December 1969 to shore up the rotation and pen during the MLB winter meeting. Next he traded his starting first baseman from 1969, Danny Cater, to the Yankees for journeyman lefty starter Al Downing. Finley lost confidence in two of his young, hard-throwing starting pitchers, Jim Nash and Lew Krausse, who never quite seemed to live up to their potential because of injuries and inexperience. Finley sent Nash packing to Atlanta for veteran outfielder Felipe Alou, the first of three Alou brothers who would eventually play for Finley and the A's in the 1970s. Later, Finley sent Krausse, outfielder Mike Hershberger, and catcher Phil Roof to the Brewers for slugging first baseman Don Mincher. Finley believed his revamping of the A's, along with the addition of new manager John McNamara, would lead to a pennant in 1970.

Reggie Jackson again became the wild card in Finley's plans for the A's 1970 season. The young superstar believed he deserved a substantial raise above his $20,000 salary and demanded $60,000 for the 1970 season. Finley, facing low attendance figures and seeing his young star's struggles in the second half of the 1969 season, offered only $40,000. Once more, both sides refused to bend. Jackson held out as spring training began and became more and more bitter toward the media's coverage during his holdout, as comments supposedly made in private began appearing in print. "It has been an educational experience," remarked Jackson. "You learn not to trust anyone."[23] Pressure mounted on Jackson as Finley played hardball in the negotiations. Jackson then lowered his asking price to $47,000 in the belief that Finley would meet him somewhere in the middle. But Finley never budged. "Catfish and Reggie are my two most important guys. I've got to keep them at the same level. And Catfish is making $40,000," Finley told the press.[24] With opening day only two weeks away, Finley finally blinked, offering to pay Jackson $45,000 and to make up the difference by paying the rent on an Oakland apartment for Jackson during the season. With only 10 days left in spring training, Jackson signed. However, he remained resentful over the contract negotiations. During his holdout, Jackson often had read Finley's snide comments in the press, and he felt betrayed.

"I was only twenty-three years old then, and I was intimidated by him. But I don't think I made any mistakes in those negotiations ... If I were treated fairly, everything would have worked out fine," Jackson later said.[25]

When the team returned to Oakland to start the season, Jackson infuriated Finley by renting an expensive apartment in the same Lake Merritt development where Finley also had a penthouse. Instead of costing Finley $2,000 for the season, the luxury apartment cost him more than $3,000. At first, Finley refused to pay for the apartment, but after an argument on the phone with Jackson, who threatened to sit out the team's opener, he paid the first two months' rent. Jackson believed he had outnegotiated the master (Finley) by renting the luxury apartment but was warned by teammates that Finley did not take kindly to being shown up by a player. Jackson, whose animosity toward Finley had grown immeasurably, ignored the advice.

The 1970 season began with the A's superstar out of shape and unfocused on baseball. As a result, he started the season very slowly. By late May, the A's were struggling, with their brooding star hitting only .200 with fewer than 10 home runs. Jackson, whose clutch hits led the team in 1969, could not deliver the big hit and continuously left runners on base. Soon, Finley and McNamara began to grouse about Jackson's performance on the field, which was affecting the team as a whole. By the end of May, the A's were in third place in the AL West with a 25–23 record and were already eight games behind the first-place Twins. McNamara, at Finley's urging, began benching Jackson against left-handed pitchers.

Jackson furthered enraged Finley by skipping his owner's annual team picnic at the Finley farm during the team's late-May visit to Chicago. The next day, during the A's game, Finley told reporters, "We've decided not to use Jackson against left-handed pitchers, and if he doesn't start hitting right-handers, there's only one thing left: He might have to be sent to our Des Moines farm team."[26]

Upon hearing the news after the game in the clubhouse, Reggie exploded. "Don't be telling me that, going to the minors," he said. "I'll tell you one thing: I won't go . . . If he would've signed me, I would've been ready. If he'd been fair, paid me the money, if he would've cared about this club, he could've had me in on time."[27] Soon, at Finley's insistence, McNamara benched Jackson against not only lefty pitchers but righties as well. Players began losing respect for McNamara, who chose not to fight his fickle owner, and the Jackson-Finley feud became a major distraction to the team. As McNamara struggled to hold the team together, Finley applied more pressure on Jackson. One late-night phone call between the two lasted nearly four hours, with Finley urging Jackson to accept a demotion to the minors and Jackson demanding a trade. But both parties held their ground, and Jackson's status remained in limbo.

During the month of June, Jackson rode the bench, and the A's floundered. Jackson played sparingly, appearing mostly as a pinch hitter or runner. "I go to the park every day," Jackson said. "The players kid me about being a $50,000 pinch runner. I work hard. I do whatever I can to help out. I wait. Nothing happens. I root for the team. I root for my replacement, Joe Rudi. A great guy . . . But there is no way he should be playing and I should be sitting. He knows it and I know it and everyone knows it, except, apparently, my boss.

"I'm angry, but I have to hold my temper. I can't pop off. Mr. Finley's my boss. He's been very good to me in many ways . . . I can't make him trade me . . . He does what he wants. He owns me. I'm a prisoner. All the players are owned by the owners . . . They're slaves to the system . . . I have no clout. He has the big stick," Jackson lamented. "No matter what, I hustle. I make mistakes, but I'm young. Aren't I supposed to make mistakes? I'm 24 years old. I'm just learning. Do they think I should be Henry Aaron?"[28]

Hearing the rumblings of the Finley-Jackson controversy in New York, MLB commissioner Bowie Kuhn was not amused. The blue-blooded, stoic Kuhn and the self-made, bombastic, and crass Finley grew to hate each other over the years, as their confrontations steadily increased. Kuhn felt that Finley acted more out of anger over Jackson's refusal to attend Finley's farm picnic than out of concern for the team's or Jackson's best interest. Kuhn said, "Most club decisions to farm players were made for good and sensible reasons, mutually benefitting both the club and player. This was not such a decision."[29] He forbade Finley from demoting Jackson to the minors and said Finley's actions were "a clear abuse of our system . . . The action was unfair because it was motivated by personal reasons unrelated to Jackson's ability."[30] His ruling carried the day. While Kuhn could not force the A's to play Jackson, his decision clearly provided a morale boost for the struggling A's star.

In response, a flabbergasted Finley demanded a hearing before the commissioner. He argued, along with attorney Bill Myers, that Kuhn "had no right to meddle in individual club-player relationships, that there were subtleties there beyond [his] fathoming, that there was no precedent for [his] action." Kuhn took the Finley appeal under advisement, but he did not reverse his decision.[31]

Interestingly, Kuhn's reaction reflected a capriciously negative and boorish attitude toward Finley that amounted to more than just a professional disagreement. In his autobiography, he described Finley: "[His] eyes were dark, riveting, cold. They fastened on what they saw like talons. Had mirth or kindness ever danced there? I think not. The voice had a rasping, low, nervous quality and was punctuated by little coughs and hesitations."[32] And their feud had only just begun.

As June turned to July, the A's struggles continued. With Jackson riding the bench and the players not hitting, the A's pitching corps kept the team in the race. The A's record stood at 43–33 on July 1. Finally, Jackson called Finley to end their feud and tell him he intended to focus on improving his play. Jackson also promised to stop mouthing off to the press. Finley felt vindicated and ordered McNamara to put Jackson back in the lineup. However, Jackson could not get on track at the plate. His power numbers improved, as he hit five homers in the month of July, but his batting average remained low, hovering around .230. At the 1970 All-Star break, Jackson was hitting a paltry .228 with only 12 home runs and 35 RBI—a year earlier he had a .282 batting average, 35 home runs and 72 RBI. Predictably, Jackson was relegated to platooning again, as the A's remained behind the division-leading Twins.

Meanwhile, problems were beginning between Finley and another of his emerging stars, Catfish Hunter. Hunter had approached Finley during his contract negotiations in the winter of 1970 about purchasing a 485-acre farm near his hometown in North Carolina. He wanted to plant crops, raise cattle, and hunt on the property as he looked toward a time when he could no longer play baseball. Finley agreed to give Hunter a loan for the property, though it wasn't clear when Hunter would be able to pay it back.

"Don't worry about it. It's no problem," Finley told him.[33] Finley wrote Hunter a check for $150,000. "When he first lent me the money," recalled Catfish, "we had a verbal agreement, never anything written down. He sent me the money straight into my bank under my name. He didn't have any attachments to it. But it was understood it was a loan. We worked out an agreement that I was to pay him back at least twenty thousand dollars a year at the end of every baseball season with six percent interest until it was paid off."[34]

Hunter and his young family appreciated the loan, and all was fine until Finley purchased professional hockey and basketball teams during the summer of 1970. "But then, three or four months into the season, Finley started asking me to pay the money back. He'd say, 'Jim, you owe me $150,000 and I've got to have it. I need it because I'm buying basketball and hockey teams.' And I'd say, 'But, Mr. Finley, you said I could pay it off $20,000 a year.' And he'd just say, 'Well, I'm sorry, but I need it.' He'd call me in the clubhouse. He'd call me off the field. He called me at the hotels on the road. He called me at home. He called my father, who was furious."[35]

Hunter tried to arrange a loan in Oakland to pay off Finley, but to no avail. Then he asked Finley to leave the team to return to North Carolina to arrange a loan there, but Finley refused to allow him to leave, even as he continuing to hound him for the money. One explanation for this repayment pressure may be that the wealthy Finley had cash-flow problems, had financial losses in his insurance business, and had made bad investments with personal wealth. In April 1970, Finley filed a $2.5 million lawsuit charging securities fraud against Parvin-Dohrmann Corporation and a few of its directors. Finley charged in the suit that he bought more than 12,000 shares in the company on assurances that the company was "very successful." A short time after his purchase, the American Stock Exchange halted trading of the company's stock, alleging price rigging. Finley never recovered all of his investment. Also, Finley's insurance brokerage company began to lose several important clients in the late 1960s and early 1970s, as medical associations found new brokers for their membership's disability insurance programs.

The insurance industry began to change, which Charlie Finley had not anticipated. In 1969 his insurance brokerage lost one of its largest disability accounts, the Southern Medical Association. Finley lost several million dollars in commissions and management fees with the change. He struggled to hold on to his largest client, the American Medical Association (AMA), throughout the early 1970s. The AMA, whose 40,000 doctors accounted for nearly 20 percent of Charles O. Finley and Company's gross revenues, eventually left the Finley disability insurance nest in 1974.

All of it led to more hounding of Hunter. "In August, when it was the worst he called me every day I was due to pitch. He didn't call me on the other days, just the days I was due to pitch," Hunter said. "I tried not to think the worst of him, but it was impossible. I was having my best year, but he hurt it badly. His calls upset me so much I didn't win a single one of my seven starts in August."[36]

Hunter even offered to turn the loan into a tax-free gift and sign a multiyear baseball contract with Finley at no additional cost to the owner. In essence, Finley could turn the loan into an upfront salary payout for three years. Finley refused, saying such an arrangement would not be fair to Hunter. In hindsight, Finley missed an opportunity, as he would have been getting Hunter at a bargain salary. Eventually, Catfish sold nearly 80 percent of the farm property to pay his debt. "I paid him that damn loan six months after I got it and had to pay $6,000 in interest to boot, but later he did refund the interest," Hunter said. He did walk away from the messy deal with 100 acres, but also with very bitter feelings toward Finley. "That's when I made up my mind that I couldn't trust him. From then on I made sure I got everything he said down on paper," Hunter said.[37]

As Finley was driving Hunter crazy, Reggie Jackson caught fire at the plate. Despite the distractions, again most caused by Finley himself, the A's closed the gap on the Twins and moved into second place. On September 5, Jackson pinch-hit in the eighth inning against the Royals in Oakland. He crushed the pitch for his first career grand slam over the center-field fence. The crowd cheered for the struggling young star. As Jackson slowly circled the bases, the months of frustration, pressure, and anger came bursting to the surface. When he reached home plate, Jackson stopped, glared at Finley in his private box, held his fist up high, and flipped the owner the bird, shouting, "Fuck you!" at a startled Finley, who raised his arms like a boxer cheering for his team and playing to the crowd of 10,000 fans. After the game, Jackson told the press, "You can't print what I said."[38] Finley seemed publicly unfazed. "It inflated my ego," a smiling Finley said. "He could've been saying a number of things. He could've been saying, 'There, I showed you I still can do it.' "[39] Finley did not take any immediate action concerning Jackson's act of defiance, instead he waited for the A's to arrive in Chicago for a Labor Day doubleheader versus the White Sox. Meanwhile, Jackson caught fire at the plate, hitting a homer the following night versus the Royals and clubbing two more homers in the doubleheader in Chicago.

Following the Chicago game, Finley asked Jackson, team captain Sal Bando, and selected others to a meeting in A's manager McNamara's suite at the Ambassador West Hotel. Jackson thought it was going to be a reconciliation meeting, something for which Finley was famous, and to strategize on the upcoming series with the division-leading Twins. Unfortunately, Charlie Finley had other ideas. Finley quickly pulled out a series of newspapers about Jackson's obscene act in Oakland and asked him what he thought about it. Jackson responded, "I'm proud of it."

"It's a disgrace to baseball. Why did you do it?" Finley asked.

"Because I hate the way you treat me, the way you treat people," Reggie shot back.[40]

They continued to go back and forth. Jackson appeared to be losing his composure. Finally, Finley presented Jackson with a statement to sign. It read, "Last Saturday, I made gestures and comments I wish I had never made. I would like to apologize to the fans, my teammates, John McNamara, and Mr. Finley."[41] Finley insisted Jackson sign it. At first, Jackson steadfastly refused. Finley became visibly agitated and red-faced. Then, Jackson looked around the room for support, but found only silent stares from Bando and McNamara. Finley pushed Jackson again to sign. He told him that if he did not sign it, American League president Joe Cronin was prepared to suspend him.

For Jackson's part, the incident at the game was totally spontaneous. "What I did after the grand slam homer just came to me. You can't plan something like that. The gesture I made was not meant to harm. It was only, 'Look, See what I can do!' Charlie wanted me to sign a statement of apology at that meeting. I never felt so alone and helpless in my life in that hotel room," Jackson recalled. "It was just like going to a police station and being put under a lamp and being whipped. He [Finley] said I owed all [his teammates, manager, and fans] a public apology. I didn't owe 'em shit. Because what I did he deserved. I was getting fucked . . . I finally signed because everyone in the room was against me. Everybody."[42]

From Chicago, the surging second-place A's headed for a critical three-game series with the Twins, but the fallout from the Jackson confrontation distracted the players, especially their dejected and angry young slugger. Reggie played a terrible series (0–9 with five strikeouts), as did the whole team. The Twins swept the A's, who fell nine games out of first place. They never threatened the Twins again in 1970.

Overall, the A's finished 1970 with 89 wins, ending up in second place, nine games out of first. Hunter paced the pitchers with 18 wins—Finley's hounding costing him a 20-win season. Starting pitchers Chuck Dobson and Blue Moon Odom, both hampered by sore arms, won 16 and 9 games, respectively. Neither pitched effectively down the stretch. Both Mudcat Grant and Diego Segui, Finley's off-season pickups, pitched well. Grant saved 24 games for the A's before Finley sent him to the Pirates in a late-season trade. Segui split time between the bullpen and rotation, but won 10 games and led the American League with a 2.56 ERA. The final high-light came on September 21, when the 20-year-old flame-throwing lefty named Vida Blue threw a no-hitter victory against the Twins. Blue provided a glimpse of things to come next season.

On the offensive side, most of the A's struggled along with their young superstar outfielder. Jackson finished the year with a mere 23 homers and 68 RBI and a lowly .237 batting average. He also struck out 135 times in only 426 official at-bats. Others fared only slightly better. Sal Bando (20 HR, 75 RBI, .263 BA), Rick Monday (10 HR, 37 RBI, .290 BA), and Felipe Alou (8 HR, 55 RBI, .271 BA) had mediocre seasons at best. Second baseman Dick Green endured a horrendous year at the plate, hitting only .190. However, there were a few bright spots. Campy Campaneris again led the league in stolen bases (42) and hit a career-high 22 home runs while batting .279. Young outfielder Joe Rudi also impressed with stellar glove play in the outfield while hitting .309 and slugging at a .480 clip to lead the team in both categories.

Despite being a part of an exciting playoff race for the second year in a row, only 778,355 fans paid to see the A's. Finley tried his usual array of promotional days and stunts, but most seats remained empty in the "Mausoleum." He even commissioned a folksy team song titled "Charlie O. the Mule" and had it played repeatedly at home games. He hired legendary Cardinals radio broadcaster Harry Caray to do the play-by-play for the 1970 season in hopes of improving the A's following. Caray resisted Finley's constant "suggestions" of ways to improve his broadcasts, the most egregious of which involved trying to convince Caray to change his famous "Holy cow" expression to "Holy mule." Needless to say, Caray refused and departed the A's after the season.

Finley could have blamed many people—Reggie Jackson, Blue Moon Odom, Dick Green, or himself—for the team's subpar performance that year. But, as always, he focused in on his manager. In the closing days of the season, Finley contrived a mini-controversy involving his catcher, Dave Duncan, who shared an apartment with hitting coach Charlie Lau in Oakland. Both had recently separated from their wives. "One day I found out that Duncan was sleeping with coach Charlie Lau," Finley told reporters. "By that I mean they were rooming together, sharing expenses. When I found out about this, I called it to their attention, asked them to break it up immediately, because as we all know, in the Army, troops don't fraternize with officers." Finley ordered the arrangement to end, but neither Duncan nor Lau moved out of the apartment. Both publicly rebuffed Finley by stating there was nothing wrong with their living arrangement. Duncan took several public shots at Finley, telling reporters, "There's only one man who manages this club, Charlie Finley, and we'll never win so long as he manages." Finley's scapegoat manager, John McNamara, remained silent on the matter.

A few days later Finley announced the firing of McNamara, connecting the action in part to McNamara's inability to control the A's players' press remarks and actions. "McNamara didn't lose his job, his players took it away from him," Finley told reporters. "McNamara would still be with us [if he'd made] statements to the press that there isn't any front office interference and how we've been helpful." However, McNamara's silence on the interference issue spoke volumes. He later said, "I've been fired since last May when the club started out under .500. I don't think it's right to blame the players for what they said in the last two weeks of the season." John McNamara became the 10th manager fired by Charlie Finley. Despite Finley's public musings, McNamara remained, up to his firing, one of the owners most loyal managers and seemed to take the continuous meddling in stride.[43]

While Finley searched for others to blame for his team's failings in 1970, such as Reggie Jackson, Dave Duncan, and John McNamara, the buck rested with the owner himself. Finley's need to control every aspect of his ball club, his inability to check his huge ego for the greater good of the team, and his tendency to bully others spoiled the A's considerable chances in 1970. Finley's bizarre hounding of Catfish Hunter for repayment of his loan mere months after the agreement forever changed the future star pitcher's view of the eccentric A's owner. The harassment negatively affected Hunter's performance during a crucial stretch of the season, and might have cost Hunter and the A's five or six additional victories.

As far as the Jackson-Finley controversies went, the acrimony clearly affected their relationship for years to come. Jackson became understandably cynical and jaded in his relationship with Finley. Finley, who believed he won the battles with Jackson in the 1970 season, tried to rebuild his relationship with his player, but only partially succeeded. Jackson and Finley—both smart, arrogant, somewhat narcissistic, and craving media attention—each wanted to have the last word. Finley should have shown more maturity and business savvy in his dealings with his young superstar, but Charlie Finley did not want to lose control over anything in his life. His inability to let the other guy (in this case Jackson) win doomed his own team's chances to win in 1970. In short, Finley's ego beat Finley's team. And the A's were bridesmaids again.

Chapter Six

On Top of the World

The championship years between 1971 and 1975 were magical for Charles O. Finley. Yes, the Oakland A's fought incessantly with one another and their owner over everything imaginable. But they had personality and character and a strange attraction that commanded everyone's attention. Even casual baseball fans knew names like Catfish Hunter, Vida Blue, Reggie Jackson, Joe Rudi, Bert Campaneris, Sal Bando, and Gene Tenace. And many, if not all, of these players still resonate today, their faces and exploits indelibly etched in our memories. Whether loved or hated, Finley and the A's got people's attention. Melvin Durslag wrote in 1971 that everyone was excited about prospects for that year's A's but "winning a pennant at Oakland couldn't start to compensate Charlie for all the trials he has endured since coming into baseball 10 years ago"; finally he would receive a measure of respect from fellow owners "who never have forgiven themselves for admitting him to their brotherhood."[1]

Finley built a baseball dynasty in California during the late 1960s, and it emerged triumphant in 1971 by winning the American League's Western Division title. Young, homegrown talent was amassed through years of excellent picks in the amateur draft, and patient player development was finally paying off. After finishing in second place in the American League

West in 1969 and 1970, the A's made the playoffs for the first time since 1931, when the Philadelphia A's lost the World Series to the St. Louis Cardinals. They finished the 1971 season with a stunning 101–60 record, 16 games over the second-place Kansas City Royals, and demonstrated a domination not often seen in regular-season play at any time. In the words of A's manager Dick Williams that February, "I don't see anyone running away from the rest of the division, unless it's us."[2]

Charlie Finley made a critical decision in hiring Williams. It, along with outstanding player development, might have been the final piece of the championship puzzle being assembled in Oakland, as Williams proved uniquely capable of channeling the talent, egos, and passions of his talented young players. He recalled that he was so successful with the A's because they were "25 guys who didn't give shit about anything but winning." Williams had been a journeyman player for several teams—including the Kansas City Athletics between 1958 and 1960—during a 13-year career. But as an on-field manager he realized his true potential, bringing the Boston Red Sox the American League pennant in 1967 before losing a dramatic seven-game World Series to the St. Louis Cardinals. Known as a strict disciplinarian, he became famous for his hard-driving, sharp-tongued managerial approach. Reflecting on his career in Oakland, Williams commented that the period from 1971 to 1973 represented "three insane, strange, sometimes incoherent years, which also happened to be the best three years of my life."[3]

Finley was his normal meddlesome self and drove Williams insane with constant phone calls and suggestions, which everyone knew were not really suggestions. Williams said that Finley was seldom in Oakland but was constantly calling there. "Charlie called me every day," Williams said. "If we won a ball game at Oakland, we had to walk all the way up the runway, quite a few stairs, to our clubhouse. And my phone would be ringing when I got in my office, and it would be Charlie. If we won, say, four to two, he would've said, 'Well, if you did this or that, you would have won six to two.'" As often as not, Williams said, when he got home after the game, Finley would call again.[4] Darold Knowles said Williams got so fed up with all of Finley's calls that during one game the phone rang in the dugout "and our trainer picked it up and answered it and said, 'It's Mr. Finley, Dick. He wants to talk to you.' And I remember Dick saying, 'Tell him I'm not here.'"[5]

As Williams prepared the A's to take the field in the spring of 1971, Finley stumped among the fellow owners for approval to try a three-ball-walk rule, which he believed would inject more offense and excitement into the game. During the latter 1960s, Major League Baseball saw a large reduction in batting averages and runs scored because of the dominance of the pitching, top to bottom, in the two leagues. There was a strong belief that this depressed fan interest and gate revenues. "While football, hockey and other sports are continuously making changes in their game regarding the rules and regulations to maintain the interest of the fans," Finley delighted in telling the media, "baseball is hibernating." Failure to deal with perceived problems by the conservative "lords of baseball," Finley added, "frustrates the hell out of me."[6]

Finley persuaded American League president Joe Cronin to allow the rule to apply in an A's preseason game with the Milwaukee Brewers on March 6, 1971. It may have enhanced the offense, but everyone thought it tedious. There were 19 walks and six home runs in the game; the A's defeated the Brewers 13–9. Naturally, the pitchers on both teams hated the change.[7] Keeper of the baseball status quo Wells Twombly wrote a scathing report of the experiment in the *Sporting News*. He called Finley a "noted revisionist" who never met a change he didn't like. "This is the same wonderful person who gave the nation lollipop-colored uniforms and pastel bases and outfielders that glow in the dark," he added. "Hardly a spring passes without good old Charlie popping up out of the turf with cunning new ideas to save baseball from itself."[8] As Ben Hochman reported, "although the idea sounded crazy and anti-establishment, Finley did attack two of baseball's biggest problems at the time—lack of offense and length of games."[9] In reality, Finley's method for increasing offense, and therefore fan interest in MLB, was probably a better answer than the decision made by owners in the 1990s to turn a blind eye to the players' bulking up through steroid use to generate much larger home-run totals.

The Athletics opened the 1971 season on April 5 in Washington, DC, against the Senators. Williams's starting nine—Felipe Alou, Sal Bando, Bert Campaneris, Dave Duncan, Dick Green, Vida Blue, Reggie Jackson, Rick Monday, and Don Mincher—were hammered 8–0. They then dropped two more games against the Chicago White Sox, and looked like a bunch of bush leaguers doing it. The struggling A's continued their home stand against the Kansas City Royals on April 9 and finally won a game. In the first six games the pitching staff gave up 40 runs. By the time the A's arrived in Milwaukee on April 12, they were playing uninspired ball and stood at a lackluster 2–4—not the performance expected of the anointed heirs to the AL West crown. Williams knew full well that he had Finley breathing down his neck.

The turning point in the A's season may have been attributable to an incident at the Chicago airport as the team boarded a bus for their hotel. Before the bus departed, flight attendants told Williams that someone had taken a megaphone used for emergency purposes, and they demanded its return. "We're on the bus, and it was a little chilly, and I said, 'Well, the bus isn't leaving till the megaphone is returned,' " Williams recalled. He heard it drop out a window in the back of the bus and then went on to scold the team, telling them that they were not playing to their potential and that they needed to get serious about their craft. Williams later learned that "it was the Cat"—Catfish Hunter, always a practical joker—who had stolen the megaphone, presumably to use later in the hotel.[10]

While it may seem a trivial incident in retrospect, Williams credited it, and his calling the team out, as the confrontation that "got us started." "They came in, and they started playing great ball, and by the end of that road trip we were in first place," he said.[11] Williams let everyone know who was boss and challenged the team of young and emerging superstars to re-focus on baseball; if they disagreed, he could get them a ticket out of Oakland. Reflecting on this incident, Williams wrote in 1990 that "as it turned out, I should have given him [Hunter] a bonus for feeding me the slow curve that enabled this team to see and feel my swing."[12]

From that point on, the A's started to play well, putting together winning streaks of five and then another seven games. By the end of April they were 17–8 and in the lead in the AL West. They never looked back. Finley remained meddlesome, but winning kept him off the team's back—for the most part. During a trip to play the Anaheim Angels, Williams recalled walking into the hotel and having the receptionist hand him a sheaf of messages from Finley. He had been calling the hotel every few minutes beginning at 3 P.M., with the last message, timed at 12:30 A.M., saying, "I will call tomorrow at 6:30 A.M." As Williams put it, "aside from such things as Charlie's phone calls, Charlie's stadium, Charlie's advice, Charlie's treatment of fans and players, Charlie's style, Charlie's lack of style—aside from all this, playing with the A's was easy."[13]

One highlight of the 1971 season was rookie phenom Vida Blue. It was obvious after he pitched a no-hitter in late 1970 that Blue would excite everyone with his fireballing. By June 1971, with the A's rolling, Blue had captured the public eye. That spring he appeared on the cover of *Sport* and *Sports Illustrated* and even *Time* magazine. Not bad for a 21-year-old pitcher who had not yet won 10 games. He was a celebrity and enjoying its perks. Finley publicly gushed about the young left-hander: "Blue is beautiful. He is what baseball needs. I am going to promote him. He is going to get more than money. He is going to get great things from this game. I am going to protect him. I will treat him as if he is a son of mine."[14]

As Blue pitched around the country, attendance soared and his wins kept piling up. By mid-June he had already won 13 games. Overjoyed with his new ace, Finley, ever the promoter, held Vida Blue Day at the Oakland Coliseum. More than 40,000 fans turned out, and Finley presented Blue with a baby blue Cadillac El Dorado with a license plate that read V. BLUE.

But pressure, along with Finley's relentless hype and lack of reflectiveness, took its toll on Blue. He did not appreciate Finley's making a big production of giving him a car during the season, effectively slighting his teammates. And the choice of a Cadillac El Dorado, in Blue's opinion, was racist. He commented under his breath, "You should have filled the trunk up with watermelons since you gave me that fuckin' Cadillac." Blue suspected Finley of relying on the stereotypes of films like *Super Fly* and *Shaft*, in which the protagonists drove Cadillacs. Finley also gave him a gas card, so every time he filled up he was reminded that "it's on Uncle Charlie."[15]

Though his motives may have been dubious, Finley treated his players uniformly regardless of race. He could be generous and paternalistic or domineering and malevolent as suited his mercurial personality. It had nothing to do with race. Later in the year, Finley was going to give Catfish Hunter a Cadillac too, as a reward for winning his 20th game, the first time he had reached that particular milestone. Hunter would go on to win 20 games each year through 1975, a total of five consecutive seasons. Hunter asked Finley to take the money he would spend on the Cadillac and instead invest it in the stock market on his behalf. Since Finley had already invested part of Hunter's salary for him, he did not consider the request anything out of the ordinary and did as asked.[16]

Finley realized that he had a gold mine in Vida Blue. Since the Vietnam conflict was under way, Finley took action to keep him out of the army and got Blue enlisted in the Army Reserves. Blue recalled, "Yeah, he gets a stroke on that one, a check mark ... I went to boot camp that winter, and I went to Fort Bragg. I did all of my training, all of my stuff, in winter. [It] pulled me for about a weekend a month for about a year, and I was in the best shape in my life, let me tell you that. And I was only twenty and turning twenty-one that July."[17]

Finley, ever the marketeer, came up with a couple of dumb ideas that affected Vida Blue. First, enamored of nicknames, he tried to get Vida Blue to change his given name to "True." Dick Green said, "Finley gave everybody names, you know. He gave Catfish his name and gave Blue Moon Odom his name and wanted to give Vida Blue another name."[18] Blue's response was a bit more abrupt: "If he thinks it's such a great name, why doesn't he call himself True O. Finley?"[19]

Finley also sought to ensure that Blue pitched during home games on Monday nights, Finley's proclaimed Family Night. This was to bring more fans to the game, since Blue was such a powerful draw that summer. "Looking back on it now," Blue said, "I realized how we got manipulated, and I was no different. And in the big scheme of things, you understand. You may not like it, and when it's your day to pitch, you pitch. But you know when they would hold me back a day, claiming that I was getting an extra day's rest, in all reality they were holding me back to pitch at home on Family Night ... since I was a natural draw anyway because of the season that I was having, and that kind of disturbed me once I got a little older."[20]

More than anything though, Finley probably contributed to Blue's arm problems down the road by overworking him.[21] The dean of Bay Area sportswriters, Glenn Schwarz, thought that Finley's overuse of Blue in 1971 probably damaged the young pitcher for the long haul. While he continued to have good years, Blue was never again the dominant pitcher who mowed down the opposition in 1971, sometimes even pitching past the 9th inning in close games. In one game he pitched 11 innings of shutout ball, while striking out 17 batters.[22] That type of overwork, even in an era before the concern with pitch counts was so strict, wore out Vida Blue. Jerry Lumpe, watching the A's that season, said he thought that "Charlie to a certain degree tried to exploit Vida . . . He was never the same pitcher after that season."[23]

As the A's entered the stretch run for the AL West title in August, Vida Blue received an invitation to visit President Richard M. Nixon, a lifelong baseball fan, in the White House. Finley delighted in this type of attention but told Nixon's staffers that either the whole team should be included or there would be no meeting with Blue. And so they arranged for a team visit on August 17 before a game scheduled that night with the Washington Senators. Finley's intervention to include the whole club in the White House visit impressed the players, and backup first baseman Mike Hegan gave him credit for insisting on a "team" concept in these matters. Even so, Blue was the focus of attention for Nixon, who, within earshot of Finley, told him, "I've read that you're the most underpaid player in baseball. I wouldn't like to be the lawyer negotiating your next contract." Finley winced. After taking the obligatory photos with the president and exchanging pleasantries between 1:14 and 1:29 P.M., the A's continued their gallop toward their first AL West title.[24]

During the season, Blue became tired of the constant media attention and the pressure. He became a mortal pitcher. His breaking ball lost a little break, and his blazing fastball slowed ever so slightly. The A's were leading the Western Division, and the only real baseball story in August 1971 was whether Blue would win 30 games. It became a national obsession. And it took its toll on Blue. After winning his 20th game in early August in Oakland, a quiet Blue admitted, "I'm glad no one will be asking me when I'll be winning my twentieth anymore. I hope no one asks me about 30." Later someone did, and Blue answered, "Man, I don't know a damn thing about it . . . Man, all I want to do right now is run, escape to some desert island to be left alone for a while."[25] Blue was tired, and it affected his play through the rest of the season and into the playoffs.

When the A's visited Chicago to play the White Sox in September, Finley took the opportunity to host a cookout for the team at his La Porte farm.

He had been doing this for many years, but this time, with the team ensconced in first place, the party was more opulent than ever before. He wanted to reward his players, and he wanted to show them off to his friends, business associates, and political acquaintances. On September 16, after the two-game series with the White Sox and before the team headed to Milwaukee to take on the Brewers, Finley had a bus bring them to his farm from Chicago. Finley had built a pool and invited everyone to swim and drink and eat and ride horses and chase cattle and engage in any mischief they could think up. The pool, for instance, had a bathhouse whose roof became a launching pad for jumps some 10 feet across the ground to cannonball into the pool, which at first caught a lot of cookout guests by surprise. A massive charcoal pit more than 10 feet long served as Finley's stove for cooking steak, chicken, sausage, lobster, and the like. As he presided over this cookout, the owner treated his players more like equals than at any other time. But as Vida Blue recalled, "everything went through him. Nothing happened unless he said, 'Put the steaks on the grill.' Now I think he was close to being a dictator . . . But he could also be the gentlest person."[26]

As he cooked on the farm, Finley indulged his addiction to the telephone. He constantly talked to people around the country, engaging in his characteristic browbeating, and listened to game broadcasts of the A's and his two recently purchased franchises—the Memphis Tams basketball team and the California Golden Seals National Hockey League team—via the phone. In the pre-cable era, the best way for him to hear these games was to open a line to the team's front office and have either Carl Finley or some staffer hold the phone to a radio broadcasting the game. He could also spout orders for underlings to relay to the manager or coach overseeing the game. Dick Williams recalled that the one thing that most impressed him about visiting Finley's farm for this cookout was that "he had a hookup box at just about every tree out in the area in case he had to plug in a phone." This enabled him to talk from anywhere on the property, and he availed himself of that opportunity seemingly all the time.[27]

These cookouts had long been command appearances for the A's players and their wives, and some of them got to the point where they would have rather had the day off. Sal Bando, for one, thought it a burden. Most enjoyed the cookouts, however. As Darold Knowles recalled:

And one of my fondest memories of that, course I grew up in the country as well, but I loved beef liver, and he had . . . this is crazy how I remember this . . . but he found out I liked beef liver, and he brought some beef liver out, and he cooked, and it was outstanding. I'll never forget that. But I also remember him yelling at our equipment manager at that time, which everybody just hated, because the guy very nicely just said . . . it was getting late, and he said, "Mr. Finley, you know, some of these guys think we ought to get on to Milwaukee"—we were taking a bus. And he jumped at his throat pretty good. And I remember everybody was kind of upset about that because he was just doing it for us, you know. And that's the way Finley was. His moods would change a lot. But I actually kind of have fond memories of the guy.[28]

Jim Schaaf's recollections of this cookout revolved around Finley's concentration on the cooking. "He loved to cook, and so he'd be out cooking the barbecue, and he'd have a band out there," Schaaf said.[29] David Finley said that for him personally, bringing friends to this event "was really, really cool."[30]

Throughout the year, Finley continued his various promotions to get fans to pay to see the A's play baseball. His most interesting promotion of the 1971 season was Hot Pants Day, which took place on June 27 at a doubleheader with the Kansas City Royals. Out of an attendance of 35,000, some 6,000 women gained free admittance wearing hot pants. It was a fashion show, and A's beat reporter Ron Bergman remembered how "we all looked forward to Hot Pants Day, and the women would parade on the second deck; you know, they'd walk from the right-field corner to the left-field corner like they used to for parades."[31]

Nonetheless, for all of his efforts to attract people to the A's games, Finley struggled to keep them coming back. He had hired an advertising firm in the off-season to help boost attendance, and it had recommended a makeover. The team would be called the A's, rather than the Athletics; the ad firm's tagline "the Swinging A's" stuck and became the moniker for the team. But Finley did not ask anyone to diagnose why fans did not frequent the games of this exciting, winning team, and the advertising firm did not offer much in the way of insight. Too bad he did not talk to his employees, who understood the problem well. Dick Williams thought it was poor service. He noticed that Finley often had "just two ticket sellers" working. "Charlie opened the front gate only, put a couple of people behind the caged windows with a bit of change, and that was it," Williams said. Many of his players and other employees commented on the disconnect between his single-minded desire to put a winner on the field and seemingly endless promotions, and his way of inhibiting ticket sales and ticking off fans. He was simply too parsimonious to pay the cost of staffing the games at an appropriate level to ensure everyone had a good time. Fans tended not to come back after experiencing how hard it was to buy tickets and get into the games.[32] Others thought that Finley's inattention to radio and television exposure meant that the A's had no fan base beyond those attending the games. Others thought that his promotions were silly. "Many of the promotions he draws up are hick-town promotions that don't go over here," sportswriter Glenn Dickey commented. "The town is a lot more sophisticated than he is."[33]

In the end, the Oakland A's breezed to the 1971 AL West title by 16 games, but they had to play a best-of-five series with the mighty Baltimore Orioles to advance to the World Series against the National League champion. The Orioles represented a formidable adversary; they were the reigning champions of the baseball world after decimating Cincinnati's famous "Big Red Machine" in the 1970 series four games to one. They were in the early years of a dynasty that ran between the late 1960s and 1980s in which they were perennial league leaders.

Finley prepared for his Oakland A's first-ever playoff appearance with actions both smart and insignificant. The smart action, as related by Dick Williams, involved sending A's scouts to travel with the Orioles and prepare an in-depth report on the opponents, even binding it in "beautiful green-and-gold books." Williams recalled that he was excited to receive this information even if the fancy cover did not impress: "I set up my rotation starting with Vida, then Catfish, then with an off-day, Vida again. So much preparation, such high hopes."[34] The insignificant action, at least for the outcome on the field, was reported in the media. "Finley ordered two dazzling outfits from his tailor and intended to wear them during the

American League playoff and World Series. One consists of a Kelly green jacket and gold trousers, the other is the reverse, with a gold jacket and Kelly green trousers. White kangaroo shoes will complete the ensembles. 'Kelly green and gold are my lucky colors,' said the Athletics' owner, 'and they work for me in any combination.' "[35]

The playoff series opened in Baltimore, and rain made Memorial Stadium a mud pit. The opening game was postponed from October 2 to October 3, but that meant the teams would lose the off day between games two and three. Consequently, Williams's plan of pitching Blue, Hunter, and then Blue again would no longer work. It really didn't matter. The A's lost the first game 5–3; an overworked Blue pitched well into the seventh inning but then gave up four runs, and Dave McNally got the win for the Orioles.

Finley sat in a box near the A's dugout through those first two games, dour and unhappy. Sometimes he fumed, sometimes he scolded and cursed. Mostly, he was taciturn. His depression was apparent to journalist Glenn Schwarz, who recalled seeing him out on the Baltimore streets past midnight after that first game. Finley displayed an unusual level of reflection during their conversation. "I ran into Finley, and he wanted me to just walk with him for a while. So we were out circling the blocks, and he wanted to relive the game." He asked Schwarz if he thought Dick Williams should have removed Blue when he got into trouble in the seventh inning or what else might have worked to preserve the win. "I came to know," Schwarz recalled, "being with him all those years, that he would pick the brain of anybody. He was always one to pull in a lot of information from everybody, including media." Of course Schwarz knew that Finley was second-guessing Williams.[36] Williams knew that too. In his 1990 memoir, he said of this game, "Go ahead, Charlie, second-guess me. I'm sure that somewhere you're still second-guessing me."[37]

Catfish Hunter went out the next day and lost the second game of the series 5–1 against Mike Cuellar, as the Orioles hit four home runs against him to put the A's in a real hole in the series. Of course, the pitchers were not entirely responsible for the losses; the A's bats fell silent at a critical time, and everyone knew that in a short series this could prove disastrous.

The A's flew back to Oakland immediately after that second loss and played again the next day. In that game, the Orioles beat the A's a third straight time, 5–3, with Diego Segui on the mound against future Hall of Famer Jim Palmer. Outfielder Rick Monday summarized the feelings of everyone associated with the A's: "I think we were surprised." It was like being run over by a train. They rationalized it by noting their team's youth and inexperience and the truly outstanding quality of the Orioles franchise. Others thought the first game's postponement had made all the difference. All vowed that they would come back in 1972.

With this sweep in the playoffs, Williams feared that Finley would sack him, as the owner had done to so many earlier A's managers. But he gained a reprieve when he was named Manager of the Year. In addition, Vida Blue received the league's Most Valuable Player and Cy Young awards. Despite faltering at the end because of overwork, Blue had twirled a stupendous season of baseball. He finished the season with a 24–8 record, eight shutouts, and 301 strikeouts. Even with his loss in game one of the playoffs, Blue's season was remarkable. These developments, as well as the overall play of the A's in taking their division, may have persuaded Finley not to pull the trigger on Williams.[38]

Over the winter, baseball's hot-stove league prognosticators and curmudgeons alike agreed that the A's would be a force to be reckoned with in the American League. The team looked poised to dominate the league the way the Yankees of old had done. For both Finley and Williams, the task during the winter was to put into place any final pieces needed to assure victory in the playoffs and the World Series in 1972. The A's had to get past the dominant Orioles to reach the World Series, and once there they had to overtake the winners of the National League pennant. The likely opponents included the Pittsburgh Pirates, who beat the Orioles in the World Series in 1971; the exceptional Cincinnati Reds, with their cadre of superb ballplayers who were among the best in the league; and the surprisingly resourceful Los Angeles Dodgers, who had outstanding pitching and timely hitting.

To accomplish this, Williams told Finley that he needed one more frontline starting pitcher. Accordingly, Finley traded center fielder Rick Monday to the Chicago Cubs for left-handed starter Ken Holtzman. Holtzman had been the third starter in an excellent Cubs' rotation that also included stopper Ferguson Jenkins and Bill Hands. The three had accounted for 60 of Chicago's wins in 1969, 47 in 1970, and 46 in 1971, but Holtzman had slipped from 17 wins each in 1969 and 1970 to only 9 in 1971. The Cubs considered him expendable, which proved a boon for the A's. Holtzman rebounded to a 19–11 record in 1972 and became a mainstay of the A's rotation, behind Hunter and Blue.

The big story of the off-season, the critical one that Finley had to resolve successfully to ensure the A's chances in 1972, was the very public contract dispute he had with flamethrower Vida Blue. Blue quite appropriately believed he deserved a healthy raise in 1972. As a first-year regular, Blue had earned only $14,750 in 1971, and on the advice of his agent, sports attorney Bob Gerst, he held out in 1972 for $115,000. Finley expressed outrage at Blue's request and claimed that his offer of $50,000 was more than generous for a second-year ballplayer without a long track record. As spring training began, Blue lowered his demand to $90,000 per year, but Finley would not budge.[39] The owner was notoriously blunt: "Well, I *know* you won twenty-four games. I *know* you led the league in earned run average. I *know* you had three hundred strikeouts. I *know* you made the All-Star Team. I *know* you were the youngest to win the Cy Young Award and the MVP. I *know* all that. And if I was you, I would ask for the same thing. And you *deserve* it. But I ain't going to give it to you."[40] On another occasion during these negotiations, Finley told Blue, "So you won twenty games? Why didn't you win thirty?"[41]

Blue's reaction was to announce his retirement, daring to take a public relations job with Dura Steel Products, a Bay Area plumbing-fixtures company. Finley was characteristically acerbic in response: "I'm happy to hear that he is entering the steel industry and starting out as a vice-president. If Vida is half as successful in steel as he has been in baseball, he has a great future ahead of him."[42] Blue did not appreciate such commentary. As Blue said at the time, "Charlie Finley has soured my stomach for baseball. He treated me like a damn colored boy."[43]

Vida Blue did not suit up until May—and only after MLB commissioner Bowie Kuhn got involved in the contract dispute. Kuhn debated whether to intervene; contract disputes traditionally had been the sole responsibility of the owners and not an MLB matter. But Kuhn itched to get into it. He believed that a star of Blue's stature was too great to lose for the season, or perhaps even permanently. He also believed, correctly, that left to his own devices, the penurious and obstinate Finley would drag out talks with Blue's agent for months. Accordingly, Kuhn searched for a precedent to support his interference. He found one in the case of Commissioner Kenesaw Mountain Landis's intervention in the contract dispute between star pitcher Paul Derringer and the Cincinnati Reds 30 years earlier; the commissioner believed the Reds had not negotiated in good faith. Kuhn then inserted himself to settle the Blue-Finley standoff. Kuhn remembered that "Finley was exacerbating an already unattractive situation by his pigheaded remarks and style." He added, "As far as I was concerned, I was the paterfamilias of the game and I could step in wherever I thought appropriate."[44]

Using his "best interest of baseball" power—Finley would say abusing that "best interest of baseball" power—Kuhn forced the two parties to sit down and not leave the table until they reached an agreement. That came on May 2, 1972, when Blue signed a contract for $63,000 with the A's. Finley fumed over the commissioner's interference in a private contractual matter; it proved to be a continuation of a series of clashes between Finley and Kuhn. "The Commissioner arbitrarily involved himself and forced himself into contract negotiations with Blue and I don't believe he had the authority to do so. I didn't like it one damn bit," protested Finley after the signing ceremony."[45]

Upon concluding the deal, however, Finley and Blue then disagreed over how it would be characterized to the public. Blue wanted to be able to claim a victory by signing for more than the $50,000 originally offered, but Finley insisted on announcing a deal that was for a $50,000 base salary—thereby claiming victory—and then adding to that a $5,000 signing bonus and an $8,000 scholarship for Blue's college education. The fight over this eventually led to Finley withdrawing the offer and stomping out of the negotiations. Kuhn ordered the offer to remain on the table. A few days later Kuhn ordered Blue and Finley to meet at the Boston office of American League president Joe Cronin to seal the deal. Finley called Kuhn several names, told him to go to hell, and announced he would not meet with Blue. Kuhn replied—and this is probably what broke the impasse—"Charlie, either you show in Boston and sign a contract with Blue, or I will make him a free agent. Take your pick." He signed Blue in Boston; the threat of losing him was too great.[46]

Unfortunately, Blue had a horrible 1972 season. He won just 6 and lost 10; most people believed the salary fight with Finley had much to do with Blue's decline in 1972. Others believed it was just a sophomore slump. The case for the latter was bolstered when Blue rebounded to win more than 20 games for the A's again in 1973 and 1975. Still others thought his young thunderbolt of an arm had been abused in 1971, reducing his career from the superstar stature he had enjoyed in that year.

Even as this contract dispute was being playing out, Finley outdid himself with two other flourishes that would define the championship A's of the 1972–1974 era. First, he bought the team new, presumably more fashion-conscious uniforms: kelly green and Fort Knox gold double-knit pullover shirts and white pants with elastic belts. When he unveiled the new uniforms, Finley expressed all the pride of an avant-garde designer. Holding up the stretchy new uniform jersey, he said, "These are slip-ons. No buttons. No zippers. Imagine—a baseball top without buttons!" These new uniforms were a mix-and-match affair, green or gold tops with white pants for everyday wear, and white jerseys for Sunday games. Finley bragged about leading the rest of MLB in adopting more colorful uniforms and predicted the same would happen this time. "I'm giving them more to snicker over," he said. "I'm introducing another new wrinkle—two-tone uniforms." Finley waxed eloquent about the vivid colors and the "polar bear whites." He gushed about how players, especially Reggie Jackson, had recommended changes to the logo and typeface on the uniforms. Reporters had a field day making fun of Finley's new career as a fashion designer.[47]

Second, Finley encouraged his players to grow a mustache and beard by promising a $300 bonus. They became known as the "Mustache Gang." In an era in which all the rest of Major League Baseball tried to present a conservative face to the public, the A's unique physical appearance related them more closely to the liberal counterculture than to the scions of big business that the owners courted.

Exactly what prompted this has been a subject of debate. Some thought Finley saw an opportunity to link his team to the strong counter-cultural current of the Bay Area. Others thought it bubbled up from inside the A's locker room. It seemed to be a little of both.

When the A's players reported for spring training on February 26, 1972, Reggie Jackson was sporting a beard, claiming he had not shaved since the American League championship series against the Orioles the previous fall. Of course, Jackson was not the first ballplayer to grow facial hair, but no major leaguer had worn it during the regular season since the Philadelphia Athletics' Wally Schang in 1914. Jackson said he liked the look, as well as not having to shave every day, and had no intention of shaving before the season started. Rather than fight the unpleasant battle of trying to get Jackson to change, the A's simply embraced the concept.

According to Sal Bando, Finley "thought that if we all grew some beard or a mustache that Reggie would shave it, and so he gave everybody money to grow mustaches."[48] Rollie Fingers, who went on to make a handlebar mustache his special brand, described how after seeing Jackson, "four or five of us pitchers decided to grow mustaches. We figured if we grew mustaches, Dick Williams would get upset and say, 'OK, guys, cut them off' and then Reggie would have to cut his off."

No one was more surprised than Fingers to learn of Finley's decision; it was indeed uncharacteristic. Finley had forced Ron Mihelic, in the A's front office, to shave his mustache by constantly belittling him. "Why don't you shave that mustache? You look a little like Stalin," Mihelic quotes Finley as saying. Likewise, Finley's son Martin was subject to his father's criticism on this front, being forced to keep his hair short.[49] But despite his private feelings, Finley took delight in making the baseball world squirm, as his fellow owners, the sportswriters, and especially Commissioner Kuhn grew more irritated over the A's and their new shaggy look. Columnist Arthur Daley grudgingly admitted at the time of the World Series that "the best team in baseball is manned by the hairy creatures managed by Dick Williams and spawned by Charles O. (for Owner) Finley. Just as the goddess, Pallas Athena, sprung full panoplied from the brow of Zeus, so did the A's emerge from the noggin of baseball's most irritating maverick, Finley."[50]

Even as the A's intended to open the 1972 season with beards and mustaches in contravention of MLB custom, they had to wait a bit to take the field because of the first major-league players' strike in the 20th century, which disrupted opening day. The strike was brought on by the Major League Baseball Players Association's insistence that the owners increase the pension fund to widen and extend coverage. Hard-liners, led by Cardinals owner August Busch, refused to negotiate. MLB owners additionally tried to smear the players and especially their union leader, Marvin Miller. At first Finley sided with the hard-liners. His sound bite, "the old truism that pigs get fat and hogs go to market," sounded like he intended retribution against his striking players.[51]

The owners initially got the better publicity; the sportswriters, long closely identified with the power brokers of the game, labeled the players as "pampered," "spoiled," "ungrateful," or worse.[52] But most of the owners, including Finley, had no stomach for a protracted struggle. A little more than a week into the strike, and after seven or eight games of lost revenues per team, the two parties accepted a settlement. The season opened on April 14, in no small measure because of Finley's work. The fight had revolved around retirement, insurance, and health care issues. Finley, more than any other owner, understood those issues because of his business, and he worked behind the scenes to forge a compromise. As journalist Ron Bergman put it, "the voice of reason was heard throughout the land. And the voice belonged to Charles Oscar Finley, owner of the Athletics. And the populace fell over each other in surprise and disbelief."[53] Finley got his fellow owners into a room and used his patented salesmanship to convince them to resolve the dispute. Perhaps Finley had a premonition of how the season would go. Ultimately, no owner would benefit more in 1972 than the man himself.

The A's roared out of the starting gate on April 15, 1972. With an opening-day starting lineup of shortstop Bert Campaneris, left fielder Joe Rudi, right fielder Reggie Jackson, third baseman Sal Bando, first baseman Mike Epstein, center fielder Bobby Brooks, catcher Dave Duncan, second baseman Dick Green, and pitcher Ken Holtzman, the A's earned a dramatic win against the Minnesota Twins on an error that allowed Rudi to score in the 11th inning. Catfish Hunter then lost the second game, but on April 18, Denny McClain—the former star pitcher for the Detroit Tigers and a 31-game winner for the World Series winner in 1968—won his first game for the A's 3–2.[54] The team piled up a 4–1 record in the first week of the season.

Great pitching is what put the A's over the top throughout 1972. But McClain, a Finley pickup and a fabled bad-boy pitcher, thanks to gambling and other demons, was released by mid-season.[55] Instead, it was the trio of Catfish Hunter, Ken Holtzman, and Blue Moon Odom that carried the A's that season. In addition, an outstanding bullpen stepped in to slam the door on the opposition should the starters falter. Rollie Fingers, of course, anchored the relief corps and set the standard for game closers in an era when that specialist position had yet to emerge. In addition, Bob Locker, Diego Segui, Darold Knowles, and Joel Horlen were reliable and effective. Oakland's relievers allowed only one run in the A's first 33-plus innings and helped ensure victory in the team's first 12 wins. Dick Williams recalled, "With great pitching from Hunter, Holtzman, and Blue Moon Odom, and great hitting from Reggie and Joe Rudie [sic] and Mike Epstein, a first baseman Charlie had picked up the previous season, we won 21 of our first 32 games and moved into first place virtually for good on May 27."[56]

The A's did have a setback, however: a game against the Kansas City Royals on May 19, when they were spanked 16–1. The vaunted A's pitching staff gave up 20 hits, Fingers gave up three runs without retiring a batter, and Don Shaw pitched three tortured innings in which the Royals put nine runs on the board. Mental errors plagued the team as fielders threw to the wrong bases and base runners missed signs and made mistakes high school ballplayers would be ashamed of. Sal Bando said it best after the game: "It was a circus; it should have been played in a tent."[57] Dick Williams was so irate about the play that he held a team meeting after the game to growl at the players. It must have worked, since through the end of May the A's had a 25–12 record.

The A's domination of the AL West made Finley a happy man. Even when they lost, and sometimes they did so spectacularly, it was a rare enough occasion that the A's owner took it in good stride most of the time. Sportswriter Jerome Holtzman told the story of the A's losing three of four to the White Sox in Finley's hometown of Chicago at the end of June. Through it all, Finley maintained a sense of humor. "The other day here in Comiskey Park, the White Sox were bombing Kenny Holtzman," Holtzman said. And that particular day the normally reliable lefty did not get an out in the first inning until after seven batters reached base. When a reliever finally got an out in the first inning, Finley "leaped to his feet, held up a lone finger, and shouted to the Chicago writers: 'Okay, you guys, that's one out?' Moreover, he did the same thing after the second and third outs."[58] Of course, it was easier to see the humor of the situation with his team sitting atop the AL West division, 20 games over .500 with a 43–23 record.

Throughout the summer, Finley traded for one player after another, casting off those viewed as less useful. Among other notable moves, he traded Curt Blefary, Mike Kilkenny, and a player to be named later to the San Diego Padres for Ollie Brown, sent Diego Segui to the St. Louis Cardinals for cash, traded Denny McLain to the Atlanta Braves for former National League MVP Orlando Cepeda, swapped several players to acquire slugger Don Mincher and glove-wiz Ted Kubiak from the Texas Rangers, and picked up weak-hit/great-glove shortstop Dal Maxvill from the Cardinals. Just as quickly Ollie Brown was gone again, as was Orlando Cepeda because of injury; other trades of lesser significance followed. All these moves became known as Finley's revolving door. The core of the team was philosophical about the owner's "here-today, gone-tomorrow" approach. "He was real cut and dried with trading or cutting or releasing or swapping a player," Vida Blue commented. "He was quoted as saying he would trade his mother if he could get the right player he felt he needed."[59] They never doubted that fact.

When the season broke for the All-Star game in July, the A's enjoyed a six-and-a-half-game lead over their nearest competitor in the AL West. In all, six A's made the team, including Reggie Jackson, who was voted as the starter in right field, but also Bert Campaneris, Sal Bando, Joe Rudi, and pitchers Catfish Hunter and Ken Holtzman. After that break, the A's continued where they had left off, dominating their division. By August 1 the A's record stood at 60–38, and they had a commanding lead in their division, but then problems arose. In a game in Kansas City, Dick Drago of the Royals hit Bando in the ankle with a fastball. Bando charged the mound and was tackled by the catcher, and both benches emptied. By the end of the melee, Reggie Jackson had torn his rib cage; he was out of the lineup for most of the month.

Despite not playing, Jackson remained both cocky and confrontational. He got into a fight with Mike Epstein over some minor events in the clubhouse, and the two ended up punching each other a few times before teammates broke it up before anyone was seriously hurt. Second baseman Dick Green said about such incidents: "There was a lot of individual egos on the team . . . When we crossed that white line to start playing ball, there was nobody that could play better as a team than we did." But before or after they would fight with each other. It was impossible to hold their aggressiveness, so effectively channeled on the diamond, in check off the field.[60]

With the loss of Jackson, the team started to falter a bit. The A's lost six of their first nine games in August and seemed to be heading for a collapse. Of course, there was little Finley himself could do about this skid—it was the responsibility of the manager to get the most out of his talented players on the field—so he considered firing Dick Williams. Speculation abounded in early August he would relieve Williams, whose contract was up at the end of the season. For once, Finley took the most appropriate action by taking none at all. He left Williams in place and then quietly renewed his contract for two more years in late August. Bert Campaneris commented at the time that this was the right move; all the speculation was tearing the team apart. "He's a good manager," Campaneris said. "I think we can get to the World Series with him." Joe Rudi added, "It eased my mind a lot. I love that man."[61]

Through it all, Williams successfully juggled the lineup to keep the A's on top of the division. He used a total of 63 different lineups during the year, not counting the pitchers, and Finley kept buying and selling players all season so the lineup possibilities appeared endless. Finding success in this setting proved even more impressive because several of Williams's star players did not have the most stellar of seasons. Altogether the A's scored 604 runs and allowed 457; not one of his hitters drove in more than 100 runs. Moreover, only Jackson and Epstein had more than 20 home runs. As a team, the A's averaged only .240, even as Joe Rudi led the regulars with a .305 average. But the A's did rate sixth in fielding percentage in the American League that year, right at the league average of .979. At some level, the 1972 A's team was greater than the sum of its individual parts.

They played well together, even as they fought with each other and Charlie Finley over matters great and small. The one huge positive that Finley enjoyed that season was the A's pitching staff. Catfish Hunter dominated with a 21–7 record and an ERA of 2.04, while Ken Holtzman went 19–11 with a 2.51 ERA, and Blue Moon Odom tallied a record of 15–6 with a 2.50 ERA. In an era before teams had specialist closers in the bullpen, Rollie Fingers posted an 11–9 record, with 21 saves and a 2.51 ERA. As a pitching staff, the A's had an outstanding 2.58 ERA, only slightly less than the Orioles' 2.53 team ERA. The A's pitching staff also combined for a league-leading 23 shutouts during the year.[62]

As the season progressed, Charlie Finley again tried to attract fans to the Oakland Coliseum through promotions and ancillary activities. The most important of these in the 1972 season, indicative of his effort to link the A's to the younger counterculture, was Mustache Day on June 18, 1972. Anyone coming to the day sporting facial hair got in free. There was some question as to what constituted an acceptable mustache. Did someone's three-day growth meet the standard or not? Finley was notoriously cheap and did not want to cut much slack. The ticket takers, however, did not relish turning fans away and tended to err on the side of inclusion, which was probably a good decision. Michael Scholl commented: "After 1972's Mustache Day, several of the A's shaved, only to grow the mustaches later in the season out of superstition. Whether it was the mustaches or not is debatable, but something worked for the 1972 Oakland Athletics, who not only ended baseball's facial-hair taboo, but also captured the World Series over the more traditional Cincinnati Reds in a series known as 'The Hairs vs. Squares.'"[63]

As he had done earlier in Kansas City in his feud with journalist Ernie Mehl, over all manner of petty and sometimes not-so-petty incidents, Charlie Finley also made war with sportswriter Ron Bergman during 1972— alienating one of the people able to help give the A's positive publicity. In the case of Bergman, then a young beat reporter covering the A's, the instigating incident came on September 16, just as the A's were completing their run for the AL West title. Bergman had written about A's broadcasters Monte Moore, Jimmy Piersall, and Jim Woods, complaining that they seemed to do little more than sing the praises of Charlie Finley during the games. "You get the impression they're in some sort of contest to see which one can make the most complimentary remarks," Bergman wrote. Finley roared back that Bergman seemed to want to make "my announcers look like prostitutes."[64] He barred Bergman from the team plane and bus, refused to make the travel arrangements for him to accompany the team, and generally tried to make his life miserable. He acted a bit like a spoiled child who failed to get what he wanted. As Bergman recalled, "if I printed something he didn't like, then he'd call me up and start screaming at me. And he'd go, 'The players hate you, and the manager hates you. I hate you. You've got the unmitigated gall'—'unmitigated gall' was one of his favorite phrases—'to write this shit.' He really got mad."[65]

The Bergman incident pointed to a central aspect of Finley's psyche. Finley and the media, perhaps Finley and everyone else, had a love-hate relationship. In part, so many of Finley's antics seemed aimed at capturing the spotlight and controlling his world. How much of this was about ensuring that Bergman and other reporters kept his name in the newspapers? If that was the case, Finley would not have been the first MLB owner to do so, and certainly not the last. It was an unbeatable combination, perhaps the real attraction for baseball ownership up to the present, and certainly something that motivated Charlie Finley.

Finley forever courted the media but also sparred with them and usually had a juicy quote about anything relating to the game. Again, Bergman captured it well. "We'd run into him in Chicago in bars and stuff like that," Bergman recalled, "and he'd buy us drinks, and he liked the whole milieu of being a baseball man. He loved hanging around with the sportswriters. We went out to dinner with him, and then he'd be pissed off at you the next day." He added:

> There were players' revolts every other week. There was a cycle,
> a four-day cycle; if things were quiet for three days, you knew
> something was going to happen, because every fourth day, some-
> thing had to happen . . . [One day a player was] talking to Charlie
> on the dugout phone, and Charlie said, "How do you like your
> uniform?" and he says to Charlie, "Well, Mr. Finley, this is really
> great and really nice." And he [Charlie] said, "How about the

white shoes? Do you like the white shoes?" The player said, "Yeah, the white shoes, they're really nice." Charlie said, "What's that noise in the background?" And he said, "Well, you know, there's a game going on right now." Charlie forgot what the game time was. So Charlie said, "Oh, geez, I'm sorry." And he hung up. Then the player told us on the team bus the next day what had happened, and it went into the paper. That guy was gone. I mean, he was in the minors the next day.[66]

Bergman thought Finley to be vindictive, as this story and the one about his kicking Bergman off the team plane and bus attest. But everyone wrote about it. Finley was good copy, and stories about him sold newspapers.

Only after the World Series victory in 1972 did dean of sportswriters Leonard Koppett put Finley in perspective: "If he wants to humiliate those who work for him, antagonize visitors, devise ways to antagonize several hundred reporters in their working arrangements, insult people and drive down everyone's throat the fact that he's the boss, it remains his right to do exactly that. It's his club and his business."[67]

One of Finley's attention-getting actions—indeed, there seems to be no other reason for him doing this—was the purchase on June 13, 1972, of the American Basketball Association (ABA) Memphis Pros. They lasted only two seasons, shutting down at the end of the 1973–1974 basketball season, but Finley owned them long enough to prove to all that his weirdness was not limited to the baseball world.

He renamed the ABA franchise the Tams, an acronym for "Tennessee, Arkansas, and Mississippi," and dressed them in his characteristic kelly green, wedding gown white, and Fort Knox gold colors, mixing and matching the combinations at his whim. He also offered the Tams the same deal as he had the A's: a $300 bonus to grow a mustache. The coach, the trainer, and several players grew full mustaches and got their promised bonuses. The team was a dreadful 20–64 for the 1972–1973 season, not unlike the first year he owned the A's. The Tams had one superb player, George Thompson, who was an All-Star every year he played in Memphis. At the end of the 1973–1974 season, Finley was fed up with the ABA and turned the team over to the league, which paid $1.1 million to buy him out. But the Tams may have distracted him somewhat from the activities of the A's, as he now had another set of employees and league officials to torment.[68]

For his NHL franchise, the California Golden Seals, Finley also adopted the same green and gold colors for uniforms he used elsewhere, including skates in those favorite colors. Like the Tams, the Golden Seals were horrendous. The team finished last in the NHL during the 1972–1973 season at 13–55–10. Neither the Seals nor the Tams drew many fans to their games and Finley quickly lost interest in them, in some part because of the contrast of the A's success on the field, which he enjoyed tremendously.

In the end, the Oakland A's rolled to the American League West championship, this time with a 93–62 record, taking command early and never relinquishing it, despite a series of instances during the summer when it appeared they might falter. As Bill Slocum appropriately concluded about the 1972 season: It was a bit of "a feeling of being inside an exciting locomotive controlled by an entertaining madman, equal parts P. T. Barnum and Caligula, and fueled by a nutty gang of misfits who serve up a never-ending barrage of amusing zingers and fisticuffs, at their opponents and sometimes each other."[69]

As the A's closed the 1972 baseball season, they had ignited a fire of expectation among all watching them. No one was more excited than Charlie Finley. The American League Championship Series opened in Oakland on October 7, 1972, with the A's clear favorites over an upstart Detroit Tigers team that had ridden to the AL East pennant by only a .5 game. The Tigers got there on the back of 22-game-winner Mickey Lolich, a surprisingly effective pitcher for more than a decade whose conditioning consisted largely of eating huge steak dinners with all the trimmings; and 19-game-winner Joe Coleman. Interestingly, no one was surprised that after Lolich retired from baseball, he became owner of a doughnut shop in Lake Orion, Michigan.

Since the A's were the solid favorites, the drama of the series turned on the hatred the two teams had shown each other all year.[70] All of their games had been tense, and the one on August 22 had sparked a full-fledged bench-clearing, eye-popping brawl that landed A's coach Irv Noren in the doctor's office. Of course, that was not unusual when Billy Martin led a team, and he had managed an over-the-hill group of Tigers to their division title. Moreover, Finley again stole the spotlight from his players by calling Martin "a liar, a phony and a 24-carat kook."[71] Finley was certainly right about Martin, but he did not call Martin a managerial genius, a true leader, and a drunken brawler, all of which were also true.

When the A's and Tigers met in game one, the collective temper was already high—and it would later become much higher. Finley asked actor George C. Scott to throw out the first pitch, and after doing so, Scott announced that he was rooting for the Tigers, much to Finley's chagrin. Lolich faced Catfish Hunter in this game, and both pitched superbly, Lolich into the 10th and Hunter until the 8th inning. With the score tied 1–1 going into the 11th inning, Al Kaline hit a solo shot to put the Tigers ahead. But the A's came back in the bottom of the 11th to win the game with two additional runs. Back-to-back singles by Sal Bando and Mike Epstein chased Lolich from the game. It looked like reliever Chuck Seelbach would win the game after Gene Tenace failed with an attempted sacrifice bunt and the runner heading for third was forced out. Then, Gonzalo Marquez came in to pinch-hit for Dal Maxvill, singling to right and driving in the tying run. Tenace, who had reached on the put-out to third during his bat, then tried to go to third on Marquez's single, and a wild throw from Al Kaline allowed him to score and win the game for the A's. The 3–2 victory made Finley ecstatic, especially after the poor showing in the playoffs the year before. He cheered, worried, and ordered, as was his wont, from his seats near the A's dugout at the Coliseum.[72]

The next day, a Sunday, Blue Moon Odom and Woodie Fryman faced each other on the mound, and the A's ran wild. Shortstop Bert Campaneris led off the game with a single, promptly stole second and then third base, and came home on a Joe Rudi hit. The A's scored four more runs in the fifth to make this into the only blowout of the series. Frustration ran high in the Tigers dugout, and Billy Martin decided to act. During the A's scoring binge in the fifth, Tigers reliever Fred Scherman threw two pitches that barely missed Reggie Jackson, sending him diving out of the way. Both sides knew that Martin was sending a message. He sent another in the seventh. After Campaneris already had made three hits, stolen two bases, and scored two runs, reliever Lerrin LaGrow threw at Campaneris, hitting him on the ankle. Campaneris staggered in pain for a moment, then turned and glared at LaGrow before flinging his bat toward the mound. The bat helicoptered about five feet off the ground toward LaGrow's left side. The pitcher was no doubt stunned and took a moment to recover, ducking out of the way just in time to avoid contact. The benches quickly cleared, and though no punches were thrown, the event punctuated the high tension of the game.

Everyone knew Martin had ordered it and intended the ankle injury to put Campaneris out of commission for the rest of the series. Joe Rudi said, "I was in the on-deck circle, and I feel the Detroit pitcher threw at him. Campy had run the Tigers ragged in the first two games, and when [Billy] Martin gets his ears pinned down, he's going to do something about it." Indeed, Martin led the Tigers rush out of the dugout and appeared to be the only one enthusiastic about a fight. He went straight for Campaneris, who ran for the A's dugout. Martin had to be stopped by the umpires. Legendary umpire Nestor Chylak, behind the plate for this game, threw both LaGrow and Campaneris out of the game.[73]

There may have been some serious premeditation to Martin's actions in getting Campaneris. David Finley recalled talking with Campaneris after the game and asking him about the bat-throwing incident. Campaneris, he said, "pulls out an article from the *Detroit Press* that said 'the only advantage . . . the A's have over us is speed. Their speed is in Bert Campaneris. How do you stop the A's? You stop their speed. How do you stop their speed? You hit 'em with a pitch. Where? Low.'" David Finley then said that Campaneris added, "That pitcher messed with my career. I thought he might be throwing at me, and when that ball hit me . . . he's messing with my life and my career, and I had no choice." Such a plan sounds totally in character for Billy Martin.[74]

Later Martin feigned innocence and put all the inappropriate behavior on Campaneris. "There's no place for that kind of gutless stuff in baseball," Martin said. "That's the worst thing I've ever seen in all my years of baseball . . . I would respect him if he went out to throw a punch but what he did was the most gutless [thing] of any man to put on a uniform. It was a disgrace to baseball." He had a lot of nerve condemning Campaneris for unsportsmanlike behavior after all of his violence and abuse over the years. No one played a more gentlemanly game or had a sweeter disposition than Bert Campaneris. The A's as a team were known for their infighting, but Campaneris always seemed a center of calm and reflection in a swirling pool. Mike Hegan said that Campaneris told him that "he, at that point, got so frustrated that LaGrow kept backing him off and throwing at his feet. It was something that was well out of character for Campy. But he just said that he snapped, and that was the first thing that he could think about, and that's what he did—unfortunately."[75] As Campaneris said, "I didn't mean to throw the bat, but you get mad in the moment and you don't think about it. As soon as it happened, I wish it hadn't happened."[76]

After the game, the A's left for the airport to fly to Detroit for game three, scheduled for Tuesday, October 10, 1972. The flight turned into a circus. A bomb scare on the plane delayed the flight for an hour and put everyone on edge. Everyone except Finley. He had a Dixieland band with him, along with family and friends, and the charter flight proved raucous. He had the band play his favorite song, "Sugartime," over and over again. Downing Scotch after Scotch, Finley was pretty well toasted by the time he grabbed the plane's intercom and sang the song for all to hear, changing the last two lines: "Put your legs around me, and love me all the time." The players, most sitting in the back of the plane, just wanted to relax and get some sleep.[77]

During the flight, Finley probably thought little about how to deal with the Campaneris bat-throwing incident, but it was the first thing he had to deal with upon arriving in Detroit. Over the objections of Finley, a late-night meeting with American League president Joe Cronin led to Campaneris's suspension for the rest of the championship series. The league also fined Campaneris $500; the decision of whether to suspend him for the World Series as well was left to Bowie Kuhn. But Cronin also decided not to suspend Billy Martin, who, everyone knew—perhaps with a wink and a nod—had engineered the incident, or Lerrin LaGrow. "Nestor Chylak said he didn't think LaGrow was throwing at Campy," Cronin said, "so he isn't being punished." He added, "Martin didn't hit anybody because the umpires subdued him quickly and there will be no action against him."[78] It was an unbelievable turn of events, and Finley was incensed. His team had lost the services of one of its best players, the fellow who kick-started the offense and anchored the defense, and Martin got away with it. Finley called a 3 A.M. press conference in his hotel room on October 10, which lasted until 4:30, to recall in excruciating detail to the media the meeting with Cronin about Campaneris, and to say that Campy's ankle was too bad to play on and that he was returning to Oakland for treatment.[79]

Cronin wanted to suspend Campaneris for the rest of the year, making him ineligible to play in the World Series should the A's advance, but Kuhn did the A's a favor, deciding instead to impose a seven-game suspension on Campaneris for the beginning of the 1973 season. Finley, ever the dramatist, held another press conference on October 12 to tell the sportswriters how he had saved Campaneris's appearance at the World Series. He told how he, along with two of his sons and manager Dick Williams, had gone to Cronin's hotel room about 10 P.M. to talk him out of a suspension. Bill Libby said that Finley told the story with the cadence of a poem, "as if he were reciting The Raven, full of flourishes and leers." When Cronin opened the door, he was wearing a long white nightgown and a sleeping cap, conjuring an image of a man out of his time and place in the "swinging seventies." The journalists had as much fun with this image as Finley. "Was he carrying a candle?" one asked. "What color was the nightgown?" asked another, causing someone to yell, "You can be damn sure it wasn't Finley green and gold." Finley laughed, and then launched into a tirade against Cronin, against Martin, and against the Tigers that lasted more than an hour. As it turned out, Cronin had changed his mind and then urged Kuhn to be lenient with Campaneris. He told Kuhn that the player was universally liked, had never been in such a fight before, and deserved to get into the World Series. He could be suspended next year.[80]

Kuhn acceded to Cronin's change of heart by allowing Campaneris to play in the World Series, claiming that he did not want to deprive the A's fans of their star, not because he wanted to help out Finley, who had been a thorn in his side for years. He looked for a precedent, and found one in the 1941 30-day suspension of the Yankees' Frank Crosetti, which was lifted for the World Series and then reinstated for the beginning of the next year. "Following that precedent," Kuhn recalled, "I suspended Campaneris for the first seven games of the 1973 season."[81] Only after negotiations with the players association and with Finley did Kuhn agree to a mere 7-day suspension; he had originally wanted a 30-day punishment.

Dick Williams recalled that Martin was crazy like a fox in this incident, getting Oakland's best lead-off man out of the series, firing up his team, and demoralizing the A's all at the same time. This one incident had turned the advantage to the Tigers. The A's lost the next two games in the series with scores of 3–0 and 4–3, before taking out the Tigers 2–1 in the final game of the series on October 12, 1972. Those were hard-fought games, but the biggest blow for the A's came in the last one, which they won to advance to the World Series. They lost Reggie Jackson in a collision with catcher Bill Freehan at the plate in an attempted double steal in the second inning. Jackson tore his left hamstring and could not play even a single inning in the World Series. All through this tension, Williams said that he slept like a baby, "that is, I woke up every two hours crying."[82]

Charlie Finley was not a man to be intimidated, and he approached the 1972 World Series with a sense of exultation, and fully believed he would finally gain the respect and support he felt he deserved. To a very real extent the A's were the underdogs in this series. Although Finley's team had fought its way to the AL pennant, they had gone to the wire with an over-the-hill Detroit Tigers team. In contrast, the Cincinnati Reds took their National League West division by 10.5 games over both the Los Angeles Dodgers and the Houston Astros, and then rolled over the 1971 champion Pittsburgh Pirates to earn their place in the fall classic. Moreover, the A's were brand-new to postseason play; it was the first trip to the World Series by the Athletics franchise since 1931, when they played in Philadelphia under Connie Mack. Alternately, the Reds were making their second trip to the Series in three years; the Big Red Machine would be perennial contenders throughout the 1970s and win back-to-back titles in 1975 and 1976.

The Big Red Machine stood in marked contrast to the Swinging A's. The Reds were the epitome of button-down efficiency, winning games and putting away opponents with ruthless competence. Conservative in style and deed, the Reds exuded confidence and superiority. They were the closest thing MLB had to the organization men in gray flannel suits so popular in the 1950s and early 1960s. They were also a seemingly lifeless bunch. Sure, there were a few personalities on the team, but mostly they had resourceful stars such as future Hall of Famers Johnny Bench, Tony Perez, and Joe Morgan, and one, Pete Rose, who would be in the Hall of Fame but for his gambling addiction and misbehavior. Overall, the Reds seemed devoid of life and blood. They were, as their nickname said it, a machine.[83]

The A's were anything but. Yes, they won games at a rate close to the Reds', but they did it in unusual, colorful ways. They had all the organization and consistency of a pie fight by a bunch of circus clowns. Of course, Finley was the head clown. The A's fought with each other, with other teams, with Charlie Finley, with the media, with everyone who came into contact with them. The A's even got into a brawl in the clubhouse after clinching the American League pennant, when Vide Blue pointed to Blue Moon Odom and gave the universal choking sign. In breaking them up, Dick Williams realized that his team "had to get to the World Series before we killed ourselves."[84]

The sportswriters labeled the 1972 series the "Hairs against the Squares" and it stuck. The series opened in Cincinnati's Riverfront Stadium, one of those saucerlike, artificial-turfed, antiseptic concrete-and-steel monstrosities that so many teams played in throughout the 1970s and 1980s. The A's, upstarts that they were, took the first game 3–2 on October 14 and also won the second 2–1 the next day before returning to Oakland for the next three games. The heroes were the unlikely Gene Tenace, a weak-hitting backup catcher and outfielder who hit two home runs in that first game, and the more likely Joe Rudi, who had a homer and made an outstanding catch to save game two. Finley sang, Finley danced, Finley ate, and most of all, Finley drank through those two joyous days. He talked to everyone about the series, about the A's, and about how he and his team would now get the respect they deserved.[85]

When the teams met in Oakland for game three on October 17, they found that torrential rains meant they could not play. The commissioner postponed this game until the next day, and before play began, Finley's ground crew contracted with helicopters to hover ever so gingerly over the outfield to help dry it out. That didn't help much, and both sides had to deal with squishy and muddy conditions. The Reds won that game 1–0 on the strength of starter Jack Billingham's stunning three-hit shutout through eight innings, with reliever Clay Carroll notching a save in the ninth. The A's bats were silent as they went down to the defeat. The one bright spot was the trick play pulled on Johnny Bench in the eighth inning. With runners on second and third and only one out, Dick Williams went to the mound when the Bench count went to 3–2, presumably telling pitcher Rollie Fingers to issue an intentional walk to load the bases so that the A's could have a play at every base. Catcher Gene Tenace stood up and moved his glove to the outside of the strike zone to signal ball four, but he returned to his crouch just as Fingers delivered a strike. The umpire called a surprised Bench out on strikes. The play likely saved a run, but with the A's bats asleep, little could be done to take back the game.[86]

The Reds and the A's split games four and five, both by one run each. So when the A's returned to Cincinnati for the final two games, they led the series 3–2. The Reds handed the A's their heads in game six, on October 21, 1972, with an 8–1 drubbing to tie the series, setting up a dramatic game seven in which the winner would take all. To a very real extent, the series turned on two first-inning misplayed balls by the Reds. One was a fly ball and the other a bad hop. This allowed the A's to score the first run. The Reds tied the score 1–1 in the fifth, but the A's went ahead in 3–1 in the sixth on the strength of a single and then back-to-back doubles by Sal Bando and Gene Tenace. Then the Reds added a run in the eighth to make the score 3–2, but Rollie Fingers shut them down to save the game and win the World Series. Tenace emerged as the star of the game, and indeed of the entire Series, by hitting safely twice and driving in two of the three A's runs. Indeed, for the whole Series, Tenace had been dominant, belting homers in his first two trips to the plate and driving in 9 of Oakland's 16 sixteen runs. His four homers for the Series set a record, and he was appropriately named World Series MVP. Lowell Reidenbaugh concluded, "And so it was at Riverfront Stadium on October 22, that the Athletics cashed in on two abnormal plays to defeat the Reds, 3–2, before a record crowd of 56,040 and win the world championship of baseball, the first major title by a Bay Area team." It was a remarkable World Series, everyone agreed. Cincinnati's manager, Sparky Anderson, summed up his experience as one of unfettered "frustration."[87]

As the final pop-out settled into the glove of Joe Rudi in the ninth inning, the A's mobbed together near the pitcher's mound in celebration. Finley climbed up on top of the A's dugout, along with wife Shirley, and began kissing her passionately for all the world to see. Dick Williams's wife also climbed onto the dugout, where the manager began kissing her as well. Later he appeared just outside the A's clubhouse and chanted, "We're No. 1! We're No. 1!"[88] The scene in the A's clubhouse was equally strange. "Under the shower, fully clothed and with champagne held high, Campy Campaneris, Dick Green, Don Mincher, and Joel Horlen harmonized the National Anthem under the sensitive direction of a nude Vida Blue," commented Reidenbaugh. In an anteroom, players' wives began chanting for Charlie Finley to appear. When he did, it was pure theater. "This is the greatest day of my life, none of you can appreciate what this means to me," he told the audience while standing with his family. When the media asked some of the children a question, Finley scolded, "You nod. I'll answer the questions." In the end, Reidenbaugh characterized the scene as "one-third Roman orgy, one-third Hollywood first nighter and one-third press conference."[89]

Mostly the great sports columnists wrote not so much about the games as about Finley during the World Series. Red Smith, who had no love for Finley, made fun of the band that he led into the Oakland Coliseum and its playing of Oakland Symphony Orchestra director Harold Farberman's new composition, the "Oakland Athletics Victory March," dedicated to, you guessed it, "Charles O. Finley and Every Single Members [sic] of the Swingin' A's."[90] *Washington Post* sports columnist Shirley Povich also belittled Finley as "a novice baseball operator with no previous experience in the game" and noted how his success now left his fellow club owners "in disbelief." "They are doing a bit of soul-searching," he wrote, "and asking where they failed if a seeming baseball dunce like that loud-talking insurance tycoon from Chicago who sells malpractice coverage to doctors can suddenly put together a pennant-winning team." But Finley had done just that; he used to his advantage good scouting and the draft system to sign superb players. Finley had owned the A's since December 1960, and he had learned much about the game during those years. He was hardly a neophyte. Perhaps Povich had a point, but in this case it seemed to be on top of his head.[91]

Povich also jumped on Finley for taking action to reward his players for their outstanding efforts in the first two games. "Put down that fellow for a $5,000 raise, retroactive," he said of Gene Tenace in recognition of his two homers in the first game of the World Series. Finley also had decided to reward both Mike Hegan and Joe Rudi for their sterling play in game two. There were rumors that he also planned to give similar rewards to other players, especially Catfish Hunter. In response, Bowie Kuhn, also channeling jealous owners, invoked a rule that owners were prohibited to give "special incentives" to employees. Finley argued that these were "retroactive raises" for the 1972 season. Did anyone believe that owners up to that point had not singled out individual players for reward in response to their outstanding play? Of course not. It was an accepted fact, but the owners pushed hard, through the commissioner's office, to damp down rewarding of an already underpaid group of players. Finley recognized this and argued that he was simply rewarding them for their efforts over the course of the year. "Tenace was getting a minimal salary," Finley said. "He was getting only $20,000," and certainly a $5,000 raise/bonus/gift, call it what you will, was a major incentive for him. Kuhn disallowed Finley's largesse and then went on to fine him $2,500 for violating the rules. Finley did reward these players later, but the actions of Major League Baseball to hold down player pay, which may have been in character for the system, certainly wasn't defensible as fair. Moreover, it was an intrusion of an owner's rights to do with his organization as he saw fit.[92]

Dave Nightengale wrote about Finley's playing host to 27 people for a night on the town, including his large family, after the series. He referred to Finley as Emperor Charles I of Oakland and characterized him as a tin-pot dictator, but a generous one who treated everyone that night. He dispensed his philosophy of "Sweat + Sacrifice = Success." He told stories, spent liberally, and engaged everyone. He confided that he prized loyalty above all else, and demanded it of all of his employees and his family.[93] It was an interesting story, but one unrelated whatsoever to the World

Series, and it demonstrates as well as any that Finley was a major part of the circus attraction of the fall classic in 1972.

When the A's returned to Oakland after the World Series, Finley led them in a parade and press conference. More than 20,000 fans showed up to greet them and Finley was in his element. Carrying a "captured" Reds' batting helmet, he tried to give a speech to a raucous crowd that could not hear him. The players took turns talking but could not be heard either. Vida Blue, who had a retiring disposition anyway, ducked out of the celebration, and when Finley realized it, he was angry that Blue had such disregard for the fans. He was simply incapable, loving the spotlight as he did, of understanding how less extroverted people could wish for a little solitude. He did agree with Mike Epstein's call to the fans in Oakland: "Let's keep this trophy for 10 years."[94] Although Finley was certainly on top of the world with his A's, as soon as all the parties at the conclusion of the World Series calmed down, he went into overdrive, trying to figure a way to ensure a repeat in 1973.

Chapter Seven

Repeat, Three-peat

"Perhaps the truest axiom in baseball is that the toughest thing to do is repeat," warned Los Angeles Dodgers manager Walt Alston.[1] It was something that Charlie Finley knew all too well. No team had repeated as World Series winners since the New York Yankees in 1961 and 1962. In fact, since World War II, only the Yankees had been repeat World Series champions; in addition to the 1961 and 1962 championships, they had taken an incredible five series in a row between 1949 and 1953. Finley fully intended for the A's to win again in 1973 and set about trying to accomplish it over the winter by ensuring that he fielded the best team possible in Oakland the next season.

At a time when the average salary was $36,566 and the MLB minimum was $15,000, Finley increased his payroll significantly in 1973, from an average of about only $28,000, to make his stars happier, although all of them still fumed that they were underpaid. Which they were. Catfish Hunter received an estimated $75,000; Reggie Jackson, $70,000; Bert Campaneris, $65,000; Joe Rudi, $50,000; and World Series MVP Gene Tenace, $35,000—figures far less than the players' market value. The salaries of three of the biggest stars of the American League—Hunter, Campaneris, and Jackson—did not match up to the those of comparable players on other teams. Finley also increased the pay of Dick Green (who threatened to retire but was lured back to the team by Finley's offer of more money), Chuck Dobson, and Rollie Fingers (who got a $5,000 raise).[2] None of these salaries came close to league standards. For example, some of the top earners in Major League Baseball that year were pitcher Bob Gibson of the St. Louis Cardinals and outfielder Carl Yastrzemski of the Boston Red Sox, who each earned a reported $150,000; Willie Mays with the San Francisco Giants, who earned $170,000; Hank Aaron of the Atlanta Braves, who got $200,000; and Dick Allen of the Chicago White Sox, who had a stunning $225,000 contract.[3]

A's players whom Finley could not sign, or apparently could not otherwise placate, he traded elsewhere. A primary case was catcher Dave Duncan, who had long disagreed with Finley on issues great and small. Finley traded him to the Cleveland Indians for catcher Ray Fosse. In departing, Duncan said he had learned much from Finley, mostly "how I don't want to live my life."[4]

One of Finley's many player transactions proved enormously significant for the A's in 1973. Bill North, known to all as Billy, was a speedy young outfielder with a lot of promise, but he failed to hit the way the Chicago Cubs wanted in the 1972 season. When Finley peddled pitcher Bob Locker to the Cubs, he got North in return. The deal was completed on November 21, 1972, soon after the World Series, and North settled into the center field position for the A's the next summer after injuries to Billy Conigliaro and Angel Mangual took them out of the lineup. He proved himself in 146 games, batting .285, scoring 98 runs, and stealing 53 bases for the season. His presence in the lineup, even more than either Conigliaro's or Mangual's, ensured that the potent A's hitters in the middle of the order had a jackrabbit on base who could score on singles or sacrifice flies. Interestingly, the A's decided to bat North for much of the season in the ninth spot in the order. In previous years this would have been the pitcher's slot, but 1973 was the first year of the designated-hitter rule in the American League—a victory for Finley after years of lobbying. The addition of North aided the run-scoring potential of the A's. He also provided the kind of defense in center field that had been missing from the A's since Rick Monday was dealt to the Cubs in 1971 and provided strength up the middle with Fosse, Green, Campaneris, and North.[5]

In all, only 13 of the players on the A's 25-man roster at the time of the

1973 World Series had been with the A's the year before. "There's a core of us who are never touched," Sal Bando commented, "but the other players are always changing. If that core ever starts slipping, we're in trouble." He concluded, "The policy puts a lot of pressure on us."[6]

As he continued to wheel and deal, Finley also took his bows for the A's winning the 1972 World Series. On January 16, 1973, he loved participating in a 1,000-person "Thank You, Charlie Finley" day at an Oakland hall.[7] He even had a special formal suit made—in green and gold—for when he received the Hoosier of the Year award presented by the Indiana Society of Chicago; he was quite proud of the fact that previous award winners included Wendell Willkie and Cole Porter. He also greatly enjoyed the dinners in his honor in his old stomping grounds of La Porte and Gary, Indiana. At the La Porte affair, more than 2,000 people showed up at the school gymnasium. Finley insisted that the sponsors keep the cost of tickets for this dinner under two dollars, "because I want it within reach of the working man and the kids." The event was presided over by Indiana governor Edgar Whitcomb and attended by Joe Rudi, Reggie Jackson, Gene Tenace, and Vida Blue. Finley was totally in his element and gracious in his acceptance of accolades. He was finally getting some respect. Even so, he was convinced he remained the redheaded stepchild of baseball. "They haven't accepted me, and I don't expect they will. I didn't inherit a team . . . I'm used to their attitude . . . [I] came out of the Gary, Ind., steel mills and made money accidentally in the insurance business. Now I'm ruining the sanctity of their game."[8]

In addition to taking bows and planning for the 1973 season, Finley also prepared the World Series champion rings that he bought for each player and other employees of the Oakland A's. Probably no owner in MLB history spent more time on this item than Finley. Reporter Dave Condon wrote about how he went to Finley's home and "found Charlie frying fish and liver, listening to a Memphis Tams' broadcast on an amplified telephone, accepting and making calls on other phones, and putting the final approval on his Athletics' World Series rings and souvenirs." He promised that they would be the most lavish ever created, and he worked hard to accomplish that feat. Condon said that several different times on several different days he "interrupted him while he was spending hours on the wording, the coloring and design." When finally completed, the ring had a one-carat diamond emblazoned with "World Series 1972." "The decision over the Reds is noted. Each player's name will be in bold letters. As a personal touch, there's the signature of Charles O. Finley, and in large engraving, Finley's pet formula 'S + S = S,' or Sweat plus Sacrifice equals Success," Condon wrote about Finley's personal motto and its place in the baseball world. Finley told him, "All my players know the health-and-happiness ideas, and that S plus S will remind 'em. If not, their wives will remind them, because each wife is getting a charm bracelet complete with a half-carat diamond, the A's Logo, and her husband's name enscribed [sic]."[9] Finley boasted that each of the World Series rings cost him $1,500, and he could not resist a swipe at his fellow owners by saying that earlier rings had cost an average of only $300 each. He also drooled over the player wives' charm bracelets and bragged that they each cost about $500. "Nothing ever has been given to the wives as nice as my charms," he was quick to add.[10]

In March, Finley went to spring training in Arizona to hand out the World Series rings to his team. He made much of how elaborate and expensive they were, and then he told them, "If you repeat and do this in '73, I'm going to make that look like a dime-store model."[11] Sal Bando said that several of the players had these rings appraised, for insurance purposes, and found that they were worth $3,500, an exceptional amount for the time.[12] Bando said that Finley also gave "a trophy to each guy, and he got the nice rings, and he got the wives a pendant, which was a duplicate of what the ring looked like. It was just really generous."[13] Finley showered these rings on nonplayers as well. A's beat reporter and onetime Finley adversary Ron Bergman said he received the same ring but without a real diamond. He didn't expect a ring and was happy to accept it, adding that ethical rules would prohibit sportswriters from accepting such a gift from an owner today.[14]

A's farm director John Claiborne said that, in displaying this generosity, Finley ran afoul of the lords of baseball. He had raised the bar on what would be expected, and they resented it: "Charlie decided to outdo them, and he got in a little trouble from the league . . . Everyone in most every other sport after that started jazzing up their rings with some type of diamond set up in the middle. It might be a group of diamonds, it might be a big diamond, whatever."[15]

Another joke Finley played on his players, although it was inadvertent since he was deadly serious about it, was his championing of an experiment with orange baseballs. Finley argued—and "argue" is the operative word here—that a baseball cover dyed alert orange, not unlike a construction worker's vest, would be easier for both players and fans to follow in the field of play. He insisted it would generate more offense since it would give hitters an advantage. "Batters can see an orange ball better, particularly at night," Finley told *Time* magazine. "If we start using this ball, batting averages will increase. That means more action, and that's what the fans want to see." He added, "Action—that's what the game needs! Let's get some goddam action in this sport!"[16]

Finley was right about the need for more action. In an era when batting averages were declining and pitching was growing more dominant with every year, pumping more offense into the game seemed important for future fan support. Finley said of his fellow MLB owners, "If they don't get wise to themselves, they won't have any game left to be sanctimonious about."[17] But Major League Baseball has always been a notoriously conservative entity, and he found few supporters for his idea despite his years of advocacy. In 1973 he talked Commissioner Bowie Kuhn into letting him try it out during spring training. He did so against the Cleveland Indians on March 29, the San Francisco Giants on March 31, and the Los Angeles Dodgers on April 4. It did not work out too well. Pitchers complained that the ball was slippery and hard to grip; batters complained that they could not pick up the seams of the ball as it spun toward them, since the normal red stitching was not present to help plot that course. Sal Bando offered his assessment: "Orange baseball was a bad idea . . . only because, when we did it, it was a day game. I mean, you couldn't see the ball that good, and it was very slippery for the pitchers to throw." Bowie Kuhn told him to knock it off with the orange balls, which Finley did, but for the rest of his life, he used the stash of them that he'd ordered as gifts.[18]

When the A's broke training camp in Arizona, they were convinced they could win the American League West once again, despite being picked to finish second, after the Chicago White Sox. Manager Dick Williams proudly announced, "We're going to win it again," because "we have the best pitching in baseball."[19] He was right. The A's had a good offensive team, led by Jackson, Bando, and Tenace, but it was superb pitching that made the A's outstanding. Three starting pitchers won 20 or more games that season, with Catfish Hunter at 21–5, Ken Koltzman at 21–13, and Vida Blue at 20–9, while Rollie Fingers turned in 22 saves, and a capable bullpen provided a lot of support. Those three 20-game winners were the most flashy of all of the accomplishments of the A's in 1973. Not since 1931, when they were based in Philadelphia and owned and managed by the legendary Connie Mack, did an A's team have three 20-game winners. In 1973, Hunter, Holtzman, and Blue dominated the American League just as Lefty Grove (31–4), George Earnshaw (21–7), and Rube Walberg (20–12) had in 1931. And the Oakland trio of dominators were ecstatic about it. Vida Blue said, "Like I always say, for a pitcher to win 20 games is like breaking the sound barrier, it's like an actor winning the Academy Award, like winning eight Gold Medals, like going around the world in 79 days."[20]

In classic Finley style, he incited charges of poor taste early in the season by unveiling the largest world championship pennant anyone had ever seen. It was, according to sportswriter Art Spander, "about as subtle as a punch in the mouth." It was "green and gold, and about half the size of Texas."[21] It didn't much matter. The A's took the AL West lead on June 28 and never looked back, finishing the year with a record of 94–68. They outdistanced the second-place Kansas City Royals by 6 games. The preseason favorite to take the AL West, the White Sox, finished a distant fifth in the division, 17 games behind the A's.

It was not the easiest run to the victory circle the A's had enjoyed. Finley wanted to get speed into the game and kept insisting on speedsters in the designated-hitter spot, but that did not work out well. Not until former Phillies slugger Deron Johnson got into that slot did they start to turn it around. Likewise, Billy North was not the opening-day center fielder, and it took a while to settle on him in that role. Moreover, as Ron Bergman analyzed it, "Williams juggled lineups looking for the right combinations. He had to find out what everyone could do and, what would help him even more later on, find out what they couldn't do."[22] Finley found several additional players to shore up gaps in the lineup throughout the year.

Outfielder Reggie Jackson, who had periodically asked to be traded away from the A's, quipped about the revolving door in Oakland: "I can stay right here in Oakland and meet all my idols." Finley acquired three players who would help the team during the final run to the pennant at the July 31 trading deadline: second baseman Mike Andrews and outfielders Vic Davalillo and Jesus Alou, the second of the Alou brothers to play for the A's. "Charlie will probably go over to the National League in September and get someone with 300–400 career homers," Jackson added.[23]

The most interesting midseason addition was Allan Lewis, a minor-league call-up. Finley had long been envious of the speedsters in Major League Baseball and had signed Lewis, nicknamed the "Panamanian Express," to bring some speed to the A's in 1967. He would periodically try to promote him to the big leagues, but Lewis lacked the baseball skills to do much more than steal bases. While his batting statistics in the minors were respectable, he never could hit when called up to the A's. Dick Williams quipped, "He's a .300 hitter, .150 left-handed and .150 right-handed."[24] Moreover, his inability to play any position—he was listed as an outfielder—was problematic. When a ball was hit in his direction, an adventure ensued. Many of the A's, especially captain Sal Bando, criticized Lewis as unworthy of a place on a major-league roster. Nonetheless, Finley loved the idea of speed and insisted on keeping Lewis there.

The regulars revolted on June 20, when Williams used Lewis to pitch-run for Deron Johnson against the Kansas City Royals. Later, in extra innings, with the score tied 4–4, Johnson's place in the order was up once again. This time he was not available, having been lifted for Lewis. Another pinch hitter went up, promptly struck out, and the A's lost the game. Bando and others exploded after the tough loss, criticizing Finley, Williams, and Lewis. "At that time, it was kind of new to us to carry a player who would not have made the team based on his baseball skills," Bando recalled. He could not understand why Finley insisted on "putting somebody on the club that, when other guys are competing who have more skills to hit and field, couldn't make the club." The presence of Lewis, who, everyone admitted, was a pleasant-enough chap but not a Major League Baseball player, was a sore point for the team the whole of 1973.[25]

Such antics as this from Finley continued to turn the A's daily existence into a soap opera. Dick Williams said that Finley was relentless in his daily involvement in team activities. "I got the idea he'd like to be everywhere at once," commented journalist Bob Bestor. "He thinks he's God, he wants to be omnipresent." More than this, as Wells Twombly concluded, "He seems to have a basic need for controversy." Kansas City sportswriter Joe McGuff added, "If you try to figure Finley out, you'll only succeed in confusing yourself . . . His capacity for turmoil is incredible. He thrives on it. He enjoys tough times so he can work his way out of them and give himself credit."[26]

Charlie Finley won a measure of pity in August 1973, when he experienced a heart attack that landed him in the hospital for nearly two weeks. On August 7, he collapsed and was rushed to the Passavant Pavilion of Northwestern University Hospital in Chicago, where he was in intensive care for several days. He remained in the hospital until August 20, when doctors sent him back to his farm in La Porte for a monthlong recuperation. His health problem removed Finley from his normal pattern of meddling in the details of the team, and during this time the A's dominated the league as never before. They went 20–7 in August; could it have been because they were left to themselves? It would be too much to make that case, especially when it was known that "he stole away for a couple of phone calls" every now and then. But Finley's absence allowed the team to carry on without worrying about his follies every day. Reporters, always looking for good copy, missed Finley enormously and even sent him a get-well card. "It's strange," Ron Bergman opined, "but you sort of miss him when he's not around."[27] Toward the end of the season, Finley made it to two A's games in Chicago, the most important of which was when the team clinched the division title on September 23, behind a 10–5 victory by Vida Blue, his 20th of the season. It was a test of Finley's health to attend the playoffs and World Series. He passed. But the response in the locker room after clinching the division was subdued. The media reported, "The players sat on their stools in the visitors' clubhouse drinking champagne, and looking like customers in a workingman's bar."[28] Perhaps the team's excitement was diminished, but certainly not the drive for excellence.

The A's played the Baltimore Orioles for the second time in two years for the privilege of ascending to the World Series, and again the series went a full five games. In the opening game, in Baltimore's Memorial Stadium on October 6, the Orioles pounded A's starter Vida Blue for a 6–0 win. The next day Catfish Hunter took the mound and beat the Orioles 6–3 with the aid of four home runs, two by Sal Bando and one each by Joe Rudi and Bert Campaneris. Returning to Oakland for game three, on October 9, the A's beat the Orioles 2–1 behind the pitching of Ken Holtzman and the power of Campaneris, who hit his second homer of the series. This gave the A's a 2–1 lead in the series, but the very next day the Orioles tied it with a 5–4 win to force a do-or-die fifth game. This time Hunter came out and pitched a five-hit shutout to beat the Orioles 3–0 to advance to the World Series.

For the second year in a row, the A's entered the fall classic as underdogs—this time to the New York Mets. (At any rate, this was the judgment of a lot of sports commentators with New York accents.) The Mets had risen to greatness in 1969 by winning an unlikely World Series over the Baltimore Orioles. Now they were back to do it again, behind the pitching of Tom Seaver, considered the best in baseball despite his 19–10 record.

At first Charlie Finley was more subdued at this World Series than he had been during the 1972 championship; he was still recovering from his heart attack, and this was his team's second time around. Dick Williams confirmed this perspective about being in the World Series for the second time: "Well, I knew I was going to leave. I was happy for the players—I was very happy for the players. But when you win your first one, and it never gets old winning them, but when you win your first one, that's the . . . big topper."[29]

Finley behaved himself in game one. The A's had won the first game of the series in Oakland, 2–1, behind a solid if unspectacular pitching performance by Ken Holtzman. He faced Mets starter Jon Matlack, 14–16 during the season, who held his own until the third inning, when the A's put up two runs after Holtzman doubled—his first hit of the season because of the institution of the designated hitter in the American League—and scored on a Bert Campaneris ground ball that rolled between the legs of Mets second baseman Felix Millan. Campaneris then stole second and scored when Joe Rudi singled. Those were the only runs the A's needed.

Charlie Finley (center) with the document approving his acquisition of majority control of the Kansas City Athletics, December 19, 1960. Flanking Finley are Judge Robert Dunne (left) and Finley's attorney, Thomas Keane. (© Corbis/Bettman Images)

Charlie Finley and his son David on the family farm in Indiana, July 1968. (© TIME & LIFE Pictures/Getty Images)

Charlie Finley and his family watching his team play from his private box at the Oakland–Alameda County Coliseum in 1968, the A's first season in Oakland. (© Ron Reisterer)

Reggie Jackson, Rick Monday, and Finley during the 1968 season. (© Ron Reisterer)

Is Rick Monday more amazed at being called out on strikes or by Finley's mechanical rabbit, which, installed soon after the A's arrived in Oakland, dispensed new baseballs as needed to the home plate umpire? (© Ron Reisterer)

Casey Stengel whispers in the ear of "Charlie O.," the mule and team mascot, as Finley looks on. (© Ron Reisterer)

The end to the contentious contract dispute between Finley and Vida Blue. The dissatisfaction of both men is evident as Commissioner Bowie Kuhn makes the announcement on May 2, 1972, with American League president Joe Cronin to his right. (© Corbis/Bettman Images)

Finley and manager Dick Williams during the 1972 season. (© Ron Reisterer)

...ign hanging from the second deck of the Oakland Coliseum during the 1972 World Series. (© Ron Reisterer)

...ver the passionate fan, Finley in the stands. (© Oakland Tribune)

Finley giving actor George C. Scott a mini-Oscar during the 1972 World Series. Earlier, Scott ha[
rejected the Oscar he had won for *Patton*. (© Ron Reisterer)

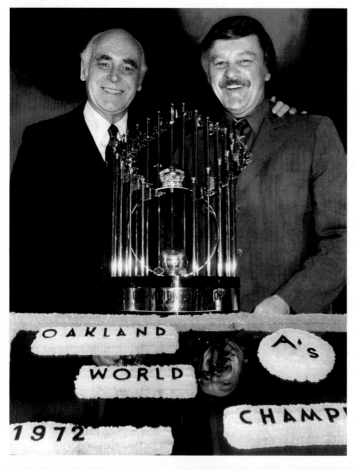

Finley and Dick Williams cel[
brating the A's first World Seri[
victory, October 1972.

(© Oakland Tribune)

he A's victory parade in downtown Oakland, led by 1972 World Series hero Gene Tenace, celebrating e first of three consecutive championships. (© Ron Reisterer)

ring training, 1973: Reggie Jackson, Finley, Gene Tenace, and Dick Williams admiring Tenace's World ries ring. (© Ron Reisterer)

Finley (front row, foreground) in his private box in 1974 with Stanley Burrell (far upper right, later to take the name MC Hammer) and his friends. Finley had hired Burrell as an office assistant, and then named him an honorary vice president. (© Ron Reisterer)

By 1976, two years after the third World Series victory, Finley had started to dismantle his team, and t Oakland fans had had enough. (© Ron Reisterer)

The Mets scored a run in the fourth, but that represented all the action in the game. Rollie Fingers and Darold Knowles relieved Holtzman and provided good support with Knowles earning the save. Knowles would go on to appear in all seven of these World Series games.

The next day the Mets took down the A's 10–7 in an ugly 12-inning match that featured Vida Blue versus Jerry Koosman, neither of whom pitched well. At the end of 9 innings the score was tied 6–6, and stayed that way until the 12th. It was then that Mike Andrews's arm suddenly stole the show. A defensive replacement at second base, Andrews committed two errors to lose the game. Charlie Finley went crazy, tried to toss Andrews off the team on a trumped-up injury, and the shenanigans that followed are the stuff of legend. The fact that Finley had recently suffered a heart attack and had a cardiologist by his side to keep him under control made no difference whatsoever. Glenn Schwarz recalled, "I think he came back as ornery as ever."[30] The *Sporting News* editorialized that Finley was just too much of a fan, which colored his judgment and ended up incurring the wrath of the baseball establishment: "Whatever version that you accept in the unfortunate Mike Andrews case during the World Series, Finley's part in it was that of a man who hates to lose. Oakland fans probably wished, too, that they could 'fire' the second baseman after his errors cost the A's the second game of the World Series."[31] It represented the first instance in which Finley's follies spilled out of the local arena onto the national stage for all to see.[32]

The Andrews affair was a low point for the A's, but it may well have been the single most important incident that pulled them together and enabled them to overpower the Mets. When the A's and Mets journeyed back to the Big Apple for game three of the World Series on October 16, the A's took the lead by defeating the Mets 3–2. The next day the Mets won 6–1, and in the fifth game of the series the Mets won again, 2–0. This set up the final games of the series in Oakland with the Mets leading three games to two. Those last two games, on October 20 and 21, were critical for the A's, and they took both to repeat as champions of the baseball world.[33]

As the A's celebrated in the infield, several thousand fans stormed the field. One rather large man also jumped to the field from the right-field seats. Tony Del Rio, all 290 pounds of him, was Reggie Jackson's personal bodyguard. Only a few people—including Finley and Williams—knew exactly why Del Rio quickly arrived at Reggie's side, along with a half-dozen police officers, to rush him to the dugout immediately after the final out. Late in the season Jackson had received several death threats from a racist known as the "Weatherman." The threats included the possibility of shooting Jackson during the World Series. Finley called the FBI into the situation, and Jackson had continuous protection, much of it provided by Del Rio. While Finley feuded often with his star player, he also went out of his way to assist Jackson and the authorities in protecting him. Finley's paternal side, which at times infuriated his players, kicked into effect during that crisis.[34] While most law enforcement officers believed the threat to be a hoax, they could not know for sure.

Jackson was the star of this World Series, the first installment of the "Mr. October" set of performances he would make famous during the rest of his career, and he nearly single-handedly destroyed the Mets during the final two games. He was a bit concerned about his performance early on, commenting, "I just hope we win this thing so I won't be the scapegoat."[35] While he took Most Valuable Player honors for the 1973 season, his first game in his first World Series was unspectacular. Then he turned it around. Beginning in game two, he went on a tear, with a .310 batting average, three doubles, a triple, a homer, and six RBIs, and was named series MVP as well.[36]

Finley went over to Jackson during the victory celebration and congratulated him for his great work, telling him he was the best player in baseball. Jackson's contributions were all the more impressive because of the death threat, which he then revealed to the media. He told the *New York Times*, "If I had got knocked off, I'd rather it be on the field."[37] "It happened just before the season ended," he added. "I got a call from Finley and for once he wasn't messing around. I went to his office and he showed me what Monte [Moore, A's broadcaster,] had received. The letter said that if I played in the playoff or the Series, it would be the last thing I ever did. This kook said he had a high-powered rifle with a long-range sight and he'd pop me from the stands. Made me feel just great." In the end, notwithstanding Jackson's considerable efforts, the A's beat the Mets in a hard-fought seven-game series because, as Melvin Durslag wrote, they were "better than the Mets, who milked their meager skills for all they were worth and made an outstanding show."[38]

As the A's celebrated their victory in the clubhouse at the Coliseum, Finley crooned, preened, and bragged like there was no tomorrow. Bowie Kuhn could hardly stand it. When it came time to award the A's the World Series trophy, he handed it over without fanfare and acknowledged only that the A's had earned it. "Charlie and Bowie were oil and water in ways that had little to do with specific issues or specific events; they were just oil and water," said Louis Hoynes, an attorney for Major League Baseball. "You could almost regard it as a religious matter—baseball was a religion to Bowie, and to Charlie it was just something to have fun with."[39]

When all was said and done, it had been a remarkable World Series, one in which the games on the field were much less significant than the drama of Finley and Kuhn. Art Spander labeled it "seven games of insanity":

> It was a World Series that should have been covered by Edgar Allan Poe instead of Red Smith, a bizarre, unnerving week of bruised egos and belligerent words and more than occasionally a grounder through the second baseman's legs
>
> ... It began with a second baseman getting fired and ended with a manager resigning. And practically everything could be laid at the feet of Charlie Finley
>
> ... But there's one thing you can say about Finley. He has stocked the A's with good players. And, despite all his egomania, more often than not they win. Only, with all the bizarre events of the World Series of '73, it almost didn't seem to matter what they did.[40]

Wells Twombly pronounced, "Never before and never again will there be a World Series to match the one just completed. It had just about everything, with the possible exception of good baseball."[41] Jimmy Piersall, the former major leaguer famous for having a nervous breakdown in public and who worked for Finley for a short time in the early 1970s, said of his team, "They get lost under all the crazy things he does ... Being around him made me feel well."[42]

Afterward, Bowie Kuhn reviewed the record of Charlie Finley in the 1973 World Series and decided to put him on notice. In an October 26, 1973, letter informing Finley of the $7,000 fine for his antics in the Andrews affair, Kuhn wrote, "I also determine that you personally shall be placed on probation . . . until further notice and warn you that further conduct not in the best interest of baseball may lead to disciplinary action against you as provided in Article 1 of the Major League Agreement." Kuhn added, and many of the A's and various observers agreed, that "the handling of this matter by the Oakland Club has had the unfortunate effect of unfairly embarrassing a player who has given many years of able service to professional baseball."[43] Kuhn had the power to discipline Finley, no doubt. Article 1 bestowed the commissioner with the authority to suspend anyone. This was an ominous threat. Finley fumed, threatened legal action, and ultimately lived with Kuhn's reprimand. Up to that time only three owners had been suspended: Fred Saigh of the Cardinals in 1953, when he was sent to prison for income tax evasion; Bill Cox of the Phillies in 1943, for betting on his team; and Horace S. Vogel of the Phillies in 1909, for charging others in the baseball family of fixing games. That was not good company, and Finley barely avoided joining this crowd—which, a few years later, would include George Steinbrenner on two separate occasions for two separate violations.

Then there was the lawsuit that Mike Andrews filed against Finley after the World Series. Released by Finley a couple of weeks after the Series ended, Andrews had difficulty catching on with another team. He believed it was because Finley had so vilified him. "Certainly this whole incident has something to do with how I was perceived by everybody, even though I did have the throwing problem. It was pretty much, 'We're not going to touch him,'" Andrews said. "I had an attorney who had been kind of my friend and agent, and he said, 'Well, we've got to do something about this because you should be getting invited to spring training.' But we settled it, and it was over with."[44] The amount asked for in the lawsuit was $2.5 million, and while the terms of the settlement have not been disclosed, it is a reasonable bet that Finley paid a substantial amount for his shenanigans during the 1973 World Series.[45]

Finley threatened legal action against Kuhn for the commissioner's actions and not-so-veiled threat of suspension. He asserted that the commissioner did not have the authority to suspend him and declared that it was his word against that of a ballplayer, saying that if Kuhn was "going to ingratiate himself with the pallplayers [sic] at my expense, he's badly mistaken." He added indignantly, "I don't know what he means (by) probation, let him explain it in court." As it turned out, Finley quietly dropped the lawsuit and toed the mark enough to avoid being suspended.[46]

During the fall of 1973, Finley was involved in a few other arguments. First, he got into a fight with Dick Williams over the manager's departure and tried to extract money and players from the Yankees in return for letting Williams out of the last two years of his contract. He eventually acceded to Williams's desire to leave the A's but refused to let him manage the Yankees. Finley signed Alvin Dark for a second stint as A's manager.[47] As repeat championship winners, the players believed they deserved serious raises, and they were right. Their recompense did not match what comparable players received from other owners in that era before free agency. Some of the sportswriters delighted in what they knew would be a lively off-season of jousting matches over salary. Reggie Jackson was the first out of the box. He demanded $150,000 for the 1974 season, considerably more than the $70,000 reported for him in 1973, but he had also won MVP honors for both the American League and the World Series. No doubt he deserved a reward. "What Jackson actually has in mind is asking his business partner and agent to start negotiations at $150,000," reported Wells Twombly.

> If Finley gags, falls down on the carpet and pretends that something dastardly has happened, the bid will probably be lowered to $140,000. It is common knowledge that Jackson will not go under $125,000, no matter how loudly Charlie whimpers. This should be an especially traumatic winter for the last feudal lord. See Charlie sitting in his office. Here comes Reggie with the following trinkets: (1) Most valuable player in the World Series; (2) Most valuable player in the American League by unanimous vote; and (3) player of the year in the American League in *The Sporting News'* poll.

After Jackson, Catfish Hunter (who wanted at least $100,000), Sal Bando, Rollie Fingers, Bert Campaneris, and others would also make their cases. Twombly was positively delighted by the prospect. "Let's have some heroic music, professor, something a man can march to while he's battling Charlie Finley for more money," he wrote. "Sic'em Reggie."[48]

A's players acquired a powerful new weapon in 1973 that they used effectively against Finley when it came time to negotiate salaries. As a result of the 1972 strike, the new MLB collective bargaining agreement provided for a salary arbitration process in which any player with a minimum of two years of major-league service who failed to come to terms with his team could ask for a three-person review board, with one owner representative, one union representative, and an independent arbitrator to assess the offer and counteroffer. Each side could argue their respective positions, and the review board could rule in favor of either the owner's offer or the player's counteroffer; the board did not have the authority to split the difference. The owner and player could reach a compromise agreement up to the point of the arbitration panel's ruling, but once the panel ruled, it was a binding decision for both parties not subject to any changes. The salary arbitration process began following the 1973 season for the 1974 contract year.

The players quickly realized the power of this process for resolving salary disputes with owners. The owners had acquiesced to this as appeasement to prevent the players' union, at least temporarily, from making further attacks on the reserve clause, which bound players to a team for life. Arbitration put the players on a more even footing with the owners when negotiating salaries. "The players now have a dignified status with the clubs," said union leader Marvin Miller. "The essential dignity of equals sitting down together just can't be overemphasized."[49] Miller viewed it as the first step toward his ultimate goal: a new system that allowed for player free agency.

Most important, the arbitration rule implemented in 1973 ensured, in the words of MLB baseball attorney Louis Hoynes, "some mechanism so that players would be paid comparably for their performance regardless of what team they played for. It was a compelling argument, and in those days we were trying very hard to find things that would satisfy the union's demands without having to get into free agency." Hoynes specifically said

Finley was viewed as a problem by the other owners because of how he underpaid his players: "He was regarded as a guy that squeezed the players unreasonably."[50]

Finley recognized immediately that arbitration would do more than anything else to boost players' salaries. First, there was the psychological issue: The owners could not lowball their offers the way they were used to doing and then wait as the players sweated as the clock ticked. Finley was notorious for starting exceedingly low, then going up slightly and browbeating a player into signing. Now that tactic was less effective, since outrageously meager final offers from owners could be overturned by the arbitration panel. Second, to avoid going into the formal arbitration process, owners were now more willing than ever to pull out all stops to settle a contract dispute on a timely basis. They no longer had the clock on their side, as had been the case previously, when players who held out suffered economically. Arbitration kept Finley from exerting the control over his players that he previously had enjoyed. Holding out for more money was the only real tool players had in previous salary negotiations—and both Reggie Jackson and Vida Blue had engineered two famous holdouts against Finley.

Finley was naturally a vocal critic of the new policy. He said at the time, "We'll be the nation's biggest assholes if we do this. You can't win . . . You'll have a system that drives up the average salary every year."[51] Son Martin Finley recalled that arbitration made his father crazy. "Of course free agency was the result of arbitration," he said, "but it was arbitration that really got my dad upset, because here was somebody telling my dad how much he has to pay the player." When it came to free agency, Martin Finley noted, it meant that the player would leave town and would no longer have to be dealt with. But with arbitration, if Finley lost, as would happen many times in the 1970s, the arbitrators would tell him, " 'Finley, he stays with the A's, and you have to pay him what he wants.' "[52]

A's players availed themselves fully of the arbitration process after the 1973 season. In that first year of salary arbitration in MLB, 29 cases were heard, of which the owners won 16 and the players won 13. Nine of those cases were by members of the Oakland A's, who argued that they were underpaid. Indeed, 18 of the A's players filed for arbitration—the most of any team—but half of them settled their cases before they came before the panel. Sal Bando, Rollie Fingers, Ken Holtzman, Ted Kubiak, Joe Rudi, Reggie Jackson, Gene Tenace, Darold Knowles, and utility infielder Jack Heidemann all went through the arbitration process. All were represented by attorneys or agents, and union head Marvin Miller also served as a counsel during the hearings for each player. Emerging sports agent Jerry Kapstein represented Holtzman, Fingers, and Knowles. Finley and his lieutenant John Claiborne represented the A's during the hearings. The arbiters agreed with the A's players five times, but Finley did manage to win four cases.

During the arbitration hearings, Finley was, as one might imagine, part theatrical actor, part super salesman, and part inquisitor. He often spoke for himself and opened the hearing by presenting the basic case for the A's before turning over the detail work to John Claiborne. Both sides used statistical studies to bolster their positions, and as Claiborne recalled, "we, of course, got our butts whipped the first two years ... I think we were something like four and seven." Part of that was because the players deserved the money, and partly it was due to the naïveté of those involved in the process. Claiborne said that he and agent Jerry Kapstein became friends in spite of their adversarial places in this arbitration process. They came to "respect each other," Claiborne said. "I respected him for what he was doing. I didn't like it, but I respected him ... the way he was doing it. But Jerry was thorough, very prepared but superficial in the fact that he didn't have baseball knowledge."[53]

Marvin Miller recalled that Finley hurt his case by involving himself too much in the process. "I really don't know why he undertook to represent the club in that proceeding instead of retaining somebody who understood what salary arbitration might be like," Miller said. "He was terribly inept. He was entertaining ... The first day I remember it was like a fairly good interpretation of Clarence Darrow. He marched up and down the room. He never sat down while he was talking. He used all kinds of flamboyant gestures and deep sarcasm in his tone and words and was terribly inconsistent ... contradicted himself one time after another." Miller concluded, "In a way, he was funny. You know, arbitrators are accustomed to not showing their reactions. They've got good poker faces, most of them, but it was hard not to break up."[54]

1974 A'S ARBITRATION HEARING RESULTS

A's Player	1973 Salary	1974 Player Request	1974 Finley Offer	Arbitration Award
Sal Bando	60,000	100,000	75,000	100,000
Rollie Fingers	48,000	65,000	55,000	65,000
Jack Heidemann	15,750	15,750	12,600	12,600
Ken Holtzman	66,500	93,000	80,000	93,000
Reggie Jackson	75,000	135,000	100,000	135,000
Darold Knowles	50,000	59,000	55,000	59,000
Ted Kubiak	30,000	42,500	37,000	37,000
Joe Rudi	50,000	67,500	55,000	55,000
Gene Tenace	33,000	52,500	45,000	45,000

As many expected, Finley lost the arbitration with superstar Reggie Jackson, who had already come down from his $150,000 demand to $135,000, but not as far as Finley's counteroffer. He won his arbitration for $135,000. Finley said he hated this experience, making this heartwarming case: "I hate the fact I have to sit across the table from a player I admire and point out his shortcomings. It can ruin your future relationship with the player." Did anyone believe that he had anything approaching a future relationship with any of his A's after all of his high jinks and shenanigans from the 1973 World Series? More likely he hated being told what to do, and by a bunch of arbiters no less, by bureaucrats.[55]

Finley won his hearing with left fielder and Gold Glove All-Star Joe Rudi. After a superb 1972 season (he was second in American League MVP balloting), Rudi struggled at times during the 1973 season because of illness and injury, but he provided several clutch hits in the 1973 postseason. It was a long process that brought Rudi to arbitration, and he wanted to reach an amicable arrangement, but Finley proved belligerent. As Rudi remembered:

> [In] '73 I didn't quite have as good a season as I had in '72, but we won the World Series. Overall I had a very good year, and so he sends down the contracts, and he said, "No raise—same salary."

You know, we won the World Series; I played decent and I hit .300 the year before. And so one afternoon—we were living in Danville, outside of Oakland—and we were just getting ready to set the table . . . I pick up the phone, and Charlie starts swearing at me. He didn't say "hi"; he didn't say "boo." "What the hell, you ungrateful son of a bitch! What are you doing sending your contract back? I thought you'd be the first one to sign your contract and be happy I didn't cut you." He had this whole canned thing built up, and he went on this tirade for a couple of minutes. And normally I'm pretty laid back, but for whatever reason, I got pissed off, and I started screaming back at him, "How the hell can you send me no raise when I won the World Series twice for you?" And he always talked about all this "not being able to repeat" and all, you know? So I started screaming back at him, and my wife is standing there looking at me like, "What the hell is going on?" And the next breath, "Hi, Joe. How are you doing? How's the family? How's Sharon? How's Mike and Scott?" He knew the wife's name and the kids' names, so he had all this stuff right in front of him, so he opened with this barrage, trying to buffalo me into signing. And as soon as I got mad and yelled back at him— boom! He's flipped the switch, and now he's Mr. Nice Guy! He starts talking, going on for five minutes about how much he loved me and on and on and on and on.[56]

Even so, negotiations were difficult. It was almost as if Finley was daring his players to take him to arbitration. One could conclude that this experience validated Finley's maverick strategy. But his successes were only occasional.

The first pitcher to face Finley and the panel was lefty starter Ken Holtzman, who won 21 games in 1973 season, made the All-Star team, and won two key games in the World Series. Holtzman sought $93,000 for 1974, but Finley offered only $80,000. "One of the first things Mr. Finley said when he got up to talk was 'Kenny, don't take it personally,' and he eventually said that I wasn't as good as my record showed," Holtzman recalled. "But, it didn't bother me, because when he said that, Jerry Kapstein said, 'Well, we're going to say things here, Mr. Finley, that you might not like, and don't take it personally.'"

Holtzman won the hearing and was paid $93,000 in 1974. All three of Kapstein's clients won against Finley in 1974—a fact not lost on the rest of the A's players, many of whom later hired him as their agent. Next up came A's All-Star third baseman and team captain Sal Bando. Bando sought $100,000 for 1974, but Finley offered only $75,000. Bando said, "After listening to Holtzman, I thought there might be a lot of mudslinging going on. But Charlie started off by praising me to the arbitrator, then tried to show why I wasn't worth a hundred grand. It was really very pleasant, and I think Charlie thought he could win just by his salesmanship, not facts."[57] Bando won and became a "hundred grand" player.

Finley might have won more hearings had he utilized more quantitative data to argue his case, rather than his own qualitative opinions. In the end, Finley ended up paying around $87,000 in additional salary in 1974 as a result of arbitration. Despite his efforts to hold the line on salaries, the A's became one of the best-paid teams in baseball. For example, the 1967 A's expended $443,000 in salaries for players, coaches, and staff. By 1974, after implementation of the players association's arbitration process, Finley paid more than $425,000 to four of his All-Stars—Jackson, Bando, Hunter, and Holtzman—with three of his stars earning at least $100,000.[58]

Marvin Miller recalled the most humorous event of the proceedings with two pitchers, Holtzman and Fingers. "Particularly, I remember on two successive days," he said, "Finley making a presentation that Ken Holtzman, a fine starting pitcher, was not really as good as his numbers because his numbers were dependent on the great relief pitching of Rollie Fingers. And the next day, when Fingers's case was up, he proceeded to say the exact opposite to the same arbitrator . . . that Fingers's great relief statistics were really dependent upon the fine starting pitchers he had."[59]

Some chose not to go to arbitration. Vida Blue was one of the A's who refrained. He said it was because he just didn't want to put himself through the turmoil. Also, he knew that he would have to sit there while his faults were discussed and that he would not have been able to remain quiet. Blue also knew he possessed a very foul mouth. "I just knew had I gone to arbitration," he said, "I was going to say 'motherfuck' the arbitrator. I was going to 'motherfuck' Finley, his attorney—I might have 'motherfucked' my attorney. I was going to 'motherfuck' myself out of baseball."[60]

As all this took place, Finley's poor health forced him to slow down. A's farm director John Claiborne recalled that the heart attack made Finley realize that he simply couldn't do whatever he wanted any longer. Claiborne said Finley had "to slow his pace down, and the pace never really came back."[61] He also quit smoking, having previously been a heavy smoker, and tried to control his diet. This lasted for only a short time, however, before he was back to his old ways.

Sal Bando recalled that the heart attack really changed Finley, not just in how much he could do but also in how he treated others. "He just didn't seem like the same person," Bando said. "He went from being so generous after the first World Series to as cheap as you can get after the second one." Bando noted with disdain how Finley "could get very demeaning to people. What he liked to do, and I know he did it with people like me, when we were in Chicago, he would call me into his office on Lake Michigan, and then he would call someone and put them on the speakerphone, and then he would just crucify them. And you had to sit there and listen to him demean the people."[62]

No question, Finley entered the winter of 1973–1974 in a much nastier frame of mind than after the first A's championship season. He approached life with more resentment, sourness, and sharpness toward everyone. Certainly this was partly because of his health, but also because his marriage broke up and he had a desperate fight over assets with Shirley that took six years to work out. Some A's players were aware of this strife, but stayed as clear of it as possible and refuse to talk about it in detail to this day.

There had been serious warning signs of impending disaster in Finley's personal life for some time, and they especially manifested themselves beginning in the fall of 1973. After spending weeks in the hospital after his heart attack in August 1973, he came home to the farm in La Porte to recuperate. Shirley stayed with him for a time but then took an extended trip. He had caregivers, so she took the opportunity to not be where Charlie was. Was she seeking to escape him and his controlling presence? David Finley certainly wished he could have also escaped him. "That was the longest month I ever had in my life," he recalled.[63] During this time, Finley apparently took out his anger at Shirley by burning some antiques she had stored in one of the outbuildings at the farm—a pattern of behavior that he had engaged in since burning the stadium lease and the bus in Kansas City more than a decade earlier, not to mention the caboose on the farm.

While few witnesses were willing to talk about it, except as unnamed sources, several people suggest that the difficulties of the marriage proved irreconcilable for a number of reasons. There had been plenty of disagreements between Charlie and Shirley Finley prior to their divorce. Often they seem to have been fueled by liquor. Finley was known to sometimes drink a lot, and it was not usually beer or wine but Wild Turkey whiskey. He was known to down a fifth without much compunction.[64] Some people around Finley believed he had a drinking problem; others did not. Chuck Dobson, who played for Finley's A's during those championship years and had his own challenges overcoming alcohol abuse, thought that Major League Baseball was something of a "haven for alcoholics" and that it was tolerated, even encouraged; the coaches "liked the players to go out after the game and drink together because the belief was that 'the team that drank together, won together.'" Dobson said that he knew Finley would go into the "coaches' office, and he'd be drinking with the manager after the games, and it wasn't beer. It was part of the deal. Yeah, I think alcohol was involved in a lot of his decisions and a lot of his tirades and things."[65]

Then there were the rumors of extramarital affairs over the years. Ron Mihelic said he had knowledge of only one such incident but had heard of many others. According to one rumor, Finley and his cousin Carl had once wound up at a woman's apartment, drinking and carrying on. When the woman's husband came home, the two Finleys threw him out the window. It is unclear whether this episode really transpired, but if it did, no charges were filed.[66]

Others have repeated stories that are second- and even thirdhand. He did love to flirt with women. Of course, they might have been, and probably most of the time were, innocent flirtations. Fern Schultz of La Porte told how Finley in his later years "liked to mingle with the women, and they enjoyed it. That was flattering to them to have Charlie pay attention to them. But I don't think any of them would ever have considered dating him, because most of them knew the baggage he carried, and they were married ladies, not interested in that kind of thing. But you could tell that he was a charmer when he wanted to be."[67] David Finley said that his father "had female friends my whole life," adding that after his divorce he "never really wanted a heavy relationship. He would date someone for an extended period of time, but he was not the 'I'm going to get married' type."[68] He often gave out little presents to women that he wanted to impress.

Mike Storen, commissioner of the American Basketball Association in the 1970s, when Finley's Memphis Tams played, related a story of visiting Finley in the hospital when he required open heart surgery later in the 1970s:

> I remember going to the hospital to visit him, and he was divorced at that time. And I got on an elevator in the hospital, and this big, robust black nurse had a zirconia diamond ring. And Charlie, for whatever reason, carried around a pocketful of those, and one of Charlie's routines, like with this nurse, was, "You're the most wonderful nurse in the world. I ought to marry you, and I'm going to give you a diamond ring as a first step to our getting married." And he'd give them to people, girls of course. So I got on the elevator and saw this nurse with this ring on, and I said, "Tell me how Charlie Finley is doing?" And she said, "Well, he's doing just fine." And, of course, [she] couldn't figure out how I knew she was one of the nurses taking care of Charlie Finley.[69]

Was this all innocent fun or evidence of infidelity? Could this behavior, innocent or not, have contributed to Charlie and Shirley Finley's divorce?

As the A's planned for the 1974 season, a series of arguments in La Porte led Shirley Finley to file for divorce. Charlie did not contest it, but he did fight over the settlement every step of the way. Filed in the La Porte Superior Court 2 on March 15, 1974, the petition cited an irretrievable breakdown of the marriage as grounds for divorce. She asked for $1,250 per week in child support, $1,900 per week in other support, and continuation of her and the children's insurance, automobiles, and the like. This was granted by the court after a dramatic two-day hearing on May 15 and 16, 1974, in which both parties were present with their lawyers. Shirley also obtained a provisional restraining order barring Charlie from the farm, which she and their minor children continued to occupy.[70]

Finley created sparks by offering Shirley a mere $100 per week to pay her bills, saying that it was more than enough for her and their family—besides, he said, he could afford nothing more. Judge Alfred J. Pivarnik, presiding over the court, questioned this assertion and demanded records. Charlie Finley fought every effort to comply and responded through his attorney in July 1974 that Shirley Finley had adequate resources to sustain herself, including a bank account of more than $8,000. He claimed that he had lost more than $1 million in income and did not have the resources to pay her the money awarded in the provisional order. This prompted the attorneys for Shirley to ask the court for an order that Charlie turn over copies of financial records, tax statements, audit reports, sale documents, and other related documents.[71] Charlie lost at every turn.[72]

His failure to comply with the rulings of the court in producing documentary records proved frustrating for Shirley Finley and her attorneys, to say the least. "They didn't produce the necessary discovery," said Leon R. Kaminski, one of the lawyers on the case. "We had no alternative than to cite him for contempt."[73] They filed such a request on June 14, 1974, and a series of legal maneuverings followed, including a request for a change of venue. In time the judge ruled that Finley had to produce the requested records. He delayed for six more years. As all of this took place, Finley decided to divest himself of his hockey and basketball teams. He had purchased the Seals of the National Hockey League in 1970, but he had never been happy with the team or anything about it. It lost money, it took up too much time of his time, and he knew nothing about hockey. It is surprising that he purchased it in the first place. He developed over time similar misgivings about the Memphis Tams of the ABA, but at least he understood something about basketball. Finley said he was selling these teams on the advice of his doctors, who told him after his heart attack that he was stretched too thin and needed to reduce his workload. The National Hockey League had tried to acquire the California Golden Seals from Finley for a year before finally buying back the team for $6.585 million in January 1974 and then selling it to another owner in California.[74] He hung on to the Memphis Tams a bit longer, but by February 1974 was actively seeking to offload the franchise. He said that he "didn't have time to run 'em all. Particularly when my heart is in baseball."[75] In June 1974, he succeeded in giving the Tams back to the American Basketball Association, which paid $1.1 million to buy him out.[76] Finley considered selling the A's as well, offering to let the franchise go for $15 million, which would have been a huge windfall from his original purchase price.[77]

He could use the money, no doubt, and that need for cash perhaps led him to really tick off his players when, after they won the 1973 World Series, he didn't repeat, much less outdo, as he had promised, the 1972 championship rings. Sportswriter Glenn Schwarz recalled that "the first one, I think, had a diamond in it, and I don't recall exactly the setting for the second, but in spring training of 1974, when the World Series rings arrived, the players went crazy, because they were cheap, with a cheap green stone, and they were calling them the '7-Up rings' and 'the un-Cola rings.' "[78]

Second baseman Mike Andrews thinks that there was more to it than Finley's divorce and the need for cash. "So with everything that happened to me," Andrews said, "he ended up taking away all the diamonds—and the way the players reacted and the manager quitting. He took all of the diamonds off of these rings and presented them at spring training the next year with just this big green piece of glass." Andrews made the best of this. He said he told his sons, "Hang on to that. That could be really valuable someday, because it's probably the only championship ring in any major sport in this country that doesn't have a diamond."[79] This may have led to one of Finley's increasingly common activities, flirting with women everywhere he went. His attorney Bill Myers recalled that "on the airlines, he always carried a flock of artificial diamond rings and was always engaged to a stewardess on that flight."[80]

There were a lot of other things that Finley did that were beyond the norm, even his norm, to save money on the team. When Reggie Jackson signed a deal with Puma to wear its cleats on the field, Finley went crazy because he had already negotiated a deal with Adidas to clad the entire team in its white shoes, and his superstar's separate deal could abrogate it. He insisted that Jackson relent and wear only Adidas on the field. He also announced that he would no longer pay for postage when the players responded to fan mail. In numerous other little ways, he cut back here and there to save a few dollars. At the time, most of those with the A's thought he was just ratcheting up his normal cheapness; they did not realize how tight his finances truly were.

With very nearly the same team as in 1973, the A's did not dominate their division in quite the same way. They played .500 ball in April and only a little better in May, ending the month with 27–21 record. The new A's manager, Alvin Dark, brought a far different approach to dealing with his players than had the hard-driving, combative, and sometimes profane Dick Williams. A born-again Christian, Dark was anything but profane, and while Dark worked the team hard, he was unwilling to dress them down in the same way Williams had when they failed to execute on the field. But Dark was likable, and he had a talented group of veterans, some of whom were All-Stars and three of whom would become Hall of Famers. Their excellence on the field soon became apparent. Through it all, Dark remained tactful, respectful, and sensitive to his players. This seemed to work; the A's rose to their natural place at the top of the AL West in mid-summer and remained there throughout the rest of the season.

During the 1974 season, Finley was less engaged with the team than he had been since purchasing it in 1960. He was preoccupied elsewhere as never before, though he still popped up periodically to annoy the players. As an example, Finley angered some veterans on the team when he insisted that Dark include on the active roster a young speedster named Herb Washington, who had not played baseball since high school, to replace Allan Lewis as the designated base stealer, even bestowing on Washington the nickname "Hurricane." Finley then hired Dodgers great Maury Wills to coach Washington on how to run the bases. Gene Tenace spoke for the other members of the team when he called it a joke that would "cost somebody who should be in the major leagues a job."[81] Dick Green thought Washington such a one-dimensional player that he told him, "If you break a leg, we'll have to shoot you."[82] As A's captain Sal Bando sarcastically put it, "That Charlie Finley, what an innovator."[83]

The A's in 1974 did not require Finley to instigate controversy in the clubhouse; their poor start and naturally competitive nature ensured plenty of turmoil. It wasn't quite the New York Yankees "Bronx Zoo" of the latter 1970s, but there were constant disagreements. The most serious, perhaps, was the fight between Bill North and Reggie Jackson over a woman on June 5, 1974, which prompted Finley to call a team meeting and berate the players. Darold Knowles recalled that this fight was "one of the better ones I ever saw." Knowles said that he had been playing bridge with Ken Holtzman, Dick Green, and Rollie Fingers when they heard shouting and saw punches. Vida Blue and Ray Fosse raced to pull North and Jackson apart, yelling for others to help out. Holtzman said he couldn't because "I gotta two-club bid." The laughter broke the tension, and both men returned to opposite parts of the clubhouse. Jackson sat out that night's game because of an injury sustained during the fight; Fosse hurt his neck and was out for most of the rest of the season, and when he returned, his play was never the same.[84]

In the end they won 90 games, lost 72 games, and finished first in the American League West, 5.5 games ahead of the Texas Rangers. After drawing slightly better than 1 million attendees in 1973, the A's attracted only 845,693 in 1974. That decrease in attendance seems to be the result of Finley's budget cuts. He failed to negotiate a television contract for the 1974 season, eventually working one out late in the spring for only a few games. He curtailed promotions and discounts for season ticket holders, driving more people away from the games. A Mad-at-Finley Club sprang up in Oakland to help show him the door.[85]

For the fourth time in four years, the A's played the Baltimore Orioles for the American League championship. Again, most people considered the Orioles the better team, even though the A's had beaten them in the playoffs the past two years. The A's made short work of the Orioles, losing the first game in the series but then winning three straight to advance to the World Series. This year the National League's standard bearer was the Los Angeles Dodgers, a team that dominated its division with a 102–60 season record and blew past the Pittsburgh Pirates in the playoffs three games to one. The Cincinnati Reds finished four games behind at 98–64, still better than any team in the American League. Since the Reds were the "Big Red Machine," the Dodgers liked to call themselves the "Little Blue Bicycle," but they were so much more. They boasted an infield of Steve Garvey at first, Davy Lopes at second, Bill Russell at shortstop, and Ron Cey at third. This infield had been playing together since 1973 and would do so until 1981. They set the record for the longest-serving infield in baseball history, and during that run, they went to four World Series, losing each time until 1981 when they beat the Yankees in a dramatic six-game series.

A lot of baseball experts expected the Dodgers to beat the A's. For one, the A's had been there twice before; they were not the same hungry team as in earlier years. They also did not get the same dominant pitching from their top three starters. Catfish Hunter finished at 25–12, but Ken Holtzman declined to 19–17, and Vida Blue to 17–15. Their winning percentages were certainly not what they had been previously. The everyday players were again led by Reggie Jackson, whose .289 average, 29 home runs, and 93 RBIs put him among the league leaders. Joe Rudi contributed with a .293 average, 22 home runs, and 99 RBIs. Sal Bando's batting average dipped to .243, but he also hit 22 homers, and drove in 103 runs, the only player on the team to crack the hundred-RBI mark. Gene Tenace continued to hit for power, 26 homers, but batted only .211 while driving in 73 runs. Of course, the steady Bert Campaneris batted .290 while providing speed at the top of the lineup. Designated-base-stealer Herb "Hurricane" Washington did not contribute much to the offense.

The 1974 World Series was never really all that close, with the A's dominating the Dodgers. The A's beat them 3–2 in game one at Dodger Stadium on October 12, with Jackson hitting a solo home run in the top of the second to put the A's in the lead—a lead they never relinquished. The next day the Dodgers won their only game in the series, 3–2, before traveling to Oakland for game three on October 15. The A's then took three straight from the Dodgers—3–2 on the strength of Hunter's seven-hit start, 5–2 with Holtzman hitting a home run to help his own cause, and 3–2 in the final game of the season, with Blue Moon Odom getting the win after relieving Vida Blue and giving way to Fingers with the save.

Just like that, the A's were the champions of the baseball world once again, the only three-peat winners other than the Yankees. As in past years, Finley was everywhere taking bows for the victory. But it was not the same sweet victory that the first had been. The years that followed would be increasingly difficult for him, personally and professionally.

Chapter Eight

Catfish Swims Away

The unraveling of baseball's most storied dynasty since the New York Yankees of the 1950s and 1960s began with a simple dispute between A's star pitcher Catfish Hunter and owner Charlie Finley over $50,000 of deferred salary compensation. The dispute could have been resolved simply, but it was not, thanks to a confluence of events, oversights, misinterpretations, arrogance, and miserly behavior by both A's owner Charlie Finley and the leadership of Major League Baseball. The outcome of this dispute fundamentally reshaped MLB employer-player relations. It opened the door for the eventual destruction of the reserve clause, the advent of player free agency, and the possibility of million-dollar salaries. All this ultimately proved more profitable than ever before for both players and owners. The losers were the fans, who had to pay rising ticket prices to see their favorite teams. It also ushered out many old-school owners with limited financial capacity, and Charlie Finley was one of them.

The Finley-Hunter contract dispute started with their annual contract negotiations in January 1974. Catfish Hunter had known Charlie Finley for nearly 10 years by this time, and Hunter always had a special place in Finley's heart and vice versa. Finley hadn't believed the scouts who'd said that Hunter would never be a major-league pitcher, and he had signed him against the conventional wisdom of MLB brains. Deep down, both men respected each other, and despite their bumpy relationship, as evidenced by the farm-loan fiasco in 1970, they remained on fairly good terms. This did not mean, however, that Hunter either completely trusted or even liked Finley. "Mr. Finley often does go out of his way to be nice to ballplayers. He's been nice to a lot of us. He's helped us make some good investments and he's made us loans. He paid some of us big bonuses to sign, but he is a tough man at contract time," Hunter admitted. "And I've seen him mistreat a lot of players. And managers. And other employees. He'll do a good thing and then spoil it by doing a bad thing."[1]

Hunter met with Finley in January 1974 to negotiate his own contract with the tightfisted owner. They agreed to a two-year contract that would pay Catfish $100,000 per year. It seemed a fair contract to Hunter. He probably could have squeezed Finley for slightly more money if he had used an agent, but then again, Finley despised player agents and might have dug in his heels at the prospect of a contract battle with Hunter. While many of his teammates headed to salary arbitration, Hunter was leery. He felt it was better to personally negotiate with Finley, as he had always done.

After reaching an agreement on money, Hunter asked Finley about inserting a deferred-compensation provision into the contract. Finley reacted amiably by stating this would be no problem and asking how much salary was to be deferred. Hunter said he would need to get the precise amount from his tax attorney in North Carolina, J. Carlton Cherry. Finley agreed; it seemed the issue was settled.

By late January, Cherry and Finley were exchanging letters and phone calls as they worked out Hunter's deferred-compensation provision to the special covenant section of Hunter's contract. It appeared to be a routine contract. Finley, always looking to save money in attorney fees and time, asked Cherry to draft the language covering the deferral. In a February 15 letter to Cherry, Finley said the Oakland club "will be very happy to cooperate in any manner possible to defer any amount of Mr. Hunter's compensation... After you have decided as to how much these payments should be made and who they should be made to, kindly advise us and we will cooperate accordingly."

Cherry sent Finley his proposed language for the special covenant to the contract. It stated, "The club will pay to any person, form or corporation designated by Mr. Hunter, the sum of $50,000 per year, for the duration of this contract to be deferred compensation, same to be paid at any time requested by Mr. Hunter." Finley quickly responded on February 24 to the proposed contract and wanted the portion of the special covenant that stated that the deferred compensation be delivered "at any time requested by Mr. Hunter" to be changed to "during the season as earned."[2] Finley then signed the contract and returned it to Hunter. Nothing seemed amiss.

During the 1974 season, Hunter tried on two occasions to provide Finley with documentation and an application for a 10-year insurance annuity contract with Jefferson Standard Life Insurance Company as the designated third party for Hunter's deferred salary. Finley claimed each time that the documentation was never forwarded to him. On August 1, Hunter personally gave Finley the deferment documentation in Finley's Chicago hotel room.

Whether Finley had ever contacted his attorneys or tax advisers about Hunter's deferred annuity is unknown. But soon after receiving the documentation from Hunter, Finley balked at purchasing the insurance annuity. He claimed that early August was the first time he realized that the deferral was to be in the form of an insurance annuity to be purchased and held by the A's ball club on Hunter's behalf. Finley claimed that under such an arrangement, he could not write off the $50,000 as a business deduction, until the time the actual annuity was disbursed.

As the month of September passed, with A's fighting for the Western Division crown, Finley and Cherry exchanged progressively contentious phone calls and letters about the salary-deferral issue. Finley held fast that he would not set a precedent by purchasing the annuity for Hunter and insisted that his understanding of the contract was similar to a deferred-payment contract he entered into with Reggie Jackson in 1973, in which a portion of Jackson's salary was deferred and paid directly to Jackson over a two-year period. Finley reportedly told Cherry on September 15 that he had no plans to purchase the annuity and had thrown the paperwork away.

Sensing the Hunter contract might bubble up to be a rather contentious issue that could affect the ongoing management-labor issues with the Major League Baseball Players Association, league commissioner Bowie Kuhn dispatched two attorneys, Barry Rona and Louis Hoynes, to Chicago to figure out the facts of the brewing controversy with Charlie Finley. Finley was not an organized person, especially when it came to the management of the A's. Papers, bills, receipts, and contracts littered his office. But the two attorneys plunged into the stacks of paper, and with much cajoling, began piecing together a paper trail concerning Hunter's contract.

Hoynes and Rona slowly began to understand what had actually happened. Hoynes said, "He made that sort of deal with Catfish Hunter believing that he had done the same thing he had done with several other players and other clubs had done with some players. It wasn't commonplace, but it wasn't extremely uncommon either. He [Finley] agreed in a little side agreement attached to the contract that he would pay the deferred amount as directed by Hunter." Ultimately, Finley and Cherry disagreed not on whether Finley owed Hunter the $50,000, but on the tax issues involved in the deferred-payment annuity Cherry wanted Finley to purchase. Finley believed that if he purchased the annuity for Hunter, it would not be tax-deferred, because its purchase was directed by Hunter, who would ultimately own the annuity. Further, the complex deal presented tax liabilities, as Finley would not be able to write the deferred salary off as an expense.[3]

Finley thought that it would cleaner and easier for him just to provide the money to Cherry and Hunter and allow them to purchase the annuity. But Cherry and Hunter wanted Finley to purchase the annuity as stated in the contract.

On September 16, Cherry wrote Finley a letter outlining his version of events over the past nine months and providing him with another annuity application form. Cherry advised Finley that failure to purchase the annuity would result in a breach of contract. Cherry told Finley in the letter that he had a 10-day grace period to respond and make amends. Finley did not respond to Cherry nor did he purchase an annuity during the grace period. The season ended with Hunter winning a career-high 25 games and propelling the A's into the playoffs for the fourth time.

Sitting on the sidelines, watching and eager to assist, was MLB Players Association director Marvin Miller. He saw the unique potential to free Hunter from his contract and to establish the true free market value of the game's greatest pitcher. However, Finley could still spoil Miller's plans by simply purchasing the annuity. Sensing upcoming legal problems and knowing that the union would likely use the dispute to attempt to win Hunter his free agency, MLB attorney John Gaherin suggested a meeting between Hunter and Finley to resolve the issue. On October 4 (only a day before the opening of the A's American League championship series against the Orioles), Finley, in the presence of league president Lee MacPhail, called Hunter to the team's offices in Oakland. Finley and MacPhail wanted to resolve the issue and offer the money to Hunter in an attempt to fulfill the contractual obligation. MacPhail recalled the dialogue of the meeting.

"Okay, Catfish, here's a check for $50,000. That's the rest of the money you have coming in your 1974 contract," Finley told Hunter.

"I can't take it," responded Catfish. "I've been advised by my attorney that the check must be sent directly to the Jefferson Insurance Company."

Then Finley asked Hunter to call his attorney into the meeting. Hunter and Cherry conferred by phone for several minutes, and then Hunter told Finley, "I'm sorry, but he said I shouldn't take it." Hunter left the meeting without the check. After the meeting, MacPhail said, "The fact that Mr. Finley did offer Hunter a check for the disputed $50,000 puts an entirely different light on the situation. I seriously doubt that Hunter will win his free agency."[4]

So far, no mention of the Finley-Hunter contract dispute had appeared in the press. That ended on October 11, 1974, the day before the start of the World Series, the A's versus the Dodgers. An exclusive *Chicago Sun-Times* story reported that Hunter and his attorney had charged Finley with breach of contract because of his refusal to purchase the $50,000 deferred annuity as directed in the contract. According to the story, Hunter claimed Finley's action, or inaction, voided the contract and would result in his becoming a free agent. The story made the front page of every sports section in the country. Finley tried to downplay the whole mess, telling the *Chicago Tribune*, "It's not even worth commenting on. But you can be assured that we do not owe any player any money." Later, Finley admitted to a minor dispute with Hunter over the language in his contract, and described it as "just a little misunderstanding."[5]

As the A's prepared for the World Series against the Dodgers, the media pounced on Hunter, who was upset about the story and reluctant to confirm the report. He'd hoped to keep the dispute a secret until after the World Series, fearing it would be a big distraction to him and his teammates. Hundreds of reporters looking for a new angle on the World Series pushed Hunter for answers. Hunter remained mum, acknowledging only that there was a dispute, but giving few details. One reporter asked Hunter if he still worked for the A's. "I wouldn't be wearing this uniform if I didn't," Hunter replied. "I don't want anything to disrupt us now with the World Series starting."

While the A's were battling the Orioles and then the Dodgers in the playoffs, players association head Marvin Miller and counsel Dick Moss maneuvered the dispute into the MLB management-labor grievance system. Upon hearing of Finley's belated attempt to pay Hunter the $50,000 on October 4, Moss said, "[The payment offer] was not in keeping with the terms of the contract and, moreover, had become irrelevant because the Oakland club already had defaulted in its performance of the contract. Owner Finley had been advised in writing of his failure, on September 16, at which time he had a 10-day grace period to make amends but failed to do so."[6]

Miller and Moss knew they had a grievance case against Finley for breach of contract. They also knew they had a decent chance of winning Hunter his free agency, but they were cautious not to play their hand until the A's season was over. If they declared Hunter a free agent at the end of the season or during the playoffs, confusion, criticism, and mayhem might lead to unfavorable press and public opinion. It was better to wait until after the World Series to move forward with the grievance. Moss filed the preliminary legal documents on October 4. He sent Finley a telegram late in the day notifying him of his breach of contract: "Because of the impending playoffs and World Series the effective date of termination shall be the day following the last game played by the Oakland Athletics in 1974." Moss then sent a letter to Commissioner Bowie Kuhn, asking that immediately following the World Series, Hunter be declared a free agent (free to sign with any club) as the result of Finley's default on his contractual obligations. Kuhn denied the request.

Only an hour after the Dodgers' Von Joshua weakly grounded out to A's closer Rollie Fingers for the final out of the 1974 World Series, the MLB Players Association filed two grievances on behalf of Catfish Hunter. The first grievance went against Major League Baseball and the commissioner for not declaring Hunter a free agent and asked that "the 24 clubs be ordered to treat Mr. Hunter as a free agent and make him whole for any damages he may suffer due to the delay in doing so."[7] This grievance relied on Finley's alleged breach of contract. The second grievance went against Finley and the A's and asked the Oakland club to pay Hunter the $50,000 owed to him and to also provide damages for the club's failure to purchase the annuity in the first place.

According to baseball's collective bargaining agreement between the players and owners, an arbitration panel was charged with resolving such player-management grievances. Under the arbitration rules, three men sat on the panel: Marvin Miller, representing the players' union; John Gaherin, chair of the owner's Players Relations Committee, representing the league and the owners; and the third arbitrator, Peter Seitz, who had become a MLB arbitrator in 1974, after serving in the same capacity for the National Baseball Association for several years. Everyone knew Miller and Gaherin would vote for their respective sides, canceling out each other's vote. The deciding vote, therefore, fell to the third arbitrator, Seitz.

Prior to the hearing, Finley and his attorneys tried to place the $50,000 into an escrow-type account to illustrate their view that the dispute was not about violating the contract clause, but rather was about the execution of the annuity and its tax implications. Seitz refused the escrow payment ploy, thus keeping all possible outcomes on the table.

Heading into the arbitration hearing, on November 26, 1974, in New York, most in the media believed it unlikely that Hunter would gain his free agency. Conventional wisdom held that the impartial arbitrator would force Finley to purchase the annuity but would keep Hunter's contract with the A's intact. Finley arrived at the hearing confident. He shook hands with Catfish Hunter and told him, "It's good to see you."[8] Both sides had their various attorneys; Dick Moss presented the case for the player, while

Barry Rona and Louis Hoynes represented Finley and the owners. In all, five people testified: Hunter, his attorney Carlton Cherry, deferred-compensation expert Mortimer Brill, Finley, and AL president Lee MacPhail. The proceedings were thorough; the transcript ran 200 pages.[9]

Finley did not make a very good witness. "The only thing I would say about Charlie is that when Charlie testifies, you don't get the feeling that you are getting the full story from him," Hoynes said. "He has the look—and this is purely subjective—he sort of has the look of somebody that is kind of making it up or at least not telling you everything he knows. He was not a good witness; he was not a convincing, sincere witness. I always felt that we never really knew everything that had gone on between Hunter and Charlie."[10]

Hoynes thought that Hunter's testimony was more convincing, but it was largely a recital of his understanding of the contract. "It was really more based on the documents," Hoynes said. "They had their text, their biblical text, that Charlie would have to pay the money as directed. I'm pretty sure those were the words, 'as directed by Mr. Hunter.'" Hoynes thought Dick Moss "just kept pounding that in, for the union . . . Charlie always looked like he was holding something back. He looked like it in the hearing room; he looked like it when he talked to us. It was very strange. Usually when you get a client, you want the client to tell you everything, and you decide how to present it. Well, Charlie really wanted to control how it was presented, so he controlled what he told us." Hoynes angrily remembered feeling that "it was clear that the arbitration [was] really about how Charlie mistreats players, and his reputation proceeded him. You could see from the beginning that Seitz wanted to teach Charlie a lesson, maybe wanted to teach baseball a lesson."[11]

Players association director Marvin Miller recalled that "it was a complex defense, but a part of it was that he had accepted what Kuhn and MacPhail and their lawyers had told him to say. And they were so far out of it that it wasn't even funny." From the standpoint of the players, Miller said, "what he [Finley] was saying made no sense at all. For example, they [Kuhn and MacPhail] told him to say that, 'Look, he really offered the fifty thousand dollars in cash or a check to Hunter, so therefore, he could not be accused of violating the contract with Hunter.' Well, the contract didn't call for a payment to Hunter. It called for the payment of that money much earlier to an insurance company, which would not be paid to Hunter until some time after he had retired as a player. And [this] defense, apparently urged by Kuhn and MacPhail and their lawyers, made no sense at all."[12]

The hearing ended with Seitz heading off to deliberate on the case and consider the hundreds of pages of documentation. Despite Finley's ambiguous testimony, most legal experts believed the third arbitrator would find some sort of compromise decision that would force Finley to pay but would keep Hunter with the A's.

Peter Seitz took nearly three weeks to announce a decision in the case. On December 13, 1974, he declared that Hunter was a free agent. In explaining his ruling, Seitz said, "He [Hunter] did not seek to enforce or seek compliance by Mr. Finley with the provisions of the Special Covenant in the player's contract. Instead, he elected to invoke the rights granted in the termination provisions in the player's contract. In contrast to enforcing that contract he asserted that the Club's actions resulted in there being no contract at all."[13] Seitz said it was clear from the beginning that Hunter's objective was to avoid taxation on current income and that Finley made no statement that the deferral was conditioned either on the club's use of the money during the deferral period or on the right of Finley to claim the deferred salary as a business expense. Hunter had escaped Finley's domain and became baseball's first true superstar free agent.

Emotions about this dramatic ruling still ran deep more than 30 years later. Louis Hoynes said, "Charlie wanted to win and expected to win. He knew that at the end of the day that fifty thousand dollars was gone ... It still makes my blood boil to think about what Seitz did. And Charlie didn't expect it ... It wasn't that Charlie expected to get the fifty thousand dollars back—he didn't—but he didn't expect to lose the contract of Catfish Hunter."[14]

However, Marvin Miller remembered things differently and faulted Finley for losing Hunter. "Charlie Finley was never a stupid man," Miller said. "He was a capable and intelligent man, but he never knew where his own limitations were. And, for example, he knew all about insurance and annuities and so on. What he didn't understand were the tax laws. He did not understand that if instead of paying an employee current salary, you agreed to pay it to a third party—and it's not to be paid to your employee until many, many years later—that you cannot count it as a current expense for tax purposes . . . A simple request to a tax lawyer about the nuances of this would've straightened him out. But he didn't do that kind of thing. He was not only the owner. He was his own general manager. He was his own scout. He was his own publicity agent. He was his own attorney, representing himself in arbitrations. And he was his own tax authority."[15]

Finley quickly sought to have the arbitration decision overturned in court. On December 18, Finley attorney Neil Papiano filed papers seeking a temporary injunction to overturn the Seitz decision in Alameda County Superior Court, claiming Seitz had "gone beyond the scope of the issue." The temporary injunction was denied. At a January 3, 1975, hearing, Finley and Papiano argued the case again before Superior Court Judge George Phillips, seeking to overturn the Seitz decision, which Papiano described as "akin to giving the death penalty for a parking violation." Phillips told Papiano, "I think the award should be confirmed." Finley and Papiano attempted to argue the case in appeals court, but lost again. It seemed that the rules of the bargaining agreement governing Major League Baseball were quite specific on the "binding" nature of an arbitration panel's decision. Finley lost one of baseball's best pitchers forever.

Meanwhile, the other 23 baseball clubs salivated at the prospect of signing the premier pitcher. However, Commissioner Bowie Kuhn tried to prevent the other clubs from negotiating with Hunter. Kuhn told their general managers, "I have not yet had an opportunity to review the decision and I am advised that the Oakland club intends immediately to seek a court restraining order to prevent Hunter from contracting with another club. Direct or indirect contact between Hunter and other clubs is temporarily prohibited."[16] But court relief never came to Finley or Major League Baseball. Miller threatened to sue if Kuhn continued his prohibition on teams' making contact with Hunter. Kuhn acquiesced and lifted his embargo on December 18. Soon afterward, representatives from 15 ball clubs made the trip to Ahoskie, North Carolina, trying to lure free agent Catfish Hunter. In the end, teams—the Yankees, Padres, Royals, and Indians—emerged as finalists to sign Hunter.

The Yankees used former Finley scout Clyde Kluttz, who had originally signed the young Hunter for the A's, as their primary interface with Cherry and Hunter during the negotiations. The move paid off. Hunter trusted Kluttz and spurned two higher offers (from the Padres and the Royals) to sign with George Steinbrenner's New York Yankees on December 31, 1974, for five years and a total compensation package worth nearly $3.5 million. Hunter would go on to win 23 games for the Yankees in 1975 and 17 more while leading them to the AL pennant in 1976. Jim "Catfish" Hunter won 224 major-league games in a 15-year career cut short by shoulder injuries and diabetes that plagued him in the late 1970s. He retired from baseball after the 1979 season and was eventually elected into the Baseball Hall of Fame in 1987, the first of Finley's Athletics to receive such an honor. Hunter died in 1999 at age 53 after battling amyotrophic lateral sclerosis, the same incurable neuromuscular disease that claimed Yankees legend Lou Gehrig in 1941.

Charlie Finley's refusal to execute Hunter's deferred-salary clause cost him the game's most prized starting pitcher—all because Finley wanted to write Hunter's deferred $50,000 salary off as a business expense in 1974. Hunter was the glue of Finley's heralded pitching staff. The A's "big-game" pitcher had few equals in all of baseball. His loss hurt the A's future chances immeasurably. Finley's penny-pinching and tightfisted ways had finally caught up with the wily owner.

In its January 4, 1975, edition, the *Sporting News* published an editorial on the whole affair:

> Never before has a professional of Hunter's caliber been freed to weigh all offers at the peak of his career. And Catfish owes it all to Charlie, who builds baseball champions, runs basketball and hockey franchises into the ground and makes enemies with remarkable ease. Long after Finley's departure, sports historians will be arguing bitterly in attempting to assess his stature. Probably nothing could please Charlie more.[17]

Had Finley been able to see the forest instead of all the trees, Hunter would have remained his ace starting pitcher, and possibly would have anchored the A's in additional championships. Finley's inability to find a win-win solution crippled his team's future. He had to be in control and could not stand the fact that Cherry and Hunter had outmaneuvered him in this arbitration.

Finley had many distractions in 1974: his declining insurance business, his failing health, and his divorce. But because he refused to relinquish control of anything in his life, his mistakes—caused by age, health, distractions, and an inability to see that an ever-more-complex world was progressing beyond his sphere of influence—began to take a toll on his empire. As for baseball itself, the Seitz ruling and the resulting bidding war for Catfish Hunter's golden pitching arm showed major-league players and their union what a star player could actually earn, free from the constraints of the reserve clause. Baseball was on the brink of a new era, all thanks to ol' Charlie Finley.

Chapter Nine

Life After Catfish

Charlie Finley knew his A's faced tough hurdles coming into the 1975 season. First, the odds of any baseball team winning a fourth straight World Series were long. Injuries, improving opposition, complacency—all conspire against any long-winning team. Finley's A's faced all three problems, plus the loss of star pitcher Catfish Hunter.

During the 1974–75 off-season, after losing Hunter in the Seitz ruling, Finley seemingly put more effort into settling contract disputes with his players before their arbitration hearings. He knew his team needed its remaining stars to compete in 1975 and possibly make it to their fourth consecutive World Series. Whether the Hunter ruling made Finley more leery of the arbitration process isn't known, but it's likely he wanted to have a greater role in deciding the final salaries of his players and pushed for settlement before arbitration. Again, the A's led the league in arbitration filings prior to the 1975 season, with 13 players seeking a hearing. Finley worked quickly to settle with 7 of these players before their hearings. Vida Blue, Billy North, Blue Moon Odom, Joe Rudi, Gene Tenace, Paul Lindblad, and Dave Hamilton all reached an agreement with their tightfisted owner. Finley also grew to hate sports agent Jerry Kapstein, who started representing more of his players. A's executive John Claiborne remembered, "He didn't like the [arbitration] process. But, again, the world was turning now as far as players, and this was what he didn't like . . . He no longer had control, and here's a lawyer telling him what his player's worth, and Charlie didn't like that—and he took it personally. He didn't like Kapstein or, quite frankly, any of the other agents."[1]

While the 1974 hearings and their aftershocks left several players disheartened and annoyed with their irascible owner, the 1975 arbitration hearings with 6 players—Bando, Fingers, Holtzman, Jackson, Fosse, and Kubiak—left most with a bitter aftertaste that lingered for the rest of their career.

Sal Bando's hearing became particularly nasty. Before it started, both Bando and Finley had traded sharp barbs in the press. The thoughtful and sensitive Bando had even tried to withdraw his case and negotiate directly with Finley to avoid another a nasty confrontation at the hearing. But Finley had refused to deal with him. Bando told *New York Daily News* columnist Dick Young, "Everything he does, there must be a battle and I'm sick of it. I think most of our men are sick of it. You get to a point where hassling every day isn't amusing anymore. I want out."[2] Finley would agree to call off the hearing only if Bando agreed to his offer of the same salary in 1975 as he'd received in 1974. Bando refused.

Finley stoked the flames of controversy by calling Bando a "pop-off" in the press and stating, "If he wishes to become the village idiot, let him be my guest."[3] Bando sharply criticized the size of Finley's front office and the manner in which he ran the A's. Finley fired back, "One thing I resent very much is that Mr. Bando took it upon himself [in two banquet appearances] to come out and state that the Oakland A's have the worst front office in baseball . . . I even thought at one time that he [Bando] had great possibilities of managing the A's, but no more. Not as long as I own the team."[4]

The arbitration hearing became a slugfest. As Bando recalled years later, "it was unbelievable. I had finished third in the American League 1974 MVP voting and finished second in the American League in RBIs, and we were world champions again. And he started drilling that my slugging percentage was down and that my fielding percentage compared to our first baseman, Gene Tenace, was down . . . And then he's trying to explain the slugging percentage, but Finley can't explain it . . . But the part that got me was that he goes, 'Mr. Arbitrator, balls go by him on the left. Balls go by him on the right. Balls go through his legs. How can I pay this guy one hundred and twenty-five thousand dollars?' Well, at that point, I can feel my veins in my neck just coming out, and my wife is grabbing my arm, holding me back, because I can just picture myself diving across the table and strangling him. And as it turns out, I lost that case only because the arbitrator knew nothing about baseball, and he saw that my slugging percentage was less than the year before."[5] Bando lost, and as a result, he received no raise in 1975.

Finley expressed a real obstinacy and nastiness in dealing with players' contracts, alienating his players as never before. He amended his earlier comment about pigs and hogs: "There's an old truism that applies to what's going on here; Hogs go to market and pigs get fat. But most of these players aren't being pigs. They aren't being hogs. They're just being gluttons. And the fans aren't going to put up with it much longer," Finley told the press.[6] In the end, Finley won four of the six salary arbitration hearings in 1975, those for Bando, Holtzman, Fosse, and Jackson.

Undoubtedly, the arbitration process and the resulting hearings severely damaged the already fragile relationship between Finley and his players. Despite Finley's telling his players after each hearing that "it is only business," many of his arguments became personal. But the bad blood did not affect the team's performance on the field. They already hated Finley and channeled this hatred to their advantage as a unifying force. The salary arbitration losses did breed additional dissension and hurt the team's chances in 1975, but the departure of Catfish Hunter was the critical blow that started the demise of the A's.

Finley knew the 1975 season would be a challenging one. He needed to improve the team's offense; find playing time for his rising young outfielder Claudell Washington; sign a new second baseman, as veteran Dick Green had retired; find some bullpen help; and get a quality starter to replace Hunter in the rotation. All tough tasks for any general manager, but Finley attacked each with vigor and surprising craftiness.

At the same time, Finley complained bitterly about low attendance and fan interest in the A's. Media reports had Finley close to selling the A's for an estimated $13 million to several different groups of local Bay Area buyers. One potential buyer was businesswoman and horse owner Marge Everett, who wanted to move the team to Seattle. Another group, led by former Giants manager Herman Franks, offered more than $15 million for the team and planned to keep it in Oakland. However, even as Finley railed about the lack of attendance at home games, he dampened sales rumors by stating, "There's no truth to it. The club is not for sale."[7]

In 1974, the World Series champs drew only 845,693 fans in the regular season. Finley attempted to increase attendance in 1975 by holding 11 half-price Monday-night family games and by adding additional promotional games throughout the season. With the A's payroll becoming one of the highest in baseball, Finley needed every dollar he could muster. However, as Finley courted fans, he could not resist badgering Oakland and the A's faithful for their lukewarm support of him and his team. "I tell you this: if the Athletics were located in any other city, they would be drawing two million people a year . . . On the road, we are one of the best draws . . . The attendance thing really gets to me. It's discouraging, disheartening and disappointing. It's not just me either. The players are proud of their accomplishments and they ache when people don't show up to watch them," Finley complained.[8] Later in the season, with the A's poised to attract more than 1 million fans, Finley continued his assault on the Bay Area for not supporting the A's. "The Bay area simply cannot support two teams," Finley whined. "If we can't draw with a championship team, how can they [the Giants] draw with one that is not even a contender?"[9] Rumors of the A's leaving Oakland for New Orleans or Seattle or Toronto circulated for most of the summer.

Finley retained Alvin Dark as manager in 1975. However, Dark feared the loss of Catfish Hunter would provide the perfect reason for Finley to fire him if the A's got off to a slow start. Finley and Dark exchanged barbs at the 35th annual Diamond Dinner in Chicago in mid-January. Dark explained in a rather joking manner to the audience that Finley had wanted to fire him several times in 1974 but could not because the team was too good. Dark opined that Finley might now use the loss of Catfish as the perfect reason to sack him. Finley did not appear amused by Dark's comments, and during his time at the microphone, shot back, "I'm intrigued that my good friend Alvin Dark had the audacity—or unmitigated gall—to use as an excuse for the possibility of being fired in 1975 the loss of Catfish Hunter." Finley added, "Managers are a dime a dozen, all he has to do is look back on the last few years and see how many I've had."[10]

As spring training approached, Finley instructed Dark to move Gold Glove outfielder Joe Rudi to first base, thus freeing up an outfield position for young, fast, line-drive-hitting prospect Claudell Washington. The move upset Rudi. "Why don't they move Reggie? He has bad legs. He gets hurt all the time. It would be much less demanding on him at first base," Rudi said.[11]

Finley responded in the press: "Rudi is a good left fielder, but Washington's speed will enable him to reach balls that Rudi couldn't reach . . . If I were 25 years younger, I probably could come out of retirement because first base is that easy to play . . . I don't care how much Rudi pops off. But sometimes when my players pop off, they don't know what they're talking about."[12]

Finley also attempted to bolster his offense by acquiring aging Cubs outfielder Billy Williams as the A's new designated hitter. Williams's offensive totals for the Cubs in 1974 (16 HRs, 68 RBI, .280 BA) easily outperformed the combined stats of the 18 players who served as the A's designated hitter that year. But acquiring Williams came at a high price for Oakland. The A's gave up 1973 World Series relief star Darold Knowles, pitcher Bob Locker, and second base prospect Manny Trillo. Trillo would go on to an All-Star career with the Cubs, Phillies, and Giants and fall a few votes short of winning the National League's Rookie of the Year award in 1975.

Dick Green's retirement left the A's with a huge defensive hole in their infield. His impressive glove work had played a significant role in the A's victory over the Dodgers in the 1974 Series. He said he had decided to finally retire after Hunter jumped from the team. "There is no use in coming back when you can't win," Green said. "And you can't win without Catfish."[13] Replacing Green would not be easy, especially after Finley traded away Trillo. "I think Green being gone will hurt you more than the loss of Hunter in the long run," opined former A's manager Dick Williams. "Greenie was the stabilizer in the middle of the infield."[14] To fill the void,

Dark and Finley decided to convert rookie third baseman Phil Garner into their new second baseman. The 25-year-old Garner, who displayed a good bat and a strong glove at third in the minors, worked with veteran infielder Dal Maxvill during spring training to improve his fielding. Dark believed that once Garner became comfortable at second, his bat would also prove to be far more potent than the light-hitting Green's.

While Finley and Dark knew it would be impossible to find one outstanding pitcher to replace Catfish Hunter, they hoped to replace his 25 wins by obtaining several good, solid pitchers. Finley's search for new pitching depth began with the acquisition of right-hander Jim Todd from the Cubs. The reliever's role would ease the workload of Rollie Fingers and lefty Paul Lindblad. As the A's broke spring training, three young starters from their minor-league system competed for Hunter's spot in the rotation: tall right-hander Glenn Abbott, lefty Dave Hamilton, and youngster Mike Norris. Twenty-year-old Norris, who pitched the previous year in the AA level in the minors, emerged as Hunter's top replacement coming out of spring training. Norris kicked off the 1975 season by firing a shutout against the White Sox in his first start. Many observers believed him to be the next Vida Blue and thought Finley had pulled another amazing find. Norris possessed three solid pitches (fastball, curveball, and changeup) and showed surprising poise on the mound. However, Norris sent Finley and the A's scrambling as calcium deposits in his elbow flared up in his third start and forced him to the sidelines for most of the season. Dark turned to Abbott and Hamilton to fill the void, but neither performed well enough to secure Hunter's spot at the front of the rotation.

Going into the 1975 season, most sportswriters picked the A's to again win the AL Western Division, but most believed they would not make it back to the World Series. The New York Yankees and their new ace, Catfish Hunter, became the new favorites to win the AL pennant. Most of the A's players viewed their new underdog status as a motivator for the season. They knew the loss of Catfish hurt their chances but were confident that they had enough remaining talent to overcome that loss.

The A's proved their rumored demise premature by making a strong start. Powered by strong hitting from Rudi, Tenace, and Washington, the A's won 12 of their first 20 games. Vida Blue and Ken Holtzman anchored the starting rotation. When Mike Norris went down with his elbow injury, Finley swung two key trades to help his starting rotation. On May 16, he traded utility infielder Ted Kubiak to the Padres for 38-year-old former All-Star starter Sonny Seibert. On May 20, he traded one of his favorites, Blue Moon Odom, to the Indians for veteran starter Dick Bosman and former Cy Young Award–winner Jim Perry. Finley deemed Odom expendable, as he had never truly recovered from an elbow injury in 1971. All three new A's pitchers were on the downsides of their careers. Perry, who was also 38, had lost his fastball and could barely go five innings per start. "I'd like to come here and pick up this club," Perry told reporters at the time of the trade. "I'm healthy and throwing good."[15] However, in his first start for the A's, Perry could only retire six batters before being lifted. At the June trade deadline, with the A's still struggling to find a quality third and fourth starter, Finley made one more deal in hopes of bolstering the A's rotation. He traded young lefty Dave Hamilton and rising outfield prospect Chet Lemon to the White Sox for veteran starter Stan Bahnsen. The three-time All-Star Lemon would turn out to be the steal of the trade for the White Sox. Meanwhile, Bahnsen, who finished his major-league career with a 146–149 record, helped to stabilize the pitching in the second half of the season.

The four new veteran pitchers Finley traded for during the 1975 season were all only average major-league starters at that point in their careers. Sonny Siebert, Dick Bosman, Jim Perry, and Stan Bahnsen moved in and out of the A's rotation as third and fourth starters throughout the season. While their individual records were not impressive, each pitched well at times. With the exception of Perry, all had ERAs around 3.50 and routinely gave Alvin Dark five or six solid innings per start. In fact, the four acquired starters combined to win 24 games for the A's in 1975, just one short of Hunter's victory total the previous year.

As the A's headed toward the 1975 All-Star break, they were punishing opposing teams with added vigor. Finley's efforts at adding offense seemed to be working, as the A's hummed on all cylinders, seemingly not missing Catfish Hunter on the mound. On July 14, 1975, they sat in first place in the AL West, with an impressive 55–32 record. Seven A's players (Jackson,

Tenace, Campaneris, Rudi, Washington, Fingers, and Blue) were selected to the AL All-Star roster. Finley joined his seven players in Milwaukee for the All-Star festivities and to attend league meetings. While most fans were excited about the All-Star game itself (the National League won the game 6–3, with Catfish Hunter taking the loss), most of the news headlines came from Charlie Finley's antics off the field.

A few weeks before the All-Star game, rumors began to make the rounds that Bowie Kuhn might not have the votes to be reelected MLB commissioner during the league meetings in Milwaukee. A "Dump Bowie Club" of a few American League owners emerged—and rumors placed Finley as the leader of this group. MLB rules called for Kuhn's reappointment as commissioner to be considered by both leagues 12 to 18 months before his seven-year term ended in August 1976. The rules stated that each league had to approve the renewal of the commissioner's term for another seven years by a vote of at least 9–3. If either league failed to provide at least nine votes for extension, then Kuhn would be ousted.

Of course, Finley hated Kuhn and vice versa. Finley never forgave the commissioner for not allowing him to demote Jackson in 1970; for interfering with his contract negotiations with Vida Blue in 1972; and for ruling against and fining him during the Andrews controversy in 1973. Finley wanted Kuhn out and moved secretly to garner the votes he needed to force him from his job. Finley's club included two other disgruntled owners: Baltimore's Jerry Hoffberger and the New York Yankees' George Steinbrenner. Kuhn had suspended the Yankees owner for two years in November 1974 after Steinbrenner was convicted in federal court of making illegal campaign contributions. In a June 1975 article in the *Chicago Sun-Times*, Finley and Hoffberger refused to comment on rumors of a budding "palace revolt," virtually ensuring that they were leading the charge. Steinbrenner told the press, "I would never vote against the commissioner because of anything he did within the perimeter of his authority . . . I will not enter into retaliatory attempts of any sort."[16]

AL president Lee McPhail had taken a poll of owners in early July, before the All-Star game, and found that 10 of them supported Kuhn's reelection. Kuhn also enjoyed strong support among the National League owners. With the revolt an apparent mirage, both leagues placed the commissioner's reelection on the All-Star game meeting agenda. Meanwhile, Finley, needing one additional vote to block Kuhn's reelection, secretly met with new Texas Ranger owner Brad Corbett at a Milwaukee bistro and convinced him to join the revolt. Corbett believed MLB needed a more dynamic commissioner to move the game forward.

The American and National leagues met separately at the Pfister Hotel the day following the All-Star game. The AL owners considered Kuhn's reelection first. A straw vote revealed that four AL clubs were opposed to Kuhn's reelection: the Yankees (being led by Steinbrenner partner Pat Cunningham, since Steinbrenner was officially suspended), Corbett's Rangers, Hoffberger's Orioles, and Finley's A's. League officials passed the news of this vote to the National League owners. Immediately, Dodgers owner Walter O'Malley recessed the NL meeting for twenty-four hours via a parliamentary procedure. Then O'Malley proceeded to caucus with several influential owners to strategize on how to bring at least one of the rebellious American League owners back in the fold. Finley went to bed that evening believing he had outmaneuvered and dethroned Kuhn as commissioner, but during the night, several National League owners met secretly with Corbett and Yankees representatives and asked them to change their vote. Bowie Kuhn recalled hearing very early the next morning the results of the arm-twisting. "At 6:00am I was awakened by a call from Walter O'Malley. Sometime during the night he had reached Corbett by telephone and applied the extraordinary O'Malley powers of persuasion. Brad agreed to join the forces of light . . . to support me," he said.[17]

The next morning owners from both leagues gathered in a joint meeting for a final vote. Kuhn gaveled the meeting to order, then left the room for the two leagues to formally vote on his reelection. The National League voted 12–0 in favor of reelection. Next, the American League tallied its numbers—the owners supported Kuhn's reelection by 10–2. The Yankees and Rangers had changed their negative votes, and Kuhn was reelected for another seven-year term.

The owners called Kuhn back into the room to announce his formal reelection and gave the commissioner a standing ovation—even Finley joined in the applause. Kuhn, who had held his tongue during the maneuvering of the past 24 hours, said, "Thank you, gentlemen, especially those who voted for me. It's too bad it took so long, but it's not surprising, considering the quality of the opposition."[18]

Hearing the shot by Kuhn, Finley jumped to his feet, unable to contain himself, and shouted, "What a joke!" The Kuhn-Finley bitterness appeared again 20 minutes later at a press conference. Kuhn had just finished his statement accepting his reelection and describing the events of the previous day as "obscene" when Finley stood in the audience and announced that he had a statement for the press. Without hesitating, Kuhn sharply replied, "Charlie, you may leave the room."[19]

"Thank you, Commissioner," Finley sarcastically replied. "That just shows more class." Finley then retired to an adjacent room, followed by a dozen reporters. Addressing the reporters, Finley expressed surprise at Kuhn's bitter tone. "I would say that the commissioner hasn't been in baseball long enough. When you're in baseball, you realize you win a few and lose a few, and when you lose, you have to lose as graciously as when you win." Six days later, Kuhn wrote Finley a short letter extending an olive branch. Finley never replied. "Reading this letter many years later, I don't know why I bothered," Kuhn wrote in his autobiography, *Hardball*. "Pearls before swine."[20] Nonetheless, Walter O'Malley saved Bowie Kuhn's job. Kuhn was O'Malley's boy, and he protected him in this and other controversies with the owners. And Kuhn would not forget Finley's rebellion.

With both the Giants and A's struggling for attendance, Kuhn also announced at the press conference his intention of moving either the A's or the Giants from the Bay Area before the end of his new term. Toward the close of the owners meeting, Kuhn tried to push an expansion resolution for consideration by all the owners. The first paragraph called for expansion into Seattle and Washington, DC, by 1977—nothing controversial. But, the second paragraph called for one of the two Bay Area teams to leave its current location. Finley reacted angrily. "That resolution was the kiss of death," he said. "I'm fighting like hell to stay in Oakland. I'm doing everything to get good attendance. We may have two teams in the Bay area, who knows? We may have one. I don't know which one it should be."[21]

Giants owner Horace Stoneham and Finley blocked the resolution, but the expansion and franchise movement remained a hot subject through the summer and autumn of 1975. Several different scenarios became public. One had the Giants moving to Toronto and the A's staying in Oakland. The scenario that generated the most media attention had the financially struggling White Sox being sold to new owners in Seattle and the A's moving from Oakland to the South Side of Chicago as the city's new second team. White Sox owner Arthur Allyn was facing severe financial problems in his business interests and was running two months behind in paying White Sox bills. He put the team up for sale, but it appeared that the American League owners might have to take over the club if Allyn was forced into bankruptcy. Finley yearned for the A's to be in his home city of Chicago. He believed his championship club could easily draw more than 2 million fans per season. However, legal issues with the A's 20-year lease at the Oakland Coliseum complicated a potential move. Finley tried to convince many owners and the commissioner to consider the possibility of the franchise shift, but in the end, Kuhn and the other owners decided against it and focused on expanding MLB with new ball clubs. Eventually, Allyn sold the White Sox to legendary baseball maverick and Finley nemesis Bill Veeck, a move that annoyed Charlie Finley and ended his hopes of moving the A's to Chicago.

The A's continued to surge during the dog days of August, playing fundamentally sound baseball and moving toward another AL West crown—all without their former star pitcher Catfish Hunter. It was the A's revamped bullpen that truly saved the pitching staff in 1975. The bullpen trio of Rollie Fingers, Paul Lindblad, and Jim Todd were forced to pitch far more often than anticipated, but threw exceptionally well throughout the season. Fingers saved 24 games and won 10 while making a major-league-high 75 appearances as the A's closer. Todd won 8 games and saved an additional 12 with an outstanding 2.29 ERA, while Lindblad won 9 and saved 7, both out of the A's pen. Manager Alvin Dark expertly used his bullpen to help supplement his weaker starting pitchers.

As the A's amazed the baseball world on the field, Finley's national notoriety reached its zenith on August 18, 1975, when he appeared on the cover of *Time* magazine dressed in his customary kelly green A's sports coat and green cowboy hat and holding a black bat, as if waiting for a pitched ball, before a background of white and orange baseballs. The title on the cover read BASEBALL'S SUPER SHOWMAN: OAKLAND'S CHARLIE FINLEY. The story remains the last major profile of the controversial owner in a national publication. It related the familiar Finley success story and focused on his team's chance of winning a fourth World Series title. It touched on his successes and controversies. It had the iconic owner passing out his orange baseballs to everyone from fans to stewardesses to players. It featured the 57-year-old Finley, who had separated from his wife in March 1974 and was currently engaged in bitter divorce proceedings, living the life of a swinging single with a Chicago lakefront bachelor pad. The five-page profile included photographs of Finley celebrating a birthday with Playboy bunnies in A's uniforms, smooching stewardesses on airplanes, cooking and supervising dinner preparations in a upscale Chicago restaurant, and playing a guitar while serenading friends at his apartment late at night. It discussed all the familiar Finley traits, including his love-hate relationship with his players, his miserly business ways, his controlling personality, his love of fine food and drink, his many health issues, his 18-hour workdays, and his desire to change baseball for the better.

"I've never seen so many damn idiots as the owners in sports," Finley sputtered in the article. "Baseball's headed for extinction if we don't do something. Defense dominates everything. Pitching is 75% of the game, and that's why it's so dull. How many times have you seen a fan napping in the middle of a football or basketball game? Hell, baseball people nap all the time. Only one word explains why baseball hasn't changed; stupidity! The owners don't want to rock the boat."

Later in the article, Finley explained how he was really very similar to most teams' general managers. "The one difference," he said, "is that this general manager also happens to the owner. It's my club, my money, and I'm gonna roll my dice as long as my money's on the table." One unnamed A's player was quoted as saying, "The problem is simple. Charlie Finley is the cheapest son of a bitch in baseball."[22] The article went on to describe how Finley continuously rocked the sport. "You can't miss Charlie," said Twins owner Calvin Griffith. "He's the P. T. Barnum of baseball."[23]

Even though Finley put forward the image of the happy bachelor and ladies' man, he struggled with the divorce proceedings between Shirley and himself. Over and over again, Shirley's lawyers tried to obtain material from him about his finances to move the process forward. He would ignore orders, give material that was not asked for, claim he did not have other documents requested, or otherwise drag out the process. He also tried to make her life miserable by demanding of her the same type of documentation that he refused to hand over. According to the local Indiana newspaper, Finley's attorney, Saul Ruman,

> filed a list of questions for Mrs. Finley to answer and a request for production of "any and all evidence of ownership of personal or real property, including bank books, statements, deeds, etc. in possession of yourself or your agents at this time." Questions for Mrs. Finley to answer include her ownership of personal property over $500, real estate, banking accounts, credit cards and accounts, and gifts to churches, priests and charitable institutions. She is also asked to itemize her expenses on a weekly basis.[24]

Not only did the judge not agree to Finley's counteroffer; he ordered the payment of "$15,000 to the county court clerk to be turned over to the wife's attorneys for preliminary fees." In the earlier order, Finley had already been ordered to pay $2,000 to Mrs. Finley's attorneys as a "nonrefundable retainer."[25]

The failure to comply with the rulings of the court in producing documentary records proved frustrating for Shirley Finley and her attorneys, to say the least. "They didn't produce the necessary discovery," said Leon R. Kaminski, one of the lawyers on the case. "We had no alternative than to cite him for contempt."[26] They filed such a request on June 14, 1974, and a series of legal maneuverings followed, including a request for a change of venue.[27]

Throughout this process, Finley sometimes failed to pay court-ordered support to his wife. The judge also ordered Finley to comply with the discovery effort and required an additional payment of $50,000 for legal fees.[28] Additionally, the judge ordered an audit of the financial resources of the Finley family for purposes of dividing its assets in a divorce settlement. Finley stonewalled on this, claiming that his wife had access to this information already. After dragging this out for two years, Finley's attorney filed a motion on July 7, 1976, stating that the discovery placed too great a burden on Finley: "The information sought by the petitioner in discovery is available to either party in this action. It is unfair and beyond the scope of the discovery rules to place the sole burden on one party to produce the information when the other party has access to the information also." Other statements followed, all suggesting that this was a burdensome requirement that required reconsideration.[29] Shirley, fed up with this constant interfamilial warfare, prompted the IRS to investigate Finley's business dealings, claiming he had failed to properly account for his income over several years in statements to the government. This set off even more desperate actions on Finley's part.[30]

Leon Kaminski recalled that although he was not a divorce lawyer and had limited experience in this type of legal proceeding, the Finley divorce seemed unusually difficult and trying. "I can't picture any other divorce case going on six years," he said. "That's probably the only divorce I've handled since the 1950s. But it wasn't a divorce case; it was a world war over assets, that's what it was." He noted that, in their efforts, they learned that Finley was no stranger to the courtroom, having been involved in numerous lawsuits over the years. It seemingly did not bother him to spend this much time in the court, having his attorney argue every point in the deliberations.[31]

Kaminski also thought that much of the case hinged on the valuation of Charles O. Finley and Company, for that would determine the divvying of assets with his soon-to-be ex-wife. Finley had every reason to get that amount down to as low of a dollar figure as possible. He took every tactic he could think of to obfuscate, delay, and minimize.

What could possibly explain Finley's incredible reluctance to answer questions? Why did he work so exhaustively to delay the proceedings? Was he merely trying to inflict as much pain on Shirley as possible? Most people want to get through divorce proceedings expeditiously, but Finley dragged his out for more than six years. He seems to have been creating as much havoc as possible while delaying the division of their property. Legally restricted from buying or selling major assets during these proceedings, he nonetheless allowed the case to continue without resolution. Meantime, Shirley Finley stayed at the farm for several months after the divorce pleading was filed, but short of funds, she moved to Florida.[32]

Also in August 1975, longtime A's executive John Claiborne resigned as the team's director of minor-league operations and de facto assistant general manager. His resignation left the A's front office with fewer than 10 full-time staffers. Claiborne became increasingly annoyed with Finley's trading away good young talent on the verge of major-league stardom for aging veteran talent, who were often injured and whose skills were declining. In particular, Claiborne had opposed trading away Chet Lemon, Manny Trillo, and young prospect outfielder Dan Ford in an attempt to replace Catfish Hunter with solid yet aging pitchers. One source reported that over a five-year period, the A's traded away 27 minor-league players while gaining back only 3 minor-league players. Finley systematically traded away or sold his young prospects for veteran role players in a desperate gamble to win championships in the short term. While his moves decimated the A's farm system for years to come, they did enable the A's to remain the class of the baseball world throughout the '75 season.[33]

The A's enjoyed one of their best overall offensive seasons in 1975, finishing second in the AL in both home runs (151) and runs scored (758). While pitching had carried the A's in their previous three championship seasons, their hitting set the pace in 1975. Reggie Jackson, Joe Rudi, Billy North, and Gene Tenace all enjoyed a solid season at the plate. Billy Williams and Phil Garner also provided timely hitting. In fact, only third baseman Sal Bando had a slump, hitting only .230 with a career-low 15 home runs and 78 RBI. Both Joe Rudi and Phil Garner adjusted well to their new positions, and by season's end, Garner's fielding was on par with Dick Green's. However, Rudi's play at first base was not up to his Gold Glove standard in left field, and in early August he tore ligaments in his left thumb while trying to check a swing; the injury sidelined him for most of August and September. Finley acquired veterans Tommy Harper and Cesar Tovar to add depth for their pennant run. Harper responded by hitting .319, stealing seven bases, and playing a solid first base in Rudi's absence. Meanwhile, young Claudell Washington struggled at times in left field, but he finished fifth in the American League, with a .308 batting average.

The A's also stole 183 bases during the 1975 season. They were paced on the base paths by shortstop Bert Campaneris (24 SB), center fielder Billy North (30 SB), and Claudell Washington (40 SB). Another Finley experiment ended in May, when the team released designated-runner Herb "Hurricane" Washington, whom Finley had signed prior to the 1974 season. Washington had no real baseball experience but still managed to steal 29 bases during the '74 season. He also committed numerous base-running mistakes that earned the ire of his teammates. The A's needed players on the roster who could do more than just run and steal bases. Increasingly, Dark needed bench players who could pinch-hit and field; Washington could do neither. Finley acquired two new fleet-footed prospects in Don Hopkins and Matt Alexander, both of whom could also play in the field and hit. Several A's were not sorry to see an end to Finley's designated-runner experiment. "I'd feel sorry for him if he were a player," said A's captain Sal Bando. The mild-mannered Herb Washington shot back in the press, "The toughest adjustment was putting up with egocentric players and a ton of bullbleep from front-runners on the team, front-runners in the media, and front-runners among the fans . . . Some of the players are nice guys. Some are jerks, too."[34] Overall, the world-class sprinter turned base stealer stole 31 bases in 48 attempts in his brief baseball career.

Despite the loss of Catfish Hunter, who beat his former teammates four times during the 1975 season, the A's emerged once again as winners of the AL West with a 98–64 record, their most regular-season wins since the 1971 season. The A's rode the backs of lefty starters Vida Blue (22–11, 3.01 ERA) and Ken Holtzman (18–14, 3.15 ERA) to their fifth-straight division crown. Both Blue and Holtzman turned in workhorse-type seasons, each starting 38 games and throwing 278 and 266 innings, respectively. The A's returned to the ALCS in 1975. Finley's A's were poised to sweep into their fourth-straight World Series. As the A's basked in the glory of their latest triumph with champagne, a few new A's were experiencing sweet victory for the first time. "Beautiful!" shouted Billy Williams. "Absolutely magnificent. Ain't no feeling like this. Never knew champagne tasted so good. Fifteen years to pour champagne."[35] Meanwhile, Finley blathered to the press about his team's latest triumph, calling the 1975 A's "the best ball club we've had in the 15 years I've owned it."[36] But the real test awaited them in the playoffs.

For the first time in three years, the A's were not clear favorites to win the American League pennant. Though they won 98 games in the regular season, they still lacked a quality third starting pitcher. This vulnerability threatened to upend them in a short five-game league championship series against East Division champs the Boston Red Sox. The first two games of the 1975 AL series were in Boston's Fenway Park, with its notorious Green Monster in short left field. Game one featured A's lefty Ken Holtzman versus Red Sox ace Luis Tiant and his array of different pitches and unorthodox motion. The Oakland scouting report warned that Tiant possessed six pitches (fastball, curveball, slider, changeup curve, palmball, and knuckleball) and could throw all with sidearm, three-quarter, or overhand motions. From the beginning of the game, Tiant and the Fenway Park infield had the A's out of sorts. The usually sure-handed Sal Bando and Phil Garner committed two errors that gave the Red Sox a quick 2–0 lead after the first inning. The game remained 2–0 as Tiant baffled the A's hitters. The wheels came off in the seventh inning, when Washington badly misplayed a ball in left field and Billy North dropped a routine flyball. Even the vaunted A's bullpen could not contain the damage as the Red Sox scored five runs in the seventh and eventually won the game 7–1. The A's defense committed four errors in the loss. "Tiant," Reggie Jackson declared after the game, "is the Fred Astaire of baseball."[37] Sitting behind the A's dugout, Finley frowned and steamed throughout much of the game.

Before game two, Alvin Dark made a few changes to the A's lineup. He moved Gold Glove outfielder Joe Rudi back to left field and the Green Monster. He moved Tenace to first base, made Washington the designated hitter, and inserted veteran Ray Fosse behind the plate in an attempt to shore up a porous A's defense. Vida Blue started the game versus Reggie Cleveland for the Red Sox. The A's offense started to respond, with Jackson blasting a two-run homer in the first inning and adding an additional run in the fourth for a 3–0 lead. Blue rolled through the Sox at first but ran into trouble in the fourth inning by giving up key hits to Carl Yastrzemski (who had a two-run homer), Carlton Fisk, Fred Lynn, and Rico Petrocelli to score three runs and chase him from the game. The bullpen could not stem the Red Sox attack, and the A's lost 6–3. As the A's went quietly in the top of the ninth, the Red Sox crowd began to serenade Finley and the A's by singing, "Goodbye, Charlie. Goodbye, Charlie..." Finley stood up from his box seat behind the A's dugout and painfully gave a half smile and waved his hands to the crowd. Finley knew his team was in trouble.

As they headed back to Oakland, the A's knew no team had come back from this type of deficit in a best-of-five series. With his team on the brink of national embarrassment, Finley ordered Campaneris moved to leadoff batter, but the A's faced a larger problem: Who would start game three? Not having Catfish Hunter finally hit home. Alvin Dark seemed to be leaning toward starting Dick Bosman in game three. After all, the rested Bosman had won 11 of his 21 starts for the A's after joining the team in mid-season. However, Finley had other ideas. He lacked confidence in Bosman and ordered Dark to start Holtzman with only two days' rest. Finley and Dark hoped Holtzman could go for five or six strong innings, enough to get to the A's strong bullpen.

Holtzman held the Red Sox in check until the fourth inning, when a costly fielding error led to a single Red Sox run and a 1–0 lead. Holtzman's arm seemingly ran out of steam in the fifth as he gave up three Red Sox runs on big singles by Denny Doyle, Carlton Fisk, and Fred Lynn, knocking the A's starter out of the game and giving the Red Sox a commanding 4–0 lead. The A's could never catch up. While much was made over the loss of Catfish Hunter, the A's poor hitting and fielding played a major role in their defeats at the hands of the Red Sox. In the end, despite a late A's rally, the Sox strong pitching and fielding—led by the great glove play of left fielder Carl Yastrzemski—hamstrung the A's All-Star hitters. The A's lost game three to the Sox 5–3. Dreams of an A's four-peat championship evaporated in the bright California sun.

Following the game, many of the A's players, including Jackson, Rudi, Bando, and Fingers, walked over to the Red Sox locker room and congratulated the new AL champs. Finley said little to the press after the game.

As the A's assessed what happened to their dynasty, many understandably pointed to Finley's mishandling of the Hunter contract and the pitcher's escape via free agency. Years later, most players continued to point a finger at Finley. "It was absolutely huge; it really was," recalled Joe Rudi. "Finley lets him get away. I mean, he was really the backbone of our team and especially our pitching staff. And so now all that pressure fell on Holtzman and Blue, who still pitched great, but we really only had two good pitchers. Then what really killed us was Finley traded almost all of our really good young players away trying to replace him . . . Pitching is everything, and we just didn't have that extra little edge that made the difference between us and the Red Sox."[38]

San Francisco columnist Art Spander best summed up the A's downfall when he wrote, "The blame for the A's demise has been placed on Finley because he lost pitcher Catfish Hunter through a contractual oversight. But Hunter might not have made that much of a difference in the playoff. The A's could have made errors behind him the way they did behind Ken Holtzman. Yastrzemski still would have made his great catches and throws. But it wasn't Finley or Hunter, or any other member of the A's who were there or not there. Rather it was the Boston Red Sox moving in to take a championship the A's thought belonged only to them."[39]

The A's watched the World Series on television for the first time in three years, and Finley began planning for the 1976 season. First thing, however, he decided to rid himself of another field manager. Finley's relationship with Alvin Dark appeared more strained than normal as the A's fell to the Red Sox. Finley privately fumed at comments his born-again Christian manager made in the *Time* magazine article. Dark was asked how it was to work for Finley and responded by saying, "It's tough. Charlie's tough and rough, and at times you think he's cruel. But he is a winner."[40] Dark also offended his owner at a local church congregation in late September. During the talk, Dark reflected on his Christian faith and on Charlie Finley. For many months, Dark feared for Finley's soul and subtly tried to show him a new way to live his life, but Finley mostly passed off his overtures with jokes and smiles. "You know—and I'm saying this with respect—Charlie Finley feels he is a fantastic big person in the game of baseball. And he is," Dark told the congregation. "He has accomplished things, and I give him credit on building up the ball club. But to God, Charlie Finley is just a very little bitty thing that's lost, and if he doesn't accept Jesus Christ as his personal savior he's going to Hell."[41]

The following day, the suburban *Haywood Daily Review*'s headline was ALVIN DARK SAYS THAT UNLESS HE CHANGES HIS WAYS, FINLEY GOING TO HELL. Dark quickly claimed the quote was taken out of context, and publicly Finley seemed amused by the headline, saying his mother did not think he was going to hell, "and she knows more about these things than Alvin Dark." Dark's comments stung Finley to the core and confirmed his belief that Dark's proselytizing needed to stop.

After the playoff loss, Finley decided not to renew Dark's contract for 1976. Dark thus became the second field manager Finley fired twice. Upon hearing the news of his dismissal, Dark told the press, "Charlie called me and he told me that he was not going to renew my contract for next year. I said, 'Thank you for the two years and all I can do is wish you the best.' "[42] Later, when pushed by the media for a response to the firing, Finley said, "I simply believe that Dark's outside [church] activities interfered with managing the club."[43] Little did Finley realize that larger change loomed on the baseball horizon—change that would rock the world of baseball and crumble the A's fading dynasty.

Chapter Ten

Finley's Fire Sale

In January 1976, as Oakland A's owner Charles Finley sat in his offices on Chicago's Michigan Avenue, the baseball world was, to most observers, spinning out of control. To a man such as Charlie Finley, who valued control over everything, the events of 1976 would forever change his ability to compete as an owner. As the United States prepared to celebrate the bicentennial of its independence, baseball was poised to enter its own revolution. Despite what Finley's many critics within baseball thought, the wily and eccentric owner could clearly read the tea leaves; he realized that the days of the owners' control over baseball's salary structure were ending. And he was forming his own plans to steer through the coming storm. Finley was a survivor, a smart and savvy businessman, and he knew better than most of his fellow owners what he needed to do to survive the inevitable changes . . . or so he thought.

For the first time since 1972, the Oakland A's were not reigning world champions. During their reign, the A's gave baseball long hair and thick mustaches, kelly green and gold uniforms, white shoes, numerous locker room fights, constant news-making controversies, and the sport's most chaotic and dysfunctional owner—Charles O. Finley. Nonetheless, the Oakland A's, a small-market team from a city overshadowed by its neighbor across the bay, remained the class of the baseball world. The players had become household names—as had their ever-present owner.

Their run of three consecutive World Series championships had ended with Boston's stunning three-game sweep in the 1975 American League Championship Series. Despite being a seasoned team, the A's had folded in those games against the Red Sox, and looked surprisingly old and vulnerable in their first postseason series without Catfish Hunter. Was this the beginning of the A's decline or just a temporary lull? Many thought it was the latter, but the demise accelerated during 1976.

Keeping with the famous Finley modus operandi, he fired manager Alvin Dark after the loss to the Red Sox and in December 1975 hired former White Sox manager Chuck Tanner to guide the A's for the upcoming season. Finley, who repeatedly bullied Dark, felt his relationship with Tanner would be different. "Tanner possesses the qualities I have been looking for in a manager for a long time," Finley extolled. "He'll be the best manager I've ever had." Few reporters at the press conference believed the sales job. "I've had him in mind since the end of the season. I expect him to lead the A's to their fourth world championship in five years," Finley added. "I'm really happy to manage a club with the ability of the A's," said Tanner at the press conference. "They didn't win it last year, but they have a lot of pride. All they need to win again is for the season to start again."[1]

During the winter of 1976, the baseball world seemed to be unraveling in nearly every arena, none more so than with collective bargaining and player salaries. The players and their union leader, Marvin Miller, paid close attention to the amount of Hunter's new contract and the willingness of owners, despite their complaints at the bargaining table, to sign star players to a rich, multiyear contracts. Finley also knew his cadre of hardheaded, rabble-rousing players would push him for equally high salaries and multiyear deals. Though he no larger had the best club in baseball, Finley still had one of the highest team payrolls. When the first salary arbitration season came, the A's accounted for 9 of the 29 cases. While Finley growled about his arbitration losses that winter, their eventual total came to only $87,000.[2]

The salary losses Finley absorbed via arbitration would pale in comparison with the ones he would suffer after Peter Seitz's second bombshell decision in December 1975. With the support of the Major League Base-ball Players Association, pitchers Andy Messersmith and Dave McNally filed for an arbitration hearing after playing the 1975 season without a contract. The players sought to overturn the decades-old reserve clause, which bound players to teams for life. They wanted to become free agents with the ability to negotiate with all teams for their services. In a stunning December 1975 decision, arbitrator Peter Seitz invalidated the reserve clause, declaring the two players free to negotiate with any team. The precedent terrified owners. Players could now play out their option year and become free agents. Finley read the writing on the wall. Retaining his star players would be next to impossible because of all that had passed be-tween them over the years.

However, his fellow team owners did not go down without a fight. Following the Seitz ruling, Major League Baseball filed an appeal to the federal district court and the federal circuit court of appeals. Both courts rejected the appeal in the spring of 1976. Desperate for leverage over the players, the owners determined that with the expiration of MLB's collective bargaining agreement during the off-season, they would lock the players out of spring training in 1976, pending a new labor agreement in which they insisted on placing limitations on free agency. As the owners strategized and tried to renew labor negotiations with the players follow-ing the Seitz ruling, Finley, ever the astute businessman, opined that his fellow owners should "make 'em all free agents." He was right; this move would have diluted the market and reduced the salaries of players as a whole. But since Finley had proposed this strategy, it had no chance of be-ing adopted; he was a pariah among the lords of baseball. Royals owner Ewing Kauffman said it best: "If Finley pointed out the window at noon and said the sun was shining, many of the owners would have said it was dark." Many owners felt Finley's idea might lead to the rich teams buying all the good players. Kauffman added, "Teams with the most money would have all the best players soon . . . Every owner seemed opposed to Finley's crazy idea." However, in 2000, Bowie Kuhn said, "Maybe Charlie was right . . . I don't say that too often."[3]

Finley's idea of making every player a free agent concerned union head Marvin Miller. "With regard to his position on free agency, I worried about it because it made so much sense from the owners' point of view having lost the case—the Messersmith case," recalled Miller. "And Finley's suggestion not to fight free agency, to keep players signed to one-year contracts and let them be free really was starting to result in the market which was crowded with players and which could do nothing except hold salaries down. I was concerned that the logic of this would finally percolate on the owners."[4] Ultimately, his fellow owners, stuck in their old mindset and not having much respect for the bombastic Finley, dismissed his idea.

As winter turned to spring, Finley turned his focus to survival and how best to remain a viable owner with a competitive team. Labor negotiations with the union were at an impasse and the lockout remained in effect. Finley knew that some form of free agency would be institutionalized, and he understood that he would be unable to retain most of his star players. However, because of Finley's wheeling-and-dealing trades of recent years—many sending away talented farmhands in exchange for aging veterans to plug gaps on the team—the A's farm system possessed few young prospects. His team had already brought up two potential stars in 1975, outfielder Claudell Washington and second baseman Phil Garner, and behind them the cupboard appeared rather bare of talent.

Finley had plenty of experience in building a competitive team from virtually nothing. He had bought the hapless Kansas City Athletics team and transformed it from the foundation up. Finley also realized that the key to surviving in the new business-labor environment would come by developing young talent through his farm system. However, a few non-baseball-related problems were also affecting his ability to further replenish his farm system. Finley, who repeatedly whined about losing money in his baseball operation when in fact his baseball operation nearly always made a profit, actually appeared to be in financial trouble. He was in the midst of an acrimonious divorce battle with his wife, Shirley, and though it was not widely reported in the press, Finley needed money to settle the case. And his successful insurance business was suffering from the recession gripping the country in 1975 and 1976, with several longtime clients abandoning the insurance magnate. Nonetheless, Finley knew he had the baseball knowledge to survive. In the spring of 1976, the question came down to whether he had the necessary cash to remain competitive in the changing baseball environment.

In late winter 1976, a cash-strapped and stubborn Charlie Finley began contract negotiations with his major stars for the upcoming season. Ever the cantankerous negotiator, Finley faced several new challenges as he began contract considerations. First, most of his star players believed they could refuse to sign a contract for the 1976 season and become a free agent after the season, per the Seitz decision. Second, his stars saw the kind of contracts signed by Catfish Hunter and, later in the spring of 1976, Andy Messersmith. The contracts included large guaranteed salaries, were multiyear agreements, and contained no-trade or trade-limiting clauses. The A's all realized they were worth much more money than Finley was paying them. Third, Finley would have to deal with the agents representing all of his unsigned players—particularly the brassy young agent Jerry Kapstein.

Over the previous two off-seasons, Finley and Kapstein had butted heads in negotiations and arbitration hearings for several A's players. They loathed each other. The Harvard-educated Kapstein became the game's first super agent. He understood the key to winning arbitration hearings. He pioneered the use of statistics and formulas to highlight a player's net worth to a team. And Finley hated Kapstein for besting him. In the spring of 1976, Kapstein represented five of Finley's star players.[5]

Finley faced the daunting task of signing his nine dissatisfied stars. Reggie Jackson, Bill North, Joe Rudi, Bert Campaneris, Sal Bando, Gene Tenace, Rollie Fingers, Ken Holtzman, and Vida Blue were poised to play the 1976 season without signing a contract, thus becoming free agents at the end of the season. In February, Jerry Kapstein began negotiations by requesting a contract of $480,000 over three years for pitcher Ken Holtzman. Finley blew up. He was outraged at the request. "Kapstein called me and said both Campy [Campaneris] and Holtzman wanted multiyear contracts . . . I told him no way, I don't give multiyear contracts . . . When he finally told me $480,000 over three years [for Holtzman], I said, 'You make me sick' and I hung up on him. He didn't tell me what the others wanted because I didn't give him a chance to tell me. I couldn't care less."[6] This became a familiar occurrence throughout the spring of 1976. All of

Finley's stars wanted huge salary increases and guaranteed multiyear contracts. For instance, Rollie Fingers and Joe Rudi wanted three year contracts at $435,000 and $375,000, respectively. Finley offered only slightly more than a third of their requests and refused to budge.

On March 15, 1976, with his stars still unsigned, Finley executed the obligatory renewals of his players' contracts for the 1976 season based on their 1975 salaries, but he cut each player's salary by the maximum 20 percent allowed by league rules. While the players expected this reaction, it only strengthened their resolve to not sign a contract and thereby become a free agent after the season. Then suddenly, on March 17, at the urging of Dodgers owner Walter O'Malley, commissioner Bowie Kuhn lifted the lockout and opened the major-league training camps. Baseball would start the 1976 season without a new labor agreement.[7]

Charlie Finley was running out of time. Facing the possibility of losing all of his star players with nothing in return, he decided to take action himself. On April 3, 1976, after weeks of rumors and speculation, he began an overhaul of the A's. He traded outfielder Reggie Jackson, pitcher Ken Holtzman, and a minor-league pitcher to the Baltimore Orioles for outfielder Don Baylor, veteran pitcher Mike Torrez, and highly touted pitching prospect Paul Mitchell. The trade of the former MVP and superstar Jackson rocked the baseball world. Prior to the trade, Jackson and Finley had been involved in serious contract negotiations. In fact, Jackson had stated publicly that he wanted to remain with Oakland. "I've got things too good here. I'd be stupid to go anywhere else . . . I feel like I'm part of the Oakland scene," Jackson told the Oakland press. Uncharacteristically, Finley was even talking about a multiyear contract with Jackson's agent. Soon after the trade was announced, Finley claimed the move was simply to obtain additional pitching for the A's. It had nothing to do with the contract squabble. "The deal was made because it will lead us to another world championship," Finley said. "I would have made the deal even if all three of the players were signed."[8]

Finley went on to say, "We felt we needed another starting pitcher. We feel Paul Mitchell is one of our starters. He is a very outstanding young pitcher." Mitchell had gone 10–1 at the Orioles' AAA Rochester club in 1975 and 3–0 in a brief stint with the O's in a September call-up. However, many of his players doubted this reasoning and felt the A's did not receive equal value in return. "I don't think the guys we got from Baltimore are as good as Kenny or Reggie," said A's outfielder Joe Rudi. Interestingly, Don Baylor, also represented by Jerry Kapstein, was not under contract for the 1976 season. Thus, Finley traded an unsigned Reggie Jackson for an unsigned Don Baylor. Finley found Baylor's contract demands just as "unreasonable" as Jackson's. Baylor quickly joined his A's teammates in looking forward to his free agency after the season.[9]

A couple of weeks later, Finley sang a different tune about his blockbuster trade. He stated in the local media that he traded Jackson because he had refused to lower his salary demands. Finley reportedly offered Jackson a three-year contract totaling $525,000. Jackson and his agent, Gary Walker, had countered with a request for an additional $75,000 a year to be deferred over a 10-year period. His request would have increased the value of the contract to $750,000. Finley balked. "I told Walker, there was no way I'd go for that," Finley groused. "There were only two courses open to me—run away, or roll up my sleeves and start fighting. I don't run away from a fight, so I simply told the agent I was going to give him an hour and a half to change his mind. If he didn't, I would trade him [Jackson]. When he failed to call back, I traded him." While Walker could not remember the exact sequence, he did recall Finley indicating he would trade Jackson if they did not lower their terms. In a matter a few hours, the most famous and talented of the A's stars was gone.[10]

To make matters worse, the A's got off to a terrible start to the regular season. Minus Jackson and Holtzman, the team seemed to be lacking chemistry and leadership. Early-season hitting slumps plagued newly acquired Don Baylor, veteran shortstop Campy Campaneris, team captain Sal Bando, and designated hitter Billy Williams. Gene Tenace, the A's regular catcher, was on the disabled list. Even the pitching was inconsistent. On May 28, the fifth-place A's had an 18–24 record and were already 7.5 games out of first place.[11]

Throughout the spring of 1976, commissioner Bowie Kuhn watched Finley's horse trading with a wary eye. Kuhn, who viewed Finley as a rather unsavory person and businessman, grew to not just dislike Charlie Finley; he grew to despise him. Kuhn, an Ivy League–educated lawyer from New

York, found few redeeming qualities in the A's owner. Finley resented the commissioner for his constant interference. Charlie O. had always resisted authority, and Kuhn particularly boiled Finley's blood. He hated Kuhn so much that he always mispronounced the commissioner's name as "coon" (as in raccoon), as a show of disrespect.

Finley was facing many uncertainties and potential problems in May 1976. First, the labor situation was at a stalemate, and the final resolution was unclear. Finley's labor advice to his fellow owners was wholeheartedly ignored. Second, Finley and most of the baseball world knew free agency was just around the corner, and he was unsure of his ability to compete in the new marketplace. Third, many of the A's players were likely to play out the season without contracts and become free agents at the end of it. Fourth, the A's were off to a slow start and, minus Jackson and Holtzman, unlikely to win the division crown. This left Finley with a short window to move the remaining players via trades if he could not sign them. And finally, Finley's old nemesis Bowie Kuhn was carefully watching the A's as the trading deadline approached. Kuhn tried keeping the A's owner on a short leash. Once again, Finley was poised to break the leash.

By June, Charlie Finley was growing anxious. While he had successfully signed one of his unsigned players—outfielder Bill North—the others remained unsigned and looked forward to leaving the land of Charlie O. at season's end. The other stars were holding out for big raises and long-term deals. Nevertheless, Finley had not lost hope of signing a few of his stars.

Prior to the June 15 trade deadline, he gathered his stars together at Comiskey Park in Chicago before an A's game against the White Sox. He told them that he wanted to sign them and that he thought of each as a son. But, Finley warned, he could not handle the no-trade clauses and guaranteed contracts they wanted. "You have those kind of contracts on your ball club, you have handcuffs on your hands; you can't maneuver," he stated. "You could have the entire club signed but not be able to trade a single player . . . That I don't approve." As for Kapstein, Finley brought out his usual rant: "You know it is awfully hard for me to make a deal when I have continuously requested your agent come to Chicago and sit down and talk to me. He has yet to come in."[12] It was Finley's best sales pitch, but no one showed much interest. For one thing, he had slashed their salaries by 20 percent. And for another, all present had heard his tales before and were growing accustomed to being lied to. Just in case Finley might hoodwink the new players in the clubhouse, Joe Rudi advised them that "anytime you hear him clearing his throat, he's lying. If you hear him say 'a-hem,' watch out."[13]

Soon after the Comiskey Park meeting, Finley started working the phone lines with several clubs, including the Red Sox and Yankees, to make blockbuster trades. He proposed many outlandish trades, including sending Rudi, Fingers, Blue, Tenace, and Bando to the Red Sox for outfielder Fred Lynn, catcher Corlton Fisk, and a couple of lesser players. He proposed trading Vida Blue for Yankees catcher Thurman Munson and one of their outfielders (Roy White or Elliott Maddox); he later changed the proposal to Rudi for Munson. Finley called nearly every team in the American League offering various deals. Finley found no takers.[14]

The day before the trade deadline, Finley placed numerous phone calls to fellow owners from his Chicago office. His tactic had changed. Instead of trading players, he now was willing to "sell" his stars for cash. He talked with Red Sox executive Dick O'Connell and Yankee president Gabe Paul. The Yankees and Red Sox were in a hot pennant race, and neither side wanted to be holding an empty bag at the trade deadline. Finley told O'Connell, "I'm offering Rudi, Blue, Baylor, or Tenace for a million apiece and Bando for half a million, are you interested?" His offer stunned O'Connell, but the Red Sox GM jokingly asked Finley if he didn't like Italians (a reference to the lesser price for Sal Bando). Finley replied, "I don't like him."[15]

O'Connell and his assistant Gene Kirby were already in Oakland awaiting their team's arrival on June 14 for a series with the A's beginning the following night. They had hoped to see Finley, only to discover that he was in Chicago. They quickly called Red Sox manager Darrell Johnson before he left for the flight to Oakland. They asked Johnson what two players he wanted. He said Rudi and Fingers. O'Connell was puzzled by this response because the Red Sox were already loaded with players and talent in the outfield; he believed they needed pitching to beat the Yankees and Orioles. As the day passed, O'Connell and Kirby were convinced that

Blue was a better choice and that they could convince Johnson of this when he arrived with the team in Oakland. However, a series of problems ensued, preventing them from talking to Johnson that evening. With the night growing late, O'Connell called Finley and agreed to take Joe Rudi and Rollie Fingers for a million dollars apiece. The first transaction was done. Then O'Connell tried to get the Detroit Tigers to keep Vida Blue away from the Yankees.[16]

Dick O'Connell called Tigers general manager Jim Campbell and strongly suggested that he offer the A's $1 million for Vida Blue before the Yankees could close a deal with Finley. It was the middle of the night on the East Coast, but Campbell called Finley and offered $1 million to match the offer Yankees president Gabe Paul had made earlier in the day. Faced with two million-dollar offers, Finley called Paul and convinced him to up his offer to $1.5 million for Blue. However, Paul drove a harder bargain than the Red Sox. The Yankees wanted Blue signed to a contract before they would complete the transaction. Finley then called Blue's agent and began negotiations. Of course, Finley did not disclose to Blue or his agent, Chris Daniel, that he had an agreement to sell Blue to the Yankees. Finley, negotiating on the Yankees' behalf, maintained his thrifty nature. He called Daniel's three-year, $600,000 proposal "astronomical." Both sides continued back and forth, finally agreeing to the terms of three years for $485,000. The Yankees jumped the gun on Finley and prematurely announced the sale. Suddenly, Blue realized that the one who had profited the most from his own value and talents was the arrogant and tightfisted Charlie O. Finley.[17]

The news of the trades spread over the newswires as fast as lightning. Finley quickly called the A's clubhouse to inform manager Chuck Tanner of the trades and talk to the departing players. Several members of the press crowded into Finley's Chicago office watching the circus master at work. Don Pierson of the *Chicago Tribune* recorded the Finley side of the conversations that night with the A's players and manager.

Finley explained to Tanner and others in the A's clubhouse that he had no alternative but to trade his stars. He stated, "I can't afford to pay these astronomical salaries they are all demanding when we're drawing so poorly in Oakland." He told Tanner, "We'll rebuild, Chuck. I'm sorry we had to do this today. The big thing, Chuck, as I'm telling the press here, was the agent Jerry Kapstein . . . He kept me in the dark continuously, right up to the last minute. Never made one trip to come in and talk to me."

Finley went on, "Is Vida there? I can't find him. The damn Yankees released the story on me and it makes me look bad because I didn't tell him . . . Rudi cried for half an hour, I know he feels bad. Let me talk to them, Chuck. All of 'em. One at a time." Finley proceeded to talk with several of the A's players.

Finally, Vida Blue got on the phone. "Vida," he said, "this is Charlie Finley. I know how you feel. The goddamn Yanks jumped the time on me . . . What do you mean, what announcement? I traded you to the Yankees . . . just you . . . for money."

Finley continued talking to Blue on the phone as reporters listened: "Vida, this will mean an awful lot to you. I've appreciated all you've done to help me and all the contributions you've made . . . Well, I appreciate you accepting this in a professional manner. I hate to see you go . . . This whole thing was brought on by one agent, Jerry Kapstein . . . I love you buddy and believe me when I tell you that." Blue had been scheduled to pitch that evening against the Red Sox. The slick-talking Finley was in rare form.

As word spread that evening from coast to coast, a reporter asked Finley if he had any more trades in the works. Finley said, "The night is young." In fact, trader Charlie did have a couple of additional sales in the works. He had contacted White Sox owner Bill Veeck and was discussing Sal Bando. Reached later, Veeck observed, "It looks as if he's pulling another Connie Mack . . . Apparently, he's conducting a fire sale, but not at fire sale prices."[18] The Rangers also tried to pick up Don Baylor for $1 million as well, but as Finley sat in his office above the Chicago skyline, commissioner Bowie Kuhn prepared to extinguish the fire sale.

Kuhn just happened to be in Chicago on June 15 attending a routine Players Relations Committee meeting. He had heard rumors of Finley offering players to other teams. He knew Finley's situation and expected him to trade a few of his stars as the trading deadline neared. The day before, rumors had spread about Finley actually selling players. Kuhn had urged American League president Lee MacPhail to persuade Finley to abandon his plans. MacPhail tried, but Finley refused to listen.[19]

On the evening of June 15, Kuhn was watching the White Sox play the Orioles at Comiskey Park. It was nice evening for a game, and he was enjoying the pitching duel between Jim Palmer and Goose Gossage. At around 9 P.M., Kuhn's assistant Johnny Johnson arrived and told him the news of Finley's sale of Blue, Rudi, and Fingers for a total of $3.5 million to the Yankees and Red Sox.[20]

Kuhn quickly called Dick O'Connell and informed him of his displeasure with the sale. O'Connell told Kuhn, "Commissioner, that's what you're there for! If you don't like it, you can kill it, and that's it." Kuhn phoned Finley at his office and said, "Charlie, I'm at Comiskey and just heard from Johnny about your sales. I don't like the look of these sales at all. I'm putting everything on hold until I can decide whether or not to stop them. I want you to know that. I've advised the Red Sox and Yankees." Finley shot back, "Commissioner, it's none of your damn business. You can't stop me from selling players. Guys have been selling players forever and no commissioner has ever stopped them." It was true. Connie Mack had emptied his teams of his star players on two different occasions by selling the players outright. Kuhn listened to the angry Finley, who sounded close to a verbal meltdown—something that would hurt both of them. Kuhn suggested that they meet that evening and talk over the situation.[21]

Everyone arrived at around 10 P.M. at the coffee shop in the Pick Congress Hotel (not to be confused with the Congress Plaza Hotel on Michigan Avenue at Grant Park). Sandy Hadden, Kuhn's second in command, and Kuhn both eyed Finley and his son Paul across the table. Finley began, "Don't butt into this, there are other things the commissioner should be doing. Don't butt into this." He then showed Kuhn the sale agreement with the Yankees and launched into his monologue of the world according to Finley. He recounted the legend of Charlie Finley and talked about his past deals and his successes. He claimed he would use the money to buy prospects and rebuild his franchise into another winner. "Commissioner, I can't sign these guys. They don't want to play for ol' Charlie. They want to chase those big bucks in New York. If I sell them now, I can at least get something back. If I can't, they walk out on me at the end of the season and I've got nothing." As an additional flourish, Finley added, "This free agency thing is terrible. The only way to beat it is with young players. That's where I'll put the money."

Finley whined about the state of his finances and how he had tried to trade the three players but found no takers. So he had reluctantly turned to a sale for cash. His argument failed to impress Kuhn, who did not believe Finley's claims of poverty and distress. While Finley's points were rational, Kuhn knew Finley's mischievous ways. Kuhn believed lying was Finley's forte—especially since the owner had just signed Blue to a long-term deal before shipping him to the Yankees. It was past midnight in Chicago, and Kuhn decided he had heard enough. "I'm still very troubled by this situation. Charlie," Kuhn said. "You've made your points, you've given something to think about . . . I can't tell you anything tonight. But, I'm freezing those players right now until I decide how to handle this." The meeting ended without further discussion.[22]

Kuhn flew back to New York and the next day convened an executive committee meeting by telephone. The morning papers on June 16 carried headlines about the sale, and the whole baseball world seemed poised for a showdown. Kuhn was still not convinced about Finley's motivations. He was equally concerned as to what precedent the sales might set. It could lead to weaker teams routinely selling off their players to stronger teams, upsetting the competitive balance in baseball. The meeting began with members of the executive committee, including team owners, stating that the deal was bad for baseball. Some of the those same owners had only 48 hours earlier tried to bargain with Finley for the players. American League president Lee MacPhail said, "If you get into this, Finley is surely going to start a fight. We're going to have the unpleasantness of court proceedings. I doubt that's very good for the game."[23]

There was also concern about how this potential controversy might affect the pending collective bargaining deal with the players' union. Many felt it would lead the union to believe Kuhn was trying to undermine free agency. Several felt Kuhn shouldn't interfere. However, one voice had yet to be heard—that of Walter O'Malley. O'Malley believed the sale sent a bad message at a time the sport needed business stability. He also shared

Kuhn's concern over balance and competitiveness. "You must not allow this to happen," O'Malley advised Kuhn. At the end of the teleconference, the committee was tied 3–3 on whether to stop the sale. Both sides presented persuasive arguments, but no decision was made. Kuhn decided to have a hearing with all parties the next day.[24]

The following day, 18 people attended the hearing in Kuhn's New York office. Charlie Finley, Dick O'Connell, Yankees owner George Steinbrenner, Yankees GM Gabe Paul, players association director Marvin Miller, and Finley attorney David Kentoff were all present to plead their cases. Finley recounted most of the same arguments he had made previously to Kuhn. After the 90-minute meeting ended, most of the attendees felt that the sales were going to be approved. Steinbrenner even flashed a thumbs-up sign to the media after the meeting. Most believed that while Kuhn did not personally approve of the sale, he did not have the legal basis to stop it. After the meeting, Finley, dapper in a gray plaid suit and yellow golf shirt and hat, confidently said, "I plan to use this money to great advantage. We'll be able to purchase a lot of players at the end of the season." Marvin Miller opined, "I don't understand what the furor is about. No rules have been violated. What has happened here has happened hundreds of times: namely the selling of players for cash." Kuhn, though, remained noncommittal: "The issue is whether the assignment of the contracts is appropriate or not under the circumstances. That's the issue I have to wrestle with. I have to consider these transactions in the best interest of baseball." Kuhn's decision would come the next day.[25]

Since the announcements of the sale and the commissioner's hold, Rudi, Fingers, and Blue had been in a state of limbo. Boston manager Darrell Johnson had already decided not to play Rudi and Fingers on June 15. He wanted to calm their nerves and allow them to recover from the shock. Both Rudi and Fingers were pictured in Red Sox uniforms on the night of June 15 but never played a game for the Red Sox. "We were ecstatic to be going to Boston . . . My wife had the whole house packed the next day. Still it was a very emotional day . . . I was an 'A' my whole life, and all of a sudden I am on the Red Sox side," reflected Joe Rudi. Essentially, they were players without a team. They were not allowed to work out with either the A's or Red Sox. But after reflecting on the situation,

Fingers said, "Hey, I'm worth a million dollars. Somehow, that just doesn't seem right." Rudi remembered years later, "We were in limbo. All of our stuff was packed in trunks . . . all of our family stuff. We had eight or ten trunks in the Boston clubhouse . . . The Red Sox took them with the team to Anaheim." Meanwhile, Vida Blue remained in the Bay Area, awaiting the outcome of the hearing. On June 17, the Red Sox left Oakland for Anaheim and their next series with the Angels. Rudi and Fingers remained in Oakland.[26]

With Finley back in Chicago on June 19, Kuhn announced his decision. The commissioner went with his own impulses and feelings and voided the sales. His carefully worded statement explained his reasoning.

> Shorn of much of its finest talent in exchange for cash, the Oakland club, which has been divisional champion for the last five years, has little chance to compete effectively in its division. Whether other players will be available to restore the club by using the cash involved is altogether speculative although Mr. Finley vigorously argues his ability to do so . . . Public confidence in the integrity of club operations and in baseball would be greatly undermined should such assignments not be restrained . . .
>
> Nor can I persuade myself that the spectacle of the Yankees and Red Sox buying contracts of star players in the prime of their careers for cash sums totaling $3,500,000 is anything but devastating to baseball's reputation for integrity and to public confidence in the game, even though I can well understand that their motive is a good faith effort to strengthen their clubs. If such transactions now and in the future were permitted, the door would be opened wide to the buying of success by the more affluent clubs, public suspicion would be aroused, traditional and sound methods of player development and acquisition would be undermined and our efforts to preserve the competitive balance would be greatly impaired. I cannot help but conclude that I would be remiss in exercising my powers as commissioner pursuant to Major League Agreement and Major League Rule 12 if I did not act now to disapprove these assignments.[27]

The reaction was nearly immediate. "The ruling is horse bleep," Finley roared. "Kuhn sounds like the village idiot. He's continuing a personal vendetta with me," the A's owner suggested. "We're going to haul his tail into court Monday. His Highness can't make decisions that are contrary to the law of the land."[28]

While public opinion seemed firmly on Charlie Finley's side, Commissioner Kuhn seemed confident in the Major League Agreement and his authority to act. Finley fumed in Chicago, talking to all who would listen about the injustice of the ruling. Seven days after the Kuhn decision, Finley filed a $10 million lawsuit in federal court in Chicago against Kuhn, claiming restraint of trade. Finley ordered Chuck Tanner not to play Rudi, Fingers, or Blue until the issue was resolved in the courts. Finley attorney Neil Papiano explained the rationale: "If Charlie uses any of the players, then, in essence, he is ratifying the commissioners position." Papiano believed that the players should not even be allowed in the clubhouse because of the previous fights and injuries in the A's locker room. Joe Rudi remembered, "Finally, after a week, Finley let us come to the park, work out before the games, and take batting practice." Thus, Tanner was forced to use a roster of only 22 players, missing three of his biggest stars.[29]

The A's played nearly two weeks without Blue, Rudi, and Fingers. The inactivity was frustrating for the players. "We were getting pretty disgusted with the whole thing," Fingers recalled. Finally, on June 24, Kuhn ordered Finley to "remove any restraints" from playing them. Finley balked. The Twins were in town, and the A's took a strike vote on June 26 after the three were not allowed to play. The vote was 20–0, with two abstaining, to strike the next day. On June 27, the team sat in the locker room in street clothes up to nearly 10 minutes before game time. The A's were once again playing chicken with their owner. "It got to the point where we had a team meeting," Fingers said, "and we told Chuck Tanner that guys weren't gonna play . . . We were gonna forfeit the game to Minnesota if we were not activated." Tanner walked into the locker room after a phone call with Finley. Billy North asked what the lineup was. "Okay here it is," said Tanner, who proceeded to read the lineup: "North, centerfield . . . Campaneris, shortstop . . . Baylor, designated hitter . . . Bando, third base . . . Tenace, first base . . . Rudi, left field . . ." The room erupted. "I'm telling you, it was mass hysteria," said Sal Bando. "It was like the World Series around here . . . All we wanted to hear was Rudi's name was in there." The A's went on to defeat the Twins that afternoon 5–3. Rudi went hitless, but Fingers pitched three and one-third innings to pick up his ninth save.[30]

For Rudi, Fingers, and Blue, the return to the lineup was bittersweet. And all three struggled afterward. Blue did not win another game until July 6, more than three weeks after the fire sale. On June 14, the A's had a 27–31 record and were 10.5 games out of first place. The A's won six and lost five games with the three players out of the lineup. The two weeks of inactivity by the three and their following struggle to regain their batting strokes or stamina on the pitching mound may have cost the A's the Western Division pennant. In July, the A's proceeded to right the ship and started winning games in bunches. They nearly ran themselves into the playoffs as they stole 341 bases, a major-league record. The A's finished 87–74, only 2.5 games behind the Kansas City Royals. "We lost to Kansas City that year . . . I think if we'd been playing, and had the opportunity to play those two weeks, we may have won the pennant that year," Fingers recalled.[31]

In November 1976, the six A's free agents applied for the reentry draft—making Finley's worst fears come true. However, Vida Blue remained an Athletic after being tricked into signing a three-year contract before the sale to the Yankees. All six A's free agents signed multiyear big-money contracts that autumn: Don Baylor and Joe Rudi signed with the California Angels; Rollie Fingers and Gene Tenace signed with the San Diego Padres; Sal Bando went to the Milwaukee Brewers; and Campy Campaneris opted for the Texas Rangers. Charlie Finley had rolled the dice in trying to sell his three stars—but unfortunately his luck had ran out.

As for the A's themselves, it was obvious the team was in a decline, the beginning which may be appropriately traced to the departure of Catfish Hunter in 1975. Joe Rudi recalled that in losing Hunter, "we lost that little edge that made the difference between us and the other teams." The decline accelerated with Finley's trade of Reggie Jackson and Ken Holtzman to the Orioles in the spring of 1976. Rudi recalled, "When he traded them to Baltimore, we knew that was the beginning of the end. Most of us who were unsigned figured that, before the year was over, we were going to be traded. So we were all standing by, waiting for the hammer to fall."[32]

Separately, the A's players who won championships from 1972 to 1974 never matched their collective success in Oakland, except for Reggie Jackson and, to a lesser extent, Catfish Hunter (three pennants, two World Series champions with the Yankees) and Rollie Fingers (MVP and Cy Young awards in 1981 with the Padres). Joe Rudi helped the Angels win their division but never matched his Oakland success; he retired in 1982. Bert Campaneris made the 1977 All-Star team while with the Rangers, but he lost his starting position the next season and played as a utility infielder until his retirement in 1983. Sal Bando was a starter for Brewers for three years and retired following the 1981 season. Vida Blue pitched for the A's in 1977, but was never again dominant, as his career became side-tracked by injury and drug problems. Kuhn appropriately concluded that Blue "was bitter and suspicious, exactly as I would find him during the rest of his career."[33]

Finley recognized that with free agency, his small-market A's could not effectively compete against the larger-market teams without a radical shift in strategy. He did not have the finances to compete with the George Steinbrenners and Gene Autrys of baseball. Finley knew he had to obtain value for his star players before they became free agents. He also realized that only by developing talent in the minor leagues could he continue to compete in the brave new world of free agency and salary arbitration.

In this, Finley pioneered the practice that owners of small-market teams still use 30 years later: Trade or sell outright your pending free agents to obtain value before you lose them, and then plow either the prospects or the money back into your minor-league system. It is how the Twins, Marlins, Indians, Tigers, A's, and other small-market teams are able to compete today. Kuhn's ruling, however, prevented Finley from carrying out his strategy. Was Kuhn motivated by his stated belief that preventing the sales was "in the best interest of baseball" or by his antipathy toward Finley?

If Dodgers owner Walter O'Malley had wanted to sell his All-Star infield because of impending free agency, it is hard to believe that Kuhn would have interceded in the same way. Simply put, Kuhn overstepped his powers in June 1976 and in the process destroyed Finley and the A's ability to compete for the next three years. One could fairly conclude that Kuhn was siding with O'Malley and other members of the baseball establishment in their dislike of Finley. But Finley would soon have his day in court and a final showdown with his nemesis Bowie Kuhn.

Chapter Eleven

Finley vs. Kuhn

As Charlie Finley entered the large meeting room at the Los Angeles Hilton during the December 1976 baseball winter meetings for a hastily called news conference, he knew the coming few months would decide his future as an owner of a major-league ball club. His once-proud championship franchise lay in shambles. Six of his frontline starters had jumped ship only weeks earlier in baseball's first reentry free agency draft. Rudi, Tenace, Baylor, Fingers, Bando, and Campaneris all signed with new clubs for multiyear, million-dollar-plus contracts. Finley drafted 24 free agents during the proceedings, but because of his limited financial resources and his tightfisted, bombastic reputation as an owner, he found no players interested in signing with the A's. Only two stars from his championship teams remained: Vida Blue and outfielder Billy North.

Finley also knew his upcoming legal showdown with MLB commissioner Bowie Kuhn, which would begin in a mere two weeks in his home city of Chicago, would determine his future in Oakland. Finley filed a $10 million lawsuit in the summer against Kuhn for voiding his fire sale of pitchers Vida Blue and Rollie Fingers and outfielder Joe Rudi for $3.5 million. Kuhn claimed his voiding of the sale preserved the integrity of the game and was in the "best interest of baseball." Finley hoped to prove in court that Kuhn's action had grossly exceeded his authority. Interestingly, Finley's colleagues voted (24–2) to indemnify Kuhn and baseball against any loss suffered in the upcoming trial. If Finley won the trial, he would also have to share in the cost of his winning verdict.

In front of a dozen reporters, Finley, in his deep, coarse voice, began a rambling 90-minute monologue that covered many subjects but mostly centered on free agency, Bowie Kuhn, and the terrible state of baseball under Kuhn's leadership. It was vintage Charlie Finley. "Without leadership, you have no stability," Finley began in his opening statement. "At this point in time, we have no stability. There is one individual who calls himself the Commissioner of Baseball who single-handedly has ruined the A's and potentially the game of baseball."

Finley went on to say, "I'm in favor of the government stepping in, not only in baseball, but all sports, before the owners destroy themselves. The owners need to be protected. They are destroying themselves." He then proceeded to complain that six of his former All-Stars signed new multi-year contracts that guaranteed them more than $9.2 million in salaries and bonuses. Had he counted former A's superstar Reggie Jackson's new Yankees contract (Finley had traded the unsigned and dissatisfied Jackson just prior to the 1976 season), it would have added up to more than $12 million in salaries and bonuses received by the former A's players.

"In defense of the players in all sports, I don't blame them. We have two problems. Number one, no leadership. Number two, the stupidity of the owners. The day of reckoning [for the owners] isn't tomorrow. It was yesterday and today," Finley ranted. "In the end, the rich clubs will end up controlling baseball. There is no way the A's, Minnesota, and a couple of other clubs can survive the battle," Finley said. "Some owners ask me where we are headed. I say to them, 'To the crapper.' "

Finley ended the press conference by stating that if he won his upcoming lawsuit against Kuhn and MLB, he planned on selling the A's and leaving baseball. He claimed to be in serious financial shape, facing a possible bankruptcy. "I'm here to tell you today, I can't compete with the other clubs. As much as I love baseball, I can't hack it," Finley said.[1]

While Finley cried constantly about the A's losing money, facts do not support his claims. For example, A's treasurer Charles Cottonaro recalled that during his tenure every year except one the team made money.[2] Although the A's were not a huge moneymaking dynamo for the Charles O. Finley and Company, moreover, Finley said years after leaving baseball that the A's division of the company actually turned a profit in 19 of the 20 years he owned the ball club (the exception being 1979). Some years were better than others, but overall Finley's A's made money. Whether or not Finley's claims of financial ruin were accurate, he did face enormous monetary hurdles in both baseball and his insurance business during the mid and late 1970s. He desperately needed to score a win over Bowie Kuhn in December 1976; he knew his future as an owner and a national figure depended on it.

The "Charles O. Finley and Company versus Kuhn" trial began on December 16, 1976, in federal court in Chicago before U.S. District Court Judge Frank McGarr. Both sides utilized dozens of lawyers, with the Finley legal team led by San Francisco attorney Neil Papiano and the Kuhn–Major League Baseball team led by Washington attorney Peter Bleakley. Finley had bucked his attorney's advice earlier by filing the lawsuit in Chicago rather than Oakland. Judge McGarr attempted to show some humor by stating at the opening of the trial that he was "going to resist the temptation to open this trial by saying 'Play ball.' "[3] Despite the judge's use of baseball terminology in his opening remark, Finley's attorneys were concerned from the outset over McGarr's lack of familiarity with baseball. Finley attorney Dennis Page recalled, "The trial was in the federal court in Chicago, and by random selection we get a judge, Frank McGarr, crusty old fellow. We went into chambers and met with him to go over preliminary things before the trial, and the subject came up as to whether he was a baseball fan. He told us without blinking an eye, 'You know, I'm really not. I don't know much about the game.' And I thought, 'Oh, my God! Of all the people we could have gotten—a judge who swears he doesn't know anything about the game of baseball!' "[4]

The Finley vs. Kuhn trial marked only the second time in baseball history that an owner had brought suit against a commissioner in court. The proceedings took 15 days and played out before a packed courtroom with dozens of reporters from around the country. In the end, the trial had 20 live witnesses, including both Finley and Kuhn, plus more than a dozen depositions, which were read into the record. The official trial transcript ran 2,059 pages and did not include the thousands of pages of pre- and post-trial briefs filed by each party. More than a hundred exhibits were presented during the trial—mostly old newspaper clippings about past baseball transactions decades earlier.

The trial boiled down into one real issue: Did Kuhn exceed his authority in voiding the sales of the A's players for $3.5 million in June 1976? The Finley legal team argued Kuhn acted beyond his authority and with malice in voiding the A's owner's sale of his three star players. Finley claimed the sales did not violate existing baseball rules and, in fact, selling players had occurred on numerous occasions throughout the history of the sport. Finley claimed he attempted to sign all of his star players but found their demands too great, and not finding any owners willing to trade other players for his, he was forced to sell them in order to avoid a total loss when they became free agents. Finley contended he planned to use the $3.5 million from the sale to purchase quality players both at the major-league and amateur levels in order to rebuild his franchise for future seasons.

The Kuhn side contended that the commissioner voided the sales on the basis that they were not in the "best interest" of baseball and that, if they had gone through, the trades would have upset the "competitive balance" of the game. Kuhn's legal team cited the ironclad authority granted the commissioner in the Major League Agreement governing baseball. They contended that the commissioner possessed unfettered powers over the business and on-field aspects of baseball and that his decisions were final.

The trial was contentious nearly from the start, with each side employing aggressive courtroom tactics. On one trial day, Kuhn's attorneys rose to voice 49 objections on various procedures and witness questions posed to American League president Lee MacPhail by Finley's attorneys. Repeatedly, Finley's attorneys tried to steer the court to examine the merits of the sales through similar past trades and sales. They attempted to ask key witnesses, "What would you have done?" and "What did you think of Kuhn's decision?" Papiano attacked Kuhn's "best interest of baseball" argument and tried to convince Judge McGarr, who would decide the case himself without a jury, that Kuhn mainly voided the deal because of the large amount of cash exchanging hands. They attempted to portray Kuhn as vindictive, canceling the sales because of personal malice toward Finley. However, Judge McGarr continuously steered both sides, particularly the Finley team, toward the real issue on trial. "Whether the commissioner did indeed have the authority [to kill the trade] is the ultimate issue," McCarr noted.[5]

The Finley team called seven key witnesses to support their case: James Enright, a retired Chicago baseball writer and author of *Trade Him*, a book about historic baseball trades and sales; Richard Moss, lead counsel for the MLB Players Association; Richard Sandor, an economist; AL president Lee MacPhail; former Texas Rangers owner Bob Short; Yankees president Gabe Paul; and Finley himself.

Economist Richard Sandor testified that Finley's $3.5 million haul for his three stars was not as much as former A's owner Connie Mack received in the early 1930s, when he broke up his championship teams. Over a period of three years, Mack sold players for more than $900,000, which, with inflation and other economic factors, translated to $4.5 million in 1977, according to Sandor. He also estimated that the 1947–1948 breakup of the St. Louis Browns netted owner Bill DeWitt nearly $1.2 million at the time, which translated to nearly $3 million in 1977. Additionally, James Enright testified about four historic instances in which club owners broke up a team by selling players for cash. Papiano hammered home the fact that these and other sales of players were allowed by previous commissioners.[6]

Later, players association chief counsel Dick Moss testified that the Major League Agreement does not provide the commissioner with the powers to arbitrarily void player sales or trades that do not violate baseball rules. On the witness stand for two days, Lee MacPhail testified that the MLB executive committee appeared split on whether to allow the trade. However, MacPhail indicated that a majority did favor allowing the sales but that Dodgers owner Walter O'Malley had said, "I'm probably a minority of one." MacPhail went on to say, "He [O'Malley] thought these assignments were damaging to baseball's competitive balance and said strong action by the commissioner was needed."[7]

Prior to the executive committee meeting, MacPhail had discussed the sale at length with Kuhn. "We both agreed it was regrettable these assignments were made," MacPhail testified. "But I advised him [Kuhn] he should not take action."[8] Later, during cross-examination, Kuhn attorney Irwin Nathan asked MacPhail whether the commissioner had the right to disapprove a player assignment. MacPhail said the commissioner did have the right.

Bob Short and Gabe Paul testified to their belief that the commissioner cannot intervene with team player assignments and that his powers were limited to enforcing the rules concerning trades and player transactions. Thus, if no existing rule was broken, Kuhn could not legally void the sales. Paul also testified that the commissioner "cannot make any determination on competitive balance." Papiano read the deposition of Bill DeWitt, who owned three major-league clubs and served as chairman of the Chicago White Sox in 1977. DeWitt explained the limitation placed on the commissioner's office to perform secretarial and perfunctory duties concerning player assignments. "There's no such thing as competitive balance or trying for competitive balance," DeWitt said. "It's dog eat dog."[9]

Interestingly, the Finley legal team could only offer DeWitt's deposition testimony instead of having him testify live in court. Only two weeks before the trial, Finley and DeWitt were both attending baseball's annual winter meetings in Los Angeles. DeWitt casually approached Finley during a break in the meeting for some small talk. The mercurial Finley was not in a good mood that day and proceeded to berate DeWitt simply for asking how he was doing. DeWitt had been scheduled as an important witness for Finley at the trial. But after Finley's explosion, he refused to attend the trial or testify on Finley's behalf. Attorney Dennis Page remembered, "So, we did have his deposition, and one of our partners sat on the witness stand and read the deposition. And it was still a powerful testimony, but it's just not the same . . . I think Charlie stubbed his toe on that one, because we were all counting on DeWitt."[10]

On December 22, Finley took the stand as his legal team's final witness. He recounted his rationale for the sale and his conversations with Kuhn before a packed courtroom. "He said he was very much concerned over the sales," Finley testified. "I told him I couldn't see why. I got pretty heated. He embarrassed me. No other owner in baseball history has been so embarrassed by a commissioner.[11]

"I didn't really talk about selling players until June 14, one day before the trading deadline. I told Kuhn that night [June 15] I tried desperately to make player-to-player deals, but all the clubs knew I was in a corner because my players were playing out their options. They [the other owners] told me 'you better sell them, Charlie, to get something back,'" Finley explained in court.[12]

"He asked me, 'Are you selling them to get out of baseball?'" Finley remembered. "I told him, 'Look, commissioner, I'm going to take this $3.5 million for three things: 1) I'm going to sign the other unsigned players on my club; 2) I'm going to participate in the re-entry draft of other free agents at the end of the season; and 3) the money will help me meet expenses during the year.'"[13]

Finley testified for nearly two days and, for the most part, gave strong and convincing testimony. However, his behavior at other times during the trial raised several eyebrows. Attorney Neil Papiano recalled, "Charlie showed up one day with a woman who would stop a train . . . She was really beautiful and well-endowed. I said, 'Charlie, don't bring her to court anymore. It's just not right, and people will be looking at her and not you.' He said, 'Okay, I'm not going to do it.' Two days later he walked in with [Royals owner Ewing] Kauffman and two gorgeous women that put the other one to shame. We sat down, and I whispered to him, 'Don't bring those whores in here anymore.' He jumped up and said loudly, 'They're not my whores; they're Ewing Kauffman's whores.' And everything went to hell. Charlie did things like that when you would least expect it."[14]

The trial took a one-week break over the Christmas and New Year's holidays. On December 31, newspapers around the country reported that Finley was having tax troubles. The story claimed that Finley failed to file personal tax returns in 1975 and that his insurance company failed to file returns from 1972 to 1975. Finley claimed that he was working on these returns and that he had not broken the law, as he had overpaid corporate taxes to the IRS in previous years. Undoubtedly, the disorganized Finley knew he was required to file federal tax returns, but with his empire slowly crumbling, a bitter ongoing divorce battle, and his focus on the

Kuhn trial, he appeared to be slowly sinking into a financial morass. For years, Finley had balanced and controlled all aspects of his business and personal life, but now he began to slip. He could no longer keep everything in order. Once again, Finley blamed others for his misfortunes. "The parties that planted this story are well aware of the fact that I am in good graces with the IRS," said Finley, who believed the story was planted to discredit him at the trial.[15]

On January 3, 1977, the trial resumed with the Kuhn team's turn at the plate. Over the next week, the Kuhn defense team called 13 key witnesses in an effort to show that the commissioner had the authority to void Finley's sales. Witnesses for Kuhn included Fred Lieb, a retired baseball writer; Joe Cronin, retired president of the American League; Phil Piton, a former baseball administrator who had served as an assistant to baseball's first commissioner, Judge Kenesaw Mountain Landis; numerous MLB team owners and general managers, among them, San Diego Padres president Buzzie Bavasi, Royals owner Ewing Kauffman, Tigers owner John Fetzer, Brewers owner Ed Fitzgerald, and Dodgers owner Walter O'Malley; and Bowie Kuhn himself. The Kuhn defense team's primary strategy evolved around demonstrating that the Major League Agreement gave the commissioner the complete and unfettered authority to void the sale of the A's players.

Both Lieb and Piton testified to the original powers Judge Landis incorporated into the commissioner's office after the White Sox World Series scandal of 1919—powers that grew in scope and were considered absolute by nearly everyone in baseball. Several owners testified to this effect. Royals owner Ewing Kauffman testified, "They [the owners] are self-confident, sometimes egotistical, and occasionally egocentric. And they need a broad, strong hand in order to keep baseball running properly."[16] Tigers owner John Fetzer agreed, "There's a degree of maverick in each of us . . . Henry Kissinger might settle a dispute between the Arabs and the Israelis . . . and could be a failure trying to settle disputes among us 25 owners . . . [The commissioner] can express judgment almost at his pleasure."[17] When asked by Finley attorney Neil Papiano about "what standard" Kuhn used in voiding the sales, Brewers owner Ed Fitzgerald replied, "The standards are his standards . . . We rely entirely upon the integrity of the individual."[18]

Next to testify was Dodgers owner Walter O'Malley. For decades O'Malley manipulated baseball and its commissioners in manners that suited the Dodgers and himself. Many believe Kuhn served as a mere puppet to the powerful Dodgers owner. O'Malley's testimony supported the strong and absolute powers of the commissioner. He also testified that he opposed the Finley sales because of the harm to the Oakland fan base. Nonetheless, Finley's attorneys pounded O'Malley on the witness stand.

"So it would have been a fraud on the Oakland fans to move the three players?" asked Papiano.

"Whether it is one, three or ten, this particular transaction, in my thinking, was that it would have been a fraud on the fans, on the public," replied O'Malley.

"Did you think it was a fraud when you moved your entire team out of Brooklyn?" asked Papiano.

"The commissioner could have slugged us down," O'Malley shot back. "And if he had, we'd be bound by his decision. And, actually, we ran that [moving the franchise] through the commissioner."[19]

On January 12, Bowie Kuhn took the witness stand before a packed courtroom. The press yearned for this final showdown of Kuhn versus Finley's high-powered attorneys. Charlie Finley, with his silver-gray toupee and his kelly green jacket, sat quietly and listened to Kuhn testify that he considered himself "the conscience of the game . . . the watchdog." Kuhn described how he had the right to void the sales in the "best interest" of the game. Kuhn recounted the hours after the sales were announced. "I reached Finley promptly," testified Kuhn. "I said, 'Charlie, these deals are disastrous for baseball. Very troublesome. I don't think we can let them stand.'"

Later, when asked to describe the powers of his office, Kuhn said, "One has to wrestle with the breadth of power . . . Awesome power . . . It must be used with sensible and rational restraint . . . but it has to be used." However, Kuhn said his decision to void the sales was not a snap judgment. Kuhn further opined, "You couldn't look at this transaction and not see this consideration."

Kuhn went on, "The sales could set a terrible precedent. It would weaken a very outstanding team in Oakland. It would upset the competitive balance in both the Eastern and Western divisions . . . The timing was very bad. It was unfair in the short- and long-term interest of the Oakland fans . . . Big cash deals are bound to be suspect . . . and shake public confidence." Finally, Kuhn testified, "I doubt if Finley would be able to put the cash [from the sale of Blue, Rudi, and Fingers] into his ball club . . . he told me his financial problems went beyond his ball club."[20]

The next day, the 15-day trial concluded. "These have been the largest crowds in the history of this court," remarked Judge McGarr as the trial wrapped up. "If we had tickets, or a popcorn concession, we could have cleaned up."[21] The judge took all the proceedings under advisement. After the trial, Finley beamed with confidence, a feeling that lasted about two months.

On March 17, 1977, Judge McGarr issued a surprisingly short six-page judgment order that decided the case in favor of Bowie Kuhn:

> This case has commanded a great deal of attention in the vociferous world of baseball fans, and has provoked widespread and not always unemotional discussion . . . The case is not a Finley-Kuhn popularity contest—though many fans so view it. Neither is it an appellate judicial review of the wisdom of Bowie Kuhn's actions. The question before the court is not whether Bowie Kuhn was wise to do what he did, but rather whether he had the authority.
>
> The questionable wisdom of this broad delegation of power is not before the court. What the parties intended is. And what the parties clearly intended was that the Commissioner was to have jurisdiction to prevent any conduct destructive of the confidence in the integrity of baseball. So broad and unfettered was his discretion intended to be that they provided no right of appeal and even took the extreme step of foreclosing their own access to the courts.

Ultimately, McGarr found inadequate evidence to support Finley's claim that Kuhn's actions were "arbitrary or capricious, or motivated by malice, ill will, or anything other than the commissioner's good faith judgment that these attempted assignments were not in the best interest of baseball . . . Whether the commissioner was right or wrong is beyond the competence and jurisdiction of this court."[22]

Finley responded to the McGarr decision in characteristic manner. "Maybe it's just 18 years of blood, sweat, and sacrifice down the drain," he complained.[23] "We'll play the next inning in appellate court."

He added, "This decision means nothing except more trouble for the commissioner . . . And it isn't going to influence the way I operate my Oakland Athletics one bit . . . I don't think he [Kuhn] has the guts to fight this one out."[24]

The stoic Kuhn admitted he was pleased with the decision. "I've said right along there was really more at stake here than a hassle between Charlie Finley and Bowie Kuhn. What is more important is the fact that the court upheld the commissioner's authority to do what he thinks is right for baseball."[25]

Finley filed an appeal in 1978, and Judge McGarr's decision was upheld at the appellate level. The Supreme Court then refused to hear the case, thereby ending the lawsuit. And Finley's hopes of recouping the $3.5 million he needed to save his team and his empire vanished. Thus did Finley begin to realize his time as a baseball owner was coming to an end.

As Finley waited for resolution to his lawsuit against Bowie Kuhn, he worked feverishly to rebuild his once-proud championship ball club. Only three starters of his regular eight remained: outfielders Claudell Washington and Bill North and second baseman Phil Garner. On the pitching side, ace lefty Vida Blue remained. Finley knew he had to rebuild, but it would take time for the team to mature. He was facing problems on many fronts. In addition to his ongoing divorce battle and the continued decline of his insurance business, his health began to deteriorate at an alarming rate; heart problems had persisted after his initial heart attack in 1973. Now in his late 50s, the once-energetic Finley found himself increasingly unable to control all of his business affairs. He began to doubt whether he possessed the fortitude to rebuild his franchise, especially in baseball's new era of big-money free agency. Again, Finley increasingly thought about either selling the A's or moving the team to another city. However, one huge obstacle stood in his way: the 20-year Coliseum lease he signed with the city of Oakland in 1968.

Nonetheless, Finley had gone to work following the loss of his star players to free agency. In November 1976, he pulled another of his classic trades. A's manager Chuck Tanner wanted to leave the team to manage the Pittsburgh Pirates but was contractually controlled by Finley and the A's for the upcoming season. The wily Finley swung a unique trade by sending Tanner, his manager, to the Pirates for veteran catcher Manny Sanguillen and $100,000 in much-needed cash. The trade marked only the second time when a field manager was a part of a major-league trade and the first instance a manager was traded for a player. (Managers Joe Gordon and Jimmy Dykes were traded for each other in the 1960s.) "I'm not trying to discredit Tanner as a manager," Finley said at the time, "but I'd trade a manger any day in the week for Manny Sanguillen and $100,000."[26]

On February 19, 1977, just one month after the conclusion of the Kuhn vs. Finley trial and before the verdict had been rendered, the A's owner again poked the baseball establishment and Bowie Kuhn in the eye by selling veteran A's relief pitcher Paul Lindblad to the Texas Rangers for $400,000 cash. "I just sold Paul Lindbald to the Texas Rangers for $400,000 cash," Finley announced at a press conference. "Kuhn's asking all the clubs before they make a deal for cash to contact him. My telegram to him in essence told him to go to hell. I'm not telling the commissioner nothing."[27]

Again, Commissioner Kuhn placed a hold on the deal and scheduled a hearing with all parties. Kuhn feared another liquidation sale of the A's. Finley calculated that Kuhn would not interfere with this transaction as both sides awaited Judge McGarr's decision. Finley believed Kuhn feared a possible embarrassing loss from the trial and therefore would not act. Finley miscalculated. Upon hearing of the commissioner's hold, Finley unloaded. "Before I called this man a village idiot," Finley blasted. "I apologize to the villages across the country. I should have said he's the nation's idiot."[28]

On March 3, 1977, Kuhn held a hearing in Texas into the proposed sale. Kuhn heard testimony from Finley, Rangers' owner Brad Corbett, and several attorneys. Finley attorney Neil Papiano again argued that Kuhn's possible rejection of the sale overstepped his authority—the same argument presented to Judge McGarr. With McGarr's decision still unknown, Kuhn reluctantly approved the sale. Kuhn said, "I am far from convinced that there is not a plan to substantially liquidate the assets of the Oakland club. But while Paul Lindblad is an established and respected major league relief pitcher, he will be 36 years old in August, hardly in the prime of his career, and cannot be classified as a star player."[29] However, in an attempt to limit future Finley sales, Kuhn arbitrarily established a $400,000-sales-price ceiling on all major-league player sales shortly after announcing his decision. Many major-league owners, including Charlie Finley, bemoaned the new ceiling. In spite of his apparent victory, Finley continued to rail against Kuhn: "Bowie Kuhn has a personal vendetta against Charlie Finley. He's trying to run me out of baseball."[30]

As the A's opened spring training in Arizona under new manager Jack McKeon, Finley continued his search for young talent and additional cash resources to shore up his precarious finances. On March 15, 1977, Finley, ever the shrewd judge of baseball talent, made a blockbuster trade that paved the way for the A's resurgence a mere three years later. He sent disgruntled and unsigned second baseman Phil Garner—who sought a million-dollar four-year contract from the strapped A's owner—to the Pirates for six players: veteran pitchers Doc Medich and Dave Giusti, and young minor-league outfielders Tony Armas and Mitchell Page and pitchers Rick Langford and Doug Bair. The deal seemed innocuous at the time but years later proved to be one of Finley's most profitable trades. Later in the spring, he traded outfielder Claudell Washington to the Texas Rangers for two minor leaguers and cash. Then, after the season began, he traded an unhappy and unsigned Mike Torrez to the Yankees for veteran pitcher Dock Ellis and two minor leaguers. Six weeks after that, he sold Ellis to the Rangers for an "undisclosed amount of cash." While Finley appeared to be selling or trading away his remaining veteran talent, he was also restocking his farm system, as he had done in Kansas City. Unfortunately for Finley, the new economics of baseball and his dwindling personal wealth made his efforts to rebuild the A's even more difficult.

Meanwhile, he again began looking at the possibility of moving the A's from the Bay Area, where most baseball people felt only one team could thrive. "There simply is no way two major league clubs can survive in this area," Finley said at a January press conference to introduce new manager Jack McKeon. "I'd love to remain in the Bay Area, but if it would help baseball to have one team here, I'd be cooperative."[31] Kuhn and other major-league owners believed that relocating the A's to Washington, DC, might resolve the attendance problems of having A's and Giants in the Bay Area. It seemed the two adversaries might have, for once, a common goal.

But Finley's cooperative attitude evaporated when he realized that Kuhn and his fellow owners planned not only to move the A's to Washington and into the National League but also to buy out the A's maverick owner. Kuhn moved secretly to secure a new ownership group in the DC region while putting together a $10 million buyout package for Finley.

"They're twisting my arm, trying to force me to sell," Finley charged. "Now I'm beginning to put all of the pieces together. This has been Kuhn's idea for a long time. He's been trying to force me into a bankruptcy situation, hoping I'd have to get out of baseball."

Finley's words appeared true when an anonymous National League owner reported, "We are for the idea of putting a team in Washington and balancing the leagues at 13 teams each, and enough of us even want interleague play [long a Finley idea to improve the public's interest in the game]. But there is no way the owners in our league would approve this arrangement if Finley owns the club. We don't want him in our league." Soon after, Finley killed the proposed deal. "I have no intention of moving my club," said Finley. "I have no intention of selling my club. The commissioner has problems in Washington"—this was a reference to ongoing congressional antitrust-exemption hearings that were plaguing Kuhn—"and I have no intention whatsoever of pulling his chestnuts out of the fire."[32]

On the field, the 1977 A's looked and played like Finley's old Kansas City A's teams of the early 1960s—they basically stunk. Only six players in the A's team photo in 1977 had been there a year earlier. Surprisingly, Jack McKeon led the young club to a near .500 record, but Finley fired McKeon as manager on June 10. He cited McKeon's lack of discipline; there were reports of bench players listening to games and drinking in the clubhouse rather than sitting in the dugout during games. Finley named former Arizona State University head coach Bobby Winkles as the new A's manager. (Winkles had served as an A's coach for Alvin Dark in 1974–1975.) McKeon moved to the front office as a Finley assistant. Soon after the change, the A's tanked, losing 14 games in a row. The team finished in last place in the American League West, a half game behind the expansion Seattle Mariners, with a 63–98 record. The A's went 37–71 under Winkles. Home attendance plunged. Despite slashing ticket prices for all Monday-through-Thursday games by half, the A's drew an anemic 495,578 fans— the lowest in MLB.

There were few highlights to the miserable season. Several of the young A's Finley obtained via trade did show some promise. Mitchell "the Rage" Page played brilliantly in the outfield and displayed a clutch bat, hitting .307 with 21 homers and 75 RBI. He also swiped 42 bases, including a league-record 26 straight without getting caught. Reliever Doug Bair also provided a lift with eight saves and a 3.47 ERA. Former farmhand Wayne Gross played a solid third base and launched 22 homers as well. But the starting rotation labored all season. Even All-Star Vida Blue, unhappy for most of the season to be stuck with the A's, struggled and nearly lost 20 games. Had Winkles not held him out of a final start in Texas, Blue might well have achieved the dubious mark. Bobby Winkles recalled, "I just wasn't going to let him lose twenty games, that's all . . . I know Charlie wanted him to lose twenty games or at least have the opportunity to do it, but I didn't pitch him."[33]

As the team's rotten season drew to a close, Finley underwent major heart-bypass surgery at Northwestern Memorial Hospital in Chicago. With his health in steady decline, Finley chose to undergo the operation, though it was rather risky at the time. He entered the hospital on September 9 after complaining of chest pains. However, he tried to put on a strong face for the public. A few days after the surgery, lying in his hospital bed, seeing the changing economics of baseball, and realizing the long road to rebuild the A's, Finley decided he needed to make a dramatic change. So he did something amazing: He reached out to Bowie Kuhn.

Charlie Finley had decided to get out of baseball. He fielded interest from prospective buyers in New Orleans and Washington, but he seemed most intrigued by billionaire oilman Marvin Davis in Denver. While he despised Kuhn, Finley also realized that he needed the commissioner's help to sell the Oakland A's. Kuhn recalled, "I knew that Finley was not going to be able to sell his club to anybody away from Oakland without the consent of his landlord, the Oakland–Alameda Coliseum, and the co-operation of the San Francisco municipal government and the Giants. To get that consent and cooperation he needed my help, a miserable spot for a proud man. And now he was asking for it, explaining that his doctors had told him he could no longer safely operate a club."[34]

Kuhn and American League president Lee MacPhail salivated at the prospect of Finley's selling the A's. On the surface, a sale to the multi-millionaire Davis seemed like it would be a dream come true. The 52-year-old Davis impressed most everyone he met with his no-nonsense business style and his imposing six-foot-four-inch, 300-pound frame. He report-edly made $60,000 per day and was a confidant of the likes of President Gerald Ford, Secretary of State Henry Kissinger, and Egyptian president Anwar el-Sadat. Davis shied away from media attention and rarely gave in-terviews, a welcome contrast to the flamboyant Finley. A native New Yorker, Davis grew up cheering for the Dodgers and Giants. Finley told Kuhn, "This guy's got more money than anybody in baseball. Hell, he could buy the other 25 clubs."[35] Still, Kuhn knew it would be tough to move the A's out of Oakland.

In December 1977, Finley announced the sale of the A's franchise to Marvin Davis for approximately $12.5 million. Davis stated his intent of moving the franchise to Denver prior to the 1978 season and pledged to pump an additional $5 million into the operations side of the A's in his first year as owner—a far cry from the shoestring budget Finley had used for years to run the club. The agreement had two key contingencies: The American League owners had to approve the sale and transfer of the fran-chise; and Finley had to work out his differences with the Oakland Coli-seum, where the A's had 10 years remaining on their lease, and deliver the club, according to the terms of the sale, "free and clear of any encum-brances." Finley needed to enlist the support of two groups with which he had feuded for years—the Oakland–Alameda County Coliseum board and the city of Oakland. For years, both groups watched Finley attempt to wiggle his way around various provisions in his Coliseum lease. They also disdained Finley's tightfisted style of running and marketing the A's.

But Oakland planned on keeping the A's. Soon after Finley announced the deal with Davis, the city of Oakland and the Coliseum board obtained a 10-day restraining order to block the sale of the team. Then, they filed a $35 million lawsuit against Finley and Davis for attempting to move the A's to Denver. Finley, Kuhn, and new Giants owner Robert Lurie worked behind the scenes to find a compromise between all parties. "The A's still have 10 more years on their contract and we're going to make a united effort to keep them in Oakland," said Coliseum general manager Bill Cunningham.[36]

Despite their public musings, the members of the Coliseum board knew the economics of their situation and the problems of the Bay Area supporting two franchises. They were also wary of a lengthy legal battle with Major League Baseball and the extremely wealthy Marvin Davis. Soon, with the help of Bowie Kuhn and Lee MacPhail, it appeared all parties might be open to a compromise that involved playing half of the Giants home games at the Coliseum. Kuhn convinced Oakland city officials of the necessity of the move and their potential legal vulnerabilities if they stood in the way of the sale. Kuhn aptly pointed out that the city was not generating enough attendance to support the club and the legal problems that could occur if Finley was forced into bankruptcy. Thus, Kuhn convinced Oakland officials that it was in their best interest to compromise—the restraining order was lifted and the Coliseum board agreed to go along with the sale, provided the Giants agreed to schedule half of their home games at the Coliseum for the remaining 10 years of the A's lease. The deal seemed set.

Giants' owner Bob Lurie knew the economics of his team's predicament. The idea of playing half of the Giants games in Oakland did not thrill Lurie, but for his club to survive, he believed the Giants needed the A's out of Oakland. "We have a lease obligating us to play all of our games at Candlestick Park," Lurie explained to Bay Area fans, "but that could be altered with the board's permission, if playing some games in Oakland would make sense."[37] It made sense to everyone except San Francisco mayor George Moscone and the San Francisco Board of Supervisors, which controlled the Giants' lease at Candlestick Park and rejected the proposed terms of the Giants playing 40 games in Oakland. San Francisco officials would allow 20 or 25 Giants games to be played in Oakland, but not 40. They also strongly rejected the idea, proposed by Oakland officials and supported by Lurie, of the Giants' removing "San Francisco" from their name and becoming just "the Giants." In late January 1978, with Finley unable to deliver the A's "free and unencumbered," the sale collapsed. Davis said, "We reached a point where we couldn't wait any longer on the Oakland deal. So now that we won't be getting the A's, I'm ready to make a pitch for a National League franchise in 1979."[38]

The fiery Finley took the failure in stride, knowing that this was just one setback in a longer effort to sell his club, but he could not resist taking a few shots at his foes in San Francisco. "It's just too bad Mayor Moscone and San Francisco aren't more aware of their problem. If they want to play that way out there, well, so can I. The end result is that somebody is going to be a loser in the Bay Area and I don't intend it to be me,"[39] vowed Finley. Meanwhile, Kuhn remained circumspect and pragmatic, but warned, "we are now threatened with a situation that could be a black eye for both cities, and baseball."[40]

In March 1978, Finley again pushed the parties into negotiations. He believed a compromise could be reached. With the cost of his divorce case rising, Finley needed to sell the team. Again, he solicited his old nemesis Bowie Kuhn for help. He also approached Davis a second time. Unimpressed, Davis lowered his offering price to $10 million, which irked Finley. Kuhn recalled the second round of negotiations, which again took Finley and the A's to the brink of a sale and a move to Denver:

> For the next three weeks, the politicians, the baseball administration and the lawyers struggled to find solutions. At last, amazingly, parity was agreed to. The team name would be the San Francisco Giants except in Oakland, where it would be the Giants. Financial payments to the Oakland Coliseum were set at $3.25 million. The internal fight within baseball was difficult when Finley would put up no more than $1 million as his share of the Coliseum payment. Even that we were finally able to persuade the clubs to accept. But, when we asked him [Finley] to waive claims of any kind against baseball, he balked.

It was a strange turn of events—and it might have changed baseball history—but Charlie Finley refused to give up his right to sue Major League Baseball. Finley told the Associated Press, "I want to sell but I won't give up my Constitutional rights. There is no way any red-blooded American would agree to sign such an idiot agreement."[41] As for his part, Marvin Davis reacted with ire: "This hasn't dimmed my interest or enthusiasm one bit. Just my enthusiasm for doing business with that nut . . . I just don't want to sit there across from Finley. When the American League can deliver the package, then we'll take it."[42]

For weeks Finley and his attorneys, who were awaiting a ruling on his appeal of the McGarr decision, had been planning a second lawsuit against Kuhn. The second suit stemmed from Kuhn's voiding of Finley's second attempt to sell star pitcher Vida Blue—this time to the Cincinnati Reds. It may well have been because of this lawsuit, and the larger enmity between Finley and Kuhn, that the Davis sale again collapsed.

At the annual baseball winter meeting in December 1977, Charlie Finley, while negotiating with Marvin Davis over the sale of the A's, decided he needed to hedge his bets for the upcoming season. Still steaming over the McGarr decision, and with few real stars left, Finley wanted to make a dramatic move to shake up his franchise. Finley needed additional young players if he was ever going to rebuild the A's. But he possessed little cash, so he decided to take one final shot at Kuhn's prohibition on cash sales of players for more than $400,000. Finley saw players earning millions of dollars via free agency and felt Kuhn had robbed him of his own personal free-agency payday by voiding his sale of Blue, Fingers, and Rudi for $3.5 million. Finley wanted his own million-dollar payout.

At the conclusion of the winter meetings in Hawaii, on December 9, the Cincinnati Reds and Oakland A's announced the trade of A's All-Star pitcher Vida Blue to the Reds in exchange for minor-league first baseman Dave Revering and $1.75 million. The cash amounted to $250,000 more than the Yankees had agreed to pay Finley 18 months earlier. Both the Reds and Finley hoped that by including the money as a part of a legitimate player trade, they would avoid Kuhn's $400,000 price limit on cash sales of players. Kuhn saw little difference. Within hours of the announcement, Kuhn stated publicly that he might again void the deal and said, "I'm ad-

vising the Cincinnati and Oakland clubs that I'm calling a hearing rela-
tive to the Blue-Revering deal. I believe it raises substantial questions as to
whether it should be approved or not."[43] In response, the parties did try
modifying the deal. "We made a specific suggestion to Kuhn as to how the
deal might be done," said Reds president Bob Howsam, "and the commissioner didn't even respond to the proposal."[44]

During the 14 hours of hearings in late January 1978, Kuhn asked
several probing questions, trying to get to the exact motivation for
the proposed deal by Finley and the Reds. Kuhn questioned whether the
deal was in the best interest of baseball; whether the deal signified
Finley's attempt to again liquidate his club's talent for cash; and finally,
whether the deal would adversely affect the competitive balance of baseball. More than a dozen lawyers attended the hearings and several
witnesses testified, including Finley, Howsam, Yankees owner George
Steinbrenner, American League president Lee MacPhail, and players association director Marvin Miller. Most everyone testified in favor of the
cash trade being approved. The commissioner appeared to be the lone
holdout over the deal.

Finley testified that he needed the money to sign amateur players and
to develop a stronger farm system in order for the A's to again become a
competitive team. However, he made no firm commitment to using the
money solely for player purchases. "I would use the money to keep the
ship afloat, meaning that this money would be used to meet the payroll
and also in signing players, also in paying bills incurred as a result of a
$1.2 million operating loss for 1977 and $600,00 in 1976," Finley testified.[45] He also tried to convince Kuhn that Revering was not just a throw-
in to avoid an all-cash deal, indicating plans to use Revering as the A's first
baseman in the upcoming season. Cincinnati Reds president Bob
Howsam said, "The purpose of every trade is to strengthen your club.
Every trade I made or that which any other baseball man makes, is with
that in mind."[46] The hearings ended with no decision, but Kuhn stated
that his decision would come shortly. An optimistic Finley told reporters,
"By gosh, it's about time I won one."[47]

On January 30, 1978, Bowie Kuhn voided yet another Finley player
transaction. In his decision, Kuhn wrote:

The proposed assignment would send Vida Blue, an established star pitcher, from Oakland to Cincinnati. Cincinnati is one of the strongest Clubs in its division of the National League . . . Thus, the proposed assignment promises materially and adversely to affect the balance in the National League West.

There is a big competitive difference between a player-for-player deal and a player-for-cash deal . . . The record before me provides no basis for concluding that the $1.75 million in cash to be received by Oakland for Vida Blue would in fact be spent on replacement talent.[48]

Kuhn concluded his statement by again asking the two clubs to restructure the trade with additional players and less money. He pledged to assist in the process if needed.

Baseball writers, pundits, players, executives, and owners railed over Kuhn's decision in voiding the Blue trade. Hoping to leave Oakland for the Reds, Blue said, "The things I could put into words wouldn't even begin to express my feelings." Union head Marvin Miller commented, "The owners have only themselves to blame . . . The ruling is an invitation to chaos." A dumbfounded Bob Howsam said, "The commissioner seems to be saying the Reds will be too strong for their division. If so, he must be asking us to give up players to weaken our club to the extent that Blue would strengthen it."[49] Finley remained uncharacteristically calm, simply vowing to sue Kuhn again.

A new deal involving Blue could not be structured with the Reds. However, Revering became an Athletic nonetheless, when Finley traded pitcher Doug Bair to the Reds for Revering and cash, reportedly just under the $400,000 limit. Finley looked for another team interested in Blue, and he found a trading partner just across the bay—the San Francisco Giants. On March 15, 1978, Finley traded Blue to the Giants for first baseman Gary Thomasson, catcher Gary Alexander, reliever Dave Heaverlo, three minor-league players, and $390,000 in cash. Vida Blue became the last of the Oakland stars to escape the Finley fun house. "It's a big weight off my back," Blue said after the trade. "It's going to be good to get away from some of the harassment I've had here . . . Now I'm going to a new team.

It's a new lease on life. It's really going to be nice."[50] Blue went on to win 18 games and pitch in the All-Star game for the resurgent Giants in the 1978 season. However, he never again pitched in the postseason. Charlie Finley had finally unloaded his last superstar from the A's championship teams.

Chapter Twelve

Charlie O.'s Last Stand

The 1978 baseball season began with a horrible start by the A's. Charlie Finley could not let go of his team and, more important, could not convince Oakland city officials to accept a buyout of the team's stadium lease. The A's also faced a severe loss of broadcast revenue for the season when Finley opted to sign a radio deal with the small 10-watt local station KALX, owned by the University of California at Berkeley and operated by students. For years, Finley had feuded with larger local commercial radio stations over broadcast rights to the A's games. He always wanted increasing broadcast-rights fees, but local stations were not willing to pay his asking price for a subpar baseball product. Because KALX's signal was so weak, most listeners outside of Berkeley and Oakland could not pick it up at night. Only a few weeks into the season, Finley abandoned the weak college station and signed with a stronger Oakland commercial station.

Finley kept the A's on an austere budget from that point forward. One reporter called the A's office early in the season and left his number with a secretary, who warned, "We do not return long-distance calls unless charges can be reversed."[1] Finley employed no full-time scouts or minor-league hitting and pitching instructors. He also kept only four major-league coaches on the roster, while many other teams employed five or six. In the front office, many teams had upwards of 60 to 100 employees in baseball operations; Finley's A's employed less than two dozen, mostly clerks and secretaries. Besides Finley and his son Charlie Jr., who was listed as the team's secretary-treasurer, the A's had only three other executives: executive vice president and PR head Carl Finley, controller Chuck Cottonaro, and minor-league director Norm Koselke. In fact, most Class AAA and AA minor-league clubs employed more front office and baseball operations staff than Finley's major-league A's. And the ones the A's did have were often part-time workers, such as a young teenager named Stanley Burrell.

Finley first met Burrell in the Coliseum parking lot during the 1973 season. The 11-year-old was, in his own words, "doing a dance with ten friends . . . just being crazy and Mr. Finley walked over and said I looked like Hank Aaron. Then invited me up to his box."[2] So strong was the resemblance, in fact, that Finley reportedly gave Burrell Aaron's nickname, "Hammer."

Hammer became a fixture in the A's dugout and front office, picking up numerous odd jobs around the organization. He helped the clubhouse managers, ran errands, and provided Finley with telephonic play-by-play broadcasts of the A's games back to his offices in Chicago. At first, Burrell simply arranged the phone calls so Finley could hear the actual radio broadcasts of the games, but later Hammer actually began doing the play-by-play himself. In a 1978 *People* magazine article, Burrell demonstrated his broadcasting talent for a reporter. "Here's the pitch," purred the youthful voice into the telephone. "Swung on and missed, one ball, two strikes, runner on first. This is station WCOF coming to you directly from Oakland Coliseum. This is the Hammer. I want all you people to know that Charlie Finley is the greatest general manager in the game. I'm a Charlie Finley man. He treats me good and he pays me good."[3] His style amused the cantankerous A's owner, who paid Burrell $7.50 per game. Despite his stingy reputation, Finley always enjoyed helping out the underdog, and Burrell fit the profile, having grown up poor with his mother, who worked as a police department secretary, and eight siblings in a cramped apartment in a very rough section of East Oakland.

Burrell seemed to make an impression everywhere. As time went on, Finley gave Hammer an honorary position as a club vice president. In the

HBO documentary *Rebels of Oakland*, Reggie Jackson recalled, "Hell, our chief executive, the guy that ran our team, that communicated [with] Charlie Finley, was a thirteen-year-old kid." Years later Burrell recalled, "Every time I come down to the clubhouse, you know, Rollie [Fingers] would yell out, 'Oh everybody, be quiet! Here comes Pipeline!' "[4] Burrell earned this second nickname from several A's players who suspected he fed Finley information on what they were saying about him. "Finley has always had someone around giving him reports on what players say in the clubhouse," said an unnamed observer in *People* magazine. "They think Hammer is that person now."[5]

A's equipment manager Steve Vucinich remembered Burrell as a clubhouse fixture. "Charlie just kind of liked having the kid around, and it got to the point where Charlie actually took him on a road trip to Toronto one time to do some business as vice president in just a joking way, but that's Charlie Finley, "Vucinich said. "Charlie upset the regular broadcasters because he had Stanley go on air and do an inning or half inning occasionally on the radio broadcast."[6]

Longtime A's announcer Monte Moore also remembered the first time Finley ordered Burrell to broadcast an inning of an A's game: "Charlie called one day before the broadcast and said, 'I want you to put Hammer on the air tonight with you.' And I said, 'What do you mean?' 'I want him to broadcast some innings,' Charlie said. I said, 'Charlie! This is a big-league broadcast.' He said, 'I want him to do it!' "[7] Burrell managed only a half inning of live radio commentary before executives from the team's flagship radio station ordered him off the air.

Hammer grew up in the A's locker room, at first surrounded by the stars of the A's championship seasons, then later, surrounded by the retreads and young players who dominated the teams of the late 1970s. As Burrell matured, his respect for Finley grew as well. "He's a great person," said Burrell of Finley. "He's done nothing but good for me." A's pitching coach Lee Stange summed up Burrell best by saying, "Stanley was a piece of work then too. He was a good kid; he never caused any problems. He'd come down on the field once in a while, and I'd harass him, but he was a pretty good kid. He had a tough job talking to Charlie for the whole game on the phone every night."[8]

Ultimately, Burrell needed to grow up and find a real job. He dreamed of playing professional baseball, but he found his baseball talent lacking. Drugs and crime always nipped at his heels on the tough east side of Oakland, but Burrell resisted and joined the U.S. Navy after high school. Several years later, Stanley Burrell, who dreamed of playing major-league baseball but lacked the skills, became an international superstar in his own right as an acrobatic rap singer and dancer known to world by his old nickname, MC Hammer.

Both the 1978 and 1979 seasons were very difficult for A's fans. Gone were the All-Stars of the early and mid-1970s. In their place was a hodgepodge of castoffs from other teams, former stars on the downside of their careers, and young rookies who were talented but extremely inexperienced. While almost everyone focused their attention on Finley's antics and efforts to sell his team, the A's minor-league system began developing another crop of superbly talented young prospects. Soon, the baseball world came to know these new players, such as Rickey Henderson, Dwayne Murphy, Tony Armas, Steve McCatty, and Matt Keough. At the same time, many young A's playing in the majors during this difficult period began developing their talents and learning how to play baseball on the major-league level.

In 1978, the A's surprisingly blazed into first place in April and May. Manager Bobby Winkles found the magic touch to turn his team of noname veterans and young rookies into winners during the first part of the season. Winkles used fatherly coaching and strict clubhouse rules, such as a dress code and bans on loud music and alcohol on plane trips, to focus his young players on their baseball tasks. "Anyone who's watching this club knows there's been a change in attitude," said Winkles. "We're playing more aggressive baseball. We're winning the one-run games."[9] Led by timely hitting, aggressive base running, and solid pitching, especially in the bullpen, the A's rushed to first place with a 24–15 record. Young players such as slugger Mitchell Page; speedy base-stealer Miguel Dilone; starters Rick Langford, John Henry Johnson, and Matt Keough; and relievers Elias Sosa and Bob Lacey played at a level beyond their talent during the first two months of the season. However, their luck ran out by late June, and the A's crashed back to reality.

The precipitating event in the A's collapse was the resignation of Bobby Winkles in late May. Like nearly all of his predecessors, Winkles grew tired of a re-engaged Charlie Finley tinkering with the roster, calling him at all hours of the day, and second-guessing his decisions, including his rule against drinking on team plane trips. So, on May 23, with his club in first place by two games, Winkles resigned as A's manager.

Finley tried to talk Winkles into staying, but his mind was made up. Finley could not reconcile why Winkles quit while the team held first place, but told reporters that Winkles "wanted to go out while his club was on top, while he was looking good."[10] Later, Finley took his customary parting shot: "I've had a lot of managers in baseball, but now I've seen the most gutless and unappreciative one I've had in 19 years."[11] As a replacement, Finley turned to his third-base coach Jack McKeon, whom he had fired only one year earlier as manager. Soon after McKeon took the helm, the A's record swooned. Attendance had risen slightly during their first-place run, but it tanked as the season progressed. However, it still surpassed the 1977 season, with 526,999 fans paying to watch the A's.

The A's lost 42 of their final 55 games in 1978 and finished in sixth place with a record of 69–93. Despite their collapse, several players gave promising performances, including a solid season from Mitchell Page (.285 BA, 17 HR, 70 RBI—all team bests). Outfielder Miguel Dilone swiped 50 bases, despite a .229 batting average; and 38-year-old veteran designated-hitter Rico Carty (.277 BA, 11 HR, 31 RBI) provided a solid bat for the team in the second half. However, solid pitching performances by three key starters—Rick Langford (7–13, 3.43 ERA), Matt Keough (8–15, 3.24 ERA), John Henry Johnson (11–10, 3.39 ERA)—gave the A's hope for the future. The bright spot on the 1978 A's team resided in their bullpen: Elias Sosa, Dave Heaverlo, and Bob Lacey all turned in a stellar season. Despite their promising performances, however, the A's struggled at the plate, hitting only 100 home runs, and committed an atrocious 178 fielding errors.

But it wasn't until the next season that Finley's A's truly hit a low point. By all measures, the 1979 A's and their owner were embarrassments both on and off the diamond. On the field, under new manager Jim Marshall—the 17th manager hired in Finley's 19 seasons—the A's compiled a franchise-worst 54–108 record. They finished last in the American

League in batting average and also committed the most errors in the league. Their promising pitching staff reeled for much of the season, with starter Matt Keough symbolizing the staff's troubles. Keough, an All-Star pitcher in 1978, tied a 73-year-old MLB record by losing his first 14 decisions in 1979. The team's offense, for its part, sank along with Mitchell Page's averages. Page fought a sore shoulder and struggled at the plate, finishing with a dismal .247 average, with just nine home runs and 42 RBI. Nearly every regular struggled during the team's first four months, and the A's lost 77 of 107 games.

The team played more competitive baseball in the second half of the 1979 season, when Marshall turned to some of his younger players. Beginning in July, the A's fielded a new young outfield that featured strong-armed Dwayne Murphy in center field, power-hitting Tony Armas in right field, and a blazing-fast, line-drive-hitting rookie named Rickey Henderson in left field. While none of the three young A's posted stellar numbers in 1979, they did provide glimpses of their very promising futures. Henderson, a future Hall of Famer, managed to hit .274 and steal 33 bases in the second half of the 1979 season.

As the A's struggled on the field, Finley began to lose interest in the team. He became disenchanted with baseball as his insurance empire struggled to meet its financial obligations; he withdrew to his offices in Chicago. The usual Finley micromanaging stopped. In fact, Charlie Finley did not attend a single A's baseball game in the 1979 season.

Moreover, Finley cut the A's operating budget to the bones and anticipated selling the team during the off-season. Three local groups showed interest in purchasing the franchise from Finley and keeping it in Oakland. The strongest group was led by local furniture magnates Sam and Ed Bercovich and included a consortium of wealthy partners, including the owner of the *Oakland Tribune* newspaper. Various proposals were exchanged between the Bercovich group and Finley, with former Finley attorney Neil Papiano serving as the broker. Talks dragged for weeks. After several negotiation sessions, Finley told the press, "I don't know how many times I've heard people say they want to buy the team, but I have yet to see a single dollar of earnest money. The price of the team is $12 million and I don't think Bercovich or anybody else can come up with the $12 million."[12]

Ed Bercovich contended that he had the financing but wanted concessions from the Coliseum to reduce the length of the A's lease to three years. As the weeks dragged on, the prospects for the deal looked grim.

As 1979 arrived, Finley whined to reporters about the stalled sale. "I stand ready and willing to sell to a local group under the Bercoviches," he said. "I've already agreed on the price. Last year, the Coliseum blew a good deal that would have brought it $3 million and half the Giants' home games. The question in my mind is, are they going to blow this, too?"[13] Finally, Finley and the Bercovich group heard from the Coliseum board, whose president Bob Nahas issued a statement saying, "We feel anything short of a five-year effort wouldn't be adequate."[14] The Bercovich deal died.

Soon a new suitor emerged with hopes of moving the team to New Orleans. Ohio shopping mall magnate Edward DeBartolo Sr., who owned three horse racing tracks and a professional hockey team, offered to buy the A's for between $10 and $12 million. Vincent Bartimo, an executive with DeBartolo, said that money was no object and, after meeting with Finley in Chicago, told reporters, "We are extremely close to finalizing the deal. It is conceivable this can be accomplished in the next few days if Mr. Finley can negotiate his way out of his stadium lease and if the American League approves the franchise transfer we could have the team here [in New Orleans] in April, 1979."[15] However, the proposed shift of the A's to New Orleans failed to win over MLB commissioner Bowie Kuhn, who still hoped a deal could be brokered with Denver oilman Marvin Davis. Finley again failed to free the A's from their Coliseum lease as the New Orleans proposal met stiff resistance in Oakland. "We have never indicated any decision to consider a release," said Bill Cunningham, manager of the Coliseum.[16] He emphasized that the Coliseum and the A's had "a binding agreement through 1987" and that they would go to court to prevent Finley or anyone else from moving the A's to another city. Finley prepared to remain in Oakland for the 1979 season.

During the 1979 season, very few Oakland fans turned out to watch the hapless team play in the damp, cool Coliseum. A game against Seattle on the chilly evening of April 17, 1979, drew national attention not because of the play on the field but rather because of how few fans attended. The paid game attendance totaled only 653 fans. The actual number that showed up for the game was closer to 250 in a stadium that seated 50,000.

A's first baseman Dave Revering actually tried to count the fans in attendance but lost track as he became involved in on-field activities. So dramatic was the shortfall that it became an embarrassing national story: The A's had filled their stadium to about 0.5 percent of capacity. "People don't want to come to the ball park because they don't want Finley to get his share of the tickets," said Donna Oneto, membership secretary of the nearly invisible Oakland A's Booster Club. "Charlie hasn't spent one red cent on promotion," said A's relief pitcher Bob Lacey. "I've played on Triple A teams that promoted more."

Days later, the Red Sox and Yankees arrived in Oakland for games that drew slightly better crowds. A half-price game versus the Red Sox on April 30 drew only 14,716 fans and the world-champion Yankees drew a miserably low total of 16,293 fans over two games on two separate days. At season's end, the A's had drawn an abysmally low 306,763 fans to their home games. As a whole, however, Major League Baseball was setting attendance records annually.

Within days of the A's embarrassingly attended game before 250 fans, the city of Oakland filed suit against Finley and his company for breach of contract, alleging that Finley failed to comply with his "obligation to endeavor in good faith to obtain maximum occupancy of the Stadium by the public by failing to reasonably promote attendance at Oakland A's baseball games." The city sought $1.5 million for lost revenues (concessions, parking, etc.) during the previous four seasons. Additionally, the city sought $10 million in punitive damages for Finley's "reckless and conscious disregard" of his promotional obligations.[17] In Chicago, Finley remained silent but steadfastly refused to spend any of his funds on promoting the A's. The suit culminated 10 years of acrimony between Finley and the city of Oakland. Each blamed the other for the A's attendance failures. Twelve years earlier, Finley had faced the same lack of support and bitterness from the fans of Kansas City and had brazenly moved the A's to Oakland, snubbing his nose at Kansas City fans. However, he was no longer in a strong position. In 1967, Finley was enjoying the apex of his financial and business success. In 1979, his world appeared to be crumbling around him. He was no longer the young, powerful businessman and deal maker he had fought so hard to become.

Adding to this, the ongoing distraction of his divorce came to a head in the fall of 1979. After years of legal thrusts and parries in the divorce proceedings, Shirley Finley's lawyer, Leon Kaminski, finally obtained an August court date for the dissolution of the marriage. Finley failed in his efforts to delay once again on that occasion. Kaminski wrote to the judge:

> We are prepared to go forward with this trial on August 6 as scheduled by the court and we object to any continuances of any nature or kind. Conveniently, we are hearing that opposing counsel is not going to be prepared and this is a matter which I feel is totally without justification, and we object strenuously to any continuance of this case. It seems to me that Charles O. Finley has had over five years to get ready to try this case, and the only thing that can be said is that this is another attempt to avoid the final disposition of this case.[18]

Through it all, Finley had remained cantankerous and reluctant to comply with any requests for information. He was cited for contempt on more than one occasion, including on October 31, 1979, for selling some of their assets in contravention of the provisions of the court, which may have had the desired result of moving the proceedings forward.[19] Finally, on December 31, Judge John Montgomery granted the final divorce. "Hearing having been had on petition for dissolution of marriage," he wrote, "the court now finds the material allegations of the petition are true and that there is an irretrievable breakdown in the marriage of Charles O. Finley and Shirley M. Finley." An "irretrievable breakdown in the marriage" was certainly an understatement, and accordingly, the judge granted dissolution of the marriage.[20] Throughout these proceedings Kaminski recalled seeing Finley sitting each day "in the back of the courtroom . . . and he always has on either arm, or on both arms, beautiful women."[21] The judge commented that Charlie and Shirley Finley shared their responsibilities in the marriage equally and decided to disperse their assets 50–50.[22]

The judge found that the Finleys owned three corporations—Charles O. Finley and Company in Illinois, Charles O. Finley and Company in Indiana, and Finley and Friday Inc. in Indiana. "After seeing everything that my dad was trying to do to make sure my mom was miserable, financially strapped, or whatever," recalled David Finley, "the first four [children] decided to go in with my mom and liquidate Charles O. Finley and Company, because they had 69 percent of it. So that, needless to say, caused a very big rift." He had thought that the liquidation would ensure that the children each received an equal share, but in his mind, it did not. He said, "The first four did not split it with the last three . . . Anyway, put that in the book in big letters, if you would."[23] Finley appealed this ruling, which dragged the case on until the summer of 1981, when the appellate court reviewing the decision supported Judge Montgomery's ruling 3–0.[24]

It is impossible to survey the record of this divorce proceeding without coming to the conclusion that Charlie Finley stonewalled and fought the proceedings every step of the way. His obstinacy won him no friends among the attorneys working on the case or the judge charged with resolving it. It also cost him considerable goodwill with his children, whom he forced into choosing sides. All of them became estranged—some for the rest of his life. Shirley Finley eventually remarried, outliving her second husband and remarrying yet again. Now more than 90 years old, she lives in Florida. Charlie Finley never remarried. He lived the life of an attractive and eligible bachelor—that is, he was about as attractive as Donald Trump, even taking to wearing a toupee and seeming to have beautiful woman on his arm at every public occasion.

In the midst of this turmoil, soon after the end of the 1979 season Bowie Kuhn and Lee MacPhail again turned to the problem of Charlie Finley and finding a buyer for the A's. Both Kuhn and MacPhail wanted the A's to move out of the Bay Area and leave the territory to the Giants. They also believed that, with the right inducements, the city of Oakland could be convinced to accept a buyout of the A's lease for the Coliseum. Kuhn wanted the A's to move to Denver and favored Marvin Davis to purchase the franchise. He also wanted to rid baseball of Charlie Finley. Again, Davis and Finley agreed to a $12 million sales price for the A's, contingent on Finley, Kuhn and MacPhail getting the A's out of their Oakland lease.

In late November 1979, all parties reached a tentative deal that appeared to release the A's from their lease for a $4 million buyout. The deal seemed to be the best Oakland could achieve. While struggling to keep the

A's, Oakland officials also feared losing their most important sports team, the NFL's Oakland Raiders. With their Coliseum lease expiring, Raiders owner Al Davis threatened to move to Los Angeles if city officials did not make substantial improvements to the Coliseum, including adding 65 new luxury boxes. Oakland officials planned to take the A's buyout funds to make improvements to the Coliseum, with the hope of keeping the Raiders. Most city officials were simply sick of arguing with Finley and wanted him to go. "I've changed my position for a couple of reasons," said incoming Coliseum board president Jack Maltester in December 1979. "First, there are just no signs of any local buyers who would keep the A's in Oakland. Secondly, I don't want Finley staying in Oakland."

Oakland mayor Lionel Wilson also feared additional litigation. "I feel we've waited Charlie Finley out as long as we can wait him out. Mr. Finley could take us into court. I've always had questions on my mind whether a court ultimately would rule that the lease could keep the A's here."[25] With Wilson and Maltester supporting the buyout, it appeared the Oakland City Council would go along with the proposed deal. But, just as quickly as the deal looked completed, it began to unravel. In December the Oakland City Council surprised everyone by voting 8–0 in favor of keeping the A's in Oakland, thus preventing their departure.

In late January, the Davis-Finley sale appeared to be further in jeopardy after the Raiders announced their intention of moving to Los Angeles. Suddenly, Oakland faced losing both professional franchises. Mayor Wilson, the Coliseum board, and the Oakland City Council dug in their heels. All vowed to prevent the A's departure. MacPhail and Kuhn attempted a last-minute resurrection of the $4 million lease buyout, arguing that the A's were being held hostage and that the buyout money could help finance the Raiders' requested changes. But the writing was on the wall. Al Davis announced his plan to move the Raiders to Los Angeles.[26] Charlie Finley and his Oakland A's would remain in Oakland for the 1980 season.

As spring training approached in 1980, Finley knew he needed to change the dynamic in Oakland. He resigned himself to the fact that he needed to find a local owner. He feared being forced into a position where he might have to sell the A's for much less than the $12 million price tag he wanted, and his team appeared in a dismal place after the 1979 season. Finley needed to once again generate excitement for the club. He needed to attract fans back to the Coliseum in order to attract a local owner willing to pay his asking price. And so Charlie Finley, the maverick, surprised the baseball world one last time.

In February 1980, Finley fired manager Jim Marshall and hired the hotheaded but brilliant Billy Martin to lead his team. Martin possessed star appeal, and the A's certainly needed a new star to lead them. He had a reputation of warring with players, owners, and umpires alike, but he won games. Most recently, he led the Yankees to the 1977 world championship, but was fired in 1978 by owner George Steinbrenner for not getting along with the owner and several star players, particularly former A's outfielder Reggie Jackson.

Many writers and observers wondered how Finley and Martin, a control freak himself, would survive each other. Finley promised to again refrain from the day-to-day field management of the club. Martin told reporters, "Charlie is the owner and general manager. Naturally he has to have a say. On the field, that's my say. Charlie and I have ironed out all these things. We know exactly what we want."[27] Martin wanted a young club to mold as he saw fit. He wanted a new team to prove to the baseball world that he still possessed his magic touch. Finley wanted Martin to turn the young A's into winners in hopes of attracting fans and a new local owner for the club. They were improbable bedfellows, but they needed each other. Few doubted the relationship would last, but fewer realized Finley's days of micromanaging the team were over. Finley focused his energies on running his struggling insurance company and finding a buyer for the A's. Soon Billy Martin and his young A's put Charlie O. back atop the baseball world. Their new aggressive, base-stealing style of baseball, nicknamed "Billy Ball," became the talk of the baseball world.

Martin convinced the young A's that they just needed to believe in themselves and they could win baseball games. Martin's team took to the field and played a brand of baseball that emphasized solid fielding, line-drive hitting, aggressive base running, and a reliance on the team's young starting pitchers. Newly inspired, the young A's fought the division-leading Royals tooth and nail all season. Led by young left fielder Rickey Henderson

(.303 BA, 111 runs scored, 117 walks), right fielder Tony Armas (35 HR, 109 RBI), and center fielder Dwayne Murphy (.274 BA, 13 HR, 102 walks, 26 stolen bases), the A's offense scored runs in droves. The trio also caught nearly everything in the air. Henderson broke Ty Cobb's AL stolen-base record (96) with 100 steals in 1980. Martin had the A's playing aggressive baseball all season—they stole home 7 times and completed 14 double steals and 1 triple steal. The team's new "Billy Ball" offense attracted many old fans back to the Coliseum, and the A's attendance jumped dramatically from 306,763 in 1979 to 842,259 in 1980.

While the A's hitters sprinted around the base paths at a record rate, it was the starting rotation that truly spurred the team's amazing turnaround. The A's starters threw a mind-boggling 94 complete games (CGs), the most by any team since 1946. The A's starting five—Matt Keough (16–13, 2.92 ERA, 20 CGs), Rick Langford (19–12, 3.26 ERA, 28 CGs,), Mike Norris (22–9, 2.54 ERA, 24 CGs), Steve McCatty (14–14, 3.85 ERA, 11 CGs), and Brian Kingman (8–20, 3.84 ERA, 10 CGs)—became arguably baseball's best rotation. No Oakland starter pitched fewer than 211 innings in 1980. At season's end, the A's finished with a respectable 83–79 record, good for second place in the AL West, behind the Kansas City Royals, and 29 games better than the previous year. Charlie had wanted Billy Martin and his young A's to make a splash and generate some positive feelings and press; instead he made Finley look like a genius.

With his club generating headlines and breaking records, Finley knew the time was right to unload the A's. He again began talking to local groups about purchasing the team. In the summer of 1980, Finley held secret discussions with Walter H. Haas Jr. (the chairman of the clothing giant Levi Strauss and a great-grandnephew of the firm's founder), his son Wally Haas, and his son-in-law, the attorney and professor Roy Eisenhardt. Cornell Maier, the president of Kaiser Aluminum and Chemical Company, brought the two parties together and assisted in the final negotiations. The Haas family had no previous experience or interest in professional baseball, but they viewed buying the A's from Finley as a philanthropic move to help the local community and keep the franchise in Oakland. Soon, both sides arrived at a palatable sales agreement. On August 23, 1980, at the Oakland headquarters of Kaiser Aluminum, and to the complete surprise of all in attendance at the hastily called news conference, Charlie Finley announced the sale of his Oakland Athletics to the Haas family and their Levi Strauss and Company for $12.7 million. Even after his years of attempting to move or sell the A's, Finley's sudden announcement stunned the Bay Area and the baseball world.

After the announcement, Finley took several questions from the press. The event became Finley's final moment in the national spotlight. As always, he took advantage of it to make a few parting shots at baseball and his enemies, particularly Bowie Kuhn. "Bowie Kuhn started my exit out of baseball," said Finley.

"The main reason I'm leaving baseball is because I can no longer compete financially. During the time we were winning championships, survival was a battle of wits. We did all right then. But it is no longer a battle of wits, but how much you have on the hip," opined Finley. "I can no longer compete. I'm going to have to leave baseball because of these idiotic, astronomical salaries. If baseball is going to survive, something should be done about compensation." Finley believed teams that lost players to free agency deserved compensation in some manner for that loss. He steadfastly believed that his proposed sales of Blue, Fingers, and Rudi in 1976 and Blue in 1978 could have provided him such compensation had Kuhn allowed them.

Finley went on to say that he had the "pleasure of smelling the roses many times, maybe more than I deserved" in his years as the A's owner. "Before I leave the game," said Finley, "I'd like to see orange baseballs introduced. I'd like to see a three-ball walk, and I'd like to see a designated runner. I'm sorry to leave the game, very sorry. Yes, I have tried to get out before, but even now as I am, I'm not happy about it. But, I'm impressed by the new owners and I'm sure they will do well for the Oakland fans."[28]

Roy Eisenhardt answered most of the questions for the new owners at the press conference. "Our philosophy is to develop a team through the farm system. We plan to spend our money at the scouting level, the minor-league level and instructional level. We have a lot of enthusiasm for baseball and we will do everything it takes to build a strong organization," Eisenhardt said.[29] Eisenhardt and the Haas family followed through on their plans of building a strong team from the bottom up, and they turned the A's into world champions again in 1989.

Finley operated the team for the remainder of the season. The A's surprisingly turned a profit of more than $1 million in 1980, all banked into the Charles O. Finley and Company coffers. American League president Lee MacPhail, who had attended the August 23 press conference as a representative of MLB and Commissioner Kuhn, publicly reflected on the Finley ownership of the A's. "Baseball has lost its number one innovator. The designated hitter, divisional play, night World Series games, colorful uniforms and opening the World Series on Saturday were all ideas that Charlie pushed before others did," said MacPhail. "But Charlie had three big problems. He was an absentee owner who never could tear himself away from the streets of Chicago. He didn't have the organization needed to market his product properly. And more than anything, he was hurt by the new [free agency] system."[30]

Bowie Kuhn watched the Finley sale from afar in New York, and it no doubt pleased him. Despite their shaky union in attempting to sell the A's to Marvin Davis and move the club to Denver, Kuhn continued his steadfast dislike of Finley, whom he felt was "abusive, disrespectful, coarse . . . and treated players like plantation hands."[31] But time was running out for Kuhn too. Major-league owners tired of Kuhn's autocratic ways and his inability to contain the players association and Marvin Miller. In 1982, the owners voted Kuhn out and eventually replaced him with 1984 Olympic organizer Peter Ueberroth.

Kuhn found life after baseball challenging. In January 1988, he set up a new law firm with attorney Harvey Myerson. But Myerson proved to be a dubious character, using the firm to swindle money both from Kuhn and their clients. Ultimately, the business wound up in shambles. A mere two years later, Kuhn—fleeing his firm's creditors—protected his remaining assets by moving to Florida, near Jacksonville. Later, he made a multimillion-dollar lump-sum payment to his creditors and began buying and selling minor-league franchises. Kuhn became reclusive and extremely religious, joining Opus Dei, the secretive Catholic sect with more than 3,000 U.S. members.[32]

On March 15, 2007, the 80-year-old Kuhn died of complications of pneumonia at a hospital in Jacksonville. He was inducted into the Baseball Hall of Fame in 2008, after being elected by the Veterans Committee nine months after his death.

In the end, Charlie Finley, who entered the baseball world with a huge flash of bluster, ideas, and ego, exited the game with little more than a whimper and a familiar whine. Finley reigned over the baseball world for nearly five years in the early 1970s, but he left it a broken and defeated man. During his 20 years as owner of the A's, he witnessed revolutionary changes in the promotional and business aspects, as well as the style of on-field play, in Major League Baseball, championing many of them himself. In the end, baseball adapted, prospered, and entered a new renaissance period of fan interest. Ironically, the most important change—player free agency, which led baseball into a future of unprecedented prosperity and popularity—spelled doom for the maverick owner from the Windy City.

Epilogue

Life (and Death) After Baseball

When Charlie Finley lost his family, his Indiana farm, and more than half of his wealth in the divorce settlement, finally ratified in 1981, it signaled a new stage in his life. Near the same time, he sold the Oakland A's and no longer had the sporting spotlight he had enjoyed for more than 20 years. He also lost much of his earning power, as the insurance industry began to change in the 1970s, moving away from brokers like himself between professional organizations and the big insurance companies. Moreover, his health, precarious since his 1973 heart attack and 1977 heart-bypass surgery, proved a troublesome aspect of his daily life. By the early 1980s, much of what had made Finley who he was had changed, deteriorated, or vanished entirely.

Charlie Finley would live until 1996, but after selling the A's, he was never the same. He continued to work in Chicago, and he appeared the whirling dervish in his dealings, but his empire was collapsing. The A's were the last of the sports franchises that had defined Finley during his glory days, with his hockey and basketball teams long since sold.[1] Much of his fortune was gone, as the $12.7 million from the sale of the Oakland A's would be largely required to pay off his ex-wife and children as well as other creditors.[2]

Finley tried to use his characteristic wits, sales skills, and drive to rebuild his fortune, but never quite succeeded. Part of this was because his poor organizational habits, always a factor in his business dealings, worsened during the last two decades of his life. The stories of files being thrown into desk drawers and stacks of paper being haphazardly tossed about his office were well known to business associates. They got more dramatic as time passed.[3]

The 1980s proved to be a tough economic environment, and Finley had difficulty leveraging his personal and business resources with reasonable borrowed investment capital.[4] He witnessed his insurance empire crumble, and the returns that he'd usually received from stock investments proved unreliable. In October 1987, a stock market collapse lopped 22.6 percent off the Dow Jones industrial average in a single day. A savings and loan industry collapse followed, and Finley, along with millions of other Americans, suffered huge monetary losses.[5] He was wiped out by this stock market crash and the subsequent collapse of the junk-bond market and never recovered. By the time of his death, he was largely without resources, still owing other creditors.[6]

For many years he continued to operate out of Chicago, spending the workweek there, where he still maintained an apartment, and returning to La Porte, Indiana, on weekends.[7] He pursued several schemes, beyond stock investments, to remake his fortune. Martin Finley said that his father tried to keep busy. "He tried to start another baseball league. He came pretty close at getting the international football league going . . . He had all the bylaws of all the leagues, and he put together what he liked and didn't like, and that kept him busy for years."[8] He even tried to buy the Chicago Cubs, but there was no way the lords of baseball were going to allow him back; the team went to the Tribune Corporation.[9]

In the late 1980s, Finley also pursued a new football design that he believed would improve the game. He applied for and received a patent for a "double grip football" that had recessed dimples, like a golf ball's. Finley argued that these would improve traction. Some versions had fluorescent yellow horizontal stripes—rather than the more common vertical ones—which were intended to help receivers and fans see the ball better while it was in flight. As Finley explained at the time, "the grip-enhanced football will be able to be thrown 5 to 15 yards farther than a regular ball and with more accuracy."[10] He tried to peddle it to sporting goods manufacturers and worked to have it adopted by various leagues and teams. He persuaded the University of Michigan to use his football the year that Desmond Howard won the Heisman Trophy.[11] He persuaded 8 bowl teams (Washington, Michigan, Nebraska, Wyoming, Arizona, Southern Mississippi, Alabama, and the Air Force) to use it in 1990, and 30 universities did so in 1991. He never convinced the National Collegiate Athletic Association to allow the use of his striped version, but for a short time his football was a moderate success.[12]

Lew Krausse recalled that Finley also went to the National High School Athletic Association, based in Kansas City, to pitch his football. He asked Krausse, who stayed in Kansas City after his playing days, to pick him up at the airport and transport him to the meeting with the association officials. As Krausse recalled, Finley said, "I've got to present this to them, and they're going to look it over and, hopefully, accept this ball to play all the football games with."[13] He was successful in convincing several high school systems to use his striped football in their poorly lit stadiums. Not surprisingly, his first positive response came from La Porte High School, which used in it in 1989. Indiana High School Athletic Association director Robert Gardner called it the best thing since Gatorade in USA Today. "I found it easier in passing and kicking situations and made the game more enjoyable for spectators." Even Notre Dame coach Lou Holtz endorsed the football. Finley used those endorsements at every opportunity, but the major manufacturers pushed back on the innovation and were able to reassert their contol over the market.[14]

Having lost the farm on Johnson Road in the divorce, he settled into another farmhouse a short distance away, on State Highway 35. He had originally purchased it for his parents to live in, but after their passing, he began to homestead there. The farmhouse, originally built in 1860 for a physician, was fabled to have been a stopover for Abraham Lincoln during one of his trips, and on the place where Lincoln supposedly had made an impromptu speech, Finley built what he called the "Lincoln Cottage." At least four additions had been made to the main house over the years, and by the time Finley moved in, it had five bedrooms, three bathrooms, and a large family room, all beautifully decorated. He built an outhouse on the property, with entrances for "Gentlemen" and "Broads," apparently with no thought to the sexism this displayed. He claimed to have borrowed more than a million dollars to rehab the barn into a massive, 72-by-32-foot lodge, complete with bedrooms, bathrooms, a kitchen, and a den. "This is Finley's showpiece," a reporter visiting the farm said of it in 1992, "and he's willing to make the expedition through its many rooms and up steep steps to its third-story observation deck to display it to full effect." It had a loft bedroom known as "Charlie O.'s Bedroom," an observation deck called "Charlie O.'s Widow's Walk," and a bar called "Charlie O.'s Bar." Finley's running joke was that these might have been named either for him or for his famous mule. He showed off his three World Series trophies in the barn, as well as other memorabilia and mementos of his glory years as a lion in the baseball world. Most striking, he had stained-glass windows put into the barn with the image of himself, Reggie Jackson, and a rooster, among other depictions.[15] Later in life, when he was less mobile than in earlier years, Finley had his bed put into the living room of the barn to avoid having to use the stairs to the upper rooms.[16]

Even on this second farm in La Porte, he managed to capture the spotlight. For example, he began holding big Christmas parties there, putting up elaborate lights and lawn scenery. The decorations grew more complex every year, and when Finley replaced his more mundane Nativity scene with live actors and animals, people came from all around to see them. Rick Knoll remembered helping arrange for police officers to direct traffic because of the congestion. Knoll also commented, "One of my best memories was Mr. Finley's last Christmas party up there. My father died in October, and Mr. Finley had the big party, and we were all up there being festive, and he took me aside, and he said, 'You know, Rick, I think this is my last Christmas party. It's just not fun anymore without your dad here.' And that was his last one."[17]

Sportswriters, especially columnists, called Finley for his views on the game, the players, the owners, the universe, you name it. Finley, as always, loved the spotlight and served up his peculiar brand of half-baked views on life with bombastic crassness. Finley's unusual insights always arrived with a trace of bitterness and absurdity.[18]

When George Steinbrenner came on the scene as the outrageous owner of the New York Yankees, who better to comment on his antics than the equally outrageous Charlie Finley? He thought Steinbrenner got off easy when the commissioner suspended him from baseball operations in 1990 for his involvement in gambling.[19] Never mind that Finley squealed like a stuck pig when Bowie Kuhn put him on notice in 1973 that if he did not straighten up his act, he might be suspended. On another occasion Finley popped off about how Steinbrenner owed him both a debt of gratitude and cash. "If it wasn't for me, the man would not have won any World Series," he said in 1987. "Look, when he won it in 1977 and 1978, his biggest players were Reggie and Catfish. I signed them both. He would have no chance of winning now if he didn't have Claudell [Washington] and Rickey [Henderson]. I signed them both."[20] Through it all, Finley painted himself as the wise elder statesman now above the fray and as an endless fount of revelations.[21]

Sometimes the sportswriters turned this Finley-Steinbrenner thing on its head. In one comparison in 1996, the bottom line was that Finley was a "ruthless, classless, crude and attention-starved showman when he was owner of the Athletics, [who] wrote the playbook for modern day owners like George Steinbrenner." In essence, it said, "Charles O. Finley made team ownership safe for George Steinbrenner."[22] Let's pause for a minute here, and offer the observation that this is one of the most ridiculous conclusions ever. For all of Finley's antics, he was not the first MLB owner who was ruthless (read Walter O'Malley and a host of others), classless (read Charles Comiskey and many others), crude (read August Busch and virtually all others), or attention-starved (read the whole lot of them). Nor were Steinbrenner's activities made possible by any aspect of pioneering on Finley's part. Indeed, if there is a connection, it may be closer to Finley's observation. Some of Finley's greatest players skipped town, seduced by big bucks given to them by Steinbrenner while winning World Series for the New York Yankees.

Finley engaged in some serious historical revisionism concerning Bowie Kuhn after leaving Major League Baseball. He said repeatedly that Kuhn forced him out of the game. He pointed to the A's fire sale of 1976 and Kuhn's critical role in forestalling it. No doubt Kuhn acted supremely catty in that particular instance, but Finley's many previous shenanigans had prompted Kuhn's overreaction.[23] But all of this was an oversimplification with a patina of falsification. He was out of baseball because he pushed his wife to divorce and had to liquidate his assets per court order to pay the settlement. Kuhn did facilitate several proposed sales of the A's in the late 1970s but no doubt also enjoyed Finley's twisting in the wind over finances as the decade came to an end.

One issue that dramatically affected Charlie Finley was the legal knock-down-drag-out of the early 1980s when Shirley Finley and their children sued him to force the liquidation of Charles O. Finley and Company and the distribution of its assets as outlined in the divorce decree. Their position was all the more salient after Finley sold the Oakland A's for $12.7 million in 1980. Moreover, because he had been ruthless during the more than six years that the divorce dragged through the court system, and constantly neglected to pay support or paid less than what he was required to pay, their patience was somewhat lacking. The Finley children and ex-wife prevailed in the court case. Attorney Arthur Holtzman commented, "It was fun in the sense that we had a good legal argument to make, we had a bright circuit court judge, and we had a good appellate panel that understood the issues and understood the real issue, which again was using that Indiana decree." Holtzman added, "It was a hard case because it's a family case. And again, we felt bad that we were representing four children and they're being fought by their father . . . This led to an estrangement obviously."[24]

It certainly did. Sal Bando recalled this incident: "It's some time after the divorce or after the legal separation, whatever went on, and he calls me down to his office on Michigan Avenue to meet with them. And when I'm there, he says, 'I'd like you to go to lunch with me.' And I've already eaten, but I go with him. He orders what he's going to order. He's just talking, and he talks about his wife and the divorce. And the next thing you know, he's crying, and he got very emotional over it. So I'm sitting there looking uncomfortable—I work for the guy."[25] Finley's sense of loss for his family grew more serious over the years.

Bea Knoll, a longtime family friend, thought that the divorce and how it unfolded weighed on him, regardless of his very real culpability in its bitterness. "I just feel like that was really eating his heart," she recalled. "That's just the way I felt, and I've never talked to anybody about it." She befriended him in his old age and tried to make his life a little more comfortable. Knoll recalled inviting him to her house for Thanksgiving because she knew he had no family to socialize with during one of the great American family holidays.[26] Sue Salach, who, with her husband, purchased the old Finley family farm on Johnson Road, recalled how she'd met Charlie in the mid-1990s and how he'd spoken eloquently of his family, showing her photos of his children and talking about how proud he was of them. She'd detected a bit of a tear in his eye and a quiver in his voice as he'd talked about their lives.

The remaining years of Charlie Finley's life proved less the triumphal twilight that he might have wanted and expected than a long, slow fade from the public eye, in which he was seen increasingly as an old curmudgeon rather than a brilliant businessman, former MLB team owner, and innovator.

All the while Finley could be both cantankerous and conciliatory; it could go either way, depending on his mood. Two stories give the flavor of his mercurial temperament. In 1984, Ron Mihelic, who'd grown up in La Porte and played with the Finley boys and later worked for the A's, was back in La Porte and ran into Charlie Jr. at a bar. They reminisced about old times, and Charlie Jr. said that he had gone over and visited his father at the new farm on State Highway 35. Mihelic decided to do the same, just to say hello and catch up on things. He thought it would be a pleasant experience. It wasn't. Finley, when he first saw him, yelled, "What the hell do you want here? Get the hell out of here." Mihelic responded, "OK, Charlie, if that's the way you want it. See ya later." He went back to his car and never saw Finley again.[27]

Another encounter turned out differently. Sportscaster Merle Harmon had worked for the station broadcasting the Kansas City Athletics in 1961 before moving on. He had numerous encounters with Finley after that one season, but only in the setting of MLB meetings and the like. Mostly they stayed in separate corners, but sometimes Finley would accost him. After Finley was out of baseball and Harmon had not heard anything from him for more than a decade, he found in the *Dallas Morning News* one day a retrospective on Finley and what he was then doing. Harmon harbored deep resentment for some comments Finley had made about one of his close friends shortly after that person had passed away. Even so, Harmon said that his wife explained that this offered an opportunity to make up, because, as the Bible says, "you're supposed to forgive and forget." A deeply religious man, Harmon reasoned that "forgiveness is something that puts your life back in order . . . [and] it's been all this time." He clipped out the story, attached a note that said simply, "Charlie, thought you might enjoy having this from the *Dallas Morning News*," and sent it to Finley. To his surprise, Finley sent a note back: "Dear Merle, I want to thank you for taking the time to send me the story out of the Dallas paper. It's given me an opportunity to do something I've always wanted to do for 25 years and that is to tell you I'm sorry."[28]

Finley had a slow decline in health in the 1990s, and what caused most of his troubles was his heart. It was a mess—never mind the banner in Oakland at the 1974 World Series that read FINLEY COULDN'T HAVE A HEART ATTACK, HE HAS NO HEART. He had high cholesterol, and had suffered a heart attack in August 1973, a bypass four years later, and other hospitalizations thereafter.[29] A's pitcher Steve McCatty quipped that Finley's bypass surgery took eight hours and "seven and a half of them was just to find his heart!"[30] In March 1981, he had emergency vascular surgery when one of the arteries in his neck became plugged, and he had to undergo balloon angioplasty.[31] Years of smoking and drinking took their toll, as did his extravagant eating habits. According to David Finley, "He could put on twenty pounds and take off twenty pounds faster than anyone you've ever seen. If he said, 'Hey, I'm going to go on a diet and lose twenty pounds,' he would . . . And he was from the South . . . fried okra, fried oysters . . . you name it, and slap the butter on it, man."[32]

Aaron Fogus, who worked as a handyman for Finley on his farm for a time, also thought that Finley's eating habits were a large part of his health problem. "I can remember going to the Michigan City area, and he would have fresh soft-shell crab flown in . . . and he'd cook them in peanut oil for me," Fogus said. They were pretty bad for his arteries and heart. So was his signature corn on the cob, eaten "Charlie Finley style." Fogus remembered that Finley would give a whole stick of butter to each person eating with him and say, "Lay it on your plate and then take your corn on the cob and just roll it on that stick." Fogus said that everyone was expected to use the whole stick in buttering the corn.[33]

In the end, Charles O. Finley's death came quite suddenly for many who knew him. After having been hospitalized several times in late 1995, Finley went back to the Northwestern Memorial Hospital in Chicago in February 1996 with heart and vascular-disease problems. His family and friends thought he would recover and be released, as with all his previous hospitalizations. Sons David and Martin Finley came to visit often, as did other family members and friends. Aaron Fogus said that he called the hospital a few times and did not realize that this was Finley's swan song. "Honestly, I didn't think he was going to die," he said. "I thought he'd be coming home like the other times." Finley had been so tough and resolute in the past that Fogus thought he would survive this as well. But, Fogus remembered, when he called the hospital to talk with Charlie once more, at first the person answering said, "Charlie's not able to come to the phone." The hospital would not say anything about Finley's condition, and this worried Fogus, who soon found out that Finley had passed away on February 19.[34]

All of Finley's family gathered for the funeral, even his ex-wife, Shirley. It was held 11 A.M. on February 22, 1996—on what would have been Charlie Finley's 78th birthday—at the Geisen Funeral Home in Merrillville, Indiana. Pastor Marvin B. Troyer of the Bethel Baptist Church, of which Finley was a member, officiated the service. Afterward, Finley was buried at the Calumet Park Cemetery in Merrillville, where Finley's parents were also buried. Those were the facts from the local newspapers, giving the standard information one would find in any obituary. What made this such an unusual funeral was the coming together of Finley's family, and the five sons serving as pallbearers, after years of strife between both Charlie and the children and in some instances the children themselves. It was also unusual because of the featured speakers. In addition to daughter Kathryn, who spoke for the family, two of Finley's greatest A's gave comments, Reggie Jackson and Jim "Catfish" Hunter, both of whom he signed to the team and who both went on to Hall of Fame careers. Jackson and Hunter had fought with Finley many times over the years, and both displayed class in coming together at the end of his life to eulogize the former A's owner. Another speaker was Bill Bartholomay, chairman of the board of the Atlanta Braves, who came as the representative of Major League Baseball.

Many of the lords of baseball were nowhere to be found in remembering one of their own, especially one who had been enormously significant in the American League for two decades. The fact that Bartholomay was the sole representative at the funeral concluded the series of snubs that Finley had endured from all the other owners over the years. Yes, Finley had often been cantankerous, but he'd also had many good ideas that were adopted and he'd built a truly successful team in the early 1970s. He deserved better from the baseball community. It was the kind of favor that Finley could always be counted on for; if Bowie Kuhn, his greatest nemesis in MLB, had died before Finley, Finley would have attended the funeral, if only to prove to the world he was a "bigger" man than Kuhn.

Reggie Jackson, despite past feuds with Finley, came forward to speak fondly of his former boss. "No distance is too far to travel for a friend," said Jackson, who went on to praise him as both an innovator and a tireless worker. Catfish Hunter was no less effusive. He recalled that he was a young, naive Southern country boy when he first signed with the A's and that Finley was more than just a team owner to him; he was also a role model. "He was never a yes man, and didn't want you to be," he commented. "Charlie wanted you to have your own opinion and think your own way." Bartholomay recited the famous Finley motto, Sweat plus Sacrifice equals Success, and commended Finley for his hard work and perseverance. He applauded the legacy of Finley for Major League Baseball, his innovations especially, but he also made a veiled reference without either praise or condemnation to Finley's many fights with others in the baseball world. He thought it appropriate to laugh about these so long after the fact and opined that a fitting tribute for Finley would be a place in the MLB Hall of Fame as baseball's super showman. This drew a strong round of applause at the funeral, but little has since been done about it in the baseball world.[35]

Martin Finley said that one incident at the funeral has been misinterpreted. A photograph of ex-wife Shirley crying, along with other members of the family, ended up in the newspapers and gave the impression that she still had affection for him. Martin said she did not. "My mom attended the funeral for us, not because she was once married to him. And there's a picture in the paper . . . at the funeral, showing my mom sobbing next to my brother, who was sobbing. And my mother goes, 'Damn that newspaper. You know what? I wasn't sobbing because your dad died. I was sobbing because your brother was crying.' "[36]

Soon as his death, sportswriters published retrospective stories about Charlie Finley and his colorful and sweeping life. Most stated the usual stuff about his innovations in the game, such as the designated-hitter rule and night World Series games, the three-peat championships of the A's between 1972 and 1974, the titanic struggles between Finley and MLB commissioner Bowie Kuhn, and the circus that was the 1973 World Series with the Mike Andrews controversy. Some obtained great quotes from his former players, such as Vida Blue saying in *USA Today* that Finley "was more famous than his players. When you're considered more newsworthy than Reggie Jackson, Mr. October, then you've really done something."[37]

But at least one reflection was more thoughtful, that of legendary *Washington Post* sports columnist Shirley Povich. In a generally positive recollection of Finley's career in baseball, Povich asked, "Was he a genius or a crackpot, a career maverick or a buffoon, a liar, an angry man, an egomaniac, good for baseball or bad for baseball?" Povich's "studied answer" raised the fundamental conundrum of Finley's life: "He was all of the above."[38]

Assessing the life and career of Charles O. Finley has become a favorite indoor sport of Oakland A's fans since his death. While Finley is known for many baseball innovations, ranging from installing fireworks-spewing scoreboards in Kansas City to adopting a big, dumb jackass mule as his team's mascot to urging the adoption of a three-ball rule for walks, one can honestly say that he was not in the mainstream of conventional baseball thought. In fact, during his 20 years as owner of the Athletics franchise, most of his fellow owners and associates viewed him as eccentric, an egomaniac, and even somewhat crazy. Bill Veeck summed it up by saying, "Finley does things without class."[39] This may have been the case, but many of the positive changes in baseball over the past 40 years originated with Charles O. Finley. Most important, Finley recognized that Major

League Baseball had failed to change with the times and needed to embrace new ways of appealing to and expanding its fan base. More than most other owners, he was committed to ensuring the survivability of MLB.

His support of the designated-hitter rule as a way of injecting more offense and excitement into the game is well known. But Finley also advocated for interleague play during the regular season to capitalize on regional rivalries, a realignment of MLB divisions to ensure maximum competition, a designated-runner rule, and, who could forget, fluorescent orange baseballs. While not every one of these ideas was originally Finley's, and some were just wacky and unsuccessful, others were completely legitimate and deserved serious consideration. In every case, he adopted them and promoted them with zeal; and in some instances, he won over his fellow owners. Finley believed Major League Baseball had to change in order to remain competitive against the increasingly popular sports of football and basketball. And he was right. MLB eventually decided to adopt divisional realignment and interleague play, but not until the year of the great labor strike of 1994 when Major League Baseball nearly collapsed.

It also agreed to adopt night World Series games after Finley's long-standing campaign to sell that concept. Using the argument that it was imperative to sell Major League Baseball, or else suffer losing its audience to football and basketball, Finley made the case that the backbone of support for the game came from the working class and that the sport must cater to them. Since these people had day jobs, they could only attend games at night, and the World Series, as the singular event in the baseball season, should be accessible as well. It took him years of campaigning, but in 1971 his fellow owners finally decided to implement night games for the World Series—initially only on the weeknights, but now all such games are played in the evening. Finley was delighted with this change. After all, he said, they were "selling baseball, and if we are wise, we will do everything possible for the greatest exposure of America's Greatest Sport's Spectacle— The World Series."[40] It was an enormously important innovation, and it allowed for an ever-increasing number of people to watch the games. The last World Series played during the daytime, in 1970, drew an average television audience of 19.4 million. The next year, with its weeknight games, the World Series drew an average of 24.2 million, and it built from there. Over time, researchers for MLB have determined that playing games in the evening has had a positive economic impact on the game. Commissioner Bud Selig said in 2009, "Our goal is to have the largest number of people watching, and the truth is the potential audience is 30 percent greater in primetime at night."[41]

Finley did not receive the credit he deserved for pioneering the "moneyball" approach of small-market teams to put winners on the field. Made famous by the Oakland A's of a later era, the moneyball approach asserts that baseball is a business and that the conventional wisdom of how to create a successful MLB franchise is incorrect for teams without extensive monetary resources. It insists that for small-market teams to win, they must scout, sign, and develop young talent who can then compete successfully against richer competitors. Using the rules of player compensation established in MLB, these teams grow young superstars and pay them only modestly until the players' seniority in the system allows them to depart as free agents. Before their departure, however, the GMs often deal them for top prospects to restock their farm system. Absent the emphasis on ornate statistical analysis undertaken in the more recent moneyball era, Charlie Finley was the godfather of this approach to running his franchise. As free agency emerged in the 1970s, he restocked his A's team with home-grown talent as his superstars departed.[42]

Charlie Finley's career in baseball was controversial from start to finish. An innovator and a promoter, he was also a huckster and charlatan. And the baseball establishment always loathed him—sometimes for valid reasons, but mostly because he did not fit into the club of staid aristocrats led by such men as Bowie Kuhn and Walter O'Malley. It is fair—in fact it may be an understatement—to say that Kuhn was channeling O'Malley and the other members of the baseball establishment in his dislike of and interference with Charlie Finley. When he called Finley "an embarrassment to baseball," Kuhn mimicked the perception of the establishment. One might conclude that O'Malley was Kuhn's puppet master, and Kuhn's actions concerning Finley reflected the desires of baseball's inner circle.[43]

The fights between Kuhn and Finley were unfortunate, although entertaining for those looking in from the outside. But they also masked a much deeper problem in the game, which of course Kuhn failed to understand. Kuhn, as guardian of the MLB establishment, wanted to maintain the status quo that had existed since the time of Judge Kenesaw Mountain Landis, with dominance resting with the owners. Kuhn, and most of the owners, never understood the changes to the game taking place in the 1970s. Finley did understand, but did not fully appreciate, those changes. He did offer solutions that, had they been adopted, would have led to a very different structure than the one now in place.

Finley regretted several of his actions, especially those in relation to the move of the A's from Kansas City to Oakland. He lived to regret ever leaving the heartland, as it built a new stadium for the replacement expansion team, the Royals, which the city turned out in droves to support. Finley said in 1985, "The biggest mistake I ever made was moving the team from Kansas City to Oakland. I shouldn't have moved away from the greatest baseball fans in the world in Kansas City."[44]

No doubt Charlie Finley was a despot and a whiner and a bully and a liar and a bullshit artist. But he was also a strategic thinker, a big-idea man, and a visionary. Failure to recognize this duality of Finley's personality has too often caused him to be dismissed as a gadfly and nuisance.

No one owner had a more significant effect on Major League Baseball between 1960 and 1980 than Charles O. Finley. He perhaps deserves a place in the MLB Hall of Fame for what he accomplished. His efforts helped to change the game. Joe Rudi made that case for his enshrinement: "I really do [think he belongs]. You've got to give the guy credit for what he did. He took a run-down, zero franchise, what they called the AAA team of the Yankees for all those years, and he built it into a dynasty."[45] Dick Williams said, "I'd vote for him. I think he was brilliant."[46] Sal Bando was just as adamant the other way: "I don't think what he did was in the best interests of the game. I think there was more damage done than there was good."[47] Neil Papiano was equivocal: "I guess yes and no. If you're talking about Charlie's innovations and what Charlie did for baseball, the answer is yes. If you talk about his arguments with baseball and his contrariness on certain things, probably no, because he didn't necessarily get along with the group. But he had many, many innovations."[48]

The innovations were real. So was the success on the field. Of course, so was the cantankerousness, the carelessness, the connivance, and the cleverness. Finley was a man of contradictions and complexity. Sportswriter Dan Holmes summarized as well as anyone the appropriate assessment of Finley: "A true genius is rarely appreciated in his own time. A true asshole almost always is. Major League Baseball quickly recognized that Charles O. Finley, maverick owner of the Athletics in the 1960s and 1970s, was the latter. They still haven't a clue that he was the former, as well."[49]

Acknowledgments

Our fascination with Oakland's Swinging A's began in the early 1970s, as we both watched Reggie, Sal, Vida, Catfish, and the gang—with their kelly green and Fort Knox gold uniforms and bushy mustaches—battle the Big Red Machine in the 1972 World Series. Flash-forward 32 years, when we decided we wanted to present a paper at the annual spring *Nine* conference on baseball history and culture in Tucson, Arizona. The aunt and uncle of Mike's wife reside in Tucson, so we had a place to stay, but we still needed a topic. After talking over our interests, we realized that we both rooted and cheered for the A's growing up and were intrigued with the team's controversial owner, Charles O. Finley. We decided to write our first joint paper comparing Charlie Finley to legendary White Sox owner Bill Veeck. Over the next two years, we presented several additional papers at Society for American Baseball Research (SABR) conferences—all on various aspects of Finley's ownership of the A's. After each presentation, we became increasingly impressed by the level of interest among baseball historians and others about the life and antics of Charlie Finley. The encouragement we received from dozens of fellow SABR members convinced us that Finley's life deserved a new examination that placed his accomplishments (particularly as owner of the A's) in historical perspective. This book is the result of nearly five years of research into Charles Oscar Finley's life.

The challenging part of this project was finding the time in our busy schedules to undertake the research and complete the manuscript, as we were already overcommitted in our full-time positions at the National Aeronautics and Space Administration (Mike) and the National Air and Space Museum (Roger). We squeezed in time in the evenings, on weekends, and on holidays for research and writing. This, of course, prevented us from spending valuable time with our families and loved ones. Special thanks goes to Stephanie Mitchell (Mike's wife) for her loving support during this project. Stephanie began telling friends that she was a weekend widow to old Charlie Finley yet always agreed to stay up late to proofread chapters of this book. Equal thanks goes to Monique Laney (Roger's friend), who also endured many solo weekends because of the project and was forced to listen to endless Charlie Finley stories whenever Mike and Roger were together. Without Stephanie's and Monique's continued energy and encouragement, this project would have failed.

During the nearly five years of working on this project, we both endured personal tragedies with the untimely deaths of our fathers, Doyle Launius and Arthur Green. Both would have enjoyed reading this book. Both valued education and expected their sons to work hard, complete college, and become successful businessmen. Instead we turned out to be an award-winning historian (Roger) and a successful government executive (Mike). Both Doyle and Arthur subscribed to the Finley mantra of "Sweat plus Sacrifice equals Success"; it is how they lived their lives. We appreciate all of their sweat and sacrifice and hope we have demonstrated some modest success in this world. We miss them every day.

Two colleagues, Paul Dickson and Brad Snyder, gave us inspiring support, encouragement, and ideas as we muddled along with the project. Both are outstanding baseball writers and we greatly benefited from their thoughts and guidance. A few years ago, we met writers Benita and Burton Boxerman at an annual SABR Seymour Medal Conference, and we appreciate their insights into Charlie Finley's life. Additionally, several professional colleagues, relatives, and friends provided encouragement, support, and advice for this book. Thanks go to Marlene and Ken Nyman, Robert Hopkins, Kristen Erickson, Ed Goldstein, Jane Tobler, Kirk Cunningham, Jane Jacobs, Jack Walton, Heike and Paul Mitchell, Leslie and Henry Jacobs, Deborah and Tom Jacobs, Judith and Tom Bolenbaugh, Dale Blocher, Lori Garver, David Brandt, Victor Lebacqz, Tom Irvine, Shanessa Jackson, Patty Currier,

Jim Stofan, David Barrett, Marguerite Angelari, Doris Green, Lela Steele, Ralph Beaty, Bob Jacobs, Vianne Launius, Andy Wirkmaa, Tom D. Crouch, Ray Doswell, Jim Gates, Michael H. Gorn, Charles J. Gross, Alvin L. Hall, Tom Heitz, Karen S. Koziara, Sylvia K. Kraemer, Howard E. McCurdy, William B. Mead, Ken Moon, Peter Rutkoff, William Simons, Paul Staudohar, Steve Steinberg, Trisha Graboske, Erik Conway, General John R. Dailey, David H. DeVorkin, James Rodger Fleming, Michael H. Gorn, James R. Hansen, Peter Jakab, Dennis R. Jenkins, Alan M. Ladwig, W. Henry Lambright, Jennifer Levasseur, John M. Logsdon, W. Patrick McCray, Karen McNamara, Ted Maxwell, Valerie Neal, Allan A. Needell, Michael J. Neufeld, Anthony M. Springer, and Margaret Weitekamp.

We are extremely grateful to family and friends who opened their homes to us as we conducted research on Charlie Finley. In particular, Kathy and Steve Jacobs (Mike's aunt and uncle) always welcomed us to sunny Tucson every spring for our annual spring training "research" trip. Their loving support and strong margaritas gave us endless energy and motivation. Additionally, Sarah Carey and Cameron Beatley provided us with many wonderful "research" weekends and an occasional Bears' game based out of their lovely home in Oak Park, Illinois.

We greatly appreciate all the former players, employees, front office executives, managers, coaches, attorneys, broadcasters, friends, and associates of Charlie Finley who were gracious enough to sit down and talk with us. It is a long and distinguished list of individuals, including Supreme Court Justice John Paul Stevens, Steve Vucinich, Lew Krausse, Joe Rudi, Aaron Fogus, Arthur Holtzman, Sal Bando, Nancy Finley, Steve McCatty, Rick Knoll, Leon Kaminski, Lou Hoynes, Mike Storen, Ron Mihelic, Chuck Dobson, Hank Peters, John Claiborne, Jerry Lumpe, Merle Harmon, Fern Schultz, Bill Grigsby, Jim Schaaf, Wayne Causey, Neil Papiano, Dennis Page, Jim Chappell, Jay Hankins, Sid Bordman, Mike Andrews, Glenn Schwarz, Darold Knowles, Marvin Miller, Chuck Cottonaro, Rollie Fingers, Bill Myer, Ron Bergman, Dick Green, Bobby Winkles, Lee Stange, Chuck Tanner, Vida Blue, Hank Bauer, Dick Williams, Bea Knoll, Tom Corwin, Ed Borkowitz, and Monte Moore.

Charlie and Shirley Finley had seven children during their marriage. Six children survive today. Martin and David Finley, the two youngest surviving sons, agreed to provide extensive interviews about their father's life in and out of baseball. We are enormously grateful for their aid in this project and their recognition of their father's important place in baseball history.

Sue and Ken Salach provided us with an intimate and very interesting tour of their beautiful farm on Johnson Road in La Porte, Indiana. Beginning in the mid-1950s and running through the early 1980s, their farm was known to most folks in the area as "Finley's Johnson Road Farm." The Salachs bought the deteriorating farm in the early 1990s and began restoring it to its former Finley glory. The Salachs took time on a bitterly cold and icy December afternoon to walk the sprawling estate and answer our numerous questions. We thank them for their hospitality, warm coffee, and lively conversation as we warmed ourselves by Finley's specially constructed flagstone fireplace in the spacious family room.

Catherine Hensley, Dana Grant, and Vianne Lauinus contributed important and timely transcription services of the many audio interviews we did for the project. They saved us an invaluable amount of time in their efforts. Sister Bonnie Boilini provided legal and general research in the Chicago and Northwest Indiana area for the project. Her keen ability to track down important legal documents and newspaper articles improved this book immeasurably. We are also grateful to the outstanding staff of the A. Bartlett Giamatti Research Center at the National Baseball Hall of Fame and Museum in Cooperstown, New York, for their assistance in locating numerous articles on Finley's life.

Four additional editors demonstrated their support and interest in this project by publishing two articles on various aspects of Charlie Finley's relationship with his players and Commissioner Bowie Kuhn. The founding editor of *Nine: A Journal of Baseball History and Culture*, Bill Kirwin, accepted our article " 'Charlie Finley Has Soured My Stomach for Baseball': Charles O. Finley versus His Players" for publication before his tragic death of cancer. We met Bill in Tucson, and he impressed us with his interest in the life of Charlie Finley. Trey Strecker stepped into Bill's huge shoes as editor of *Nine* and made sure our article received top billing in the spring 2008 issue of the journal. Special appreciation also goes to Randy Merritt and Phil Osterholt of Sandlot Media, who published the short-lived magazine *108: Celebrating Baseball*. They published our article titled "The Great Baseball Fire Sale" in the summer 2007 issue of *108*. We appreciate their support and wish their magazine had fared better in the marketplace. It was a wonderful if short-lived baseball magazine.

We spent a weekend in August 2008 in Kansas City at a reunion of many players and employees of the Kansas City Athletics. The reunion gave us the opportunity to connect with many former A's players and to hear firsthand many funny and outrageous stories about Charlie Finley. Thanks to Jeff Logan, who organized the reunion and later formed the Kansas City Baseball Historical Society, and Linda Haskins, an independent filmmaker producing a Kansas City A's documentary for a local PBS station in the Kansas City area. We eagerly await Linda's final project and congratulate her on this exciting accomplishment.

Over the years six books have been written about the Athletics and their owner Charlie Finley. These works served as important resources for us throughout this project. Three were written in the mid-1970s: *Charlie O.: Charles Oscar Finley vs. the Baseball Establishment* by Herbert Michelson; *Charlie O. and the Angry A's: The Low and Inside Story of Charlie O. Finley and Baseball's Most Colorful Team* by Bill Libby; and *Champagne and Baloney: The Rise and Fall of Finley's A's* by Tom Clark. These three books, all journalistic accounts by sportswriters, were important resources in our understanding of Finley and the A's. Unfortunately, all three authors have passed away, but we felt they deserved our sincere acknowledgment and appreciation. John Peterson's *The Kansas City Athletics: A Baseball History, 1954–1967* is simply the most comprehensive book written to date on the time of the A's in Kansas City. We were fortunate to meet Mr. Peterson at the A's reunion in Kansas City in 2008 and are grateful for his encouragement of our project. *Baseball's Last Dynasty: Charlie Finley's Oakland A's* by Bruce Markusen provided a superb scholarly account of the championship seasons of Finley's A's. And finally, Ron Bergman's *Mustache Gang: The Swaggering Saga of Oakland's A's* provided a highly entertaining recap of the 1972 Oakland A's and the team's irascible owner.

Our agent, Chris Kuppig, showed great support and enthusiasm for the Finley project from the beginning of our association with him. He provided invaluable insights, advice, and editing for our final book proposal.

Chris also demonstrated a shrewd eye for the business side as he negotiated our final deal. Simply put, this project would not have been published without Chris's assistance.

George Gibson, publishing director for Walker & Company and Bloomsbury USA, believed in this biography and Charlie Finley's importance in the history of baseball. We owe George a great deal. Benjamin Adams served as editor of our manuscript. His editorial insights and shepherding of the book through the wickets of publication are most appreciated.

Finally, we'd like to thank Charles O. Finley. We never had the opportunity to meet or interview him. Most everyone we interviewed said Charlie could be a great friend; you just didn't want to work for him. It is unlikely he would have agreed with several of this book's conclusions—a few he might have enjoyed and even laughed about, and others he would have likely called us at two o'clock in the morning to gripe and cuss about in his deep, coarse voice. Charlie's mantra of "Sweat plus Sacrifice equals Success" is branded into the minds of everyone who knew him. We kept his mantra in the back of our minds as we worked toward this important goal. In this book, we attempt to put Charlie Finley's life into a new perspective, one that highlights his importance in shaping the evolution of Major League Baseball even as it acknowledges his demons and weaknesses. We hope we did him proud.

Notes

Prologue: October 14, 1973

1. Interview with Mike Andrews, May 12, 2008.
2. Baseball Almanac Web site, interview with Mike Andrews by Mark Liptak, http://www.baseball-almanac.com/players/mike_andrews_interview.shtml (accessed May 12, 2009).
3. Tom Clark, *Champagne and Baloney: The Rise and Fall of Finley's A's* (New York: Harper & Row, 1976), p. 177.
4. Bill Libby, *Charlie O. and the Angry A's: The Low and Inside Story of Charlie O. Finley and Baseball's Most Colorful Team* (Garden City, NY: Doubleday & Co., 1975), p. 267.
5. Interview with Mike Andrews, May 12, 2008.
6. Interview with John Claiborne, October 30, 2008.
7. *New York Times*, October 18, 1973.
8. John Rosengren, *Hammerin' Hank, George Almighty and the Say Hey Kid* (Chicago, IL: Sourcebooks, 2008), p. 282.
9. *New York Times*, October 18, 1973.
10. Bowie Kuhn, *Hardball: The Education of a Baseball Commissioner* (New York: Times Books, 1987), p. 135.
11. *New York Times*, October 18, 1973.
12. Ibid.
13. *Washington Post*, October 16, 1973.
14. Libby, *Charlie O. and the Angry A's*, p. 269.
15. Ibid., p. 271.

16. *Sporting News*, November 3, 1973, p. 3.

17. *New York Times*, October 17, 1973.

18. Clark, *Champagne and Baloney*, p. 186; *Sporting News*, November 3, 1973, p. 24.

19. *Washington Post*, October 18, 1973.

20. Rosengren, *Hammerin' Hank, George Almighty and the Say Hey Kid*, p. 289.

21. *New York Times*, October 18, 1973.

22. Clark, *Champagne and Baloney*, p. 182.

23. Libby, *Charlie O. and the Angry A's*, p. 275.

24. *New York Times*, October 21, 1973.

25. Libby, *Charlie O. and the Angry A's*, p. 276.

26. Ibid.

27. Clark, *Champagne and Baloney*, p. 186; *New York Times*, October 22, 1973; Dick Williams and Bill Plaschke, *No More Mr. Nice Guy: A Life of Hardball* (New York: Houghton Mifflin, 1990). p. 173.

28. Jerome Holtzman, *The Official 1974 Baseball Guide* (St. Louis: The Sporting News, 1974), p. 278.

29. Libby, *Charlie O. and the Angry A's*, p. 279.

30. Libby, *Charlie O. and the Angry A's*, p. 279; Williams and Plaschke, *No More Mr. Nice Guy*, p. 174.

31. Libby, *Charlie O. and the Angry A's*, p. 279.

32. Ibid., p.280; Rosengren, *Hammerin' Hank, George Almighty and the Say Hey Kid*, p. 298.

33. Libby, *Charlie O. and the Angry A's*, p. 280.

34. Daniel R. Levitt and Mark L. Armour, *Paths to Glory: How Great Baseball Teams Got That Way* (Washington, DC: Potomac Books, 2004), p. 255.

35. Libby, *Charlie O. and the Angry A's*, p. 280.

Chapter 1: S + S = S

1. Ron Fimrite, "Charlie O. Eyes a Pennant or Three," *Sports Illustrated*, October 9, 1972, available online at http://vault.sportsillustrated.cnn.com/vault/article/magazine/MAG1086628/index.htm (accessed March 1, 2009); Bill Libby, *Charlie O. and the Angry A's: The Low and Inside Story of Charlie O. Finley and Baseball's Most Colorful Team* (Garden City, NY: Doubleday & Co., 1975), pp. 1–2.

2. Mark Armour, "Charlie Finley," Baseball Biography Project, available online at http://bioproj.sabr.org/bioproj.cfm?a=v&v=l&pid=16949&bid=1146 (accessed March 20, 2009).

3. Wayne Flynt, *Alabama in the Twentieth Century* (Tuscaloosa: University of Alabama Press, 2004), pp. 129–33.

4. Movie Quote Database, "Sean Thornton Quotes," available online at http://www.moviequotedb.com/movies/quiet-man-the/character_1962.html (accessed March 1, 2009).

5. Libby, *Charlie O. and the Angry A's*, p. 39; Herbert Michelson, *Charlie O.: Charles Oscar Finley vs. the Baseball Establishment* (Indianapolis, IN: Bobbs-Merrill, 1975), pp. 12–13.

6. USDA Fact Sheet, "Shell Eggs from Farm to Table," August 20, 2008, available online at http://www.fsis.usda.gov/Factsheets/Focus_On_Shell_Eggs/index.asp (accessed March 12, 2009). Quote in Michelson, *Charlie O.*, p. 13.

7. John T. Dunlop and Walter Galenson, eds., *Labor in the Twentieth Century* (New York: Academic Press, 1978), p. 27.

8. Quoted in Michelson, *Charlie O.*, p. 18.

9. Interview with Neil Papiano, September 22, 2008.

10. Quoted in Michelson, *Charlie O.*, pp. 18, 19, 20; John C. Trafny, *Gary's West Side: The Horace Mann Neighborhood* (Mount Pleasant, SC: Arcadia Publishing, 2006).

11. Libby, *Charlie O. and the Angry A's*, p. 40.

12. Interviews with Hank Bauer, February 7, 2005; Dick Green, April 14, 2008; Jay Hankins, August 8, 2008; and Vida Blue, February 27, 2005.

13. Interview with Bill Myers, July 28, 2005.

14. *La Porte: Now and Then* (La Porte: n.p., 1982), pp. 67–68; William P. Vogel, *Kingsbury: A Venture in Teamwork* (New York: Todd & Brown, 1946); Libby, *Charlie O. and the Angry A's*, pp. 40–41; Michelson, *Charlie O.*, p. 25.

15. Ibid.

16. Libby, *Charlie O. and the Angry A's*, pp. 41–42; Michelson, *Charlie O.*, pp. 26, 29.

17. Thomas Dormandy, *The White Death* (New York: New York University Press, 2000).

18. Interview with Martin Finley, October 14, 2008.

19. Libby, *Charlie O. and the Angry A's*, p. 42.

20. Ibid.; *Life*, September 6, 1968, p. 71.

21. Libby, *Charlie O. and the Angry A's*, p. 42.

22. Ibid.

23. Ibid., p. 43.

24. Tom Clark, *Champagne and Baloney: A History of Finley's A's* (New York: Harper & Row, 1976), p. 8.

25. Don Kowet, *The Rich Who Own Sports* (New York: Random House, 1977), p. 125.

26. Libby, *Charlie O. and the Angry A's*, p. 44.

27. Michelson, *Charlie O.*, p. 37.

28. John E. Peterson, *The Kansas City Athletics: A Baseball History, 1954–1967* (Jefferson, NC: McFarland & Co., 2003), p. 120.

29. Michelson, *Charlie O.*, p. 37.

30. Libby, *Charlie O. and the Angry A's*, p. 44.

31. Ibid.

32. Ernest Mehl, *The Kansas City Athletics* (New York: Henry Holt, 1956), p. 70.

33. Libby, *Charlie O. and the Angry A's*, pp. 45–46.

34. John Helyar, *Lords of the Realm: The Real History of Baseball* (New York: Villard Books, 1994), p. 73.

35. Libby, *Charlie O. and the Angry A's*, pp. 46–47.

36. Interview with Ron Mihelic, November 8, 2008.

37. Interview with Martin Finley, October 14, 2008.

38. Michelson, *Charlie O.*, p. 88.

39. Interview with David Finley, November 18–19, 2008.

40. Interview with Rick Knoll, December 15, 2008.

41. Robin Orr, "Sports Millionaire Charles O. Finley," *Parade*, January 23, 1973, pp. 9–13.

42. Interview with Tom Corwin, February 18, 2009.

43. Interview with David Finley, November 18–19, 2008.

44. Interview with Martin Finley, October 14, 2008.

45. Interview with Rick Knoll, December 15, 2008.

46. Michelson, *Charlie O.*, p. 89.

47. Peterson, *Kansas City Athletics*, p. 121.

48. Bill Veeck, *Veeck as in Wreck: The Autobiography of Bill Veeck* (Chicago: University of Chicago Press, 2001 ed.), p. 363.

49. Peterson, *Kansas City Athletics*, p. 111.

50. *Sporting News*, December 28, 1960.

51. Peterson, *Kansas City Athletics*, p. 116.

52. Libby, *Charlie O. and the Angry A's*, p. 48.

53. *Sporting News*, December 28, 1960, p. 7.

54. *Sporting News*, January 11, 1961, p. 2; Michelson, *Charlie O.*, p. 91.

Chapter 2: The Savior of Kansas City?

1. *Sporting News*, December 28, 1960.

2. Herbert Michelson, *Charlie O.: Charles Oscar Finley vs. the Baseball Establishment* (Indianapolis, IN: Bobbs-Merrill, 1975), p. 91.

3. Joe McGuff, "The Finley Story," *Kansas City Star*, 1980.

4. Rex Lardner, "Charlie Finley and Bugs Bunny in K.C.," *Sports Illustrated*, June 5, 1961, p. 25.

5. *Kansas City Star*, August 23, 1961.

6. Don Kowet, *The Rich Who Own Sports* (New York: Random House, 1977), p. 128.

7. John E. Peterson, *The Kansas City Athletics: A Baseball History, 1954–1967* (Jefferson, NC: McFarland & Co., 2003), p. 126; Roger D. Launius, *Seasons in the Sun: The Story of Big League Baseball in Missouri* (Columbia: University of Missouri Press, 2002), pp. 56–57.

8. Jack Torry, *Endless Summers: The Fall and Rise of the Cleveland Indians* (Chicago: Diamond Communications, 1995), p. 58.

9. *Sporting News*, January 11, 1961, pp. 1–2.

10. *Sporting News*, August 30, 1961, p. 5; Bill Libby, *Charlie O. and the Angry A's: The Low and Inside Story of Charlie O. Finley and Baseball's Most Colorful Team* (Garden City, NY: Doubleday & Co., 1975), p. 57.

11. Ibid. The actual contract with Lane called for $200,000 spread over eight years according to Peterson, *Kansas City Athletics*, pp. 124–26.

12. *Sporting News*, January 11, 1961.

13. Interview with Hank Peters, November 5, 2008.

14. *Sporting News*, December 28, 1960, p. 7.

15. Lardner, "Charlie Finley and Bugs Bunny in K.C.," p. 26.

16. Libby, *Charlie O. and the Angry A's*, p. 48.

17. *Kansas City Star*, February 16, 1961.

18. Lardner, "Charlie Finley and Bugs Bunny in K.C.," p. 26; *Sporting News*, January 11, 1961.

19. Interview with Rick Knoll, December 15, 2008.

20. *La Porte Herald-Argus*, May 28, 2002; interview with Fern Schultz, October 13, 2008.

21. Peterson, *Kansas City Athletics*, p. 129.

22. Ibid.; *Kansas City Star*, January 11, 1961, p. 2.

23. Lardner, "Charlie Finley and Bugs Bunny in K.C.," p. 26.

24. Interview with Merle Harmon, October 15, 2008.

25. Lardner, "Charlie Finley and Bugs Bunny in K.C.," p. 26.

26. Tom Clark, *Champagne and Baloney: A History of Finley's A's* (New York: Harper & Row, 1976), p. 11.

27. Nick Acocella, "Finley Entertained and Enraged," ESPN.com, available online at http://espn.go.com/classic/biography/s/Finley_Charles.html (accessed March 10, 2004).

28. Peterson, *Kansas City Athletics*, p. 210.

29. Interview with Bill Grigsby, October 6, 2008.

30. Lardner, "Charlie Finley and Bugs Bunny in K.C.," p. 26; Michelson, *Charlie O.*, p. 128.

31. Peterson, *Kansas City Athletics*, p. 129.

32. McGuff, "The Finley Story"; *Sporting News*, August 30, 1961, p. 5.

33. Interview with Hank Peters, November 5, 2008.

34. Libby, *Charlie O. and the Angry A's*, pp. 60–61.

35. Gene Fox, *Sports Guys: Insights, Highlights and Hoo-hahs from Your Favorite Sports Authorities* (New York: Addax, 2002), p. 42; Libby, *Charlie O. and the Angry A's*, p. 154; interview with Bill Grigsby, October 6, 2008.

36. Libby, *Charlie O. and the Angry A's*, p. 60.

37. Ibid., p. 57; *Sporting News*, August 30, 1961, p. 6; *Kansas City Star*, August 23, 1961; *Sporting News*, June 23, 1961.

38. *Sporting News*, June 21, 1961, p. 20.

39. Michelson, *Charlie O.*, pp. 100–101.

40. Interview with Lew Krausse, April 25, 2005.

41. *Kansas City Star*, June 17, 1961.

42. Michelson, *Charlie O.*, p. 95; *Sporting News*, August 30, 1961.

43. Peterson, *Kansas City Athletics*, p. 146.

44. Libby, *Charlie O. and the Angry A's*, p. 155; *Kansas City Star*, June 19, 1961.

45. Interview with Lew Krausse, April 25, 2005; Peterson, *Kansas City Athletics*, p. 147.

46. *Kansas City Star*, August 17, 1961.

47. Interview with Jim Schaaf, August 17, 2008.

48. Interview with Bill Grigsby, October 6, 2008; Bill Grigsby, *Grigs! A Beauuutiful Life* (Chicago: Sports Publishing, 2004), p. 96.

49. Fox, *Sports Guys*, p. 68.

50. *Kansas City Star*, August 17, 1961.

51. *Daytona Beach Morning Journal*, August 18, 1961; Libby, *Charlie O. and the Angry A's*, p. 64.

52. *Kansas City Times*, August 18, 1961.

53. *Dallas Times*, August 18, 1961.

54. *Kansas City Star*, August 23, 1961.

55. Peterson, *Kansas City Athletics*, p. 151; interview with Merle Harmon, October 15, 2008.

56. Interview with Merle Harmon, October 15, 2008.

57. Libby, *Charlie O. and the Angry A's*, p. 64.

58. *Sporting News*, August 21, 1961, p. 5.

59. *Sporting News*, September 5, 1961, p. 22.

60. *Sporting News*, August 30, 1961, p. 5.

61. *Kansas City Star*, August 23, 1961.

62. Michelson, *Charlie O.*, p. 96.

63. *Kansas City Star*, August 23, 1961; *Sporting News*, August 30, 1961, p. 5.

64. *Kansas City Star*, August 26, 1961.

Chapter 3: In the Doldrums

1. *Sporting News*, February 14, 1962, p. 27; April 8, 1962, p. 12; April 18, 1962, p. 34.

2. John E. Peterson, *The Kansas City Athletics: A Baseball History, 1954–1967* (Jefferson, NC: McFarland & Co., 2003), p. 163.

3. Herbert Michelson, *Charlie O: Charles Oscar Finley vs. the Baseball Establishment* (Indianapolis, IN: Bobbs-Merrill, 1975), p. 125; *Sporting News*, July 27, 1963, p. 2; Furman Bisher, *Miracle in Atlanta: The Atlanta Braves Story* (Cleveland, OH: World Publishing Co., 1966), p. 13.

4. *Sporting News*, June 2, 1962, p. 4.

5. *St. Louis Post-Dispatch*, June 20, 1962.

6. *Kansas City Times*, September 19, 1962; *Kansas City Star*, September 19, 1962; *Sporting News*, September 29, 1962, p. 16.

7. *Kansas City Star*, September 19, 1962; *Sporting News*, September 29, 1962, p. 16.

8. *Sporting News*, October 6, 1962, p. 16.

9. Ibid., October 13, 1962, p. 18.

10. Ibid., November 24, 1962, p. 28.

11. Charles O. Finley to Ford C. Frick, November 7, 1963, Major League Baseball Hall of Fame Archives, Cooperstown, NY.

12. *Kansas City Times*, September 19, 1962; *Kansas City Star*, September 19, 1962; *Sporting News*, September 29, 1962, p. 16; October 6, 1962, p. 16; and October 13, 1962, p. 18.

13. *Sporting News*, October 6, 1962, p. 16; December 22, 1962, p. 26.

14. Ibid., September 29, 1962, p. 16; October 6, 1962, p. 16.

15. Ibid., October 20, 1962, p. 25; November 17, 1962, p. 20; interview with Charles Cottonaro, March 4, 2005.

16. Kevin J. Delaney and Rick Eckstein, *Public Dollars, Private Stadiums: The Battle Over Building Sports Stadiums* (New Brunswick, NJ: Rutgers University Press, 2003); Gerald W. Scully, *The Market Structure of Sports* (Chicago: University of Chicago Press, 1995).

17. *Sporting News*, June 2, 1962, pp. 1, 4.

18. *Sporting News*, June 22, 1963, p. 19.

19. Interview with Hank Bauer, February 7, 2006.

20. Interview with Lew Krausse, April 25, 2005.

21. *Sporting News*, January 18, 1964, p. 2; *Kansas City Star*, April 10, 1963.

22. Bisher, *Miracle in Atlanta*, pp. 13–14.

23. *Sporting News*, January 8, 1964, p. 2.

24. Fox, *Sports Guys*, p. 70; Joe McGuff, *Why Me? Why Not Joe McGuff?* (Prairie Village, KS: Joseph McGuff, 1992), p. 73.

25. Interview with Hank Peters, November 5, 2008.

26. *Sporting News*, January 18, 1964, pp. 2, 4; February 1, 1964, pp. 1–2; February 29, 1964, p. 14.

27. Ibid., January 18, 1964, p. 2.

28. Ibid., August 3, 1963, pp. 1–2; August 31, 1963, p. 2; January 4, 1964, p. 18; January 18, 1964, p. 4; February 1, 1964, pp. 1–2; February 15, 1964, pp. 1, 4; February 29, 1964, p. 14.

29. Ibid., February 8, 1964, p. 8.

30. Interview with Hank Peters, November 5, 2008.

31. Jack Etkins, *Innings Ago: Recollections by Kansas City Ballplayers of Their Days in the Game* (Kansas City, MO: Normandy Square Publications, 1986), pp. 126–27; *Kansas City Times*, December 25, 1963.

32. *Sporting News*, January 11, 1964, p. 8.

33. Interview with Joe Rudi, May 7, 2004.

34. *Sporting News*, March 7, 1964, p. 8; *Chicago Daily News*, January 6, 1964.

35. *New York Times*, January 7, 1964.

36. *Washington Post*, January 19, 1964.

37. *Sporting News*, March 7, 1964, p. 8; November 14, 1964, p. 22.

38. Ibid., January 18, 1964, p. 4.

39. Interview with Ron Mihelic, November 8, 2008.

40. Interview with Jerry Lumpe, October 15, 2008.

41. Steve Treder, "The Pennant Porch Pie-in-the-Face," *Hardball Times*, February 28, 2006, available online at http://www.hardballtimes.com/main/article/the-pennant-porch-pie-in-the-face (accessed April 16, 2009).

42. *Sporting News*, February 15, 1964, p. 4; interview with Wayne Causey, November 1, 2008; *Washington Post*, March 27, 1964.

43. Interview with Rick Knoll, December 15, 2008.

44. "Beatles Video Unearthed after 44 Years," Telegraph.co.uk, November 11, 2008, available online at http://www.telegraph.co.uk/news/3273941/Beatles-video-unearthed-after-44-years.html (accessed April 18, 2009).

45. "Photos of Unique Beatles Rarities," available online at http://www.rarebeatles.com/photopg7/kansa64.htm (accessed April 18, 2009).

46. "Kansas City Municipal Stadium," Ballpark Tour, available online at http://www.ballparktour.com/Former_Kansas_City.html (accessed April 18, 2009).

47. Michelson, *Charlie O.*, p. 97.

48. *Kansas City Star*, April 6, 1965.

49. Interview with Hank Peters, November 5, 2008.

50. Whitey Herzog, *You're Missing a Great Game* (New York: Berkley Books, 2000), pp. 49–50.

51. Tom Clark, *Champagne and Baloney: The Rise and Fall of Finley's A's* (New York: Harper & Row, 1976), p. 22.

52. Jim Hunter and Armen Keteyian, *Catfish: My Life in Baseball* (New York: McGraw-Hill, 1988), pp. 28–29.

53. Bill Libby, *Charlie O. and the Angry A's: The Low and Inside Story of Charlie

O. Finley and Baseball's Most Colorful Team (Garden City, NY: Doubleday & Co., 1975), pp. 181–82.

54. Hunter and Keteyian, *Catfish*, p. 3.

55. Libby, *Charlie O. and the Angry A's*, pp. 181–82.

56. Interview with Martin Finley, October 14, 2008.

57. Interview with David Finley, November 18–19, 2008.

58. Michelson, *Charlie O.*, pp. 152–53.

59. Ibid.

60. Libby, *Charlie O. and the Angry A's*, pp. 189.

61. Interview with Hon. John Paul Stevens, September 23, 2005.

62. Interview with Neil Papiano, September 22, 2008.

63. Interview with Bobby Winkles, March 17, 2005.

64. Peterson, *The Kansas City Athletics*, p. 310.

65. Interview with Bobby Winkles, March 17, 2005.

66. Bruce Markusen, *Baseball's Last Dynasty: Charlie Finley's Oakland A's* (Indianapolis, IN: Masters Press, 1998), p. 9.

67. Peterson, *Kansas City Athletics*, p. 312.

68. Interview with Vida Blue, February 27, 2005.

69. Alvin Dark and John Underwood, *When in Doubt, Fire the Manager: My Life and Times in Baseball* (New York: E. P. Dutton, 1980), pp. 111–12.

70. Peterson, *Kansas City Athletics*, p. 210.

71. Michelson, *Charlie O.*, p. 99; Hunter and Keteyian, *Catfish*, p. 256; interview with Lew Krausse, April 25, 2005.

72. Interview with Jim Schaaf, October 6, 2008.

73. Ibid.

74. Ibid.

75. Ibid.

76. Peterson, *Kansas City Athletics*, p. 210.

77. Libby, *Charlie O. and the Angry A's*, pp. 54–55.

78. Interview with Jim Schaaf, October 4, 2008.

79. Ibid.

80. Ibid.

81. Libby, *Charlie O. and the Angry A's*, pp. 75–76.

82. Ken Harrelson and Al Hirshberg, *Hawk*, (New York: Viking, 1969), p. 144.

83. Peterson, *Kansas City Athletics*, p. 221.

84. Harrelson and Hirshberg, *Hawk,* pp. 145–146.

85. Interview with Jim Schaaf, October 4, 2008.

86. Libby, *Charlie O. and the Angry A's,* p. 76.

87. Interview with Jim Schaaf, October 4, 2008.

Chapter 4: Endgame in Kansas City

1. *Sporting News,* November 6, 1965, p. 22.

2. Interview with Hank Peters, November 5, 2008.

3. "Sport: Alvin Dark: Dugout Disciple," *Time,* July 3, 1974, available online at http://www.time.com/time/magazine/article/0,9171,911357,00.html, accessed February 11, 2010.

4. John E. Peterson, *The Kansas City Athletics: A Baseball History, 1954–1967* (Jefferson, NC: McFarland & Co., 2003), p. 225.

5. Alvin Dark and John Underwood, *When in Doubt, Fire the Manager: My Life and Times in Baseball* (New York: E. P. Dutton, 1980), pp. 111, 124; Peterson, *Kansas City Athletics,* p. 227.

6. Interview with Jim Schaaf, October 6, 2008.

7. Peterson, *Kansas City Athletics,* p. 227.

8. Ibid., p. 250.

9. Ibid., p. 251.

10. Ibid.

11. Dark and Underwood, *When in Doubt, Fire the Manager,* p. 126.

12. *Sporting News,* July 15, 1967, p. 15.

13. *Sporting News,* July 29, 1967, p. 15.

14. Lee Lowenfish, "A Tale of Many Cities: The Westward Expansion of Major League Baseball in the 1950s," *Journal of the West* 17 (July 1978): 71–82; Neil J. Sullivan, *The Diamond Revolution: The Prospects for Baseball After the Collapse of Its Ruling Class* (New York: St. Martin's Press, 1992), pp. 48–73; Neil J. Sullivan, *The Dodgers Move West* (New York: Oxford University Press, 1987); "Franchise Shift," in Jonathan Fraser Light, *The Cultural Encyclopedia of Baseball* (Jefferson, NC: McFarland & Co., 1997), pp. 280–82; James Edward Miller, *The Baseball Business: Pursuing Pennants and Profits in Baltimore* (Chapel Hill: University of North Carolina Press, 1990), pp. 14–15; James Quirk, "An Economic Analysis of Team Movements in Professional Sports," *Law and Contemporary Problems* 38 (Winter–Spring 1973): 42–66.

15. Leonard Koppett, *Koppett's Concise History of Major League Baseball* (Philadelphia: Temple University Press, 1998), p. 256.

16. *Sporting News*, July 22, 1967, p. 9; *Sporting News*, July 29, 1967, p. 15.

17. *Kansas City Star*, July 21, 1967.

18. *Kansas City Star*, August 1, 1967; Peterson, *Kansas City Athletics*, p. 255.

19. *Kansas City Star*, August 8, 1967; *Chicago American*, October 18, 1967.

20. Dark and Underwood, *When in Doubt, Fire the Manager*, pp. 127–28; *Sporting News*, September 2, 1967, p. 18.

21. Interview with Lew Krausse, April 25, 2005; *Sporting News*, September 2, 1967, p. 18.

22. Dark and Underwood, *When in Doubt, Fire the Manager*, pp. 128–29.

23. Herb Michelson, *Charlie O.: Charles Oscar Finley vs. the Baseball Establishment* (Indianapolis, IN: Bobbs-Merrill, 1975), p. 106; interview with Lew Krausse, April 25, 2005.

24. Interview with Monte Moore, June 16, 2009.

25. Bill Libby, *Charlie O. and the Angry A's* (Garden City, NY: Doubleday and Company, 1975), pp. 80–81.

26. Dark and Underwood, *When in Doubt, Fire the Manager*, pp. 129–30.

27. Ibid., p. 130.

28. Peterson, *Kansas City Athletics*, p. 243.

29. *Sporting News*, September 2, 1967, pp. 16, 18.

30. Ken Harrelson and Al Hirshberg, *Hawk* (New York: Viking, 1969), pp. 186–87.

31. Ibid., p. 189.

32. Ibid., pp. 190–93.

33. Peterson, *Kansas City Athletics*, pp. 245–46.

34. Interview with Lew Krausse, April 25, 2005.

35. *Sporting News*, September 30, 1967, p. 8.

36. Ibid., October 14, 1967, p. 13.

37. *Chicago Tribune*, October 12, 1967.

38. *Chicago Sun Times*, October 18, 1967.

39. Michelson, *Charlie O.* p. 137.

40. *Sporting News*, November 4, 1967.

41. *Kansas City Star*, October 19, 1967.

42. Michelson, *Charlie O.*, p. 137; *Kansas City Star*, October 19, 1967; *Chicago Sun-Times*, October 19, 1967.

43. *Sporting News*, November 4, 1967, p. 33.

44. Tom Clark, *Champagne and Baloney: A History of Finley's A's* (New York: Harper & Row, 1976), p. 39.

45. *Sporting News*, November 4, 1967, p. 33.

46. Libby, *Charlie O. and the Angry A's*, pp. 65–66.

47. Peterson, *Kansas City Athletics*, p. 270.

48. Michelson, *Charlie O.*, p. 138.

Chapter 5: Oakland A's Rising

1. *Sporting News*, November 1, 1967, p. 29.

2. Ibid., November 11, 1967, p. 29

3. Ibid.

4. Ibid.

5. Herbert Michelson, *Charlie O.: Charles Oscar Finley vs. the Baseball Establishment* (Indianapolis, IN: Bobbs-Merrill, 1975), p. 140.

6. Ibid., pp. 141–42.

7. *Sporting News*, January 13, 1968, p. 34.

8. Ibid., April 13, 1968, p. 39.

9. Interview with Chuck Dobson, November 8, 2008.

10. Interview with Ron Bergman, April 22, 2008.

11. Quoted in Michelson, *Charlie O.*, pp. 165–66.

12. Interview with Hank Bauer, February 7, 2006.

13. Reggie Jackson with Mike Lupica, *Reggie: The Autobiography of Reggie Jackson* (New York: Ballantine Books, 1984), p. 52.

14. Interview with Chuck Dobson, November 8, 2008.

15. Ibid.

16. Bill Libby, *Charlie O. and the Angry A's: The Low and Inside Story of Charlie O. Finley and Baseball's Most Colorful Team* (Garden City, NY: Doubleday & Co., 1975), p. 108.

17. Ibid.

18. Interview with Chuck Dobson, November 8, 2008.

19. Interview with Hank Bauer, February 7, 2006.

20. Interview with Ron Bergman, April 22, 2008.

21. Libby, *Charlie O. and the Angry A's*, p. 109.

22. Interview with Sal Bando, June 13, 2005.

23. Libby, *Charlie O. and the Angry A's*, p. 110.

24. Jackson and Lupica, *Reggie*, p. 74.

25. Michelson, *Charlie O.*, p. 168.

26. Ibid.

27. Ibid.

28. Libby, *Charlie O. and the Angry A's*, p. 114.

29. Bowie Kuhn, *Hardball: The Education of a Baseball Commissioner* (Lincoln: University of Nebraska Press, 1997 ed.), p. 127.

30. Ibid.

31. Ibid., p. 128.

32. Ibid., p. 126.

33. Bill Libby, *Catfish: The Three Million Dollar Pitcher* (New York: Coward, McCann & Geoghegan, 1976), p. 76.

34. Ibid.

35. Ibid.

36. Ibid., p. 77.

37. Ibid., p. 78.

38. *Sporting News*, September 26, 1970, p. 19.

39. Ibid.

40. Libby, *Charlie O. and the Angry A's*, pp. 118–19.

41. *Sporting News*, September 26, 1970, p. 19.

42. Michelson, *Charlie O.*, pp. 172–73.

43. *Sporting News*, October 17, 1970, p. 25.

Chapter 6: On Top of the World

1. *Sporting News*, June 12, 1971, p. 5.

2. Ibid., February 13, 1971, p. 31.

3. Dick Williams and Bill Plaschke, *No More Mr. Nice Guy: A Life of Hardball* (New York: Harcourt Brace Jovanovich, 1990), pp. 119–20.

4. Interview with Dick Williams, January 21, 2008.

5. Interview with Darold Knowles, May 1, 2008.

6. Williams and Plaschke, *No More Mr. Nice Guy*, pp. 119–20.

7. *Sporting News*, March 20, 1971, p. 40.

8. Ibid., March 27, 1971, p. 28.

9. Ibid., June 8, 1999, p. 27.

10. Interview with Dick Williams, January 21, 2008.

11. Ibid.

12. Williams and Plaschke, *No More Mr. Nice Guy*, p. 126.

13. Ibid., p. 129.

14. Ibid., p. 131.

15. Interview with Vida Blue, February 27, 2006.

16. *Sporting News*, October 2, 1971, p. 8.

17. Interview with Vida Blue, February 27, 2006.

18. Interview with Dick Green, April 14, 2008.

19. Paul Dickson, *Baseball's Greatest Quotations: An Illustrated Treasury of Baseball Quotations and Historical Lore* (New York: Collins, 2008, rev. ed.), p. 63, from Richard Deming, *Vida* (New York: Lancer, 1972).

20. Interview with Vida Blue, February 27, 2006.

21. Interview with Ron Bergman, April 22, 2008.

22. Interview with Glenn Schwarz, May 7, 2008.

23. Interview with Jerry Lumpe, October 15, 2008.

24. Bruce Markusen, *Baseball's Last Dynasty: Charlie Finley's Oakland A's* (Indianapolis, IN: Masters Press, 1998), p. 56; *Sporting News*, September 4, 1971, p. 18; Conversation No. 566-1, August 17, 1971, Nixon Presidential Materials, available online at http://www.nixontapeaudio.org/logs/566.rtf (accessed May 25, 2009).

25. Bill Libby, *Charlie O. and the Angry A's: The Low and Inside Story of Charlie O. Finley and Baseball's Most Colorful Team* (Garden City, NY: Doubleday & Co., 1975), p. 141.

26. Interview with Vida Blue, February 27, 2006.

27. Interview with Dick Williams, January 21, 2008.

28. Interview with Darold Knowles, May 1, 2008.

29. Interview with Jim Schaaf, August 17, 2008.

30. Interview with David Finley, November 18–19, 2008.

31. Interview with Ron Bergman, April 22, 2008.

32. Williams and Plaschke, *No More Mr. Nice Guy*, p. 128; interviews with Ron Mihelic, November 8, 2008; Sal Bando, June 13, 2005; Dick Williams, January 21, 2008; Wayne Causey, October 1, 2008; Dick Green, April 14, 2008.

33. *Sport*, July 1974, p. 68, as quoted in Markuson, *Baseball's Last Dynasty*, pp. 49–50.

34. Williams and Plaschke, *No More Mr. Nice Guy*, p. 131.

35. *Oakland Tribune*, October 16, 1971.

36. Interview with Glenn Schwarz, May 7, 2008.

37. Williams and Plaschke, *No More Mr. Nice Guy*, p. 131.

38. Ibid., pp. 132–33; Markuson, *Baseball's Last Dynasty*, pp. 70–72.

39. *Sporting News*, February 26, 1972, p. 32.

40. Quoted in John Helyar, *Lords of the Realm: The Real History of Baseball* (New York: Villard Books, 1994), p. 136.

41. Quoted in Danielle Gagnon Torrez, with Ken Lizotte, *High Inside: Memoirs of a Baseball Wife* (New York: Putnam, 1983).

42. *Sporting News*, April 1, 1979, p. 29.

43. Ibid., May 20, 1972, p. 21.

44. Bowie Kuhn, *Hardball: The Education of a Baseball Commissioner* (Lincoln: University of Nebraska Press, 1997 ed.), pp. 131–33.

45. Ibid., May 13, 1972, p. 8; May 20, 1972, p. 21.

46. Kuhn, *Hardball*, p. 133.

47. *Sporting News*, March 11, 1972, p. 46.

48. Interview with Sal Bando, June 13, 2005.

49. Interviews with Ron Mihelic, November 8, 2008; Martin Finley, October 14, 2008; Dick Green, April 14, 2008.

50. Arthur Daley, "A Last Look," *New York Times*, October 23, 1972.

51. *Sporting News*, April 15, 1972, pp. 3, 8.

52. Robert F. Burk, *Much More Than a Game: Players, Owners, and American Baseball Since 1921* (Chapel Hill: University of North Carolina Press, 2001), pp. 174–77.

53. *Sporting News*, April 29, 1972, p. 21.

54. Markusen, *Baseball's Last Dynasty*, pp. 89–91.

55. Daniel E. Ginsburg, *The Fix Is In: A History of Baseball Gambling and Game Fixing Scandals* (Jefferson, NC: McFarland and Co., 1995), pp. 228–36; Kuhn, *Hardball*, pp. 67–73.

56. Williams and Plaschke, *No More Mr. Nice Guy*, pp. 133–34.

57. Harold Peterson, "The Week, AL West," *Sports Illustrated*, May 29, 1972, p. 74.

58. *Sporting News*, July 22, 1972, p. 8.

59. Quoted in Markusen, *Baseball's Last Dynasty*, pp. 107–108.

60. Interview with Dick Green, April 14, 2008.

61. *Sporting News*, September 2, 1972, p. 9.

62. *Total Baseball* (New York: Viking, 2006), pp. 48–49, 121–22, 128, 350–51, 606, 672, 766, 787, 824, 888–89, 1051, 1211, 1329, 1429–30, 1497, 1505.

63. Michael Scholl, "June 18, 1972: Baseball's First Mustache Day," available online at http://web.baseballhalloffame.org/news/article.jsp?ymd=20080618&content_id=7792&vkey=hof_news (accessed May 23, 2009).

64. *Sporting News*, September 23, 1972, p. 7.

65. Interview with Ron Bergman, April 22, 2008.

66. Ibid., April 22, 2008.

67. *Sporting News*, November 4, 1972, p. 6.

68. Ibid., October 14, 1972, p. 44; *New York Times,* July 1, 2009, and July 9, 1972.

69. Bill Slocum, "Champagne Is Funny," review of Ron Bergman, *Mustache Gang: The Swaggering Saga of Oakland's A's* (New York: Dell Publishing, 1973), January 11, 2006, available online at http://www.amazon.com/Mustache-Gang-swaggering-saga-Oaklands/dp/B00070OEEQ (accessed May 24, 2009).

70. *Washington Post*, October 7, 1972.

71. Quoted in Markusen, *Baseball's Last Dynasty*, p. 131.

72. *New York Times*, October 8, 1972.

73. Libby, *Charlie O. and the Angry A's*, pp. 210–11.

74. Interview with David Finley, November 18–19, 2008.

75. Bruce Markusen, "Card Corner—Campy," December 16, 2008, available online at http://www.bronxbanterblog.com/2008/12/16/card-corner-campy (accessed May 25, 2009).

76. *San Francisco Chronicle*, October 9, 2006.

77. *Sporting News*, October 28, 1972, p. 10; Bergman, *Mustache Gang*, pp. 221–22.

78. *New York Daily News*, October 10, 1972.

79. Libby, *Charlie O. and the Angry A's*, pp. 212–13.

80. Ibid., p. 213.

81. Kuhn, *Hardball*, p. 139.

82. Williams and Plaschke, *No More Mr. Nice Guy*, pp. 143–44; *Washington Post*, October 13, 1972.

83. *New York Times*, October 9, 1972, October 15, 1972, October 16, 1972.

84. Williams and Plaschke, *No More Mr. Nice Guy*, p. 145.

85. *New York Times*, October 13, 1972, October 15, 1972, October 19, 1972, October 20, 1972.

86. *Chicago Tribune*, October 19, 1972; *Sporting News*, October 28, 1972, p. 3.

87. *Sporting News*, November 4, 1972, p. 13.

88. Ibid., p. 25.

89. Ibid., p. 3.

90. *New York Times*, October 19, 1972.

91. *Washington Post*, October 18, 1972.

92. Ibid.; *New York Times*, November 2, 1972; *Chicago Tribune*, November 2, 1972; interview with Rollie Fingers, August 12, 2005.

93. *Chicago Daily News*, October 15, 1972.

94. *Sporting News*, November 11, 1972, p. 37.

Chapter 7: Repeat, Three-peat

1. *Los Angeles Herald-Examiner*, February 27, 1975, as quoted in Paul Dickson, *The Unwritten Rules of Baseball: The Etiquette, Conventional Wisdom, and Axiomatic Codes of Our National Pastime* (New York: Collins, 2009), p. 209.

2. *Sporting News*, February 10, 1973, p. 37; April 14, 1973, p. 31; interview with Joe Rudi, May 7, 2004.

3. Baseball Almanac, available online at http://www.baseball-almanac.com/index.shtml (accessed June 9, 2009).

4. *Sporting News*, April 14, 1973, p. 31.

5. Interview with David Finley, November 18–19, 2008; Bruce Markusen, *Baseball's Last Dynasty: Charlie Finley's Oakland A's* (Indianapolis, IN: Masters Press, 1998), pp. 201–202.

6. *Los Angeles Times*, October 4, 1973.

7. *Sporting News*, January 6, 1973, p. 30.

8. Wells Twombly, "Charlie O., the Missouri Mule," *New York Times Magazine*, July 15, 1973, p. 32.

9. *Sporting News*, January 6, 1973, p. 29.

10. Ibid., January 6, 1973, p. 30.

11. Interview with Mike Andrews, May 12, 2008; *Sporting News*, March 24, 1973, p. 33.

12. Ibid., June 9, 1973, p. 14.

13. Interview with Sal Bando, June 13, 2005.

14. Interview with Ron Bergman, April 22, 2008.

15. Interview with John Claiborne, October 30, 2008.

16. "Charlie Finley: Baseball's Barnum," *Time*, August 18, 1975, available online

at http://www.time.com/time/magazine/article/0,9171,917734-7,00.html (accessed June 12, 2009).

17. Twombly, "Charlie O.," p. 32.

18. Oakland A's press release, March 15, 1973, Major League Baseball Hall of Fame Archives, Cooperstown, NY; *New York Times,* January 26, 1973; December 29, 1996; interview with Sal Bando, June 13, 2005.

19. *Sporting News,* March 24, 1974, p. 33.

20. Ibid., August 25, 1973, pp. 3, 44.

21. Ibid., May 26, 1973, p. 20.

22. Ibid., July 21, 1973, p. 13.

23. Ibid., August 25, 1975, p. 3.

24. *New York Daily News,* October 15, 1972.

25. Markusen, *The Last Dynasty,* pp. 208–209.

26. Twombly, "Charlie O.," p. 36.

27. *Sporting News,* September 15, 1973, p. 3; Oakland A's press release, August 17, 1973, National Baseball Hall of Fame Archives, Cooperstown, NY; *Sporting News,* September 8, 1973, p. 30; August 25, 1973, p. 24.

28. *Sporting News,* October 13, 1973, p. 7.

29. Interview with Dick Williams, January 21, 2008.

30. Interview with Glenn Schwarz, May 7, 2008.

31. *Sporting News,* November 3, 1973, p. 12.

32. Ibid., pp. 5, 7, 11.

33. David S. Neft and Richard M. Cohen, *The World Series* (New York: St. Martin's Press, 1990), pp. 345–50; Joseph Reichler, ed., *The Baseball Encyclopedia* (New York: Macmillan, 1982, fifth ed.), p. 2191.

34. *New York Times,* October 22, 1973.

35. *Sporting News,* October 27, 1973, p. 28.

36. Ibid., November 24, 1973, p. 33.

37. *New York Times,* October 22, 1973.

38. *Sporting News,* November 3, 1973, p. 14.

39. Interview with Louis Hoynes, November 24, 2008.

40. *Sporting News,* November 3, 1973, p. 3.

41. Ibid., p. 14.

42. Ibid., p. 21.

43. Ibid., p. 5.

44. Interview with Mike Andrews, May 12, 2008.

45. *Los Angeles Times*, October 11, 1974.

46. *Chicago Tribune*, December 1, 1973; *New York Times*, November 17, 1973; *New York Daily News*, November 17, 1973.

47. *Sporting News*, December 28, 1972, p. 38; December 29, 1973, p. 27.

48. Ibid., December 1, 1973, p. 8; December 8, 1973, pp. 51–52.

49. Herbert Michelson, *Charlie O.: Charles Oscar Finley vs. the Baseball Establishment* (Indianapolis, IN: Bobbs-Merrill, 1975), p. 272.

50. Interview with Louis L. Hoynes, November 24, 2008.

51. John Helyar, *Lords of the Realm: The Real History of Baseball* (New York: Villard Books, 1994), pp. 152–53.

52. Interview with Martin Finley, October 14, 2008.

53. Interview with John Claiborne, October 30, 2008.

54. Interview with Marvin Miller, August 4, 2004.

55. *Chicago Tribune*, May 26, 1974.

56. Interview with Joe Rudi, May 7, 2004.

57. Michelson, *Charlie O.*, pp. 277–78.

58. Ibid., p. 271.

59. Interview with Marvin Miller, August 4, 2004.

60. Interview with Vida Blue, February 27, 2006.

61. Interview with John Claiborne, October 30, 2008.

62. Interview with Sal Bando, June 13, 2005.

63. Interview with David Finley, November 18–19, 2008.

64. Interview with Tom Corwin, February 18, 2009.

65. Interview with Chuck Dobson, November 8, 2008.

66. Interview with Ron Mihelic, November 8, 2008.

67. Interview with Fern Shultz, October 13, 2008.

68. Interview with David Finley, November 18–19, 2008.

69. Interview with Mike Storen, November 17, 2008.

70. In Re the Marriage of Shirley M. Finley, Petitioner, and Charles O. Finley, Respondent, County of Porter Superior Court, 1974 term, Cause No. 74 PSC 724, Provisional Order, June 3, 1974, Porter County Courthouse, Valparaiso, IN; *Arena* (Chicago, IL), March 27, 1974, p. 10; *Wisconsin State Journal*, March 27, 2007; *Morning Herald–Evening Standard* (Uniontown, PA), March 20, 1974; *Oakland Tribune*, March 27, 1974; *Salt Lake Tribune*, March 27, 1974.

71. In Re the Marriage of Shirley M. Finley, Petitioner, and Charles O. Finley, Respondent, County of Porter Superior Court, 1974 term, Cause No. 74 PSC 724,

Motion to Stay Provisional Orders Pending Appeal, July 18, 1974; In Re the Marriage of Shirley M. Finley, Petitioner, and Charles O. Finley, Respondent, County of Porter Superior Court, 1974 term, Cause No. 74 PSC 724, Petitioner's Request for Production of Documents, July 29, 1974, both in Porter County Courthouse, Valparaiso, IN; *Times-Recorder* (Valparaiso, IN), May 19, 1974; *Independent Press-Telegram* (Long Beach, CA), May 18, 1974.

72. *Times-Recorder*, June 4, 1974; July 19, 1974; *Oakland Tribune*, June 5, 1974.

73. Interview with Leon R. Kaminski, December 9, 2008.

74. *Sporting News*, November 10, 1973, p. 10; *New York Times*, January 14, 1973; *Louisville Courier*, June 21, 1974.

75. *Chicago Tribune*, February 9, 1974.

76. *Los Angeles Times*, June 21, 1974; November 10, 1974, p. 24.

77. *San Francisco Examiner*, January 9, 1974.

78. Interview with Glenn Schwarz, May 7, 2008.

79. Interview with Mike Andrews, May 12, 2008.

80. Interview with Bill Myers, July 28, 2005.

81. *Sporting News*, April 6, 1974, p. 18.

82. Quoted in Markusen, *Baseball's Last Dynasty*, p. 287.

83. Jon Miller, *Confessions of a Baseball Purist* (New York: Simon & Schuster, 1990), p. 140.

84. Interview with Darold Knowles, May 1, 2008; interview with Sal Bando, June 13, 2005.

85. *New York Times*, June 4, 1974; "Pyrotechnics by Finley," *Time*, June 3, 1974, p. 64; *Oakland Daily News*, October 17, 1974.

Chapter 8: Catfish Swims Away

1. Bill Libby, *Catfish: The Three Million Dollar Pitcher* (New York: Coward, McCann & Geoghegan, 1976), p. 78.

2. *The Sporting News 1975 Official Baseball Guide* (St. Louis: Sporting News, 1975), p. 290.

3. Interview with Louis Hoynes Jr., November 24, 2008.

4. *Sporting News 1975 Baseball Guide*, pp. 286–87.

5. Ibid., p. 286.

6. Ibid.

7. Ibid., p. 288.

8. AP story, November 26, 1974.

9. *Sporting News 1975 Baseball Guide*, p. 289.

10. Interview with Louis Hoynes Jr., November 24, 2008.

11. Ibid.

12. Interview with Marvin Miller, August 4, 2004.

13. *Sporting News 1975 Baseball Guide*, p. 292.

14. Interview with Louis Hoynes Jr., November 24, 2008.

15. Interview with Marvin Miller, August 4, 2004.

16. *Sporting News 1975 Baseball Guide*, p. 294.

17. *Sporting News*, January 4, 1975, p. 3.

Chapter 9: Life After Catfish

1. Interview with John Claiborne, October 30, 2008.

2. Bruce Markusen, *Baseball's Last Dynasty: Charlie Finley's Oakland A's* (Indianapolis, IN: Masters Press, 1998), p. 351.

3. AP story, February 16, 1975.

4. *Sporting News*, March 15, 1975, p. 37.

5. Interview with Sal Bando, June 13, 2005.

6. Herbert Michelson, *Charlie O.: Charles Oscar Finley vs. the Baseball Establishment* (Indianapolis, IN: Bobbs-Merrill, 1975), p. 279.

7. *Sporting News*, January 25, 1975, p. 45.

8. Ibid., April 26, 1975, p. 20.

9. Ibid., May 31, 1975, p. 37.

10. Ibid., February 8, 1975, p. 33.

11. Ibid., April 12, 1975, p. 12.

12. Ibid.

13. Ibid., January 11, 1975, p. 31; interview with Dick Green, April 14, 2008.

14. *Sporting News*, April 19, 1975, p. 5.

15. Ibid., July 7, 1975, p. 11.

16. Bowie Kuhn, *Hardball: The Education of a Baseball Commissioner* (New York: Times Books, 1987), p. 146.

17. Ibid., p. 150.

18. *Sporting News*, August 2, 1975, p. 7.

19. Ibid.

20. Kuhn, *Hardball*, pp. 152–53.

21. *Sporting News*, August 2, 1975, p. 26.

22. *Time*, August 18, 1975, p. 49.

23. Ibid., pp. 42, 50.

24. *Vidette-Messenger* (Valparaiso, IN), June 12, 1974.

25. Ibid., June 4, 1974; July 19, 1974; *Oakland Tribune*, June 5, 1974.

26. Interview with Leon R. Kaminski, December 9, 2008.

27. Ibid.; *Vidette-Messenger*, February 28, 1976.

28. *Oakland Tribune*, June 10, 1976; *Waterloo* (IA) *Courier*, October 4, 1977.

29. In Re the Marriage of Shirley M. Finley, Petitioner, and Charles O. Finley, Respondent, County of Porter Superior Court, 1974 term, Cause No. 74 PSC 724, Order, June 7, 1974; In Re the Marriage of Shirley M. Finley, Petitioner, and Charles O. Finley, Respondent, County of Porter Superior Court, 1974 term, Cause No. 74 PSC 724, Motion to Reconsider Pursuant to Trial Rule 52.5, July 7, 1974, both in Porter County Courthouse, Valparaiso, IN; *Vidette-Messenger*, August 28, 1975; *Billings* (MT) *Gazette*, June 10, 1976.

30. *Modesto* (CA) *Bee*, February 16, 1976; *Vidette-Messenger*, February 18, 1976.

31. Interview with Leon R. Kaminski, December 9, 2008.

32. Interview with David Finley, November 18–19, 2008.

33. *Sporting News*, August 23, 1975, p. 10.

34. Ibid., May 24, 1975, pp. 13, 16.

35. Ibid., October 11, 1975, p. 17.

36. Ibid., p. 27.

37. Roger Angell, *Five Seasons: A Baseball Companion* (Lincoln: University of Nebraska Press, 2004 ed.), p. 292.

38. Interview with Joe Rudi, May 7, 2004.

39. *Sporting News*, October 25, 1975, p. 17.

40. *Time*, August 18, 1975, p. 50.

41. Alvin Dark and John Underwood, *When in Doubt, Fire the Manager: My Life and Times in Baseball* (New York: E. P. Dutton, 1980), pp. 11–12.

42. UPI story, October 17, 1975.

43. *Sporting News*, November 1, 1975, p. 21.

Chapter 10: Finley's Fire Sale

1. *Sporting News*, January 3, 1976, p. 38.

2. John Helyar, *Lords of the Realm: The Real History of Baseball* (New York: Villard Books, 1994), p. 152.

3. Ibid., pp. 173–74; Charles P. Korr, *The End of Baseball as We Knew It: The Players Union, 1960–81* (Urbana: University of Illinois Press, 2002), p. 183.

4. Interview with Marvin Miller, August 4, 2004.

5. Helyar, *Lords of the Realm*, p. 202.

6. *Sporting News*, February 21, 1976, p. 36

7. Ibid., April 3, 1976, p. 34.

8. Ibid., April 17, 1976, p. 16.

9. Ibid., p. 16.

10. Ibid., May 1, 1976, p. 30.

11. Ibid., June 12, 1976, pp. 21, 26.

12. Helyar, *Lords of the Realm*, p. 184.

13. Don Baylor, *Nothing But the Truth: A Baseball Life* (New York: St. Martin's Press, 1989), p. 92.

14. Helyar, *Lords of the Realm*, p. 183.

15. Ibid., p. 185.

16. Ibid., pp. 185–86.

17. Ibid., p. 187.

18. *Chicago Tribune*, June 16, 1976.

19. Helyar, *Lords of the Realm*, p. 188.

20. Bowie Kuhn, *Hardball: The Education of a Baseball Commissioner* (Lincoln: University of Nebraska Press, 1997 ed.), p. 175.

21. Helyar, *Lords of the Realm*, p. 188; Kuhn, *Hardball*, p. 176.

22. Kuhn, *Hardball*, pp. 176–77; Helyar, *Lords of the Realm*, p. 192.

23. Helyar, *Lords of the Realm*, p. 193; Kuhn, *Hardball*, p. 177.

24. Helyar, *Lords of the Realm*, pp. 193–94; Kuhn, *Hardball*, p. 177.

25. *Sports Illustrated*, June 28, 1976, p. 24.

26. Ibid.; interview with Joe Rudi, May 7, 2004.

27. Kuhn, *Hardball*, p. 178.

28. *Chicago Tribune*, June 19, 1976; Kuhn, *Hardball*, p. 179; *Sports Illustrated*, June 28, 1976, pp. 24–25.

29. Bruce Markusen, *25 Years Ago: The Anniversary of Finley's Fire Sales*, BaseballPrimer.com, 2001, pp. 2–3; interview with Joe Rudi, May 7, 2004.

30. Markusen, *25 Years Ago*, p. 3; *Sporting News*, July 10, 1976, p. 7.

31. Markusen, *25 Years Ago*, p. 3.

32. Interview with Joe Rudi, May 7, 2004.

33. Kuhn, *Hardball*, p. 132.

Chapter 11: Finley vs. Kuhn

1. *Sporting News*, December 25, 1976, p. 34.

2. Interview with Charles Cottonaro, March 4, 2005.

3. *Sporting News*, January 1, 1977, p. 34.

4. Interview with Dennis Page, September 22, 2008.

5. *Chicago Tribune*, December 21, 1976, p. C1.

6. *Sporting News*, January 1, 1977, p. 34.

7. Ibid., January 8, 1977, p. 30.

8. Ibid.

9. Ibid.

10. Interview with Dennis Page, September 22, 2008.

11. *Chicago Tribune*, December 23, 1976, p. B1.

12. Ibid.

13. Ibid.

14. Interview with Neil Papiano, September 22, 2008.

15. *Chicago Tribune*, December 31, 1976, p. B4.

16. Ibid., January 8, 1977, p. 3.

17. Ibid., January 11, 1977, p. C4.

18. Ibid.

19. *Sporting News*, January 29, 1977, p. 30.

20. *Chicago Tribune*, January 13, 1977, p. C1.

21. Ibid., January 14, 1977, p. C1

22. *Sporting News Official 1978 Baseball Guide*, p. 333.

23. Ibid., p. 334.

24. *Chicago Tribune*, March 18, 1977, p. C1.

25. *Sporting News Official 1978 Baseball Guide*, p. 333.

26. *Sporting News*, November 20, 1976, p. 47.

27. *Chicago Tribune*, February 20, 1977, p. B1.

28. Ibid., March 4, 1977, p. C1.

29. *Sporting News Official 1978 Baseball Guide*, p. 335.

30. *Chicago Tribune*, March 4, 1977, p. C1.

31. *Sporting News*, February 12, 1977, p. 41.

32. Ibid., March 26, 1977, p. 23.

33. Interview with Bobby Winkles, March 17, 2005.

34. Bowie Kuhn, *Hardball: The Education of a Baseball Commissioner* (Lincoln: University of Nebraska Press, 1997 ed.), p. 245.

35. *Sporting News Official 1978 Baseball Guide*, p. 314.

36. *Sporting News*, January 7, 1978, p. 44.

37. Ibid.

38. Ibid., February 4, 1978, p. 59.

39. Ibid., February 11, 1978, p. 50.

40. Ibid., February 25, 1978, p. 59.

41. Kuhn, *Hardball*, p. 251.

42. *Sporting News*, April 15, 1978, p. 13.

43. *Sporting News Official 1978 Baseball Guide*, p. 335.

44. Ibid., February 18, 1978, p. 46.

45. Ibid., March 11, 1978, p. 62.

46. *Sporting News Official 1978 Baseball Guide*, p. 337.

47. Associated Press, January 25, 1978.

48. *Sporting News Official 1978 Baseball Guide*, p. 336.

49. *Sporting News*, February 18, 1978, p. 47.

50. Ibid., April 1, 1978, p. 44.

Chapter 12: Charlie O.'s Last Stand

1. *Sporting News*, May 6, 1978, p. 30.

2. *People* magazine, June 5, 1978.

3. Ibid.

4. *Rebels of Oakland: The A's, the Raiders, the '70s*, HBO documentary, 2003.

5. *People* magazine, June 5, 1978.

6. Interview with Steve Vucinich, June 21, 2005.

7. Interview with Monte Moore, June 16, 2009.

8. Interview with Lee Stange, April 18, 2006.

9. *Sporting News*, May 6, 1978, p. 16.

10. Ibid., June 10, 1978, p. 7.

11. Ibid., March 10, 1979, p. 14.

12. Ibid., September 30, 1978, p. 12.

13. Ibid., December 16, 1978, p. 51.

14. *Sporting News Official 1979 Baseball Guide* (St. Louis, MO: Sporting News, 1979), p. 316.

15. Ibid.

16. Ibid.

17. *Sports Illustrated*, May 21, 1979, p. 38.

18. Leon R. Kaminski to Judge John Montgomery, "Finley Dissolution," June 15, 1979, Cause No. 74 PSC 724, Porter County Courthouse, Valparaiso, IN.

19. In Re the Marriage of Shirley M. Finley, Petitioner, and Charles O. Finley, Respondent, County of Porter Superior Court, 1979 term, Cause No. 74 PSC 724, Order on Finding of Contempt, October 31, 1979, Porter County Courthouse.

20. In Re the Marriage of Shirley M. Finley, Petitioner, and Charles O. Finley, Respondent, County of Porter Superior Court, 1979 term, Cause No. 74 PSC 724, December 31, 1979, Porter County Courthouse.

21. Interview with Leon R. Kaminski, December 9, 2009.

22. In Re the Marriage of Shirley M. Finley, Petitioner, and Charles O. Finley, Respondent, County of Porter Superior Court, Cause No. 74 PSC 724, Decree of Dissolution, December 31, 1979, Porter County Courthouse.

23. Interview with David Finley, September 18–19, 2008.

24. In Re the Marriage of Shirley M. Finley, Petitioner, and Charles O. Finley, Respondent, County of Porter Superior Court, Cause No. 74 PSC 724, Objections to Respondent's Motion for Stay of Execution, January 16, 1980, Porter County Courthouse; In the Court of Appeals of Indiana, Fourth District, Charlie O. Finley, Appellant-Respondent, v. Shirley M. Finley, Appellee-Petitioner, No. 3-370 A 202,, June 26, 1981, Porter County Courthouse; *Syracuse (NY) Herald-Journal*, June 26, 1981; *Arizona Dispatch* (Casa Grande), August 2, 1979; *New York Daily Herald*, June 26, 1981.

25. *Sporting News*, December 18, 1979, p. 54.

26. Bowie Kuhn, *Hardball: The Education of a Baseball Commissioner* (Lincoln: University of Nebraska Press, 1997 ed.), p. 257.

27. *Sporting News*, March 8, 1980, p. 20.

28. United Press International, August 24, 1980.

29. Ibid.

30. *Sporting News Official 1981 Baseball Guide* (St. Louis, MO: Sporting News, 1981), p. 317.

31. Kuhn, *Hardball*, pp. 126, 143.

32. Brad Snyder, *A Well-Paid Slave: Curt Flood's Fight for Free Agency in Professional Sports* (New York: Viking, 2006), p. 328.

Epilogue: Life (and Death) After Baseball

1. Interview with David Finley, November 18–19, 2008.

2. *Washington Post*, August 24, 1980.

3. Interview with Charles Cottonaro, March 4, 2005; interview with Bill Myers, July 28, 2005.

4. Olivier Blanchard, *Macroeconomics* (New York: Prentice Hall, 2000, 2nd ed.), pp. 144, 541.

5. Robert Sobel, *Panic on Wall Street: A Classic History of America's Financial Disasters—with a New Exploration of the Crash of 1987* (New York: E. P. Dutton, 1988); Mark Carlson, *A Brief History of the 1987 Stock Market Crash with a Discussion of the Federal Reserve Response* (Washington, DC: Divisions of Research and Statistics and Monetary Affairs, Federal Reserve Board, 2007).

6. Interview with Rick Knoll, December 15, 2008; *South Bend* (IN) *Tribune*, February 14, 1997.

7. Interview with Bill Myers, July 28, 2005.

8. Interview with Martin Finley, October 14, 2008.

9. Burton A. Boxerman and Bonita Boxerman, *Ebbets to Veeck to Busch: Eight Owners Who Shaped Baseball* (Jefferson, NC: McFarland & Co., 2003), pp. 152–75.

10. *National Sports Daily*, August 17, 1990, p. 9.

11. Interview with David Finley, November 18–19, 2008; interview with Bill Myers, July 28, 2005.

12. *New York Post*, September 25, 1991.

13. Interview with Lew Krausse, April 25, 2005.

14. *USA Today*, September 1, 1989; September 26, 1990; February 20, 1996; interview with David Finley, November 18–19, 2008; interview with Bill Myers, July 28, 2005.

15. *Chicago Tribune*, October 15, 1992; *South Bend Tribune*, October 22, 2001.

16. Interview with Aaron Fogus, March 20, 2005.

17. Interview with Rick Knoll, December 15, 2008.

18. *St. Louis Post-Dispatch*, August 27, 1980; *New York Daily News*, September 3, 1980; April 20, 1981; July 29, 1981; *New York Times*, September 27, 1981; *Albany Times-Union*, April 20, 1985; *Newsday* (New York, NY), August 17, 1988; *USA Today*, October 4, 1990; *Oakland Tribune*, October 20, 1990;

August 18, 1993; *Utica Observer-Dispatch* (NY), July 18, 1993; *Globe and Mail* (Toronto), April 13, 1995.

19. *Chicago Tribune*, August 2, 1990.

20. *New York Post*, July 24, 1987.

21. *New York Daily News*, May 2, 1985; *Utica Observer-Dispatch*, August 9, 1992.

22. *New York Post*, February 23, 1996.

23. *New York News World*, April 24, 1987; *Albany Times-Union*, April 20, 1985; *New York Daily News*, April 20, 1981; Ron Bergman, "Former A's Owner Charlie Finley: A Rebel with a Cause," *The Show*, May 1990, pp. 42–43.

24. Interview with Arthur Holtzman, January 30, 2009.

25. Interview with Sal Bando, June 13, 2005; *Sporting News*, April 20, 1974, p. 5.

26. Interview with Bea Knoll, December 15, 2008.

27. Interview with Ron Mihelic, November 8, 2008.

28. Interview with Merle Harmon, October 15, 2008.

29. *New York Times*, September 19, 1976.

30. Interview with Steve McCatty, December 17, 2008.

31. *New York News World*, April 24, 1981.

32. Interview with David Finley, November 18–19, 2008.

33. Interview with Aaron Fogus, March 20, 2005.

34. Ibid.

35. *Hammond* (IN) *Times*, February 23, 1996.

36. Interview with Martin Finley, October 14, 2008.

37. *USA Today*, February 20, 1996; *New York Post*, February 23, 1996; *New York Post*, February 20, 1996; *Atlanta Journal-Constitution*, February 21, 1996.

38. *Washington Post*, February 21, 1996.

39. Tom Clark, *Champagne and Baloney: The Rise and Fall of Finley's A's* (New York: Harper & Row, 1976), p. 11.

40. Charles O. Finley to Ford C. Frick, November 7, 1963, Major League Baseball Hall of Fame Archives, Cooperstown, NY.

41. Tom Singer, "World Series Games Will Start Earlier," May 12, 2009, available online at http://mlb.mlb.com/news/article.jsp?ymd=20090517&content_id=4791706&vkey=news_mlb&fext=.jsp&c_id=mlb (accessed January 10, 2010).

42. Michael Lewis, *Moneyball: The Art of Winning an Unfair Game* (New York: W. W. Norton, 2003).

43. Bowie Kuhn, *Hardball: The Education of a Baseball Commissioner* (New York: Times Books, 1987), pp. 126–27.

44. *Kansas City Star*, January 24, 1985, p. 4.

45. Interview with Joe Rudi, May 7, 2004.

46. Interview with Dick Williams, January 21, 2008.

47. Interview with Sal Bando, June 13, 2005.

48. Interview with Neil Papiano, September 22, 2008.

49. Dan Holmes, "Charlie Finley's Legacy," January 28, 2001, available online at http://www.thebaseballpage.com/columns/holmes/010128.htm (accessed March 10, 2004).

Index

A NOTE ON THE AUTHORS

Roger Launius is a curator in the Division of Space History at the Smithsonian's National Air and Space Museum. **G. Michael Green** is a senior planner for the National Aeronautics and Space Administration. Both Launius and Green are members of SABR, the Society for American Baseball Research.